ENDS OF EMPIRE

CRITICAL AMERICAN STUDIES SERIES

George Lipsitz, University of California–Santa Barbara

Series Editor

ENDS OF EMPIRE

Asian American Critique and the Cold War

Jodi Kim

Critical American Studies Series

University of Minnesota Press
MINNEAPOLIS
LONDON

Portions of an earlier version of chapter 2 were published in "'They're a Billion Bellies Out There': Commodity Fetishism, the Uber-Oriental, and the Geopolitics of Desire in David Henry Hwang's *M. Butterfly*," in *Culture, Identity, Commodity: Diasporic Chinese Literatures in English*, ed. Kam Louie and Tseen Khoo, 59–78 (Hong Kong: Hong Kong University Press). Portions of an earlier version of chapter 4 were published in "'I'm Not Here, If This Doesn't Happen': The Korean War and Cold War Epistemologies in Susan Choi's *The Foreign Student* and Heinz Fenkl's *Memories of My Ghost Brother*," *Journal of Asian American Studies* 11, no. 3 (2008): 279–302; copyright The Johns Hopkins University Press; reprinted with permission of The Johns Hopkins University Press; and as "An 'Orphan' with Two Mothers: Transnational and Transracial Adoption, the Cold War, and Contemporary Asian American Cultural Politics," *American Quarterly* 61, no. 4 (2009): 855–80; copyright The Johns Hopkins University Press; reprinted with permission of The Johns Hopkins University Press.

In chapter 4, excerpts from the poem "Fragments of the Forgotten War," by Suji Kwock Kim, are reprinted by permission of Louisiana State University Press.

Published by the University of Minnesota Press
111 Third Avenue South, Suite 290
Minneapolis, MN 55401-2520
http://www.upress.umn.edu

Library of Congress Cataloging-in-Publication Data

Kim, Jodi.
Ends of empire : Asian American critique and the Cold War / Jodi Kim.
p. cm. — (Critical American Studies)
Includes bibliographical references and index.
ISBN 978-0-8166-5591-5 (hc : alk. paper) — ISBN 978-0-8166-5592-2 (pb : alk. paper)
1. Asian Americans—History. 2. Asian Americans—Ethnic identity. 3. Asian Americans—Politics and government. 4. Asians in literature. 5. Asians in motion pictures. 6. Cold War. 7. United States—Foreign relations—Asia. 8. Asia—Foreign relations—United States. I. Title.
E184.A75K54 2010
973.´0495—dc22
2009044277

For

MY MOTHER

CONTENTS

INTRODUCTION

Unsettling Hermeneutics and Global Nonalignments

"Aid to the disinherited countries," says Truman. "The time of the old
colonialism has passed." That's also Truman. Which means that American
high finance considers that the time has come to raid every colony in the
world. So, dear friends, here you have to be careful. I know that some of you,
disgusted with Europe, with all that hideous mess which you did not witness
by choice, are turning—oh! in no great numbers—toward America and
getting to looking upon that country as a possible liberator. "What a god-
send!" you think. "The bulldozers! The massive investments of capital! The
roads! The ports!" "But American racism!" "So what? European racism in the
colonies has inured us to it!" And there we are, ready to run the great Yankee
risk. So, once again, be careful! American domination—the only domination
from which one never recovers. I mean from which one never recovers
unscarred.

    AIMÉ CÉSAIRE, *Discourse on Colonialism*

In Chang-rae Lee's novel *Native Speaker,* narrator Henry Park theorizes on
the etymology of "gook," a racial epithet that most Americans came to know
during the Vietnam War. Stretching the spatial and temporal boundaries of
this presumed Vietnam-era racial grammar, Henry, a Korean American, traces
it back to the Korean War (1950–53). When asked by his white American
wife, Lelia, if he had really felt "lucky" when reading his junior encyclopedia
for a classroom presentation about U.S. military intervention in Korea, he
responds, "More or less, when I was little. Sometimes, even now. You know,
it's being with old guys like Stew that diminishes you."[1] Stew, Henry's father-
in-law, is a World War II and Korean War veteran and represents for Henry
a generation of men who personify Cold War logics.[2] Henry tells Lelia, "It's
that coloring those old guys have about the face and body, all pale and pink
and silver, those veins pumping in purple heart. It says, 'I saved your skinny
gook ass, and your momma's, too.'"[3] Even as an adult, particularly in the face

of "diminishment" by older, powerful white men like Stew, Henry cannot help but internalize this Cold War imperialist and racist inscription, the fiction that a benevolent America "saved" his "skinny gook ass, and [his] momma's, too." We see here the peculiar yet enduring temporality of Cold War racial grammars and epistemologies. U.S. imperialist Cold War military intervention in Korea racializes Korean immigrants and Korean Americans prior to their arrival (or birth) in the United States, and continues to racialize them in the protracted aftermath of the Korean War itself. We also see how such Cold War racial optics have come to shape, in anachronistic yet powerful ways, Henry's process of seeing and knowing himself. Henry explains to his confused wife, who thinks the word "gook" was meant for Southeast Asians, his theory on the origins of the word. He theorizes that when American soldiers entered a Korean village during the Korean War, the villagers would shout "*Mee-gook! Mee-gook*."[4] The soldiers interpreted this as "Me gook," as in "I am a gook." The word "*Mee-gook*," however, means America/Americans in Korean. What are we to make of this misinterpretation, what could be read as a pedagogical failure on the soldiers' part, the failure to recognize the Korean hail properly? It did not occur to the soldiers that the Korean villagers would be speaking in Korean, their own language. And in hearing the phonetic "*Mee-gook*" as English, the (mis)translation only works if it is assumed that Koreans can only speak in broken, ungrammatical English where the subject form "I" is replaced with the object form "me." We might say that this grammatical "objectification" registers a kind of "ontological" objectification of Koreans by the American soldiers. Moreover, it does not occur to the soldiers that the Koreans would be hailing them, calling them out as Americans perhaps to alert the other villagers or to express their own surprise. Rather, the soldiers assume that the Koreans are providing a useful lesson to the soldiers by identifying themselves. The uniformity of the chorus of "*Mee-gook*" by the villagers would suggest, however, that it is not a self-identification, because one usually identifies oneself by one's name. Surely the Korean villagers did not all have the same name!

Given this compelling theorization, Lee's narrator might be surprised to learn that the word "gook" actually antecedes the Cold War by many decades and marks America's long-standing history of military intervention and war not only in Asia, but in other parts of the world. In *The Blood of Government: Race, Empire, the United States, and the Philippines,* Paul A. Kramer traces the term back to the United States' war of colonial conquest in the Philippines (the Philippine–American War), which began officially in 1899, and surmises that the term "gu-gu," or "goo-goo," used by American soldiers as a pejorative term against Filipinos, is "almost certainly the linguistic ancestor of 'gook.'"[5] "Gook," therefore, has an older etymology than commonly presumed, and indeed has varied racial designations beyond the Asian. David Roediger traces the term's multiracial application to Asians, Haitians, and Arabs, as well as its gendered usage in designating "tarts," specifically "camp-following prostitutes." He argues in "Gook: The Short History of an Americanism" that the "broader pan-racist past of *gook* provides almost a short history of modern U.S. imperial aggression and particularly of the connections between racial oppression and war."[6] This enduring, varied, and infamous etymology of "gook" serves as a genealogy of the United States' protracted triangulation of race, empire, and war, and reveals the peculiar resonance and recursiveness of Cold War epistemology, a resonance that exceeds and outlasts the event itself. In *Native Speaker,* many decades after the war, Henry can only imagine himself as a "skinny gook ass," even though he was not yet born during the war, and was actually born in the United States. Thus, Henry's classroom encounter with Korea's history and later speculations on the etymology of "gook" index not only the Korean War, which has largely led to the post–World War II migration of Koreans to the United States, but also how the Cold War as an entrenched production of knowledge has shaped how Americans narrate this history of military intervention and how Korean and Asian Americans have come to know their very selves.

I begin with a discussion of *Native Speaker*'s reimagining of "gook"—as at once a racial epithet, an index of the United States' long-standing "pan-racist" and imperialist war-making, and as a Cold War epistemology—because it encapsulates this book's focus on the complex ways in which contemporary Asian American cultural productions critically reframe the Cold War. Beginning officially with Churchill's famous Iron Curtain speech in March 1946,[7] and putatively ending with the fall of the Berlin Wall in November 1989, the Cold War remains for many reasons a fascinating period of U.S.—indeed of world—history. One reason for this fascination is the suspicion that while the Cold War, when seen simply as a historical event or epoch, might have ended in 1989 (or after the failed Soviet coup of August 1991), it continues to enjoy a persisting recursiveness when seen as a structure of feeling, a knowledge project, and a hermeneutics for interpreting developments in the "post"–Cold War conjuncture.[8] In other words, the Cold War is not only a historical period, but also an epistemology and production of knowledge, and as such it exceeds and outlives its historical eventness. This constitutes what I call the *protracted afterlife* of the Cold War. Indeed, we witness this afterlife again and again in the U.S. government's "War on Terror" in the aftermath of 9/11, which began over a full decade after the end of the Cold War (as a historical era) in 1989. The War on Terror has been waged, for example, through explicit comparisons to and as an extension of the Cold War. In particular, the familiar Manichaean logics and rhetorics of the Cold War have been strategically redeployed in such discursive constructions as the "axis of evil," which of course resonates with the Cold War's "evil empire." It seems, then, that Cold War epistemologies and military architectures do enjoy a protracted afterlife. As pithily observed by Tobin Siebers, "The history of the Cold War is in part a history of false endings."[9] Several decades after the beginning of the Cold War, we see a renewed vigor in its logics and rhetorics of fear, anxiety, and preoccupation with manifold boundaries as rearticulated through the War on Terror.

A history of false endings also entails, as I elaborate in this interdisciplinary cultural study, a broader consideration of the narratives that seek to chart the Cold War's historical life, its beginnings and middles as well as its endings, or as evoked by my project title, its ends. By the plural "ends," I mean to mark and connect four senses of the word. First, we can think of "ends" as these *temporal* terminations or multiple endings of the Cold War as a historical era. Second, "ends" also delineate the *spatial* contours, as in extremity or furthermost points or places, where the global Cold War was waged. Third, "ends" signifies as well the *functional*, meaning the aims, objectives, purposes, and effects of the Cold War. Lastly, "ends" point to fragments and remnants, whether the physical remains and ruins of Cold War violence (as shown in the cover image of this book), the human ruin or death produced by such violence, or the necessarily fragmentary attempts to grasp, remember, and narrate Cold War history.[10] I gather, thread, and interrogate these multiple ends of the Cold War as America's "ends of empire." Specifically, I investigate how what is taken to be the bipolar Manichaean rivalry between the United States and the Soviet Union was triangulated in Asia, and how contemporary Asian American cultural productions critically index and give complex cultural form to this vexed triangulation. I demonstrate how Asian American cultural productions shift, reframe, and critically extend dominant Cold War culture and historiography by showing the ways in which they stage the Cold War as a geopolitical, cultural, and epistemological project of gendered racial formation and imperialism undergirding U.S. global hegemony. I theorize, moreover, how Asian American cultural forms make visible the centrality of Asia to that project. Produced within the linked contexts of the migrations and displacements precipitated by the Cold War in Asia and domestic and global gendered racial formations, the Asian American cultural works I analyze contain a transpacific and transnational scope and imaginary that refract narrow national(ist) schemas. My analysis thus contributes to a large body of critical scholarship on the Cold War's multiple and overlapping triangulations throughout the globe, including Africa, Latin America, and the Middle East.

Ends of Empire, then, offers a critique of American empire in Asia through an interdisciplinary analysis of Asian American cultural productions and their critical intersections with Cold War geopolitics and logics. I argue that Asian American cultural politics and critique provide a productive occasion to investigate the mutually constituted gendered racial optics and imperial logics of the Cold War in Asia as a particularly entangled and enduring episode in the history and culture of U.S. empire. Moreover, I contend that Asian American cultural politics stage not only how the multiple ends of empire animate and reinvigorate the historical life of American empire, but also how such ends are incomplete, full of contradictions, impossibilities, and at times certain failures. That is, the critical longings, enactments, and embodiments that are displayed in the Asian American cultural works I analyze allow us to imagine alternatives to empire, as in a singular "end" or termination of empire. Furthermore, my book conceptualizes Asian American critique as an *unsettling hermeneutic* and reads Asian American cultural politics against the grain of American exceptionalism and nationalist ontology. By *unsettling hermeneutic*, I wish to suggest, on the one hand, how Asian American critique unsettles and disrupts the dominant Manichaean lens through which the Cold War is made sense of and in turn generates meaning. I also aim to suggest, on the other hand, how conceptualizing Asian American critique as an *unsettling hermeneutic* generates a new interpretive practice or analytic for reading Asian American cultural productions, and the very formation of contemporary "Asian America(n)," in new ways. *Ends of Empire* thus critically defamiliarizes the "United States of America" and the contemporary formation of "Asian America(n)" by interrogating their violent and contradictory conditions of possibility in the post–World War II conjuncture.

In privileging Asian American cultural forms, namely literary and cinematic texts, as a generative site for critiquing American empire in Asia and conceptualizing Asian American critique as an *unsettling hermeneutic*, this book does not seek to provide a comprehensive (cultural) history of the U.S.

Cold War in Asia, nor does it seek to "explain" Asia under the U.S. Cold War. Rather, as I have suggested, the book's aim is to provide a critical cultural indexing of how the Cold War in Asia was a complex and manifold project of American empire and gendered racial formation, and to demonstrate how an analysis of Asian American cultural forms productively generates such a critical indexing. The *contemporary* Asian American cultural forms I analyze, produced in the prolonged aftermath of the inaugural height of the Cold War, reveal how the U.S. Cold War's violent displacements and migrations constitute in large part the conditions of possibility for the post–World War II formation of Asian America. In doing so, such Asian American cultural texts interrogate how this protracted Cold War imperialist relation between Asia and America contradictorily configures the "Asian American" subject not only as immigrant, racial (minority) formation, or putative liberal citizen-subject of the U.S. nation-state, but also as postimperial exile or "refugee" who simultaneously is a product of, bears witness to, and critiques imperialist and gendered racial violence. Thus, *Ends of Empire* situates culture and cultural forms as the site where knowledge and meaning are at once constituted and unraveled, where the officially unknowable reckons at once with the already known and the impossibility of knowing. Asian American cultural forms are palimpsests of partially visible and partially erased imaginings and longings, themselves sketched over already partial official nationalist scripts. Rather than claiming that Asian American cultural texts express a positivistic will to knowledge and countermemory, a wholesale rendering visible of that which official nationalist culture and history render invisible, I want to suggest that it complexly grapples with an impossibility and at times a certain refusal. This is to say that while ethnic minority cultural forms have often been interpreted in terms of a politics of resistance or alterity, I conceptualize Asian American culture as also engaging in a *politics of refusal*. In refusing the seductive will to total knowledge or revelation of the "truth" of the "Asian American experience," what it means to be Asian American, or what the United States "really did" in Asia during the Cold War, Asian American culture enacts what in anthropological terms has been called "ethnographic refusal."[11] Asian American culture thus refuses to be a cooperative native informant. Yet this politics of refusal is not the space of complete silence, meaninglessness, or illegibility. Instead, as Audra Simpson compellingly argues within the context of indigenous politics, "What is theoretically generative about these refusals? They *account* for the history [of conquest and resistance]," and they "speak volumes, because they tell us when to stop."[12] How,

then, do Asian American cultural forms "speak volumes" about the Cold
War in Asia, and critically "account for" or index that gendered racial imperialist history, culture, and production of knowledge, precisely through a series
of what we might call generative refusals? Asian American critique as an *unsettling hermeneutic* or analytic for interpreting Asian American cultural forms
and the Cold War as a multivalenced object of analysis reads such refusals as
generative moments.

More specifically, my book offers a threefold theorization. First, it conceptualizes Asian American critique and cultural politics in ways that mark
the contradictions and ambivalent entanglements of American empire and
gendered racial formation as the context out of which the post–World War II
Asian American subject emerges and constitutes itself as such. That is, I offer
a conceptualization of Asian American critique and cultural politics that
locates their critical strength and value not in celebratory narratives and discourses of Asian American culture and identity formation nor in lamentations of or jeremiads against racialized victimhood in liberal multiculturalist
America, but in an interrogation of how and why "Asian America(n)" was
constituted in the first place, and also might be disarticulated, in particular
instances.[13] This is to ask what gives the unruly and heterogeneous category
of "Asian American" its discursive, institutional, embodied, and material
coherence and legibility, but also to challenge the conditions of possibility or
grounds for that coherence and legibility. I invoke the possibility of the *coherent incoherence* of "Asian America(n)" as a way of marking this complex
genealogy.[14] Ultimately, I hope to reveal how the concerns of Asian American
critique and cultural politics cannot be contained as simply those of what is
by now often dismissed as the unsophisticated or exhausted identity politics
of the "minority" subject. Rather, the subjects and objects of Asian American
critique and cultural productions provide critical indexes of the vexed, violent, and often ambivalent registers of what could be called the identity politics of the U.S. nation-state in the latter half of the twentieth century and
beyond: the Cold War. As such, my analysis makes an intervention in U.S.
Cold War literary and cultural history and criticism, whose privileged objects
have been canonical works of the "liberal imagination" and "nuclear criticism," and have thus far not considered Asian American works at a sustained
level.[15] Indeed, my analysis attempts to challenge the privileging of hegemonic European and American perspectives and texts in Cold War historiography in general and Cold War cultural criticism in particular.[16] This is not
a simple call for an inclusion of neglected texts or voices, but an investigation

of how hegemonic nationalist paradigms, categories, frameworks, and hermeneutics themselves undergo necessary revision. Moreover, I argue that
Asian American critique and cultural politics exceed their literal and figurative domestication within the corrals of U.S. liberal multiculturalism. Indeed,
their global genealogy—issuing from the globality of the Cold War itself—
conjoins them to "Nonaligned" or "Third Way" Cold War cultural texts and
critiques produced throughout the world.

Second, *Ends of Empire*'s analysis of Asian American cultural forms generates a critical genealogy of the Cold War *as* a genealogy of American empire,
one that reframes the Manichaean U.S.–Soviet Cold War rivalry and shows
how it was, as I have stated, triangulated in Asia. This is not to argue that
Asia was the only site affected by the Cold War. Rather, it is to shed light on
how the Cold War, as a Western interimperialist war, which can also be seen
as a civil war *within* the West, made much of the rest of the world its bloody
terrain. In asking "What is this thing called American empire?" my aim is
not to argue that American empire is somehow exceptional or unique. Instead, I read against the narratives of American exceptionalism as well as their
critiques, and my goal is to elaborate the *specificity* of American empire by
locating what could be called the imperialist gendered racial political unconscious of the Cold War in Asia as a composition at once material, ideological,
and rhetorical. By privileging Asian American literary and cinematic texts,
my hope is not simply to recuperate the "forgotten" or occluded histories
and cultures of U.S. Cold War intervention, militarism, and violence in Asia,
but to investigate such histories and cultures as a point of entry into discussions and theorizations of the politics of our knowledge of and about American empire. How is American empire itself a politics of knowledge and
epistemology? The story I wish to tell, in other words, is not simply about
what the United States "did" in Asia, but it is also about the conditions of
possibility and impossibility for such a telling, querying, and knowing.

Third, my goal is to offer a further reframing of the Cold War by approach-
ing it not solely as a historical epoch or event, but as itself a knowledge project
or epistemology, which is always also a pedagogy, and asking how it continues to generate and teach "new" knowledge by making sense of the world
through the Manichaean logics and grammars of good and evil. In this way,
the Cold War exceeds what Derrida calls the "eventness of the event."[17] It is
a reading practice through which the United States comes to construct and
know itself and its Others. This reading practice, moreover, not only provides a geopolitical scheme for making sense of the world, but also provides

what Donald Pease calls a "cultural scene of persuasion" for interpreting literature. Pease notes that it has produced, for example, a canonized reading of Moby Dick in which Ishmael triumphs over Ahab's totalitarian will. He critiques "the power of a cultural context to designate . . . the terms in which a text must be read in order to maintain cultural power" and argues that "unlike other paradigms in the public sphere, the Cold War does not adjudicate or mediate discussions. Instead, it derives all its force by simply being persuasive. As *the explanation,* it appears persuasive without having undergone the work of persuasion."[18]

In what follows, I will provide an elaboration of my first two goals: a theorization of the critical strength of Asian American critique and cultural politics and a discussion of the Cold War as a project of American gendered racial formation and empire. In the next chapter, I will elaborate on the third goal by providing a critical genealogy of Cold War logics and epistemology through a close analysis of how "Asia" figures as a gendered racial trope in key U.S. government documents. I track how these documents collectively cohere as an imperial archive and generate a Manichaean reading practice for making sense of the world, and in the subsequent chapters, I demonstrate how contemporary Asian American literature and film critically "respond" to, disarticulate, and imagine alternatives to this imperial project.

Asian American Critique, Cold War Compositions, and Global Third Ways

Ends of Empire locates Asian American critique at the intersection of American studies, ethnic studies, critical race studies, and postcolonial studies.[19] Because U.S. imperialist exploits and gendered racial logics abroad in Asia as well as the internally colonizing structures and discourses of racialization at home mark the Asian American subject as both racialized minority and as postimperial "exile" or "refugee," such an articulation of these fields that have developed alongside—but not necessarily in conversation with—one another is productive. Indeed, as I have observed, post–World War II Asian migration to the United States, which expands and institutionally produces the category or subject called "Asian American," is a significant symptom, legacy, and material sign of the constitutively linked history of American empire in Asia and the history of American gendered racial formation both in its domestic and global modalities.[20] My book aims to reckon with this vexed, conjoined constitution by considering the dialectics of the histories and cultures of American empire and gendered racial formation. In other words, I show

how these histories and cultures engender their very critiques. Thus, my conceptualization of "Asian American critique" is neither, as I have stated, a celebration of Asian American assimilation or resistance nor a foray into what has been pejoratively perceived as the strident and unsophisticated identity politics of the "minority" subject as racialized victim or token within liberal multiculturalist America. Rather, I wish to argue that Asian American critique can be conceptualized as an *unsettling hermeneutic* that provides a crucial diagnosis of what could be called the identity politics, and politics of identification, of the U.S. nation in the latter half of the twentieth century: the Cold War.[21] As a significant project of American empire and gendered racial formation in Asia, the Cold War at once consolidated, destabilized, and reconstituted America's self-identity and identification. That is, I take my inspiration from scholars such as Grace Kyungwon Hong, who has powerfully articulated "'women of color feminism' and 'racialized immigrant women's culture' not as identity categories but as analytics" for tracking and describing American modernity.[22] Similarly, in the context of Native studies, Andrea Smith critiques an approach that is "content-driven" (one that seeks an ethnographic revelation of the essential "truth" of Native American "identity" and knowledge) and advocates instead a methodology of "generative narratology" that centers performative narratives and decenters dominant content-driven frameworks.[23] In a parallel vein, I situate Asian American critique in this project as an *analytic,* which is decidedly not a reified identity category, for apprehending the specificity of American empire in Asia in the second half of the twentieth century.

Through such a conceptualization of Asian American critique, *Ends of Empire* reveals the critical genealogies of U.S. imperialism found in the literary and cinematic cultural productions of Asian Americans. These critical genealogies capture what is repressed in U.S. national memory, and they account for and connect what is left out of hegemonic European and American perspectives and texts in U.S. Cold War historiography and cultural criticism, composed largely of detailed diplomatic histories and cultural studies of the U.S. domestic sphere in the 1950s and such developments as McCarthyism.[24] By marking the cultural texts in my study as Asian American cultural politics, I mean to highlight the complex ways in which Asian American cultural productions not only contain a politics of form, but also thematize and provide a critical anatomy of what could be called the "form of politics." The form of politics signals the formal thematics, logics, and rhetorics governing particular political discourses or narratives. And in this instance, that discourse is the Cold War. As such, Asian American critique and cultural politics generate, as I will elaborate in the next section, a different context or frame for reading the Cold War itself, disrupting its seeming coherence while simultaneously interrogating its recursive recyclings in the contemporary post–Cold War, post-9/11 period. In other words, the Cold War is itself an object of analysis and not simply a congealed historical context for my reading of Asian American cultural politics. By conjuring what has been banished, and by staging, imagining, and remembering differently what has been willfully forgotten, the Asian American literary and cinematic forms I analyze hover around the edges of America's official Cold War imperial archive, culture, and nationalist ontology. They do not always or necessarily seek entrance into this formation. They do not call for an expansion of the Cold War literary and cultural canon. Rather, I show how these specific cultural texts I have chosen for my study unsettle and disrupt the terms and assumptions under which this canon coheres as such, posing questions more about canonicity itself and less about the contents of the canon. Asian American cultural forms seek what Lisa Lowe calls a "tireless reckoning" in ways that discombobulate this nationalist ontology and ask: how has the United States, in the post–World War II conjuncture, constituted itself as a global imperium?[25] I argue that *Cold War compositions* play a crucial role in this process. Cold War compositions are at once a geopolitical *structuring,* an ideological *writing,* and a cultural *imagining.*[26] Produced in multiple sites and in a variety of forms and genres, Cold War compositions give witness to how the Cold War is a multivalenced object of analysis that exceeds its apparent containment by the Manichaean logics of good and evil, or what Michael Rogin calls "political demonology."[27] As such, Cold War compositions in their related manifestations as historical era, geopolitics, epistemology, and cultural production call to mind what Laura Hyun Yi Kang, following Foucault, conceptualizes as "compositional subjects" in her compelling interrogation of "the terms and conditions by which Asian/American women have been rendered legible, visible, and intelligible" in various disciplinary terrains.[28] My book critically tracks the Cold War in Asia as a "compositional subject."

The Cold War constitution of Asian American cultural politics is a significant critical feature of Cold War compositions. Specifically, as cultural imaginings that are constituted by the Cold War but dialectically critique their very constitution, Asian American cultural texts and productions are critical Cold War compositions that confound the Manichaean logics of official nationalist Cold War histories, epistemologies, and ontologies.[29] In this way,

Asian American cultural politics critically registers its vexed emergence and constitution as an index of the Cold War in Asia and its protracted afterlife, and makes visible the imperialist logics, gendered racial optics, and shifting historical stakes under and through which American empire at once articulates and disarticulates itself. This is not to argue that all Asian American cultural producers or productions are somehow "resistant" or "oppositional." Such a bipolar logic of "dominant" versus "resistant" would merely reproduce the formal Manichaean—the "bad" versus "good" dyad—of the Cold War itself. Rather, it is to reveal how these cultural productions trace, uncover, and interrogate U.S. Cold War imperialism as the violent conditions of possibility for why it is that Asian Americans are here in the first place. In other words, it is to expose that "We are here because you were there."[30] Or as Victor Bascara writes, Asian Americans are "living proof" of the history of U.S. imperialism in Asia, and their cultural productions bear the traces of that history.[31] That is, while the master narratives of Asian migration to the United States chart a putatively desirable and desired teleology troped as the American Dream—an escape from an unstable, economically devastated, and politically repressive homeland to safe haven in an America full of freedom and opportunity—the home that one leaves often needs to be left precisely because of the havoc wreaked by U.S. imperialist intervention there. And the contradictions of the American mythos inspire dreams of the ultimately unknowable, of what might and could have been had "you" never been there, and "we" never been here.

While Asian American cultural politics has been co-opted as a feature of liberal multiculturalism in the wake of the so-called culture wars of the 1980s, it need not be contained by it and by the rubrics of American "ethnic" literature, whose operative terms are the commodified aesthetization of racial or ethnic difference and a simultaneous strategic evasion of an interrogation of "difference" as it constitutes differences of power, freedom, and access to resources. Within this context, difference also constitutes differential proximities to life itself and the category of the human. Linked to the new social movements and "identity politics" of the 1960s and '70s, the culture wars were constituted by debates seeking to revise and expand the canon of American literature and culture. Traditionally marginalized groups—especially racialized minorities and women—sought inclusion. In addition to an expansion of the content of the canon, they sought methodological revisions in how that canon would be interpreted. "Race, class, gender" analysis has become a shorthand signifier for this critique. The culture wars, then, and the discourse

of multiculturalism, are symptomatic of broader disagreements on the meaning of American pluralism. Indeed, as Nikhil Pal Singh writes, a Cold War
understanding of pluralism as liberal consensus achieved within a diverse
polity, or *e pluribus unum*, is pitted against post-1960s understandings of
pluralism as a description of wide divisions in the polity (marked most acutely
by racial and cultural difference). Whether pluralism is construed as utopic
achievement or dystopic description, however, what remains the same on
both sides is that the U.S. nation-state is relied upon as "a stable container of
social antagonisms and as the necessary horizon of our hopes for justice." As
such, Singh demonstrates, the Cold War and the culture wars bear more than
nominal similarity, and "although the cold war may have been 'won,' it never
actually ended."[32] Moreover, as Denise Ferreira da Silva observes, starting
in the late 1960s, the nation (later to be replaced by culture) framed projects
of racial emancipation, but the question that remains to be asked is why
"the *racial* could not become the sole basis for an emancipatory project."[33]
The stakes of my project, then, do not align with an expansion of the U.S.
"national" multicultural canon in the terms articulated during the culture
wars and now co-opted into a liberal multicultural corpus. One does not
have to be cynical to observe that this liberal or corporate multiculturalism,
with its politics of symbolic, imagistic, or cultural representation has *replaced,*
rather than complemented, substantive political representation or redistribution of wealth and power. This logic of substitution was also previously
witnessed, as Penny Von Eschen argues, with the multicultural internation-
alist projects of Cold War cultural ambassadorship.[34] My hope is thus to read
Asian American cultural politics against the grain of liberal multiculturalism. Such a reading practice critically defamiliarizes the "United States of
America" and "Asian America(n)."

This untethers the contemporary Asian American cultural forms I study,
which were produced in the prolonged aftermath of the inaugural height of
the Cold War, from the constraints of their institutional recognition as "ethnic" American literature and culture and allows them to take flight beyond
the borders of a reified nation-state and enter a global cultural formation
that imagines alternatives to the imperialism of the Cold War. As such, *Ends
of Empire* traces what Lowe calls "the international within the national," which
is a marking of U.S. internationalism, or its history of empire.[35] In critically
exposing this history, and the amnesias it has inspired and required, contemporary Asian American cultural politics is in conversation, albeit in a
belated form, with the global "Third World" Movement, formally articulated

at the historic Bandung Conference in 1955. This Asian–African conference was the most significant effort by nations around the world to remain independent from Cold War politics. The notion of a third world, derived from the French *tiers état*, or third estate (the largest but least represented social group before the Revolution), signified a global majority finding its way out of colonial subjugation. Moreover, eschewing domination by either the United States or the Soviet Union, Asian and African nations declared their neutral or nonaligned status and sought a third way between the "monopoly capitalism of the West" and the "political and cultural totalitarianism of the East," a path that would reject Cold War binaries.[36] These principles of self-determination and nonalignment grew into the Non-Aligned Movement, founded at a 1961 conference in Belgrade.[37] Similarly, in the contemporary period, even as Asian American cultural politics might be complicit with or co-opted by U.S.-led corporate globalization (marked by increasing privatization or what David Harvey calls the capitalist imperialism of "accumulation by dispossession"), its Third World, Bandung, or anti-imperial genealogy puts it in conversation with anti-globalization movements around the world.[38] Indeed, as Cedric J. Robinson argues, "While the official world contestation, the Cold War, has been taken to have subsumed all other conflicts, it is now possible to cast the competition between the two imperial hegemons, the United States and the Soviet Union, as a historical sidebar to the struggles to obtain or vanquish racial domination."[39] In a parallel vein, Thomas Borstelmann observes that "in retrospect, the conflicts between the great powers of the Northern Hemisphere after 1945 distracted attention from the period's perhaps more significant long-term development: the emergence of the world's nonwhite majority from white colonial rule into national independence."[40]

Seen in such a light, and notwithstanding the Soviet Union's at times ambiguous geopolitical and racial positioning between the West and East, this Western interimperialist war, as I will be elaborating in the next section, was also a civil war *within* the West taking place amidst and against global decolonization movements as well as struggles for racial democracy in the United States that saw antiracism and decolonization as linked projects.[41] Indeed, as Cynthia A. Young powerfully demonstrates, the coalition of people in the United States—activists, artists, students, and workers—who were inspired by decolonization movements around the world as well as the "long and distinguished history of anticolonial, antiracist, and anticapitalist agitation among leftists of color in the United States" saw their own situation in global terms, and thus collectively constituted a "U.S. Third World Left."[42]

Given this international context, Asian American critique and cultural politics bespeak a genealogy that exceeds their problematic "domestication" (literally and figuratively) within the corrals of U.S. liberal multiculturalism. Their global genealogy conjoins them to "nonaligned" or "third way" Cold War cultural texts and critiques produced in seemingly disparate sites, such as cultural forms produced in Asia in Asian languages that index U.S. militarism and imperialism; South African literatures of the 1980s that oppose the U.S.-sanctioned apartheid state; or the magical realist, Boom, post-Boom, and testimonial texts as well as the Third Cinema of Latin America that imagine alternatives to U.S.-sanctioned or engineered military coups, neoliberalism, and globalization. Thus reframed, Asian American critique's unraveling of the enabling incoherence (or seeming coherence) of Cold War logics is also in alignment with work such as that of Arturo Escobar, which articulates a powerful critique of "development" in Latin America as not only a set of practices or policies, but as a discourse. The U.S. Cold War state, in collusion with regional governments, created "underdevelopment" in the first place. Yet this enforced underdevelopment is targeted by development discourse as a problem that needs fixing, given how development discourse defines development solely through the lens of Western capitalist modernity.[43]

I depart, then, from debates within Asian American studies that ask whether the field has been or should be national (domestic) or international (diasporic). Certainly, given the long history of the formal and informal ways in which Asian Americans have been held at a distance and excluded from America's national ontology (whether legislated as immigration exclusion, denial of naturalization, mass internment/incarceration, and racialized and gendered labor exploitation and stratification, or manifested as the persistent perception and treatment of Asian Americans as foreign and exotic), Asian American studies has been propelled by a concern with "domestic" identity politics issues. An organizing principle of this has been a teleological emplotment of an albeit uneven yet ultimately successful "claiming of America" by minority subjects who have historically been barred from physical, legal, and/or discursive inclusion in the U.S. nation-state by hegemonic nationalist institutions and narratives. Yet as Sucheta Mazumdar astutely observes, we need to take to task the dominant discourse regarding the history of the field. She demonstrates that contrary to the putatively cultural nationalist, domestically focused origins of the field, its very genesis was international in scope, given that it was linked to and coeval with decolonization movements around the world and the protest against the Vietnam War as a racist, imperialist war.[44]

In other words, the "international within the national," or America's history of empire, dialectically generated a critique that necessarily linked the national and international contexts of racial oppression. The domestic civil rights movement and what Borstelmann suggests might be called "the international civil rights movement" of anticolonialism were conjoined.[45] As such, the triangulation of the Cold War in Asia witnessed another triangulated relationship that was composed of the United States as colonizer or imperialist, racialized minorities at home as "internal colony," and subjugated nations and populations abroad as colony or neocolony. Such a triangulation of colonizer/imperialist, internal colony, and (neo)colony bespeaks not only the imperialist and gendered racial genealogy of the U.S. Cold War in Asia, but the international genealogy of Asian American studies. Moreover, the very constitution of the Asian American subject was not strictly a national(ist) project but an imperialist transnational one forged through, on the one hand, the Asian American movement's critique in the 1960s and '70s of U.S. imperialism and racism in Asia, and, on the other, through later Asian migration to the United States as a result of that very imperialism.[46] This dialectical formation of Asian America, as at once critic and effect or trace of American empire and gendered racial formation, is given form in the Asian American cultural productions I analyze.

In the following discussion, I elaborate this triangulation of the Cold War in Asia as a project of American empire and link it to the institutional recognition of Asian American literary and cultural studies and the so-called culture wars of the 1980s.

The Cold War's Imperialist Gendered Racial Political Unconscious

While the Cold War is metaphorically cold when seen from the vantage point of the United States and (Western) Europe, it was literally hot and bloody in much of the rest of the world, the terrain on which the West's Cold War was actually waged and fought. Indeed, the peculiar metaphoricity of the term "Cold War" itself was not simply symptomatic of an innocuous Euro-Americanism. Rather, the metaphorics and logics of the Cold War engaged in significant performative and ideological work. Most notably, they cloaked and obfuscated the violence of U.S. global hegemony and of its "ends of empire" on racialized bodies and terrain. I begin this section, then, with a brief etymological tracing of the term "Cold War," marking in particular its paradoxical, oxymoronic, and metaphorical nature. As Anders Stephanson has noted, the term is metaphoric, oddly narrativeless, and atemporal.[47] It is said to be derived from *"la guerre froide,"* a French expression used in the 1930s, but its U.S. usage is generally dated back to a 1947 speech by Bernard Baruch, the U.S. representative on the Atomic Energy Commission, in which he claimed that "we are in the midst of a Cold War." It was then popularized by journalist Walter Lippmann, but had been used as early as 1945 by the English writer George Orwell in his article "You and the Atom Bomb." Orwell captured the paradoxical elements of the Cold War, characterizing it as a state of armed paralysis or hostility that could not erupt overtly, a "peace that is no peace" in which a superpower is "at once unconquerable and in a permanent state of 'Cold War' with its neighbors."[48] Indeed, the National Security Act of 1947, one of the central inaugural documents of Cold War logic and policy, as well as the creation of the national security state, echoed this Orwellian notion by transforming the Department of War into the Department of Defense (as well as chartering the National Security Council, the CIA, and later the National Security Agency)[49] and rhetorically replacing the traditional conception of war with such euphemisms as "security," "stability," "balance," and yes, "peace."[50] The Cold War is unique precisely because of its paradoxical nature as an ideological and cultural battle fought in order to prevent not only conventional military warfare, but also a hitherto unimagined nuclear annihilation. Hence, it generated a host of oxymoronic terms such as "dual hegemony," "limited nuclear war," "peace-keeping missiles," and "win the peace."[51] However, as I noted above, the Cold War is rhetorically paradoxical, oxymoronic, and metaphorical only when considered from the Euro-American perspective of the Western superpowers. When seen from the perspective of much of the rest of the world—the terrain on which the Cold War was literally waged—the term is erroneous. Indeed, as argued by Andrew Hammond:

> The "Cold War" is an erroneous term for a global conflict which, spanning several continents and a multitude of coups, civil wars, insurgencies and interventions, was characterized by ongoing armed aggression. . . . For a Western population, certainly, the military confrontations may have appeared distant phenomena. . . . Globally, however, the Western experience is a clear exception to the norm. In all, the Soviet sponsoring of left-wing regimes and the US rollback of communism resulted in over a *hundred wars* through the Third World and a body count of over 20 million. *In Asia alone, some 11 million died in the fighting in Korea, Laos, Cambodia, and Vietnam.*[52]

Seen in this light, as I elaborate later, the Cold War can be seen as a signifi-
cant, and significantly protracted, Western interimperialist war *between* the
United States and the Soviet Union (and thus also a civil war *within* the
West) over who would be the rightful inheritor of territories and bearer of
Western political philosophical traditions within the context of the breakup
of the classical European empires in the aftermath of World War II. The
Cold War represents a key historical transition in imperial formations, from
one that had been largely formal territorial colonization to more informal
or neoimperial forms of political, economic, military, and cultural domination that stop short of territorial annexation. It thus constitutes the genealogy for the contemporary manifestation of U.S. neoimperial hegemony and
corporate-led globalization. This is not to suggest that informal or nonterritorial means of control did not exist in the period before World War II, nor
to suggest that formal territorial control has been completely absent since
World War II. Rather, it is to mark the Cold War of the second half of the
twentieth century as an imperial governmentality whose dominant logics
have operated (and continue to do so) through a flexible combination of
nonterritorial imperial tactics that include military intervention or occupation, war, treaties, mutual security agreements, covert CIA operations, trade
barriers and agreements, economic support or aid, humanitarian aid, and
the work of international organizations such the United Nations and the
World Trade Organization, as well as World Bank and International Monetary Fund "structural adjustment policies" and loans.

During the Cold War, we see the United States applying these imperial
tactics to Asia, and "Asia" as a region gathering increasing coherence and
strategic importance for the United States in economic, military, and political terms. The "loss" of China to communism in 1949 would overdetermine
U.S. Cold War (ad)ventures in Asia. Anticolonial nationalisms in Korea, Vietnam, and elsewhere would be interpreted as metonyms or specters of a
"Red Asia." This, as well as the long-standing hypnotic power of imagining
a billion Chinese consumers, would haunt Cold War logics and geopolitics.
After Mao's Communist victory in 1949, Washington deployed an effective
rhetorical construction, the "domino theory," to articulate the fear that if left
unchecked, adjoining Asian nations would successfully fall like a row of dominoes to communism.[53] The sense of urgency, to which this image graphically
contributed, provided the justification for a strong doctrine of (military) containment that reduced and simplified complex and heterogeneous formations, on the one hand, and expanded the category of "communism" to capture

or ensnare these formations, on the other. Put simply, so many developments were reductively labeled "communist" that the label itself had to be expansive and flexible, yet singular enough to be synonymous with "evil."[54] Containment as doctrine and policy, however, did not stop short of containment; it was an attempt to install governments and economic systems favorable to U.S. interests in the name of "democracy" and "collective security." Just as the "civilizing mission" of nineteenth century European colonialism had provided the ideological cover for conquest, this "democratizing mission" provided the rhetorical justification for the United States in its effort to establish and maintain imperial control over Asia.[55] Thus, the vexed triangulation of the Cold War in Asia saw, as I will elaborate in the chapters that follow, the "loss" of China to Mao's Communist victory in 1949, the U.S. occupation of Japan in the aftermath of the atomic bombings of Hiroshima and Nagasaki (1945–52), a "police action" in Korea (1950–53), a protracted "conflict" in Vietnam (circa 1959–75), and an instantiation of North Korea as part of the "evil empire," and later as "axis of evil" (2002).

Indeed, much of the contemporary post-1965 Asian American population has been formed as a result of U.S. Cold War interventions in Asia. The immigration legislation that made this possible, the landmark 1965 Immigration Act, was itself passed with Cold War considerations at the forefront. As the purported model and champion of democracy at home and abroad, the United States made itself vulnerable to criticisms of its racism and hypocrisy. One response to this was the 1965 Immigration Act, which did away with the racially exclusionary "national origins" quota system that had formally been in place since the 1924 National Origins Quota Act, and replaced it with a new preference system and hemispheric quotas.[56] More specific pieces of immigration legislation that amended the 1965 act, such as the 1975 Indochina Migration and Refugee Assistance Act, the 1980 Refugee Act, the 1982 Amerasian Immigration Act, and the 1987 Amerasian Homecoming Act, are also indexes of U.S. Cold War "hot wars" in Korea and Vietnam. While one way to interpret this immigration history is to see it as a liberalization of policy and a progressive opening of America's doors to Asian migration, doors that had begun to close as far back as 1875 with the Page Law effectively prohibiting the entry of Chinese women, *Ends of Empire* reads such legislation—and the contemporary Asian American population they occasioned—as symptomatic of U.S. imperial Cold War presence in Asia and gendered racial formations both "here" in the United States and over "there" in Asia. While the hallmark of Asian American history has been thought to be the very exclusion of Asians from the United States through restrictive immigration legislation, the Asian American cultural works I analyze in this project imagine the relative "inclusion" of Asians in the Cold War era through a different set of immigration acts not as a progressive, liberal democratic correction or reversal of a previously racist era, but as an imperial governmentality whose logic is one of *expulsion* (out of Asia) rather than an inclusion–exclusion dyad. Thus, this book owes a great intellectual debt to Lowe's important paradigm-shaping work *Immigrant Acts*. I build on Lowe's rigorous critical genealogy of the institution of American citizenship within the context of capitalist modernity by articulating it with the gendered racial "institution(s)" of American empire during the Cold War as they are made visible in the wide range of Asian American cultural texts I consider.

The dominant inclusion–exclusion dyad governing Asian American immigration history tends to elide a critical analysis of imperialism as a catalyzing force of displacement and migration. This elision abets the Cold War as a dominant structure of feeling and knowledge that needs to forget its own imperial longings and tactics, and how such longings and tactics were subtended by a gendered racial architecture. Such a concealment is effected via an abstract universalism and an espousal of "democracy" defined as individual rights and the universal right to own private property. Indeed, one revealing example of the presumed universality of this notion was its inclusion in the UN Declaration of Human Rights. This abstract universalism further manifested itself, as Neil Smith observes, in a denial of the significance of territory and geography, most notably in Henry Luce's influential *Life* magazine cover editorial entitled "The American Century" (1941). How, asks Smith, "does one challenge a century? . . . Insofar as it was beyond geography, the American century was beyond empire and beyond reproof."[57] Such abstract universalism, as Singh notes, might have been nominally anticolonialist, but was "also quite explicitly a new imperialism in the sense that it conceived of the United States as the leader of a new stage in the development of an international civilization created by the expansion of European capitalism and colonialism."[58] In the U.S. capitalist geopolitical imaginary, through which the "expansion of European capitalism and colonialism" is given form, Asia and the Pacific have figured centrally. Indeed, in the late Cold War years of a more recent past, beginning in the mid-1970s, we see the emergence of what Christopher Connery calls "Pacific Rim Discourse," an "imagining of U.S. multinational capitalism" that is at once a reaction to and an assimilation of East Asian economic success into the "us" of Western capitalism.[59]

The "American Century" also strategically repressed or attempted to contain the gendered racial formations of the Cold War. In *The Blood of Government*, Kramer offers a transnational historical study of that previous bloody imperial conquest that marked the turn of the century into the American Century, a conquest of the Philippines that has been largely forgotten or rendered exceptional. Kramer posits a complex, mutually constitutive relationship between race and empire, writing of the "racial politics of empire" and the "imperial politics of race" in ways that eschew functional reduction of one to the other. Instead, he argues that "[i]t was not simply that [racial] difference made empire possible: empire remade difference in the process."[60] Likewise, race and gender, and theories of gendered racial development, provided a significant organizing and overdetermining principle for U.S. figurations of and imperial violence in Asia during the Cold War. This does not mean, however, that U.S. domestic racial formations were simply "exported" to Asia. Indeed, transnationally configured gendered racial economies predate the Cold War itself and find an immediate historical antecedent in World War II. As John W. Dower observes, American racial perceptions of the "hated Japanese enemy in World War II . . . proved to be free-floating, and easily transferred to the new enemies of the Cold War: to Soviet and Chinese Communists, the Korean of the early 1950s, the Vietnamese enemy of the 1960s and 1970s, and hostile 'Third-World' movements in general. In every instance, the code words and formulaic metaphors of race and power were evoked to distinguish between the good self and heinous, alien Other."[61] I would add that such racial projections were not only fungible enough to be applied to "foreign" alien Others, but also "domestic" alien Others, most notably Japanese Americans during World War II. At the same time, they were also dynamic and transformative enough that former enemies like the Japanese could be properly reformed or racially rehabilitated as proper Cold War allies, as I will discuss in chapter 3. Through such an optics, in a reverse scenario, the Russians, former World War II allies, transmogrified from racially similar Westerners to the racially dissimilar "oriental" Soviet Cold War enemies. As I elaborate in the next chapter, the Soviet Union itself was racialized as "Asiatic," and Marx himself was deemed to be a "spiritual heir" of Genghis Khan.[62] Yet contradictorily, in another instance of the strange career in the racialization of Marx, his genealogy was considered to be decidedly Western. American policy makers could not see or respect, for example, anticolonial Asian nationalisms as anything other than an Asian genuflection before a Western God called Marx. Behind closed doors, it was argued that Asia and her "gooks" needed to be "saved" from such an ideological or quasi-religious duping. This, conjoined with theories of "Anglo-Saxon" masculinist racial superiority and such proposed schemes as compulsory eugenics programs, constitutes what could be called the *gendered racial political unconscious* of the Cold War.

While during the Cold War U.S. State Department officials did make routine admissions that white supremacy was the "Achilles heel" of U.S. foreign relations, they were referring to racism strictly in the domestic context and the damage it did to the United States' international prestige as the champion of democracy and freedom.[63] On the one hand, this public relations issue was managed by the federal government through the formation of what Mary L. Dudziak calls "Cold War civil rights," a particular commitment to racial justice that putatively promoted social change at home but was ultimately circumscribed by the primacy of anticommunism within the narrowly accepted range of civil rights discourse and politics. Most notably, for example, such a circumscription preempted discussions of "broad-based social change, or a linking of race and class."[64] In other words, as Jodi Melamed writes, a "racial liberalism" took earlier antiracisms (which had been connected to "heterogenous struggles of people of color," anticolonial movements, and economic justice) and sutured them to an official antiracism and U.S. nationalism. "This suture produced a liberal nationalism that normed and restricted the field of race politics, such that antiracist discourse itself came both to deflect counternationalisms . . . and to mask the workings of transnational capitalism."[65] On the other hand, even as the charge of white supremacy on the domestic front was at once acknowledged, muted, and elided through this promotion of "Cold War civil rights," "racial liberalism," and "liberal nationalism," what was simultaneously disavowed was how white supremacy also structured U.S. foreign relations itself. That is, while white supremacy at home might have been an "Achilles heel" attracting negative public relations, that same white supremacy provided the lens through which anticolonial movements abroad would be interpreted and crushed both within America's Manichaean Cold War snare as well as in future or subsequent Cold War historiography. And as I demonstrate throughout this study, Asian American cultural producers, the racialized and gendered imperial subjects who "return" to the metropole as a result of U.S. imperial Cold War interventions in Asia, carry the transgenerational memories of this twinned acknowledgment and disavowal.

The gendered racial political unconscious of the Cold War in Asia is intricately connected to the imperialist political economy of the Cold War. Susan Koshy writes that during the Cold War, the communist threat and the ideological battles it generated created an environment where political strength still owed a huge debt to military strength, and that it was not until the end of the Cold War that "the focus on trade intensified, inaugurating the shift from the Cold War to the Trade War era."[66] While I largely agree with this, I would like to examine more closely the assumed, taken-for-granted moment of inauguration. Precisely what did the formal end of the Cold War actually end and what in turn did it inaugurate? The obvious response of course is that it witnessed the demise of the Soviet Union and its corresponding communist threat, making way for U.S. hegemony and its corresponding ethos of liberal democratic freedom and capitalist free market ideology. However, this teleological narrative of the second half of the twentieth century, in which the Cold War is "won" by the forces of good against the forces of evil, captures only the dominant, Manichaean narrative. I would like to complicate this by posing the following question: Was not the Cold War *itself* a trade war? To articulate this query is not simply to quarrel with (this particular) periodization of the Cold War as an antecedent to the trade war, but to ask why we are so collectively invested in making such periodizations in the first place. I suspect that our overdetermined investment in celebrating the "end" of the Cold War and our triumphalist references to a post–Cold War era and corresponding New World Order as the "end of history" (not as apocalyptic demise but as teleological endpoint or arrival)[67] are actually symptomatic of a profound ambivalence about what such a victory might mean, and that it may be a Pyrrhic one.[68]

So, to repeat the question at hand: But was not the Cold War *itself* a trade war? Indeed, Oswaldo de Rivero argues that the battle between capitalism and communism during the second half of the twentieth century was not a conflict between totally different ideologies. It was, rather, "a *civil war between two extreme viewpoints of the same Western ideology:* the search for happiness through the material progress disseminated by the Industrial Revolution. Both capitalism and communism are products of the Industrial Revolution's manufactures. The first represents the individualist and democratic approach based on the market and inspired by Anglo-Saxon thinking; the second embodies the collectivist and authoritarian approach stemming from German political philosophy: two predatory interpretations of the same ideology of material progress."[69] De Rivero deconstructs the putative relationship between

capitalism and communism as that of radical alterity, arguing instead that
capitalism and communism can be seen as two sides of the same coin: both
carrying a Western genealogy, and both proceeding from the Industrial Revolution, and thus not posing a challenge to Western modernity. That is, they
are two extreme viewpoints within the same Western political philosophical
tradition. The question they pose is the same: how best to attain happiness
through the material progress afforded by the Industrial Revolution. They
differ only in the proposed method by which to answer the question. As such,
the Cold War *between* capitalism and communism is actually a "civil war"
within the selfsame Western modernity. As Odd Arne Westad argues, both
the United States and the Soviet Union saw themselves as the successors of
Western modernity, and the Cold War was waged over which one would be
the sole rightful successor, and would thus be able to articulate its own concept of Western modernity and attempt to universalize it.[70]

Given these insights, I would like to suggest that in terms of political economy, the Cold War was one particular phase in the much more established
Western trade wars in the globalization of capitalism and the competition
for markets and resources both natural and human. Giovanni Arrighi writes
that after World War II, there was a "structural impasse" in the world economy that blocked the "recycling of liquidity back into the expansion of world
trade and production." Eventually, "the impasse was broken by the *'invention'*
of the Cold War. What cost-benefit calculations could not and did not achieve,
fear did. . . . [T]he genius of Truman and of his advisers was to attribute the
outcome of systemic circumstances that no particular agency had created
or controlled to the allegedly subversive dispositions of the other military
superpower, the USSR. By so doing, Truman reduced Roosevelt's vision of a
global New Deal to a very shoddy reality indeed, but at least made it workable." It was "made workable" through massive rearmament during and after
the Korean War (1950–53), which "solved once and for all the liquidity problems of the post-war world economy."[71] Within this context, as I will explain
further in the chapters that follow, we can detect the increasing political economic significance of Asia as a region, particularly Japan. But briefly put,
there are two important implications to be noted here: first, what can be
termed a "neocolonial" restoration of economic and trade patterns modeled
on previous colonial relations; and second, an increasing reliance on military Keynesianism, with the wars in Korea and Vietnam serving as key "pump
primers." In terms of the first implication, the liquidity problems, most
notably the dollar gap, in the post–World War II economy were shaped by

what William S. Borden calls a "decisive paradox": the overwhelming economic supremacy of the United States, which caused a significant imbalance in the world economy, threatening foreign nations with insolvency vis-à-vis the United States and making them unable to purchase or afford American goods.[72] This imbalance was corrected via an "industrial-capitalist alliance" in which Germany, as the "spark plug" or "engine" of European production and trade, and Japan, as the Asian analog of Germany, were positioned as cornerstones. As Borden explains, this had some important implications, not the least of which was that it required the United States to revive colonial trade patterns in which Europe and Japan would trade manufactured goods to Asia, Africa, and Latin America in exchange for essential raw materials and food. This restoration of colonial economic relations, without the burdens of actual formal colonial rule, "can best be termed 'neocolonial.'" The United States could then realize its goal of establishing multilateral relations with both industrial and nonindustrial nations throughout the world, and sustain its hegemonic role, by controlling Third World economies (which were nominally *politically* independent) through such mechanisms as the World Bank and the IMF.[73] Within this scheme, Japan was positioned as America's junior Cold War partner in Asia, and its continued economic recovery relied on Southeast Asia as its source of raw materials rather than extensive trade with and ideological corruption by communist China. Such a neocolonial relation would overdetermine U.S. intervention in Southeast Asia and provoke protest from Southeast Asian nations, who decried neocolonial dependence on Japan and promoted local industrialization instead. Representative Carlos Romulo, for example, articulated Filipino resistance at the U.S.–Japan peace conference, with U.S. Ambassador to the Philippines Myron Cowen having to explain in August 1951 that "to Philippinos [*sic*], as to other Asians, [the] status of raw materials suppliers connotes colonial subservience. Any western tendency to discourage indigenous industrial development therefore is automatically suspect as [a] ruse to retain dominance economically despite [the] relinquishment of political control."[74]

Second, if we are to see post–World War II American foreign policy as responding to the twenty-five-year world crisis in capitalism that began in 1930, a key feature of this response or "solution" is an increasing reliance on military Keynesianism.[75] By 1949, while the European Recovery Program (also known as the Marshall Plan) witnessed a parallel recovery program in U.S.-occupied Japan, additional mechanisms were required to reduce the dollar gap and stimulate the world economy. In the face of a fiscally conservative

Congress reluctant to lower tariffs or appropriate ever-larger sums of foreign economic aid, efforts to militarize the Cold War found success when North Korea crossed the 38th parallel on June 25, 1950. The ensuing Korean War, as I elaborate further in chapters 3 and 4, opened a flood of congressional appropriations that rearmed Europe and the United States, helped fund France's efforts to maintain colonial control over Indochina, and sparked a tremendous war boom whose significant beneficiaries were Germany and Japan. Indeed, Secretary of State Dean Acheson called the opening weeks of the Korean War the greatest four weeks in American history,[76] while Japan, whose economy was substantively boosted through the offshore military procurements program, viewed the war as a gift from the gods. Later, Korea itself (along with Japan) would benefit similarly from America's Vietnam War. The Korean War thus marked the "beginning of the end" of the twenty-five-year economic crisis of the West and an increasing convergence or integration of economic and military aid.[77] Moreover, by 1954 what Borden calls the "Pacific alliance" between the United States and Japan was solidified through a range of mutual security agreements that formally cemented Japan into the American Cold War bloc in return for "military protection, continued procurement subsidies, and an American military protectorate in Southeast Asia."[78] Therefore, as Thomas J. McCormick writes, the Korean War inaugurated a two-decade period (1950–73) variously called the Second Cold War, the Vietnam Era, and the Long Boom. This period witnessed the increased militarization and globalization of the Cold War and coincided with and "in some ways helped produce the most sustained and profitable period of economic growth in the history of world capitalism," rewarding America's upper and middle classes but not commensurately benefiting its working class.[79]

Thus, what makes the Cold War phase of the crisis of capitalism unique is not so much the threat posed by the communist bloc, but in the *longue durée,* it is the transfer of political, military, and economic hegemony from Europe to the United States and the shift from European territorial colonialism to a less formal, but no less insidious, U.S. (neo)imperialism. McCormick observes that the Soviet Union's "very existence on the other side of that new Great Wall" helped make this transformation possible, to the extent that some observers suggested that the "Russian threat was so useful that if it had not existed, it would have had to be invented. Indeed, it was so useful that it was, at least, exaggerated."[80] The Soviet threat, metaphorized as a set of falling dominoes, echoes an earlier French metaphor vis-à-vis the potential loss of Indochina: the "ten pin theory." Within this scheme, it was feared that the fall of one piece of the French empire (even a marginal one like Vietnam) might cause other pieces (even noncontiguous, more significant ones like Algeria) to tumble, like a bowling ball striking the headpin and knocking over all the pins in succession. This logic of empire was adopted by U.S. policy makers by 1960, encompassing not only Asia and the Pacific Rim in a proximate geographical line of (falling) dominoes, but also the "ten pins" of America's extensive informal global empire in other regions of the world (the Caribbean, Latin America, and so forth). As such, argues McCormick, the famed domino theory was really two theories in one, for "empires were of a piece, and the loss of one member affected the organic health of the whole."[81] In other words, while the United States waged the Cold War to contain the double threat of Soviet communism and totalitarianism, it was also an effort to spread capitalism and "democracy," or American empire. In accounts of the Cold War, much has been made of this motive of containment. I would like to ask, however, precisely what was the United States attempting to contain? On the one hand, as I have stated, it was of course the conjoined "evils" of communism and totalitarianism. On the other hand, examining the concomitant effort to spread capitalism, I would like to suggest that part of this effort actually necessitated a peculiar *containment* of capitalism itself. This is to say that the United States has had and continues to have a vested interest in monitoring, manipulating, and maintaining the flow of capital into particular channels: channels that augment its economic, political, and military strength. And this self-interested selectiveness necessarily involved a certain containment of the free flow of capital. In the zero sum game of Cold War geopolitics and competing spheres of influence, such a tethering of capital to the U.S. nation-state was required. If left untethered, it was dangerous and could actually be used as investments in communism.

Cold War, Civil War, Culture Wars

The imperialism of the Cold War, as an enduring moment in the crisis and expansion of U.S. global capitalism, can in turn also be said to have aided the avoidance of a civil or class war in the United States. By exporting surplus capital abroad, imperialism can function as a substitute for actual social reform at home.[82] In keeping with this exporting function of imperialism—exporting not only finance capital but also class struggle and civil strife—the imperialism of the Cold War was, on the one hand, coeval with a civil rights movement and what has been called, as I discussed previously, the "culture wars" in the United States. On the other hand, it was also coterminous with decolonization movements around the world, and attempted to interpellate and induct the anticolonial nationalisms of Third World nations into yet another Western imperial formation. It could be said that this Western inter-imperialist war helped prevent a civil war *within* the United States itself. Thus, in lieu of a civil *war*, we witnessed civil rights *movements*; and in lieu of a *class* war, we witnessed *culture* wars. The Cold War, construed as an opposition of capitalist democracy and communist totalitarianism, provided what Robinson calls a "discursive cloak" or an "an ideological machine with which to preserve imperial and colonial 'adventures' among darker peoples and to suppress democratic movements at home." He argues that this Manichaeanism of the Cold War, the capitalism versus communism dyad, obfuscated (even as it violently suppressed) a decades-long global "race war," and masked the "transcendent and more enduring dualism": the racial order, à la Fanon, of a Manichaean colonial domination.[83] In other words, as I see it, while the "Cold War" as a signifier functioned as a "discursive cloak" to mask a global race war, the Cold War as a set of interimperialist practices subtended by racialized and gendered taxonomies itself constituted a race war within and upon subjugated populations and nations.

In conceptualizing the imperialism of the Cold War, I am building on Ann Laura Stoler's observation that American empire is a "blurred genre":

> As I have argued elsewhere, blurred genres are not empires in distress but imperial politics in active realignment and reformation. A combination of high-profile treaties, unwritten agreements, and unacknowledged coercive tactics, financial bodies, and agribusinesses serving as surrogate states are empire's common features. . . . Distinctly marked boundaries and transparent transfers of property represent a limited range of imperial forms and their orientations. Thus a starting point may be not to begin with a notion of empire based on a British imperial steady-state, but with a notion of empire that puts movement and oscillation at the center. . . . The United States is not a phantom empire just because it is a flexible one.[84]

The Cold War in Asia was such an "imperial architecture" in "active realignment and reformation," whose effectivity depended on the secrecy, invisibility, and partial visibility of it *as* a project of empire. This is to say that the Manichaean logics of the Cold War, articulated as the battle between democracy and capitalism, on the one hand, and totalitarianism and communism, on the other, provided a compelling covering rationale. Yet amid empire's ambiguities, tensions, and claims to democratic inclusion—the paradoxes, contradictions, and oxymorons that Amy Kaplan calls "the anarchy of empire," taken from a poem by W. E. B. Du Bois—we are left with the enduring effects of the practice of empire.[85] We are left, in other words, with the violence of war, structured inequalities, strategically imposed uneven development, a vast military architecture throughout the globe, the loss and destruction of millions of lives, the graves of the dead, and the still lingering yet scarred bodies of those who know the weapons of mass destruction (such as Agent Orange) most intimately. These effects are not the "unintended" consequences of empire, but constitute the very conditions of possibility for empire's continual expansion and reconstitution.

The Asian American cultural productions I examine in this project collectively provide a critical genealogy of the Cold War as a genealogy of American empire, revealing empire's enduring effects and contemporary reformations. In particular, these cultural imaginings shed light on the bloodiness of the Cold War's racialized and gendered taxonomies of domination, labor exploitation, biopolitical manipulation, and expulsion. They thematize and theorize the Cold War as a gendered racial formation that provides the ideological glue, if you will, between what Michael Hardt and Antonio Negri call the "concept of Empire" and the "practice of Empire." While the concept "is always dedicated to peace—a perpetual and universal peace outside of history," the practice is "continually bathed in blood."[86] This disjuncture between concept and practice is revealed further when we consider the temporality of the teleology of the Cold War. Asian American cultural stagings of the Cold War suggest that in a reverse chronology of sorts, the rhetoric of the Cold War discursively instantiated the teleological arrival or endpoint of the experiment of American liberal multiracial democracy not with the victorious end of the Cold War in 1989, but during its inaugural height in the 1950s. In other words, the Cold War victory is not the ultimate realization of American liberal democracy as the best system, but seen in another light, it can be said to unravel or undo what was already narratively constructed in the 1950s as a foregone conclusion or fait accompli, decades before the war was actually "won." The so-called liberal consensus of the 1950s effaced discussions of labor, class exploitation, racial inequality, and colonialism through the charged logics of anticommunism.[87] We see a return of this repressed, if you will, not in the form of an actual class or civil war, but in the social movements of the 1960s and eruptions of dissensus such as the "culture wars" of the 1980s. So even this return of the repressed can be seen as a placeholder

for or deferral of civil war and, as envisioned by British political economist
J. A. Hobson writing over a century ago, a "social reform in the form of a
substantive redistribution of wealth."[88] These fissures, however, along with
the complicated and unpredictable economic and political developments in
the post–Cold War conjuncture, have made the 1950s a privileged object of
nostalgia.

It could be argued, then, that Asian American critique and cultural productions constitute one "beneficiary" or legacy of the culture wars. Gaining
institutional status and cultural capital, Asian American literary and cultural
production as well as its academic study have witnessed an impressive growth
since Elaine H. Kim's important pioneering 1982 study *Asian American Literature: An Introduction to the Writings and Their Social Context*.[89] Asian
American culture and its interpretive apparatus, however, need not be "contained" by the more unsettling effects of the culture wars and the Cold War.
They need not, for example, set the nation-state or the rubrics of liberal
multiculturalism as the necessary horizon of their critical imaginings and
longings. A more dialectical imagining sets contingent, moving horizons,
and as I suggested previously in this introduction, Asian American critique
is an *unsettling hermeneutic* that disrupts the constitution of American nationalist ontology, just as Asian American cultural politics exceeds its "domestication" within the corrals of U.S. liberal multiculturalism. This study, then,
is an attempt at such a dialectical imagining.

Ends of Empire begins in the first chapter with a critical interrogation of
how official U.S. Cold War government documents cohere as an imperial
archive, epistemology, and grammar, constituting a privileged site for the
"invention" of a Manichaean reading practice through which dominant Cold
War knowledge gets congealed as "authoritative" knowledge. I trace the narrative, affective, and rhetorical registers of these canonized documents and
detect how they are deployed to construct an exceptionalist U.S. national
Bildung against a gendered racial conjuring and projection of Asia, or the
specter of a "Red Asia." This tracing sets the stage for and begins to show
how the Asian American cultural productions I analyze in the subsequent
chapters respond in complex ways to a discursive regime that precedes them,
and thus "discombobulate" and make critical interventions into the very terms
and geopolitical, epistemological, and cultural contours of this regime. Each
of these chapters, ordered via the chronology of America's acute Cold War imperial projections of and encounters with China, Japan, Korea, and Vietnam,
provides a sustained analysis of how Asian American literary and cinematic

cultural works produced in the prolonged aftermath of the inaugural height of the Cold War critically imagine such imperial projections and encounters and offer alternative possibilities. The epilogue links the Cold War to the more recent War on Terror, and discusses this linkage in terms of the broader implications of my study. In thus juxtaposing historical documents with cultural forms and putting them in conversation with one another, I want to demonstrate precisely how the Cold War was (and continues to be) an epistemological project produced in multiple sites and in a variety of forms and genres, one in which certain sites, genres, and modes of analysis are privileged over others. Moreover, I query official nationalist constructions of "authoritative" knowledge and read historical documents as themselves particular kinds of cultural *texts*. In so doing, I situate culture as itself a powerful articulation (and at times disarticulation) of knowledge. The U.S. governmental archive and Asian American cultural texts both produce knowledge, albeit different kinds of knowledge, about the Cold War, and together they constitute a complex, dialogical encounter.

I construct and organize my chapters in this manner, through a rough chronology and a situating of successive Asian national sites, in order to highlight the sheer temporal and spatial expanse of the Cold War in Asia and thus to demonstrate that U.S. militarist imperial intervention in Asia is not aberrant or contained to one nation, but is an enduring and durable project with cumulative effects and "ends," or what Stoler calls "dramatic durabilities of duress."[90] To the extent that the Cold War was itself—and provided the Manichaean cover for—an unruly set of engagements not in one nation but rather most of Asia (defined as a strategically important region), it warrants a parallel potentially "unruly" scope that offers a *comparative and relational* reckoning with its logics. That is, the Cold War's doctrine of "containment" was itself paradoxically a globally expansive project, one whose critical interrogation and analysis cannot thus be easily or neatly "contained." As such, while I could have chosen to restrict my study to one national site, and while such studies are important, doing so would have entailed a different set of questions and a different argument altogether. My relatively broad scope, however, does not include *every* Asian nation or region where the Cold War was directly or indirectly waged, such as the Philippines, Laos, Cambodia, and Okinawa, because I have chosen nations where the Cold War was "publicly" and directly waged in protracted ways as sites of immediate contention and competition between the United States and the Soviet Union. Moreover, we do not have as yet a sizable corpus of Filipino-, Laotian-, Cambodian-, or

Okinawan American cultural productions that critically thematize the Cold War. In the Filipino American case, of course, there is a large body of cultural work on the United States' long period of formal colonial rule in the Philippines before the Cold War and on the persistence of neocolonial domination. Furthermore, my chapters are organized through the distinct yet linked national sites of China, Japan, Korea, and Vietnam rather than through various thematic rubrics not in order to privilege the nation-state as the proper unit of analysis or mode of organization, but simply because the geopolitical actors, categories, and sites of the Cold War and its "hot wars" are nation-states and because specific thematic rubrics might not be even or equally salient across all national sites. Finally, the organization of my chapters serves to highlight the wide range of Asian American cultural forms that collectively generates an *unsettling hermeneutic* of the Cold War. That is, just as the U.S. Cold War in one Asian national site proved not to be aberrant or singular, a critical reframing of the Cold War found in one particular Asian American cultural text proves not to be aberrant or singular.

In chapter 1, "Cold War Logics, Cold War Poetics: Conjuring the Specter of a Red Asia," through a sustained analysis of important U.S. government documents that have been canonized in the Cold War historical archive, such as the writings of George F. Kennan (1946, 1947), the Truman Doctrine (1947), NSC 68 (1950), and NSC 48/1 (1949), I map how the invention of a Manichaean reading practice and its attendant narrative strategies cast the Cold War as a world historical contest between two radically alternative ways of life. America is figured in this contest as uniquely and solely qualified to champion and promote "good" (meaning democracy and capitalism) against "evil" (meaning communism and totalitarianism). These documents thus collectively cohere as a nationalist developmental narrative or *Bildungsroman* of American exceptionalism, and in suggesting and rationalizing specific courses of action for America, they at once unveil and obfuscate America's imperialist longings and intentions. In particular, I trace and critically detect in my analysis the Orientalism of anticommunism. Significantly, this Orientalism takes form and finds articulation *before* the Communist victory in China, and through its logics, the Soviet Union is itself already racialized as Asiatic. I interrogate, moreover, the rhetorical and narrative force of a gendered racial conjuring of the specter of a "Red Asia," and ask how it becomes legitimated as authorized knowledge and comes to overdetermine and rationalize official Cold War policy, especially military interventions, in Asia. How does "Asia," as at once a rhetorical figure or trope and a geopolitical region, gain visibility, coherence, and increasing strategic importance in America's imperialist geopolitical imaginary? Indeed, I have chosen the particular documents I have named above not only because of the significant roles they have played in producing Cold War geopolitical and cultural knowledge, but also precisely because such a production of knowledge and Manichaean reading practice have influenced Cold War policy, particularly in Asia.

Chapter 2, "The El Dorado of Commerce: China's Billion Bellies," considers the metaphorics of America's long career of "China watching," saturated by the desire for the fabled Chinese market and its Cold War "loss" to Mao's Communist victory in 1949. I analyze government documents, Cold War films, and Asian American literature, such as the so-called "China White Paper" of 1949 (a thousand-page tome of compiled government documents explaining the "loss" of China), the Cold War film par excellence *The Manchurian Candidate* (1962), and the various incarnations of the Butterfly genre, culminating in David Henry Hwang's play *M. Butterfly* (1988). The chapter interrogates the peculiar metaphoricity of China and traces how the bipolar Cold War rivalry between the United States and the Soviet Union gets triangulated when the historical "yellow peril" merges with the "red menace" in China. I show how the specter of a "Red Asia," or "red peril," if you will, thus comes to haunt Cold War logics and geopolitics in Asia, and how China in some ways displaces the Soviet Union as America's principal Cold War threat.

Then, in chapter 3, "Asian America's Japan: The Perils of Gendered Racial Rehabilitation," I examine how Japanese American cultural producers critically reveal the Cold War in Japan, specifically the U.S. occupation of Japan at the conclusion of World War II and in the aftermath of the atomic bombings of Hiroshima and Nagasaki. I analyze Steven Okazaki's documentary *Survivors* (1982, updated 1994), David Mura's memoir *Turning Japanese* (1991), and Ruth L. Ozeki's novel *My Year of Meats* (1998), and demonstrate how these works thematize the atomic bombing of Hiroshima, Japanese American internment, and the occupation of Japan as linked U.S. imperial projects of what I call gendered racial rehabilitation.

The next two chapters expose the Cold War's "hot wars" in Korea and Vietnam. Chapter 4, "The Forgotten War: Korean America's Conditions of Possibility," considers how Korean American cultural imaginings offer an unsettling hermeneutic of the Korean War that does not posit naïve or wholesale retrieval as the desired or even possible corrective to historical and narrative erasure, but rather attends to the war as a complex problem of knowledge that saturates both American nationalist discourse and Korean America's public or "admitted" knowledge about the conditions of possibility for its very formation in the post-1945 conjuncture. I argue that in Susan Choi's haunting novel *The Foreign Student* (1998), Heinz Insu Fenkl's autobiographical novel *Memories of My Ghost Brother* (1996), and Deann Borshay Liem's highly personal documentary *First Person Plural* (2000), the Korean War appears not simply as a congealed historical episode or epistemological object that is given narrative form after the event, but also as an imperialist and gendered racial Cold War epistemology in the making. What does it mean to want to represent or "remember" a war that has been "forgotten" and erased in the U.S. popular imaginary, but has been transgenerationally seared into the memories of Koreans and Korean Americans, and experienced anew every day in a still-divided Korea?

Chapter 5, "The War-Surplus of Our New Imperialism: Vietnam, Masculinist Hypervisibility, and the Politics of (Af)filiation," turns from the "Forgotten War" to the Vietnam War or so-called conflict, a military intervention that is perhaps America's most debated and protracted Cold War project of empire and gendered racial formation in Asia. It is a war or defeat that the U.S. would like to forget but by which it is persistently haunted. I examine the PBS documentary *Daughter from Danang* (2002), Aimee Phan's short story collection *We Should Never Meet* (2004), and Trinh T. Minh-ha's experimental feature-length film *Surname Viet Given Name Nam* (1989), and analyze the complex ways in which these cultural works show a Vietnam that is different from America's Vietnam. Moreover, these works ask how the masculinist hypervisibility of representations of America over "there" in Vietnam fails to reckon with Vietnamese Americans over "here" in the United States. In this instance, then, visibility is neither some teleological endpoint of political recognition or empowerment nor transparent access to "knowledge" about the Vietnam War, but a persistent problematic and preoccupying symptom that reveals America's anxieties about its defeat. I argue that such Vietnamese American cultural productions make important interventions in the masculinist hypervisibility of the Vietnam War in America's popular imaginary and imperial memory. They challenge that hypervisibility by displaying the complicated "return" of Vietnamese subjects (as "refugees" and adopted "orphans" of "Operation Babylift") to the American metropole.

Finally, *Ends of Empire*'s epilogue, "Imagining an End to Empire," reveals how Cold War epistemology continues to generate and teach "new" knowledge about Asia by linking the Cold War to the more recent War on Terror. How are post-9/11 discursive constellations, such as the "axis of evil," at once new yet anxiously conjured recyclings of Cold War inscriptions, such as the "evil empire"? I interrogate the multiple senses of the "ends" of empire: the temporal, spatial, and functional ends of empire that extend and reinvigorate the historical life of American empire, as well as the many ostensible terminations of empire. These plural ends of empire perpetually defer a singular end, or *an end,* to empire.

1

COLD WAR LOGICS, COLD WAR POETICS

Conjuring the Specter of a Red Asia

I begin this chapter by returning us briefly to Chang-rae Lee's *Native Speaker*, the novel with which I opened the introduction. Even as the Korean War emerges in this text as a *problem* of knowledge rather than a transparent *object* of knowledge that is given narrative form after the event, it is a persistent present or presence that informs and haunts the narrator's subjectivity even though he was born many years after the war. Because the Korean War resulted in the division of the country into a U.S.-controlled South and communist North, in the U.S. neoimperial imaginary there are "good" Koreans and there are "bad" Koreans. In *Native Speaker*, Lee inserts an account of the pedagogical moment in which his narrator, Henry Park, experiences the lesson of what it means to be a good or bad Korean. This moment literally takes place in the classroom when Henry decides to do an oral report on the Korean War. Henry recalls, "I read my junior encyclopedia. . . . The entry didn't mention any Koreans except for Syngman Rhee and Kim Il Sung, the Communist leader. Kim was a *bad* Korean. In the volume there was a picture of him wearing a Chinese jacket. He was fat-faced and maniacal. Bayonets were in the frame behind him. He looked like an evil robot."[1] Pressed to do a presentation that would be favorably received by his class, Henry decides to be a "good Korean" instead of the "*bad* Korean," the "Mao lover's Mao." To save himself from certain embarrassment, Henry prepares a report that parrots Cold War rhetoric: "the threat of Communism, the Chinese Army, how MacArthur was a visionary, that Truman should have listened to him. How lucky all . . . Koreans were."[2] Given this prescriptive and indeed pre-scripted route that Henry ultimately takes, we might wonder why he chose to do a report on the Korean War in the first place. We learn that Henry's report is not simply an attempt to fill a gap in his knowledge of geopolitics and history, but more deeply an effort to get to know his own family history. He is curious about the Korean War, precisely because his father "never talked about the war."[3] For Henry, the Korean War thus represents a paradoxically conjoined event. On the one hand, it remains a personal family history that refuses to be told, that exceeds signification. On the other hand, the Korean War becomes for Henry an entry in his junior encyclopedia and the moment of his pedagogical interpellation as a "good" Korean. Henry's lack of knowledge, and the Manichaean Cold War rhetoric that stands in for knowledge, index the Korean War not as a congealed and transparent historical event that can be accessed and given facile narrative form (as a junior encyclopedia entry would suggest), but as a complex problem of knowledge. This problem of knowledge saturates not only American nationalist Korean War history and broader Cold War history, but Korean American subjectivity and the very conditions of possibility for the post–World War II formation of Korean America in the first place.

Native Speaker thus provocatively demonstrates this chapter's focus on tracking the rhetorical, affective, and discursive registers of the Cold War's anticommunism. Specifically, I examine the ways in which narrative and rhetorical strategies, or what could be called "Cold War poetics," are deployed to construct an exceptionalist U.S. national *Bildung* against a gendered racial conjuring and projection of Asia. This chapter thus sets the stage for and begins to demonstrate how the contemporary Asian American cultural productions I analyze in the chapters that follow respond in complex ways to a discursive and epistemological regime that precedes them and critically disarticulate a dialogue already in progress. What are the contours of this dialogue, and how does the critical intervention of Asian American cultural forms transform the very terms of this dialogue? My tracking occurs through a sustained reading of select classic Cold War government documents that have been canonized in the historical archive and that have contributed significantly to the "invention" of a Manichaean reading practice that casts Cold War geopolitical relationships as a contest between alternative ways of life, between a universal American "good" and a gendered racial "Asiatic" "evil." These documents are George F. Kennan's "Long Telegram" and "The Sources of Soviet Conduct"; NSC 68; and NSC 48/1.[4] Taken together, these documents not only suggest and map particular courses of action for the United States, but they offer a nationalist developmental narrative or *Bildungsroman* of American exceptionalism in which imperialist desires are at once revealed and veiled by casting America as uniquely qualified to champion the cause of freedom and democracy throughout the world. In my analysis, I highlight how the Soviet Union was itself racialized as Asiatic (before the Communist victory in China), and critically detect the Orientalism of anti-communist rhetorics. Moreover, I ask how the rhetorical and narrative force of a gendered racial conjuring of the specter of a "Red Asia" becomes congealed as authoritative Cold War knowledge that overdetermines and rationalizes military interventions in Asia. In other words, these Manichaean and gendered racial discursive articulations of the Cold War, or the production of dominant Cold War knowledge, render the Cold War as at once the utterly "knowable" fight against the certain and incontrovertible evils of communism as well as the utterly "unknowable" of critical analytics that fall outside of this dominant Manichaean geopolitical structuring and reading practice. The perverse temporal logic of the Cold War, as I noted in the introduction, posits that which is yet to be, or remains to be seen, as an always already. As Donald Pease writes, "in the Cold War as drama, the Cold War paradigm *pre*occupies all the positions—and all the oppositions as well . . . since the Cold War paradigm confines totalizing operations to the work of the other superpower, the Cold War drama is free to expose even its own totalization of the globe as the work of the other superpower."[5] Thus, as I demonstrated above in my brief opening discussion of *Native Speaker,* Henry Park's schoolboy relationship to the Korean War is figured simultaneously through his knowledge of the putative certainty of Cold War anticommunist logics and his lack of critical, alternative knowledge that might disrupt such logics.

I have chosen to focus in this chapter on classic Cold War government documents for a few related reasons. First, I want to emphasize how Cold War epistemology is an intersecting multisited and multigeneric discourse. Second, my aim is to interrogate the ways in which certain sites, genres, and modes of analysis of this discourse have been privileged over others. Namely, while government documents such as the ones I analyze have been privileged or canonized in the historical archive to support dominant interpretations of the Cold War as a bipolar rivalry between the United States and the Soviet Union, I read them against the grain of such an overdetermined interpretive scheme. By focusing on the documents' discursive and affective registers, I reveal the Cold War's gendered racial and imperialist moorings, longings, and triangulations in Asia. Indeed, as William Pietz argues, while Cold War discourse would seem to bear a negative relation to colonial discourse, the relationship between the two can actually be seen as comparable and continuous.[6]

Moreover, in juxtaposing historical documents with cultural forms, I query official nationalist constructions of "authoritative" knowledge and read historical documents as themselves cultural *texts* rather than reifying them further as "objective historical evidence." In so doing, I situate culture as itself a crucial articulation, and at times disarticulation, of knowledge. Finally, I have chosen the particular documents I have outlined above because of the significant roles they have played in producing Cold War geopolitical knowledge and because of the extent to which they have influenced Cold War policy, especially in Asia, precisely through such a production of knowledge.

On the "Oriental Secretiveness and Conspiracy" of the Russian Mind

I shall begin with George F. Kennan, one of the principal architects of the Cold War. Although he would later distance himself from the official Cold War policy and parlance of "containment" that he so famously made popular (claiming in his memoirs in 1967 that he read his "Long Telegram" at that time with "horrified amusement"), his writings had a sensational effect on Washington Cold War policy makers due in no small part to the narrative force of his prose.[7] Indeed, what came to be famously known as the "doctrine of containment" appears first in Kennan's two highly cited classic Cold War documents, the so-called "Long Telegram" from Moscow and the article "The Sources of Soviet Conduct," published anonymously as "X" in *Foreign Affairs*. What narrative strategies allowed Kennan's particular use of the word "containment" to become an organizing principle of Cold War ideology and architecture? Containment—as narrative and doctrine—took on a life of its own, if you will, in ways that far exceeded Kennan's intent. While his thesis immediately found a vast audience in Washington, at the same time, in what has been pointed out as an "irony of history" by Yonosuke Nagai, Washington chose not to respond to Ho Chi Minh's repeated pleas (no fewer than eight) from the autumn of 1945 through February of 1946 asking for American support at the United Nations for Vietnamese independence from French colonial rule.[8]

Kennan's eight-thousand-word telegram, cabled on February 22, 1946, from Moscow when he was the American chargé d'affaires there, is in his words "neatly divided, like an eighteenth-century *Protestant sermon,* into five separate parts" (so that the whole would not look so "outrageously long"). It was ostensibly cabled to Washington in response to the Treasury Department's request for detailed information on the Soviet Union's refusal to join the International Monetary Fund (IMF) and World Bank.[9] In his *Memoirs,*

Kennan expresses his excitement that his opinion was being asked, after years of "unechoing silence" from Washington, and observes that "the occasion, to be sure, was a trivial one, but the implications of the query were not. It was no good trying to brush the question off with a couple of routine sentences describing Soviet views on such things as World Banks and International Monetary Funds. It would not do to give them just a fragment of the truth. Here was a case where nothing but the whole truth would do. They had asked for it. Now, by god, they would have it."[10] Before turning to a close look at the text of this (in)famous "telegraphic dissertation," I would like to examine Kennan's own words on the reception of his work. For his assessment is as interesting, and curiously revealing, as the telegram itself. He writes:

> The effect produced in Washington by this *elaborate pedagogical effort* was nothing less than sensational. It was one that changed my career and my life in very basic ways. If none of my previous *literary efforts* had seemed to evoke even the faintest tinkle from the bell at which they were aimed, this one, to my astonishment, struck it squarely and set it vibrating with a resonance that was not to die down for many months. It was one of those moments when official Washington, whose states of receptivity or the opposite are determined by *subjective emotional currents* as intricately imbedded in the *subconscious* as those of the most complicated of *Sigmund Freud's* erstwhile patients, was ready to receive a given message. . . . The President, I believe, read it. The Secretary of the Navy, Mr. James Forrestal, had it reproduced and evidently made it required reading for hundreds, if not thousands, of higher officers in the armed services.[11]

Indeed, the usually budget-conscious State Department copied the entire document for wide distribution, explaining that it was "not subject to condensation,"[12] and Kennan, up until this point a career diplomat, was recalled from Moscow by Secretary of the Navy Forrestal and appointed as the leading foreign policy expert at the new National War College. I am especially interested in Kennan's reference to his telegram as at once an "elaborate pedagogical" and "literary" effort, and as I previously quoted, as a "Protestant sermon," coupled with his understanding of the role that the "subconscious" and "subjective emotional currents" play in the making of ostensibly objective policy decisions. This self-conscious acknowledgment and conjoining of the pedagogical, literary, and religious forms of his prose suggest that he took language, and the power of rhetoric in influencing reception and policy decisions, quite seriously. He employed rhetorical strategies, a self-described "florid showmanship in prose,"[13] to argue for geopolitical "strategies of containment" of Soviet expansion and communist domination.[14] In this sense, Kennan is a scribe of Cold War poetics par excellence, and the persuasive force of his writing, whose effect has been "nothing less than sensational," owes as much to its subjective, rhetorical, and affective registers as it does to the putatively objective, realistic policy analysis it offers. These registers would overdetermine the "sensational" reception and interpretation of his work.

Turning now, then, to a close reading of the Cold War poetics and logics of the "Long Telegram," or the *why* of the persuasive force of Kennan's writing, we see that it is replete with tropes and metaphors of disease, pathology, contamination, and penetration, on the one hand, and health, manliness, and vigor, on the other. In my analysis, I would like to focus on what I detect to be the racialized and gendered Orientalism of these tropes and metaphors. Perhaps not surprisingly, Kennan's demonization of Soviet power and its "outlook," while so exaggerated as to seem parodic, reveals some fascinating contradictions and ambiguities. He begins his treatise by explaining the "basic features" and "background" of the Soviet outlook. He teaches us that the Kremlin's rule and view of world affairs spring from a deep-rooted sense of insecurity, and that the Soviet Union is thus "neurotic," "traditional," "instinctive," "archaic in form, fragile and artificial in its psychological foundation," and unwilling to compromise with rival powers.[15] This in and of itself, what Kennan calls "only the steady advance of uneasy Russian nationalism," is not necessarily sufficient cause for concern or alarm (700). However, this nationalism, in the "new guise of international Marxism, with its honeyed promises to a desperate and war torn outside world, it is more dangerous and insidious than ever before" (700). Constructing a narrative of racial development, Kennan then suggests that such an espousal of Marxism—and thus a lapse into communism—are coeval with "oriental secretiveness and conspiracy":

> In atmosphere of *oriental secretiveness and conspiracy* which pervades this Government, possibilities for distorting or poisoning sources and currents of information are infinite. The very disrespect of Russians for objective truth—indeed, their disbelief in its existence—leads them to view all stated facts as instruments for furtherance of one ulterior purpose or another. There is good reason to suspect that this government is actually a conspiracy within a conspiracy. (701, emphasis added)

References to "archaic," "traditional," "secretiveness," "conspiracy," "distort-ing," "ulterior purpose," and "conspiracy within a conspiracy" rely on and exploit the historically persistent conjoined discourses of oriental primi-tivism and inscrutability. Moreover, the connection between Marx and the "oriental" is especially fascinating, and we see it also expressed by Secretary of the Navy Forrestal, the ardent promoter of Kennan's writings and career. In a letter to Raymond Moley on February 13, 1946, Forrestal complained that there was too much reverence for "imported theories" in American uni-versities. This unfortunate trend had begun, he claimed, with the acceptance of German philosophy in the nineteenth century, and Karl Marx was the spiritual descendent of Fichte, Kant, and Hegel. But, as Lloyd C. Gardner notes, "(in a discarded draft of this letter, he had referred to Marx *as a direct spir-itual heir of Genghis Khan*.) Forrestal's emotional obsession was a parody of the old fear that European radicalism would finally terrorize the world as a German head on a Russian peasant. Forrestal made it out as a *German head on a Mongol warrior*."[16] Similarly, a few decades before Forrestal, Secre-tary of State Robert Lansing, serving under President Woodrow Wilson, had blamed the ascent of Bolshevism in Russia on the putative Asian influences of the expansive bicontinental nation, equating the rule of Lenin with "the Asiatic despotism of the early Tsars."[17] In a 1942 lecture, Kennan himself had argued that the Bolshevik Revolution of 1917 had peeled away "the western-ized upper crust" of the old tsarist ruling class, exposing the Russians in their true form as "a 17th-century semi-Asiatic people."[18] Significantly, such in-stances of the Orientalist racialization of Marx(ism) *preceded* the 1949 Com-munist victory in China. Moreover, the Manichaean racialization of Soviet Russia in general relied on old fears of the "yellow peril" and the battle with Japan in World War II. For example, during cabinet debates on atomic pol-icy in September 1946, Forrestal argued that entering into an atomic control agreement with the Russians would be a perilous move because, like the Japa-nese, they were essentially "oriental" in their mindset and therefore not to be trusted.[19] In both Kennan and Forrestal, then, we see a great investment in rendering America's Cold War other *as* an "Other" by racializing it (the Soviet Union) and its ideological father (Marx) as essentially oriental and Eastern, eliding the ways "European radicalism" *qua* Marxism and what we could call American liberal pragmatism are two strains within the selfsame Western political philosophical tradition.

The racial optics of Kennan's "Cold War Orientalism"[20] are imbricated with gendered logics. Soviet power is figured as a hypermasculine, raping force.

We see a preoccupation with "communist penetration" throughout the telegram, and a fixation on the maintenance of boundaries that are at once ideological, racial, and gendered.[21] Interestingly, while Soviet power and government, and the Communist Party, are cast as hypermasculine, Russia and Russian people are cast as feminine. Indeed, throughout the telegram, Kennan is careful to distinguish between the Kremlin and the Russian people. He writes, for example, that "We here are convinced that never since termination of civil war have mass of Russian people been emotionally farther removed from doctrines of Communist Party than they are today" (707). A few months after he wrote the telegram, Kennan compared the Soviet people to a "woman who had been romantically in love with her husband and who had suddenly seen his true colors revealed . . . there was no question of divorce. They decided to stay together for the sake of the children. But the honeymoon was definitely over."[22] This analogy in the form of a romantic melodrama, Frank Costigliola observes, "fit a favorite narrative of Kennan in which the Russian people figured as feminine (and often an object of desire), the Soviet government appeared as a cruel masculine authority, and he stood forth as the unrequited but true lover of the Russian people."[23]

In the "Long Telegram," while the Soviet Union is itself gendered and racialized, the particularly vulnerable targets of its "unceasing pressure for penetration" are similarly cast (706). Here, we also witness the imperialist logics of Kennan's sermon. He notes that a wide variety of U.S. national institutions and bodies are susceptible to communist penetration. Each one in this wide variety, as Kennan enumerates them, is marked by race, gender, class, or ideology: labor unions, youth leagues, women's organizations, racial societies, liberal magazines, and so forth (704). These bodies are figured as divisive elements in the U.S. body politic and potential sources of disruption of "national confidence." He writes, "All persons with grievances, whether economic or racial, will be urged to seek redress not in mediation and compromise, but in defiant violent struggle for destruction of other elements of society. Here poor will be set against rich, black against white, young against old, newcomers against established residents, etc." (705). Even as he acknowledges social antagonisms and stratifications in capitalist America, he disavows them by targeting the subjects who are most oppressed by them as possible communists, polluting agents, and threats to national, and by extension Western, cohesion. Similarly, he warns that the colonies and "dependent peoples" of the West are also susceptible to Soviet penetration, noting that "mistakes and weaknesses of Western colonial administration will be mercilessly exposed and exploited" (705). For Kennan, a merciless exposure of Western colonialism would not be a positive thing.

What is to be done against this possible Soviet penetration or rape? The United States must demonstrate an even more masculine will, one of "cohesion, firmness, and vigor" (707). Kennan casts himself, and the United States, as the analyst or doctor, and the Soviet Union as the psychologically and physically unhealthy analysand or patient: "We must study it with same courage, detachment, objectivity, and same determination not to be emotionally provoked or unseated by it, with which doctor studies unruly and unreasonable individual" (708). Ironically, the kind of detached, dispassionate, objective, and unemotional stance he is here prescribing is precisely what is lacking in his own telegram, and what had broken down during his passionate diplomatic mission.[24] Kennan's final prescription is that since "world communism is like malignant parasite which feeds only on diseased tissue . . . much depends on health and vigor of our own society" (708). In order to protect the world against this epidemic, much like the way a body's immune system distinguishes between self and non-self, Washington had to draw an anti-Soviet defense line along the existing boundary of the Soviet Union, giving substance to Stalin's fear of capitalist encirclement and setting into motion a vicious cycle of suspicion and toughness on both sides. Moreover, as I have been suggesting, to the extent that the communist Soviet regime is deemed to be essentially oriental or Asiatic within Kennan's narrative scheme, the trope of disease is racialized. That is, the carrier of disease is oriental, and those infected or afflicted with the epidemic of communism will thus be orientalized. Indeed, the figuration of racialized bodies as the very embodiment of disease, and the concomitant fear that they have the ability to cross multiple boundaries—particularly of space, race, or class—build on an enduring historical discourse of the "yellow peril."[25]

Kennan's epidemiological troping is part and parcel of his conjoined teleology of racial, gender, ideological, and national development.[26] What is lacking in terms of logical and evidentiary force is countervailed by the rhetorical force of a nationalist *Bildung*, whose logics construct a narrative of a masculine, Anglo-Saxon, and capitalist America that is to serve as a model and source of guidance for the other nations of the world. By taking advantage of the historically persistent potency of these logics, and applying specific literary strategies, Kennan made it very difficult for readers to disagree with his claims. For example, in one of many colorful passages, he writes, "behind all this *will be* applied an insistent, *unceasing pressure for penetration and*

command of key positions in administration and especially in police apparatus of foreign countries. The Soviet regime is a police regime par excellence, reared in the dim half world of Tsarist police intrigue, accustomed to
think primarily in terms of police power. This should never be lost sight of
in gauging Soviet motives" (706, emphasis added). While rhetorically powerful, this passage, as with the telegram as a whole, leaves much to be desired
in terms of evidence and specificity. How, for example, will "unceasing pressure for penetration and command" be applied, and in which particular
"foreign countries"? And where is the evidence to support the claim that the
"Soviet regime is a police regime par excellence"? As such, Kennan's grammars and rhetorics interpellate readers both by effectively foreclosing or
preempting disagreement, and by setting the terms of the debate.

Kennan followed his "Long Telegram" several months later with "The
Sources of Soviet Conduct," published in July 1947 in *Foreign Affairs*, soon
after his appointment as the head of Secretary of State Marshall's Policy Planning Staff. Scholars refer to this piece as the "X" article because Kennan published it anonymously as "X." X's anonymity, however, would not last for long.
The pedagogical effort undertaken to such sensational effect in "The Long
Telegram" is built upon and congealed to even greater heights in the X article.
The article makes explicit what the telegram only implies: that what is being
offered is a "psychological analysis" of "the political personality of Soviet
power."[27] As in the telegram, we are taught that this political personality is
immature, controlled by "instinctive desires," "impatience," and "impulses and
emotions" (567). Such immaturity, moreover, is gauged along a spectrum of
racial development, one that finds infancy or childhood in the "oriental" or
"Asiatic" and full maturity in the "Anglo-Saxon." In explaining Soviet behavior from the point of view of a putatively objective expert, Kennan writes,
"Their sense of insecurity was too great. Their particular brand of fanaticism,
unmodified by any of the *Anglo-Saxon* traditions of compromise, was too
fierce and too jealous to envisage any permanent sharing of power. From the
Russian-Asiatic world out of which they had emerged they carried with them
a skepticism as to the possibilities of permanent and peaceful coexistence of
rival forces" (568, emphasis added). This racial and civilizational discourse,
in which the sober Anglo-Saxon traditions of "compromise" are pitted against
a fanatic, jealous, and uncompromising Russian-Asiatic or oriental outlook,
is a prominent theme throughout the article. Indeed, the Orientalism of Kennan's Cold War logics is subtended by an assumption that the "Russian-Asiatic
world," or what he alternately calls the "Russian or oriental mind" (573), is

essentially what he deems it to be, and the litany includes fanatic, jealous, secretive, duplicitous, suspicious, and unfriendly (573). Because this is taken to be the *essential* nature of the political personality of Soviet power, its verity requires no demonstration.

Kennan follows his diagnosis with a prescription for how to contain the Soviet disease. While Soviet power is impatient and impulsive, because the "theory of the inevitability of the eventual fall of capitalism has the fortunate connotation that there is no hurry about it" (572–73), it can also afford to be patient. As such, "Its political action is a fluid stream which moves constantly, whenever it is permitted to move, toward a given goal. Its main concern is to make sure that it has filled every nook and cranny available to it in the basin of world power. But if it finds unassailable barriers in its path, it accepts these philosophically and accommodates itself to them. The main thing is that there should always be pressure, *unceasing constant pressure,* toward the desired goal" (573–74, emphasis added). Repeating here the reference to "unceasing pressure" that we see in the "Long Telegram," Kennan this time adds a concrete prescription for United States action to contain the Soviet stream: "In these circumstances it is clear that the main element of any United States policy toward the Soviet Union must be that of *a long-term, patient but firm and vigilant containment of Russian expansive tendencies*" (575–76, emphasis added). Kennan's diagnosis of the problem, the pathological political personality of Soviet power, and his prescription, a policy of firm containment (repeated throughout the article), offered Washington policy makers a clear, simple, reductive, and compellingly Manichaean view of Soviet foreign policy and U.S.–Soviet relations.[28] Given the deterioration of Soviet–American relations between 1944 and 1946, he provided the clarity that the Truman administration had already been seeking eagerly, and he articulated a policy of containment that had already found strong support within the administration. His colorful rhetoric contributed to the termination of the United States' wartime policy of cooperating with the Soviet Union, arguing that the United States must "continue to regard the Soviet Union as a rival, not a partner, in the political arena" (580). Yet while Kennan's policy of containment was largely interpreted as military containment, what his article makes clear, and what Washington officials passed over, was that the one privileged site of containment he advocated was precisely *not* military, but had much more to do with U.S. domestic policies and politics. Indeed, as Douglas Field has observed, Cold War scholars have recently called for a reexamination of the narrative of containment. Rather than continuing to use this overused (and thus imprecise) rubric, Field argues that the Cold War was characterized by "an anxiety over manifold boundaries, whether racial, sexual, political, or cultural."[29]

A close reading of the closing paragraphs of Kennan's article suggests that what has been called a policy of containment appears as a trope of American exceptionalism, a nationalist narrative of American self-identity. Soviet power is thus a complex Orientalist phantasm that serves as America's self-consolidating Other and mediates the Cold War relationship between the two superpowers. While Kennan is largely unclear about what a policy of containment might or should actually entail, he does spell out one specific project as the most significant and important in the containment of Soviet power and expansion. This project turns out to be internal to the United States, what Kennan calls the country's "internal life," "responsibilities [as] a world power," and "spiritual vitality" (581). He culminates his psychological analysis of the political personality of *Soviet* power with a psychological analysis of the political personality of *American* power. If America fulfills its manifest destiny as a "nation among nations" (582), Kennan argues, Soviet power will inevitably crumble. As such, he renders moot his foregoing analysis of this power. For as long as America fulfills its promise as an exceptional, exemplary nation, it does not matter what kind of political personality Soviet power possesses. Within this economy, knowing thyself takes precedence over knowing thine enemy. Moreover, Kennan repeatedly stresses the need to create the *impression* that America is living up to its promise so that communism can likewise *appear* "sterile and quixotic" (581). Impressions and appearances, it seems, are just as (if not more) important than actualities. The Cold War, then, as an imperial epistemology, constitutes in part the fabrication, production, and instruction of impressions and appearances—narratives—whose referents, were they to be known, might tell quite a different story.

But precisely what are the problems of America's "internal life," and its "responsibilities [as] a world power"? And what constitutes "spiritual vitality"? In revealing pieces of correspondence written before the "Long Telegram," pieces that he later had removed from his collected papers, Kennan provides some policy recommendations for strengthening, uniting, and purifying America's body politic. Feeling disillusioned and alienated after a 1938 bicycle trip through his native Wisconsin, Kennan had critiqued the atomization and individualism of American society, comparing it unfavorably to the collective, public sociability of Russian society, and accusing Americans of having "forgotten how to think or act collectively" or deal responsibly with "community problems."[30] He concluded that America needed a community-building "cataclysm," and the Soviet regime, with its aims for global communist penetration, would provide such a welcomed cataclysm. In the meantime, Kennan recommended that an educated elite unselfishly dedicated to public service direct the "hearts and minds" of Americans toward a healthy, worthwhile goal, and reform the U.S. government into a benevolent yet "authoritarian" regime. As justification for his sanitation project of purifying a disintegrating American body politic, Kennan relied on gendered and racialized taxonomies and topographies, arguing, for example, that the right to suffrage should be taken away from the majority of women, immigrants, and African Americans. He deemed these groups to be too "bewildered" and "ignorant" to vote for good leaders.[31] He was particularly fearful that a disintegrating, disunited America had transmogrified into a "matriarchy" full of women who held excessive power in all aspects of American life and society and had a particularly corrupting influence in politics by placing "enormous power in the hands of lobbyists, charlatans, and racketeers." American women were seen not only to exercise unnatural power, but to demonstrate an unnatural constitutional or bodily development: "She has become, in comparison with the women of other countries, delicate, high-strung, unsatisfied, flat-chested and flat-voiced." Kennan's preferred female type was the Russian woman, who possessed the "powerful maternal thighs of the female Slav." In order to reverse this unnatural order of things, Kennan recommended that American women restrict their participation in civic life to "family picnics, children's parties, and the church social."[32] While Kennan had previously pointed his accusatory finger at upper- and middle-class women, by 1944, witnessing greater numbers of women entering the workforce and participating in the war effort, he blamed women of all classes for maintaining the matriarchy, or the source of America's unraveling. Fearing the inversion and destabilization of traditional gender roles, as well as a subversion and abolition of America's racial hierarchy, Kennan proposed a restoration of what he calls in the X article America's "best traditions," especially its "Anglo-Saxon traditions of compromise" (582, 568).

Such a restoration is necessary if America is to pass the "test" presented to it by the Soviet challenge. It is here, at the culmination of his article, that Kennan is most explicit in rhetorically shaping the policy of containment as a nationalist *Bildung*. Alan Nadel observes that containment is to be achieved not only through counterforce, but also by counterexample. He writes: "These increased strains, attempts to frustrate by containing the flow, suggest less the tactics of a twentieth-century statesman than those of Aristophanes' *Lysistrata.* They do not constitute the foundations of a foreign policy so much as they do the motivations for a national narrative."[33] Indeed, instead of complaining about the Soviet challenge, the "thoughtful" American will "experience a certain gratitude to a *providence* which, by providing the American people with this implacable challenge, has made their entire security as a nation dependent on their *pulling themselves together* and accepting the *responsibilities of moral and political leadership that history plainly intended them to bear*" (582, emphasis added). By alluding to a "providence," Kennan not only echoes America's powerful foundational mythos of manifest destiny, but also draws a perhaps unwanted parallel between the religiosity of America's exceptionalist calling to be a "nation among nations" and the Soviet regime's "messianic movement" (582). He desires "a *spiritual vitality* capable of holding its own among the major ideological currents of the time" (581, emphasis added). But this global, imperializing spiritual vitality begins right at home: it depends on purging the American body politic of its corrupting gendered, racial, and working-class subjects, who are not figured as members, however marginalized, of the American polity, but as targets of communist penetration and thus as agents of America's unhealthy disintegration. They are the contagious carriers of the disease of communism, and do not get counted as constitutionally "American," legally and materially, when he refers to "American people" "pulling themselves together" (582). Indeed, communism's messianism, its "magical" appeal to the world, is precisely the kind of power that Kennan wants for America and its capitalist ideology. Lloyd C. Gardner has observed that in the article we see the "Presbyterian elder wrestling with a Bismarckian geopolitician."[34]

While Kennan thus takes up tropes of race and gender to tell an allegorical tale about the evils of Soviet communism, he also targets raced and gendered bodies in the pedagogical registers of his fable about America's exceptionalist national development and mission. What he would like his audiences to learn is that America is being led astray, and that a restoration of its "best values" is in order. Such a restoration would involve a temporal rollback to a fictive time of pure patriarchal, Anglo-Saxon hegemony. In other words, America's future teleology actually resides in the past, and an invented past at that. While Kennan, as I mentioned earlier, would later remove his proposal for the disenfranchisement of women, immigrants, and African Americans from his collected papers, what remains significant about his work is his ability to frame the U.S.–Soviet Cold War rivalry within the historically catalyzing discourse of American exceptionalism, one that saw—and continues to see—America as "a nation among nations," or the apotheosis of the nation-state form itself. Though the specific policy decisions and actions that would ensue from Kennan's narrative of containment *as* the narrative of American exceptionalism would be debated and sometimes contradict one another, the terms of those decisions, actions, and debates would be at once circumscribed, over-determined, and authorized by the power of this self-consolidating mythos.

NSC 68's Revised Hegelian Dialectic

Ironically, Kennan would later be critical of the prolonged military interventions and massive military build-up carried out in the name of containment. He would be especially disapproving of the Truman Doctrine for adopting a universal "containment line" and failing to specify particular regions of interest. Indeed, although President Truman's speech to Congress on March 12, 1947—what became known as the Truman Doctrine—was in immediate response to what were seen as Soviet expansion efforts in Greece and Turkey, it called for a vigilant containment of Soviet-inspired communist totalitarianism whenever and wherever it occurred.[35] Walter LaFeber observes that Truman's request for $400 million in aid to Greece and Turkey was not a "drastic departure" in U.S. foreign policy. For the year before, in 1946, the United States had already spent $260 million in aid to Greece alone. What *was* "radically new," LaFeber argues, was the "reasoning" in Truman's speech, that Greece and Turkey were not experiencing civil conflicts, but were the locus of a global battle between good and evil, between freedom and totalitarianism.[36] Indeed, to return us briefly to the novel *Native Speaker,* this emergent and soon dominant Cold War structure of feeling is precisely why Henry Park feels so "diminished" and conflicted, and why he feels that the "coloring" of "old guys" like his white father-in-law, Stew, says, with such moral authority and superiority, "I saved your skinny gook ass, and your momma's, too."[37] In order to manufacture the consent and secure congressional appropriations for such a "saving," Senator Arthur Vandenburg of Michigan, Republican leader in the Senate Foreign Relations Committee, had advised Truman to "scare hell" out of the American people.[38] In his pithy speech, Truman did precisely that by dividing the world sharply into Manichaean halves, asking support for a global battle against communist totalitarianism. Secretary of State Acheson assumed that the Greek revolution had been instigated by the Soviets, and successive administrations would make the same assumption about civil wars and anticolonial nationalist movements throughout the world, especially in Asia. The U.S. ambassador to Greece also echoed Acheson's reasoning, saying, "Any empire that bases itself on revolution always has expansionist tendencies." LaFeber wryly observes that "the ambassador was alluding to the revolution of 1917, not 1776."[39] What the Manichaean anticommunist logics of the Truman Doctrine elides, however, is the extent to which it was used to save the American and European economies. Truman himself noted that his doctrine and the Marshall Plan (the $17 billion recovery plan for Europe) were "two halves of the same walnut."[40] Indeed, as I have observed of the political economy of the Cold War, the Cold War can be seen as a trade war. LaFeber notes of the immediate post–World War II period that "Americans embarked upon the Cold War for the good reasons [anticommunism] given in the Truman Doctrine, which they understood, and for real reasons [problems within the Western economies], which they did not understand. . . . From 1947 on, therefore, any threats to [the] Western system could be easily explained as communist inspired, not as problems which arose from difficulties within the system itself. That was the most lasting and tragic result of the Truman Doctrine."[41] Although Truman's speech was immediately inspired by events in Greece and Turkey, the global battle against totalitarianism that it proposed to wage soon found its terrain in Asia. The protracted episodes that are made visible in the Asian American cultural productions I analyze in the chapters that follow are behind-the-scenes intervention in the Chinese civil war until the Communist victory in 1949; the military occupation of Japan, starting at the conclusion of World War II and continuing until 1952; a war in Korea (1950–53); and another war in Vietnam spanning a few decades, beginning with aid to the French colonial apparatus at the end of World War II and ending with the fall of Saigon in 1975. These interventions witnessed the triangulation of the bipolar U.S.–Soviet rivalry in Asia, among other regions. The "loss" of China to communism in 1949 would provide an overdetermining scheme through which developments and events in Asia would be interpreted.

Kennan and Truman's Cold War logics found a military valence in National Security Council (NSC) paper number 68, or NSC 68, issued on April 14, 1950. In the words of LaFeber, "NSC-68 proved to be the American blueprint for waging the Cold War during the next twenty years," and as I have been suggesting, much of this "waging" took place in Asia.[42] Interestingly, Kennan objected to the drafting of the document at all, critical of the ways in which his own "containment doctrine" had been used to rationalize the militarization of the Cold War. Furthering his apparent about-face, he was unconvinced of

NSC 68's claim that the Soviet regime had an aggressive design for world conquest and was also wary of the massive military build-up it promoted. However, Secretary of State Acheson overruled him and other objectors.[43] In the wake of the United States' loss of its atomic monopoly when the Soviet Union successfully tested an atomic bomb in August 1949, Acheson hoped to build global positions of strength. The Soviet Union, figured as a monstrous and menacing trope in NSC 68, provided a compelling justification. The only problem, meanwhile, was that the Soviet Union appeared "quiet and contained." Indeed, LaFeber argues that "NSC-68 was a policy in search of an opportunity. That opportunity arrived on June 25, 1950, when, as Acheson and his aides later agreed, 'Korea came along and saved us.'"[44] But as Nagai observes, "it should not be reasoned that in the absence of the unprogrammed Korean War, the U.S. Cold War strategy would have veered away from the NSC 68 orientation . . . [its] worldview . . . had already taken root in government and public opinion."[45] Moreover, between 1947 and 1950, before the officially recognized "beginning" of the Korean War in June 1950, the United States had already been intervening in Asia, recognizing its importance in the Cold War and already fighting a "two-front" war.[46] In fact, as I elaborate in chapter 3, the Cold War in Asia can be dated back to World War II, before the defeat of Japan. During the Yalta Conference of February 1945, at which the leaders of Great Britain, the United States, and the Soviet Union hammered out plans for the postwar international order, the United States and the Soviet Union had already exhibited mutual doubts and suspicions. Nakajima Mineo argues that "even the failure of the United States, Great Britain, and China to inform the Soviet Union of their final ultimatum to Japan and the American insistence on keeping secret the existence of the atomic bomb were part of the Cold War." He notes further that a great deal of research has demonstrated that although the United States knew Japan was sending out peace feelers through Moscow, it decided to subject Japan to atomic bombings as a means to prevent Soviet participation in the war against Japan. As such, although the beginning of the Cold War in Asia is generally dated to the officially recognized outbreak of the Korean War in June 1950, this was "more aptly the beginning of hot war in Asia. The Cold War had begun much earlier."[47] Still further, as I will elaborate in chapter 4, even the beginning of the hot war in Asia, or the assumed outbreak of the Korean War on June 25, 1950, can be disputed as a hegemonic periodization constructed from the perspective of the United States, and one that thus fails to recognize skirmishes of a civil conflict that had its genealogy in the Japanese colonization of Korea and was precipitated by the division and occupation of Korea by the Soviet Union and the United States into a North and a South along the 38th parallel at the end of World War II.

Let us turn now, then, to NSC 68, and trace its presuppositions, rhetorics, and narrative strategies, particularly as they articulate a nationalist *Bildung* and project the fear of a "Red Asia." In an effort to respond to criticisms that he made decisions piecemeal and lacked a long-range strategic plan, Truman directed the National Security Council to conduct a "reexamination of our objectives in peace and war and of the effect of these objectives on our strategic plans."[48] The resulting seventy-page "top secret"[49] typescript, NSC 68, was penned by the State Department's Policy Planning Staff, whose new director, Paul H. Nitze, had just succeeded Kennan.[50] Ernest May writes that "in part because Nitze did not hoard authorship, as Kennan might have, few lines seem quotable for pithiness or elegance. But the style is less that of a bureaucratically produced staff paper than of a committee-written speech."[51] Indeed, in Secretary of State Acheson's words, "The purpose of NSC-68 was to so bludgeon the mass mind of 'top government' that not only could the President make a decision but that the decision could be carried out. The task of a public officer seeking to explain and gain support for a major policy is not that of the writer of a doctoral thesis."[52]

Entitled "United States Objectives and Programs for National Security," NSC 68 provides an analysis of the Cold War (referred to as "the present crisis"), maps out four possible courses of action, and recommends one.[53] Within the internal logics of the paper, we see that given the analysis offered, the recommended course of action—"a rapid build-up of political, economic, and military strength in the free world" (24)—remains the only viable option. In an abridged lesson in political theory, NSC 68 goes on to explain the "fundamental purpose" of the United States, in contradistinction to the "fundamental design" of the Kremlin. Even the seemingly slight difference in the use of these section headings—"fundamental *purpose*" versus "fundamental *design*"—already signals an axiological hierarchy. Whereas "purpose" suggests something positive, as in a worthwhile goal or aspiration, "design," in its senses as both constitution/makeup and intention, suggests something immalleable and suspicious. The United States' fundamental purpose, we are told, is set forth in the Constitution, its preamble, the Bill of Rights, and the Declaration of Independence. Namely, it is to "maintain the essential elements of individual freedom" (26). The fundamental design of the Kremlin, however, is to "retain and solidify . . . absolute power, first in the Soviet Union and second in the areas under their control" (26).

In order to achieve this fundamental design of the Soviet Union, the "integrity and vitality" (27) of the United States must at all costs be destroyed. But why must this be so? The answer lies in the framing of the conflict between the United States and the Soviet Union as nothing other than the conflict between freedom and slavery, a revised Hegelian lordship and bondage schema in which the slave does not aspire to transcendence and freedom but aspires to destroy freedom itself. This struggle unto death is described in the following way:

> The Kremlin regards the United States as the only major threat to the achievement of its fundamental design. There is a basic conflict between the *idea of freedom* under a government of laws, and the *idea of slavery* under the grim oligarchy of the Kremlin, which has come to a crisis with the polarization of power . . . and the exclusive possession of atomic weapons by the two *protagonists*. The *idea of freedom*, moreover, is peculiarly and intolerably subversive of the *idea of slavery*. But the converse is not true. The implacable purpose of the slave state to *eliminate* the challenge of freedom has placed the two great powers at opposite poles. It is this fact which gives the present polarization of power the quality of crisis. (27, emphasis added)

I would like to note the peculiar ways in which this passage, much like the document as a whole, relies on narrative conventions and strategies in order to make its "truth" more compelling. The United States and the Soviet Union are described as "protagonists," as if they are two characters in a novel. Moreover, the conflict we are presented with is not one between freedom and slavery, but between "the *idea* of freedom" and the "*idea* of slavery." What does it mean, then, that the conflict is figured as a conflict of ideas? Indeed, NSC 68's elaboration of the "idea of freedom" turns out to be an abstract philosophical exercise channeling eighteenth-century notions of freedom, with an as yet unnamed ideal type called a "free society." Rather than explaining the specificity of how freedom is exercised in the United States, it offers platitudes of what a "free society" values: the individual as an end in him- or herself, diversity, deep tolerance, lawfulness, and so forth (27). Revealingly, however, in a demonstration of how a free society values and welcomes diversity, it relies on the metaphor of the marketplace: a free society is "a market for free trade in ideas, secure in its faith that free men will take the best wares, and grow to a fuller and better realization of their powers in exercising their choice" (28). And in an interesting reversal of previous figurations of communism as a disease or epidemic, in this economy, we are told that "the idea of freedom is the most *contagious* idea in history" (28, emphasis added). As such, the Soviet regime (the slave society) must expunge the contagion *that is* freedom before it reaches epidemic heights. Freedom would then be replaced with a "perverted faith" that compels absolute submission, and this perverted faith turns out to be a replacement for God. That is, "the system becomes God, and submission to the will of God becomes submission to the will of the system" (28). This equivalence via substitution is necessary. For if "God" remained outside the system, devotion to a higher authority, and therefore a spirit of resistance, would prevent complete submission.

By thus framing the ideological differences between the United States and the Soviet Union in such starkly antithetical and ultimately mutually exclusive terms, the authors of NSC 68 heighten the drama. Moreover, throughout the document, the reader is, as Acheson had hoped, "bludgeoned" with the politics of fear. The Kremlin's "design for world domination" is a much-repeated refrain, as are such phrases as "the integrity and vitality of our system is in greater jeopardy than ever before in our history" (52). Toward the end of the document, in conjunction with specific policy recommendations, we see some rhetorical shifts or sleights of hand. First, what had been characterized as the defensive goal of "containment" (of blocking further expansion of Soviet power, exposing its untruths, inducing a "retraction" of its control and influence, and of fostering the seeds of its destruction), transforms into a policy "intended to check and to *roll back* the Kremlin's drive for world domination" (41, 72, emphasis added). Second, the subjunctives used throughout the document turn into indicatives. We are told initially that "budgetary considerations will need to be subordinated to the stark fact that our very independence as a nation *may be* at stake" (73, emphasis added). But by the concluding paragraph of the document, we are told that "the whole success of the proposed program hangs ultimately on recognition by this Government, the American people, and all free peoples, that the *cold war is in fact a real war* in which the survival of the free world *is* at stake" (81, emphasis added). The insistence that "the cold war is in fact a *real* war" contains many ironies. As the Cold War soon turned "hot," the people of Korea, Vietnam, and many other parts of the globe certainly required no convincing that it was "in fact a *real* war." Further, within the logics of the document, the recognition of this "realness" of the Cold War depends on the legibility and "recognition" of the document's phantasmatic construction of the Soviet Union as a monstrous and dangerous force. As I have discussed previously, part of this phantasmatic construction relies significantly upon a racial logic of casting the Soviets as "oriental" and "Asiatic," and thus as wholly Other. Indeed, NSC 68's explicit recommendation, a considerable and specifically military investment in the Cold War, depends on the rhetorical force of the theory of Soviet world domination that the document projects. In the spring of 1950, before the drafting of NSC 68, President Truman's budget for the military—the army, navy, and air force—was a combined $13 billion. This constituted a little under a third of the total federal government budget and just under 5 percent of gross national product (GNP). A year later, however, after the official adoption of NSC 68, Truman requested more than $60 billion for the armed services, a figure representing over four and a half times the previous year's, almost two-thirds of the total federal budget, and 18.5 percent of a rapidly growing GNP.[54] The military portion of the federal budget would be substantial, to say the least, throughout the Cold War and beyond.

Interestingly, the "Orient" does make an appearance in NSC 68, less as the "oriental secretiveness of the Russian mind" but more literally as the geographical sites of East, South, and Southeast Asia. While NSC 68 is generally not specific about particularly vulnerable regions, it does single out Asia a few times throughout its analysis:

> The ideological *pretensions* of the Kremlin are another great source of strength. . . . They have found a *particularly receptive audience in Asia,* especially as the *Asiatics* have been impressed by what has been plausibly portrayed to them as the rapid advance of the USSR from a backward society to a position of great world power. Thus, in its *pretensions* to being (a) the source of a *new universal faith* and (b) the model "scientific" society, the Kremlin cynically identifies itself with the genuine aspirations of large numbers of people, and places itself at the head of an *international crusade* with all of the benefits which derive therefrom. (35, emphasis added)

Here again, we see the familiar troping of the Soviet Union as a religion, described earlier in the document as a "perverted faith" and now as a "universal faith" and "international crusade." Although the regime is full of "pretensions" in its efforts to win an international following, it has managed to find a "particularly receptive audience in Asia." In describing Asia as particularly impressionable, the writers of NSC 68 implicitly cast the "Asiatics" as politically immature and naïve, and their society as "backward" within the telos of capitalist modernity. According to this discursive economy, particularly after the "loss" of China to communism in 1949, just several months before the drafting of NSC 68, Asian anticolonial nationalisms and civil wars could only be read and seen through the single lens of Cold War logics.

While Asia is thus constructed as a feminized object to be "saved" from Soviet imperialism, the terms of such a rescue, and the presumption that it requires saving at all, betray NSC 68's own imperial longings. It is worth quoting at length:

> [T]he Communist success in China, taken with the politico-economic situation in the rest of South and South-East Asia, provides a springboard for a further incursion in this troubled area. Although Communist China faces serious economic problems which may impose some strains on the Soviet economy, it is probable that the social and economic problems faced by the free nations in these areas present more than offsetting opportunities for Communist expansion. . . . At the same time, a strengthening of the British position is needed if the stability of the Commonwealth is not to be impaired and if it is to be a focus of resistance to Communist expansion in South and South-East Asia. Improvement of the British position is also vital in building up the defensive capabilities of Western Europe . . . throughout Asia the stability of the present moderate governments, which are more in sympathy with our purposes than any probable successor regimes would be, is doubtful. The *problem is only in part an economic one.* Assistance in economic development is important as a means of holding out to the peoples of Asia some prospect of improvement in standards of living under their present governments. *But probably more important are a strengthening of central institutions, an improvement in administration, and generally a development of an economic and social structure* within which the peoples of Asia can make more effective use of their great human and material resources. (49–50, emphasis added)

During the drafting of NSC 68, the Soviet Union still occupied the privileged position as America's principal Cold War Other. This would later, as I elaborate in the next chapter, undergo a revision. In the meantime, particular focus is on the British Commonwealth in South and Southeast Asia. These nations, though nominally postcolonial and free from British colonial rule, are still dependent on Britain, and NSC 68 articulates a desire to strengthen this neocolonial dependency. As suggested in the passage above, "a strengthening of the British position is needed if the stability of the Commonwealth is not to be impaired and if it is to be a focus of resistance to Communist expansion in South and South-East Asia." Moreover, there is also an implied narrative about the United States taking on Britain's role, as it already had in Greece and Turkey, and was also in the process of doing vis-à-vis the French in French Indochina or Vietnam. The stability of the governments of Asia is put into question, and the problem, it is argued, is "only in part an economic one." The real problem, it turns out, is that the Asians are not capable of governing themselves effectively. Echoing Kennan's logics of racial development and Truman's logics of nation building in Greece, NSC 68 promotes "*a strengthening of central institutions, an improvement in administration, and generally a development of an economic and social structure* within which the peoples of Asia can make more effective use of their great human and material resources." Since the British no longer possessed the strength or the money, the United States will presumably take on the task of imperial subsidizer, supervisor, and teacher. Indeed, these kinds of tasks form in part the core of NSC 68's concrete policy recommendations.

NSC 48/1 and a "White-Colored Polarization"

Several months before the dissemination of NSC 68 in April 1950, in the wake of Mao's October 1949 declaration of Communist victory in China, the National Security Council also began drafting a series of documents, numbered 48, specifically on Asia. The "loss" of China heightened the visibility of Asia on the horizon of Washington's Cold War architects, and the "outbreak" of the Korean War in June 1950 would further intensify the perceived vulnerability of Asia. I turn now to NSC 48/1, the first of the NSC's Cold War documents specifically on Asia and the final script of Cold War poetics that I examine in this chapter. Much as NSC 68 is considered by historians to be the blueprint for the militarization of the Cold War, NSC 48 is regarded as the blueprint for the United States' postwar foreign policy in Asia. Written in the immediate aftermath of the Communist victory in China, Asia appears in NSC 48/1 as a weak, impressionable child who is an easy target of Soviet communist penetration but who, given the proper tutoring and guidance, can mature into a capitalist region friendly to the United States. Similar to Kennan's notions of racial development, NSC 48/1 figures the United States, its European allies, and Australia and New Zealand, the "white" nations of the British Commonwealth close to Asia, as the exemplars and spearheads in the teleology of democratic nation-state formation and maturation. Significantly, alongside the fear of Soviet communist infiltration, NSC 48/1 articulates a twinned ambivalent American discourse: a simultaneous projection and denial of imperial longing and policy, paired with a simultaneous recognition and denial of Asian agency.[55]

Dated December 23, 1949, NSC 48/1, a report titled "The Position of the United States with Respect to Asia," proceeds from the presupposition that "the Asians share poverty, nationalism, and revolution."[56] As such, the document claims, "The United States position with respect to Asia is therefore that of a rich and powerful country dealing with a have-not and sensitively nationalistic area, and of competition together with friendly countries against the USSR for influence on the form and direction of the Asiatic revolutions" (226). From the outset, even as NSC 48/1 hints at Asian agency by drawing our attention to Asian "nationalism" and "revolution," this recognition is overdetermined and ultimately overwritten by America's Cold War national security interests and racialist understanding of national development. Asia, defined as "that part of the continent of Asia south of the USSR and east of Iran together with the major off-shore islands—Japan, Formosa [Taiwan], the Philippines, Indonesia, and Ceylon [Sri Lanka]," is deemed to be "in the throes of political upheaval" and revolution, including "the prevalence of terrorism" (226, 228). Even as Asia's "revolt against colonial rule" and anticolonial nationalisms are recognized, they are quickly overshadowed by the gendered Cold War logics of assuming that Asia is a "fertile field" for "communist control and Soviet influence" (248, 228). Such control and influence, combined with "traditional social patterns antithetical to democracy" and the lack of "leaders practiced in the exercise of responsible power" (especially in Southeast Asia), betray an ambivalence about Asian agency (240, 248). NSC 48/1 thus recognizes Asian agency, but only to trope it as a weak object of Soviet control or figure it as an instance of negative agency—that is, as undemocratic and irresponsible agency.

Given this volatile context, NSC 48/1 recommends courses of action for the United States that will stabilize the Asian economy and point Asia away from communism. Here, the question of imperialism at once guides and circumscribes the recommendations. On the one hand, the document is careful to point out that the United States needs to avoid charges of imperialism. Moreover, it recognizes "that the long colonial tradition in Asia has left the peoples of that area suspicious of Western influence" (249). In this context, however, "Western influence" does not seem to include Marxism, nor does it seem to include the Soviet Union, construed as an "Asiatic power" (228) given its racialization as oriental, its ambiguous (or at times fortuitous) geographical location between Europe and Asia, and its influence in the region. The problem, NSC 48/1 cautions, must be approached "from the Asiatic point of view in so far as possible and refrain from taking the lead in movements which must of necessity be of Asian origin" (249). This judiciousness and restraint are at once contradictory and disingenuous. How can movements necessarily "be of Asian origin" and at the same time be dominated by the "instruments of communist conspiracy" (227)? And what exactly is an "Asiatic point of view"? According to the characterization made previously in the document, such a view would seem to be "antithetical to democracy" and bereft of "responsible power." Similarly, on the question of imperialism, even as a concession is made to the "Asiatic point of view," we see an ambivalence that is at once predictable and curious. NSC 48/1 argues that the United States should not do anything in Asia, such as occupying Formosa (Taiwan), that would bring about "charges of 'imperialism'" (244). What is to be avoided, then, is more the *charge* of imperialism, and less imperialism as such. Also, the document suggests that "It would be to the interest of the United States to make use of the skills, knowledge and long experience of our European friends and, to whatever extent may be possible, enlist their cooperation in measures designed to check the spread of USSR influence in Asia" (249). What might the "skills, knowledge and long experience" of the Europeans be in this context, except precisely those of colonial rule and administration? NSC 48/1 goes even further by enlisting the aid and cooperation of the "members of the British Commonwealth, particularly India, Pakistan, Australia, and New Zealand" (249). In an interesting, explicit reference to race in a document haunted and thus far only coded by racial logics, it is argued that "the cooperation of the *white* nations of the Commonwealth [Australia and New Zealand] will arrest any potential dangers of the growth of a *white-colored polarization*" (250, emphasis added). That is, enlisting both Asian and white Commonwealth nations as a multiracial cooperative alliance will prevent a polarization along racial lines. Moreover, the task facing the United States and its white European and Commonwealth friends is figured as a "burden" (250), recalling the "white man's burden" of colonial conquest and rule. The logic of NSC 48/1 thus assumes that a "white-colored polarization" does not already exist in a decolonizing Asia. This demonstrates Cedric Robinson's claim, as I discussed in the introduction, that the Cold War is taken to have subsumed all other conflicts, but that we can see it as a "historical sidebar" to global race wars, including and especially movements of decolonization.

In thus alluding to the possibility of a "white-colored polarization," NSC 48/1 at once reveals and denies how the Cold War intersected with and overdetermined global race and anticolonial wars.

NSC 48/1, along with the other canonized Cold War government documents I have analyzed, thus coheres as an imperialist projection and becomes a privileged authorized site through which a Manichaean Cold War reading practice gets invented. In this chapter, then, I have traced through America's Cold War governmental archive the narrative construction of an exceptionalist American *Bildung* against which the Soviet Union appears as an Asiatic phantasm, as well as the imperialist and gendered racial conjuring of Asia itself within this scheme. In the next chapter, I turn to a close examination of how such Cold War logics played out in China. I analyze how a range of texts, from government documents and Cold War films to Asian American literature, imagines the fabled Chinese market and its "loss" to Mao's Communist victory in 1949. Noting in particular the ambivalent metaphorics of this imperialist and gendered racial projection, I trace how the once fabled China market transmogrifies into the specter of a "Red Asia."

2

THE EL DORADO
OF COMMERCE

China's Billion Bellies

China has not been a nation for Americans, but a metaphor. To say "China" is instantly to call up a string of metaphors giving us the history of Sino-American relations and fifty years of "China watching" by our politicians, pundits, and academics: unchanging China, cyclical China . . . who lost China, containment or liberation . . . whither China-after-Mao . . .

BRUCE CUMINGS, *Parallax Visions: Making Sense of American–East Asian Relations at the End of the Century*

Grandmother and the aunts wrote letters on the deaths of every last uncle. If the uncles could have figured out what the Communists wanted of them, they would have complied, but Communism made no sense. It was something to do with new songs, new dances, and the breaking up of families. Maybe it had to do with no sex . . .

MAXINE HONG KINGSTON, *China Men*

In her novel *China Men,* Maxine Hong Kingston provides a genealogy of America's wars in Asia in the latter half of the twentieth century. In a chapter near the end of the novel entitled "The Brother in Vietnam," Kingston charts how World War II, the Chinese civil war, the Korean War, and the Vietnam War rendered successive groups of Asians and Asian *Americans* as the new enemy, the new gook. This string of U.S. interventions in Asia is thematized as the "The War" by Kingston's young Chinese American narrator in a composition, but her teacher corrects her by asking, "Which war?"[1] Yet in grouping the multiple wars under the singular sign "The War," Kingston turns our attention to the continuity of U.S. intervention in Asia during the Cold War. This continuity is one not only of enduring historical time, but also of Cold War Manichaean logics. Indeed, as I will be discussing in the next chapter,

World War II bled into the Cold War in Japan, and as I analyze in this chapter, the "loss" of China to communism in 1949 would haunt and overdetermine the Korean and Vietnam wars. The epigraph immediately above is Kingston's young narrator's distillation of the family stories she has heard about communism in China. The intersection of American anticommunism and the anticommunism of the narrator's own family (residing both in the United States and in China) emerges as a problem of knowledge. Just what is this strange new development in China called "Communism," and why does it make "no sense"? Attempts to make sense of it come through cultural metaphors and metonyms—as "new songs," "new dances," and possibly as "no sex." As Bruce Cumings encapsulates in the first epigraph, within the logics of U.S. global capitalism and of Western capitalist modernity more broadly, this metaphoricity of China long predates 1949. Indeed, to imagine China has been to imagine a metaphor, trope, or figure, most famously signified as an "open door" for the West's market interests. What is different about the metaphoricity of Communist China, however, is the very "closing" of China's door for capitalist interests. In the wake of this economic and political closure, there lies as well a closure or gap of knowledge about "Communism," and the symptom of this gap appears through another set of metaphors.

In this chapter, then, I focus on what could be called the metaphorics of America's long career of "China watching," saturated by the desire for the fabled Chinese market and its Cold War "loss" in 1949. On the one hand, the mesmerizing longing for the fabled Chinese market and its possibilities has exceeded its material realization. On the other hand, China's growth and increasing openness to and competitiveness within capitalism in the post–Cold War conjuncture have seen this longing transform into a squeamish fear of the awakening of a "sleeping giant." The ambivalent registers of this historical longing and contemporary fear have of course temporally overlapped in some instances, but they can also be seen as bookends for 1949, the year of America's "loss." This loss would overdetermine Cold War logics and geopolitics in Asia, as the specter of a "Red Asia"—a merger of the historical "yellow peril" and "red menace"—catalyzed attempts to "save" the rest of Asia from communism. In my analysis of this specter of a Red Asia, I examine how cultural productions make visible the metaphorics of America's simultaneous longing and fear as an imperialist and gendered racial projection. In particular, alongside readings of historical and governmental documents, I analyze the classic Cold War conspiracy thriller *The Manchurian Candidate* and the gendered racial trope or figure of Butterfly, the self-sacrificing Asian woman who makes an appearance in a multiplicity of genres and cultural forms, culminating in David Henry Hwang's "deconstructivist" play *M. Butterfly*.[2] What does it mean that China can only be imagined as a loss? How did this loss, and the fear of a Red Asia, triangulate the bipolar Cold War antagonism between the United States and Soviet Union? Indeed, as will be evident as the chapter unfolds, Communist China comes to rival and in many ways supplant the Soviet Union as America's principal Cold War threat.

Many Open Doors

Before turning, then, to *The Manchurian Candidate,* the "Butterfly genre," and *M. Butterfly,* I provide in this section a reading of the "prehistory" of America's Cold War in China in order to situate my analysis of these important cultural texts. The Cold War between the United States and the Soviet Union, and a form of nonterritorial imperialism or "treaty port imperialism" realized via the signing of uneven treaties, find an interesting gendered racial prehistory or preview in China. While most studies of imperialism in China have focused on Britain, there is also a largely forgotten history of U.S. imperialism there. Almost exactly a century before the "loss" of China to Mao's Communist victory in 1949, the United States formalized its "informal" imperialism in China through the Treaty of Wanghia (1844), a treaty of "Peace, Amity, and Commerce." This treaty made Canton and four other previously closed ports open for free American trade and, most crucially, granted Americans in China the right of extraterritoriality, making them subject not to Chinese laws, but only to the laws of the United States. Exclusive *territorial* jurisdiction has been thought to be a sine qua non of the sovereignty of the modern nation-state, so the extraction of *extraterritorial* jurisdiction, through which the United States claimed the right to apply its laws beyond its territorial borders, compromised the substantive sovereignty of China. Caleb Cushing, the first American minister to China and later U.S. attorney general, far exceeded his assigned task of exacting trade concessions matching those granted to the British. Remarking, "I do not admit as my equals either the red man of America, or the yellow man of Asia, or the black man of Africa," he preferred instead the "marvelous qualities of Anglo-Saxon blood," and exacted the right of extraterritoriality in response to what he perceived to be China's arrogance and superiority complex.[3] In subsequent decades, with the passage of Chinese Exclusion Acts starting in 1882 (and before that the effective exclusion of Chinese women through the 1875 Page Act), maintaining China as an "open door" for Western trade went hand in hand with hypocritically closing America's doors to Chinese immigration. When criticized for the unevenness of this situation, and for actually violating the 1868 Burlingame Treaty and its amendments, in which the United States had agreed to permit Chinese immigration, the United States responded with a legal sleight of hand: that the right to control immigration is a fundamental right of the sovereignty of the nation-state, and that a nation cannot give it away, even if it wished to do so. And yet the United States did not object to China giving or signing away its sovereign right of exclusive territorial jurisdiction. Thus, not only did the open door swing only one way, but also the sanctity of nation-state sovereignty. Indeed, Teemu Ruskola argues that "in the Treaty of Wanghia the United States laid the foundation for this imperial practice in Asia,"[4] refining the British precedent so that Britain itself and other European nations with imperial interests in Asia would come to emulate it as a model.

In the 1890s, several decades before the inaugural height of the Cold War in the 1940s to '50s, the United States and Russia opposed one another as each sought to exploit China economically, especially Manchuria. From the 1890s until 1917, the United States attempted to contain Russian excursions into China. President Theodore Roosevelt declared that Russians are "utterly insincere and treacherous; they have no conception of the truth . . . and no regard for others." Calling the tsar a "preposterous little creature," Roosevelt feared that Russia was trying to "organize Northern China against us."[5] In 1899, in an effort to keep U.S. economic interests safe in China, and to ensure that China would remain a level playing field for the major imperialist players who held treaty powers there, Secretary of State John Hay sent his famously titled "Open Door Notes" to the British ambassador. In these notes, Hay expresses three conjoined concerns: that no power should have "exclusive" rights in China, that China should remain an "open market for the commerce of the world," and that the "integrity" of China should not be compromised. He asks Britain to make a formal declaration of its "sphere of interest" and intentions in China, and seeks its support in urging other nations to do the same.[6] Hay's logic relies on the false assumption that being an "open market" for the world, assured through uneven treaties wrought by the Western powers, had not already compromised China's integrity and sovereignty. This rhetoric of integrity at once justifies and masks what is in fact a blueprint for the joint imperialist exploitation of China. Within the context of domestic politics in the United States, the open-door policy emerged as a compromise between business interests and a highly vocal and articulate anti-expansionist, anti-imperialist minority. As such, it has been described by Thomas J. McCormick as "a most interesting hybrid of anti-colonialism and economic imperialism."[7] The push for the open door by the business lobby, as Delber McKee argues, was not based on the relatively small stake of America's actual investments in China in 1900, but on "dreams about the future. . . . Former minister to China Charles Denby made that point clear in his remarks at the annual meeting of the [American Asiatic] Association in 1900. 'The Eldorado of commerce,' he proclaimed, 'lies before us in the Far East.'"[8] As I have observed, the contradiction between this open-door policy and the coextensive immigration exclusion or closed door against Chinese people wishing to migrate to the United States, which lasted from 1875/1882 to 1943, was interestingly obscured.

William Appleman Williams argues that "the empire that was built according to the strategy and tactics of the Open Door Notes engendered the antagonisms created by all empires, and it is that opposition which posed so many difficulties for American diplomacy after World War II."[9] At the end of World War II, the continued pursuit of the fabled Chinese market saw U.S. intervention in the Chinese civil war. Locating the future interests of the United States in the Western Hemisphere and the Pacific, Truman believed that the security of Asia (and of U.S. interests there) depended on supporting Chiang Kai-shek's Nationalists against Mao's Communists in the Chinese civil war. Everett F. Drumright, chief of the Division of Chinese Affairs, dispensed with the rhetoric of a democratic, free, and sovereign China, arguing instead that such considerations as "democracy in China [or questions] as to the relative efficiency of the two contending factions" were not of primary importance. Rather, the guiding principle of U.S. actions in China should be the "promotion of the security of the United States."[10] This called for massive involvement in China in support of the Nationalists, and implied that the United States could and should oppose democracy in China (and elsewhere should the need arise) if it threatened America's national security interests. Such a policy, argues Akira Iriye, justified a historic break from the World War II Yalta Agreement of maintaining a balance of power between the United States and the Soviet Union in China after the war.[11] It would soon face criticism not only from members of the United States' own State Department, but also from Mao's Communists. John Carter Vincent, director of the Office of Far Eastern Affairs of the State Department, raised the "question as to whether we are not moving toward establishment of a relationship with China which has some of the characteristics of a de facto protectorate with a semi-colonial Chinese army under our direction."[12] The presence of American troops in China as World War II ended and civil war erupted was seen as intervention in Chinese domestic affairs and thus as a violation of Chinese sovereignty.[13] Observing the continuing presence of American troops in China, a June 7, 1946, editorial in *Chieh-fang Jih-Pao* argued, "Although we have repelled the Japanese imperialist bandits, we have not gained national independence. We are even being murdered by foreign arms."[14] Mao observed that American assistance to Chiang's Kuomintang was an act of armed intervention that widened the division in China and exacerbated chaos and poverty. On July 7 a Communist declaration asked why the American "reactionaries" were so eager to "assist" China. The answer, it suggested, was imperialistic aggression, and U.S. imperialism was considered to be more formidable and dangerous than Japanese imperialism. The collusion between domestic and foreign reactionaries threatened the independent survival of the Chinese people.[15]

American policy makers interpreted the Chinese civil war through the lens of Cold War logics. A memorandum issued by the Joint Chiefs of Staff in June 1947, for example, refuted the argument that the Chinese Communists were more nationalistic and indigenous and less Soviet-inspired, and claimed that they, "as all others, are Moscow inspired and thus motivated by the same basic totalitarian and anti-democratic policies as are the communist parties in other countries of the world. Accordingly, they should be regarded as tools of Soviet policy."[16] This refusal to recognize Asian nationalism as a movement in its own right would later have tragic consequences, most notably in Korea and Vietnam. According to the memorandum, because Japan was disarmed and occupied, the only "Asiatic" government capable of challenging Soviet expansion in Asia was the Chinese Nationalists. While the Joint Chiefs of Staff recognized that the Nationalists were corrupt and showed signs of political weakness (a recognition similar to the one vis-à-vis the Greek government in the famous Truman Doctrine), the more significant issue was to ensure their continued survival as a pivotal point of Soviet resistance in the Far East. As such, the Joint Chiefs of Staff recommended that the Soviet threat should be met with effective countermeasures, including a program of "carefully planned, selective and well-supervised assistance" to the Nationalists.[17] Cold War logics, as articulated in this memorandum following the Truman Doctrine, dictated that U.S. foreign policy would only be effective if Soviet expansion in any part of the world, and not just in Greece and Turkey, were consistently countered. As this congealed as the dominant structure of feeling and knowledge, critics such as Vincent were effectively silenced and reassigned to more neutral embassies in such places as Switzerland. In the meantime, the United States continued to aid the Nationalists, particularly through programs that helped to modernize its army and through the sale, provision, and shipment of arms to China and the Pacific Islands. Though the "Asia-firsters" in Congress were outnumbered by the "Europe-firsters," in order to get his European Recovery Program (the so-called Marshall Plan) passed, Marshall promised a China Aid Program. In April 1948 a European Recovery Program of $4 billion and a China Aid Program of $460 million were simultaneously enacted. Although such aid to China, which altogether ultimately amounted to about $3 billion,[18] was not enough to ensure a Nationalist victory, it certainly succeeded in antagonizing the Communists and deepening Cold War tensions between the United States and China.

In the wake of Mao's Communist victory in late 1949, Chiang's supporters in Washington, known as the China Lobby, targeted Secretary of State Dean Acheson for the historic "loss." Having its origins in the Chinese embassy during World War II, the China Lobby had worked to promote pro-Chiang propaganda in the United States, paying for its activities through the illegal smuggling of narcotics. Until 1948, however, the group had remained relatively insignificant. But with the heightening of the Chinese civil war and Mao's significant victories, it transformed itself into an effective pressure group with the support of wealthy conservative Americans and key congressmen, such as Senator Kenneth Wherry, who had declared, "With God's help we will lift Shanghai up and up, ever up, until it is just like Kansas City."[19] (One wonders what Senator Wherry would say if he were to see Shanghai now . . .)

Secretary Acheson responded to his critics by publishing *United States Relations with China* (1949), the so-called China White Paper, a one-thousand-page tome of compiled government documents supporting the Truman administration's position that the Chinese civil war had been beyond the control of the U.S. government. In his "Letter of Transmittal" introducing the volume, Acheson writes the following. It is worth quoting at length:

> The reasons for the failures of the Chinese National Government appear in some detail in the attached record. They do not stem from any inadequacy of American aid. . . . [The Kuomingtang's] leaders had proved incapable of meeting the crisis confronting them, its troops had lost the will to fight, and its Government had lost popular support. . . . A realistic appraisal of conditions in China, past and present, leads to the conclusion that the only alternative open

to the United States was full-scale intervention on behalf of a Government which had lost the confidence of its own troops and its own people. . . . Intervention of such a scope and magnitude would have been resented by the mass of the Chinese people, would have diametrically reversed our historic policy, and would have been condemned by the American people. . . . In the recent past, attempts at foreign domination have appeared quite clearly to the Chinese people as external aggression and as such have been bitterly and in the long run successfully resisted. Our aid and encouragement have helped them to resist. In this case, however, *the foreign domination has been masked behind the façade of a vast crusading movement which apparently has seemed to many Chinese to be wholly indigenous and national.* In these circumstances, our aid has been unavailing. The unfortunate but inescapable fact is that the ominous result of the civil war in China was beyond the control of the government of the United States. . . . It was the product of internal Chinese forces. . . . Meanwhile our policy will continue to be based upon our own respect for the [United Nations] Charter, our friendship for China, and our traditional support for the *Open Door* and for China's independence and administrative and territorial *integrity.*[20]

Acheson frames the loss of China as a China lost to itself. In other words, the Communist victory is explained as having resulted from two significant Chinese failures: the ineptness of the Nationalist forces and the blindness of a great majority of Chinese people. According to Acheson's patronizing logic, the Chinese people have been duped by the "vast crusading movement" of Soviet-inspired Marxism, a foreign influence that disguises itself in Chinese indigenous and national garb. He is, however, confident that the Chinese people will eventually come to their senses and recognize communism as the "foreign imperialism" that it is, and throw off this "foreign yoke."[21] He articulates an interpretive frame that will be echoed throughout the Cold War: that indigenous nationalist movements in Asia are necessarily Soviet-directed attempts at communist penetration. Moreover, in calling communism "foreign imperialism," he reveals an unintended irony. For the "Open-Door Policy" that the United States and other Western powers had practiced in China for decades was itself an instance of the very foreign imperialism that he derides. Indeed, Acheson not only constructs a Cold War "scene of persuasion"[22] that will be echoed later, but himself explicitly echoes John Hay's declaration. He closes his "Letter of Transmittal" with the promise that the United States will continue to respect the "Open Door" and China's "administrative and territorial integrity."

Interestingly, as Iriye notes, while Acheson refers to "foreign imperialism" in his preface to the China White Paper, he does not explicitly accuse the Soviet Union of violating the Yalta Agreement. He makes one vague reference to the conduct of the Soviet Union in Manchuria, but Manchuria had been assigned to it as its sphere of influence, and the Soviet Union had evacuated its troops from the region.[23] Despite this, he still interprets Mao's victory as a Soviet victory and accuses the Chinese Communist leaders of having foresworn their Chinese heritage and announcing "subservience to a foreign power, Russia, which during the last 50 years, under czars and communists alike, has been most assiduous in its efforts to extend control in the Far East."[24] Indeed, the documents that follow within the volume do not support Acheson's claim of systemic Soviet expansion efforts in Asia. On the contrary, Iriye argues that until the first half of 1949, when a Communist victory was at hand, Soviet foreign policy was one of caution and remained committed to maintaining diplomatic ties with the Nationalists. Though the Soviet Union did open offices in Manchuria and northern China in order to deal informally with the de facto Communist regime there, it did not want to face a rupture with the Nationalists.[25]

Acheson and Truman announced on October 12, 1949, that the United States would not recognize the new Chinese regime headed by Mao. Soon thereafter, America's interpretation of the status of communism in China, identified by Acheson in 1949 as a "foreign yoke," undergoes an interesting transformation. In 1951 China is still viewed as a Soviet puppet regime, or what Assistant Secretary of State Dean Rusk calls "a colonial Russian government—a Slavic Manchukuo on a larger scale . . . not the government of China."[26] By 1955, however, Secretary of State Dulles makes an analytic distinction between the Russian and Chinese "brands" of communism, and argues that the Chinese variety poses a greater threat in Asia than the Russian one because it controls a larger population and enjoys a cultural prestige in Asia that Russia does not. He urges the Western nations not to surrender the free Asian nations to China. Chinese control of Japan, with its growing industrial capacity, would be disastrous, as would be Chinese control of the rich natural resources (oil, rubber, tin, iron, etc.) and strategic locations held by Southeast Asia. Moreover, he holds out the Philippines as an example of how the West "can create independence in Asia," implicitly proposing that nearly fifty years of U.S. colonial rule is the necessary precursor to "independence."[27] To a large extent, then, by the time of America's deepening involvement in Vietnam in the mid- to late 1950s, and in light of Chinese participation in the Korean War, China displaces the Soviet Union as the formidable Cold War enemy, even as Chinese communism had initially been deemed to be Soviet inspired. U.S.–Soviet relations are characterized as "peaceful coexistence," and in a speech at Johns Hopkins University on April 7, 1965, President Johnson explains and justifies U.S. involvement in Vietnam by conjuring the "deepening shadow of communist China," and by claiming that "the contest in Vietnam is part of a wider pattern of aggressive purposes." He argues that the United States must fight in Vietnam, for the alternative to fighting would *not* be a negotiation of a neutral noncommunist South Vietnam. The actual and only possible alternative, according to Johnson's Cold War logics, would be a Chinese-controlled Southeast Asia, and by extension, a "Red Asia." As such, the United States could not withdraw, because doing so would result in a complete, dangerous shift in the global balance of power.[28] Indeed, Aruga Tadashi argues that "the Cold War with the Soviet Union ended with John F. Kennedy's 1963 American University speech and the conclusion of the partial nuclear test-ban treaty immediately thereafter. Thenceforth American–Soviet rivalry became like a more or less normal rivalry between two major powers. The Cold War with China, on the other hand, continued. The Kennedy and Johnson administrations regarded the People's Republic of China as an expansionist power bent on communist aggrandizement by inciting national liberation movements in developing areas if not by using its own military movements."[29] Moreover, as Allen S. Whiting observes, the death of Stalin in 1953 removed the "personalized devil figure" from Cold War politics, particularly in terms of American propaganda and perceptions. The political demonology erected around the figure of Stalin is replaced by the lunatic chairman, particularly as imagined and projected by Secretaries of State John Foster Dulles and Dean Rusk.[30] Thus, we witness a triangulation of Cold War rivalries. China, in championing the rights of smaller nations and opposing both U.S. imperialism and Soviet "revisionism," overshadows the Soviet Union as America's principal Cold War threat (until the 1972 rapprochement following Nixon's historic trip) and experiences a fissuring of its own relationship with the Soviet Union. The Sino–Soviet alliance of February 1950 begins to unravel in the late 1950s into the Sino–Soviet split, and by the late 1960s, the Soviet Union itself displaces the United States as the greater threat *to China*.

It is with this Cold War constellation, in and through which China comes to occupy a privileged position in America's imperial and gendered racial imaginary, that I am concerned in this chapter. As the figure of the monstrous merger or marriage of the historical "yellow peril" and the "red menace," the

Chinese are depicted through long-standing and recycled tropes of American Orientalism.[31] In this configuration, the Chinese are inscrutable . . . the Chinese are conformist automatons . . . the Chinese are political fanatics . . . I will now turn, then, to *The Manchurian Candidate*'s metaphorics of what could be called the "red peril."

A Chinese Cat Smiling Like Fu Manchu

The 1962 Cold War political satire *The Manchurian Candidate,* a cinematic adaptation of Richard Condon's 1959 novel, is set in the aftermath of the Korean War, as its principal character Raymond Shaw returns from combat and is awarded a Congressional Medal of Honor for killing an entire company of a Chinese Communist infantry and saving all nine members of his patrol. As the intricate plot unravels, however, we learn that Raymond is no hero. Indeed, the narrative of his heroic deed turns out to be a cover for what actually transpired in Manchuria. Betrayed by their Korean interpreter, Raymond and his men, led by Commanding Officer Bennett Marco (played by Frank Sinatra), were captured by Russian and Chinese Communist soldiers and subjected to an intense brainwashing procedure for three days. Upon his return home to the United States, Captain Major Marco is reassigned to Army Intelligence and does not remember the events in Manchuria.[32] He is, however, soon plagued by a recurring nightmare, which turns out to be a flashback of the brainwashing sessions he and his men underwent. He has a moment of epiphany midway through the film. He says, "I remember. I remember. I can see that Chinese cat standing there smiling like Fu Manchu . . ." Who is this "Chinese cat," and what does it mean that he becomes legible and visible, to Sinatra's character as well as the movie audience, through a comparison to Fu Manchu? The "Chinese cat," it turns out, is Dr. Yen Lo, the chief brainwasher.[33]

As a Cold War film par excellence, *The Manchurian Candidate* at once satirizes and reinstates America's intersecting fears and paranoia of subversion and infiltration on multiple fronts, ranging from the disruption of traditional family values and normative gender roles to communist penetration from within and without.[34] As the character who embodies the merger of the historical "yellow peril" and the "red menace," Dr. Yen Lo plays an especially colorful role in this constellation of fears. In referring to him as "Fu Manchu," Bennett Marco cites an enduring Orientalist discourse in American popular culture and politics. In the late nineteenth century, as larger numbers of Chinese were recruited to the United States (especially to California and other parts of the West Coast) as cheap labor, they were targeted as the "yellow peril,"

Dr. Yen Lo (center) brainwashes the captured American soldiers (from *The Manchurian Candidate*, 1962).

a teeming oriental horde invading U.S. shores. The fear of and agitation against a perceived Chinese takeover of America were articulated in yellow peril narratives, constituting a multigeneric discourse of American Orientalism.[35] In fiction, the yellow peril was perhaps most famously and melodramatically embodied in English novelist Sax Rohmer's Dr. Fu Manchu, who made his first appearance in 1911 and 1912 in London magazine serials. In 1913 these serialized stories were then collected and published as a novel, *The Mystery of Dr. Fu-Manchu* (published in the United States as *The Insidious Dr. Fu Manchu*). This creation of the British colonial imaginary quickly traveled to U.S. shores, as would Rohmer himself, and took on a life of its own.[36] Rohmer describes Dr. Fu Manchu, a highly skilled assassin, as "tall, lean and feline, high-shouldered, with a brow like Shakespeare and a face like Satan, a close-shave skull, and long, magnetic eyes of the true cat-green. Invest in him with all the cruel cunning of an entire Eastern race, accumulated in one giant intellect, with all the resources of science past and present. . . . Imagine that awful being, and you have a mental picture of Dr. Fu-Manchu, the yellow peril incarnate in one man."[37] By relying upon every stereotype of Chinese cunning and evil circulating in the West in the late nineteenth and early twentieth centuries, as William Wu writes, "Rohmer ensured that future Chinese villains would evoke memories of Fu Manchu for many years to come."[38] Indeed,

Bennett Marco evokes this memory for movie audiences many decades later in 1962. *The Manchurian Candidate*'s Dr. Yen Lo is an ever more insidious Dr. Fu Manchu, a Cold War Fu Manchu, for he is not a "highly skilled assassin" himself but brainwashes others to become highly skilled assassins, to do the dirty work of killing for him. He brainwashes Americans, like Raymond, to assassinate other Americans.

In this classic Cold War film, why is the figure of the chief brainwasher, who is affiliated with the "Pavlov Institute" in Moscow, not himself Russian but rather Chinese? If the Cold War was a bipolar rivalry between the United States and the Soviet Union, what is the discursive and ideological effectivity of constructing a principal villain who is Chinese? In the wake of the Communist victory in China in 1949, and within the domestic context of changing gender roles, the circuits of paranoia set into motion in *The Manchurian Candidate* are ideologically inflected specifically through tropes of gender and race. The evil of communism, in other words, is conflated with the evils of "momism" (an inappropriately powerful or domineering mom)[39] and that of the Asian racial other. In the film, the American operative at the highest echelon of the conspiracy turns out to be none other than Raymond's ambitious mother, Eleanor Iselin (played by Angela Lansbury). Alongside this gendered fear, the trope of "brainwashing" works to produce a heightened sense of racialized fear precisely because audiences in 1962 had already been introduced to this term and concept as something practiced by Chinese Communists. The term was coined by journalist and CIA aide Edward Hunter in 1950, with reference to "re-educational" practices in Communist China.[40] In his book *Brain-washing in Red China: The Calculated Destruction of Men's Minds* (1951), he writes, "The plain people of China have coined several revealing colloquialisms for the whole indoctrination process. With their natural facility for succinct, graphic expressions, they have referred to it as 'brain-washing' and 'brain-changing.'"[41] He concludes his book by making an explicit link between brainwashing and nuclear annihilation: "The unique and terrible thing about this mass indoctrination is that it is planned and directed by central governing authorities. This is psychological warfare on a scale incalculably more immense than any militarist of the past has ever envisaged. This is what has to be stopped and counteracted, and the mentally maimed must be cured if we ourselves are to be safe from 'brain-washing' and 'brain-changing'—and 'liquidation' and 'evaporation.'"[42] It seems, then, that it is not only Cold War victory, but also the very survival of the human race that is at stake in counteracting such "oriental" tactics. For Hunter, brainwashing thus constitutes the new yellow peril, or what happens when the yellow peril meets or also becomes the red menace.

As I discussed earlier, China comes to compete with and perhaps displace the Soviet Union as America's principal Cold War threat, and *The Manchurian Candidate* preys and plays on such fears. It reminds its American audience of Chinese involvement in the Korean War, and the real-life fear that American POWs had indeed been brainwashed through a mysterious oriental technique of mental torture.[43] The film also articulates the threat of communist and gendered racial penetration into America's domestic space by having the two Asian characters, Dr. Yen Lo the Chinese brainwasher and Chunjin the Korean interpreter (who turns out to be a North Korean spy), travel to the United States.[44] This movement simultaneously recycles and complicates familiar gendered racial tropes of Asian male presence in the United States: that of the laundryman and houseboy, effeminate or emasculated figures who engage in domestic or "women's" labor. Dr. Yen Lo comes to supervise a "refresher" session on Raymond's brain and comments that his brain has not only been "washed, but dry cleaned." Here, the "Chinaman" is not performing menial physical labor *for* the white man, but is conducting highly skilled intellectual labor *on* the white man so that he will do the dirty work of killing for the Chinaman. Moreover, U.S. society itself becomes the Chinaman's analysand when Yen Lo comments on the "uniquely American symptoms of

Eleanor Iselin exerts great power over her son, Raymond Shaw.

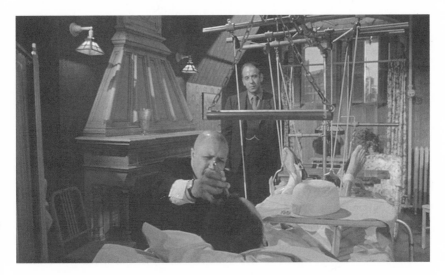

Dr. Yen Lo comes to the United States to continue brainwashing Raymond Shaw.

Chunjin, a North Korean spy, follows Raymond Shaw to the United States and works as his houseboy.

guilt and fear." Similarly, when Chunjin comes knocking on Raymond's door asking to be his "houseboy," his real task is to spy on him for Communist North Korea. These tropes and labors get resignified, even as the new signi-fications fortify competing stereotypes of oriental duplicity, cunning, and inscrutability by tethering them to long-standing historical fears of the "yel-low peril."

The Manchurian Candidate also plays on such racialized paranoia by sug-gesting that the real, or at least competing, source of brainwashing is much closer to home. While there was no evidence found of Chinese brainwashing of American POWs in the Korean War, some of what Hunter and his con-temporaries warned against turned out to bear similarities to the United States' own CIA experiments in "mind control" techniques.[45] Moreover, the film displays the power of television, mass communication, and advertising. Even Dr. Yen Lo and his wife, Madame Yen, have succumbed to the seductive powers of capitalist advertising. They are exposed as supreme hypocrites who delight in capitalist consumption when Dr. Yen Lo reveals that he must go shopping at Macy's for the long list of items that Madame Yen has given him. We also see that TVs, and references to them, appear repeatedly in the film. In one climactic scene, for example, Raymond's ambitious mother, Eleanor Iselin, married to Senator John Iselin (a thinly disguised, if at all, McCarthy), hopes to become the next First Lady by "rally[ing] up a nation of television viewers into hysteria, to sweep [them] up into the White House with powers that will make martial law seem like anarchy." By thus preying and playing on these racialized and gendered Cold War fears, the film both heightens and critiques such fears.

In the following sections, I turn to an examination of how such American fears, desires, and projections condense around the gendered racial figure of Butterfly, who appears in a variety of cultural forms constituting what could now be called the "Butterfly genre." How is Butterfly mobilized as an embod-iment of and metaphor for America's imperialist desires in Asia? In partic-ular, I analyze David Henry Hwang's play *M. Butterfly* as an Asian American parodic limning of Mao's Cultural Revolution, and read how that revolution thwarts and complicates America's gendered racial fears and longings.

The Butterfly Genre

If *The Manchurian Candidate* imagines Asian presence in the United States as a sinister, polluting element threatening to undermine the very founda-tions of the nation, how have cultural forms also imagined the U.S. presence in Asia? What better dramatic form to tell the story of U.S. adventures in Asia, and of East–West relations in general, than through the figure of Butterfly, that tragic, suicidal Asian woman used, duped, and ultimately cast off by a Western man? The prehistory of what could now be called the Butterfly genre, a tracing of its genre-fication and the fixation of the figure of Butterfly as a trope, indexes a prehistory of America's preoccupation with the fabled Chinese market in the globalization of capitalism in the late nineteenth and early twentieth centuries, for the emergence of Butterfly in the popular imagination curiously intersects with the emergence of the Asian market in the geopolitical landscape.

What emerges as well in this prehistory is a continuous citational chain in which we discover that the figure of Butterfly actually predates Puccini's famous opera. Indeed, writes Christina Klein, "Madame Butterfly is more of a genre than an individual narrative. Genres exist as an intermediate category between the specificity of an individual text and the much larger arrangements of social, political, and economic life. Genres perform a mediatory function, and by studying how they evolve, one can chart changes over time in textual form in relation to the changes over time in social relations."[46] What mediatory function does Madame Butterfly serve, and how, moreover, has it evolved since its inception? Developed between 1887 and 1904 in four interrelated works of different genres and different nationalities, the story first appeared in 1887 in a French novel, *Madame Chrysantheme*, by Pierre Loti, the pseudonym of French naval officer Louis-Marie-Julien Viaud. Then, in January 1898, an American periodical, *Century Magazine*, published "Madame Butterfly," written by John Luther Long, a Philadelphia lawyer and Japanophile, as a short story based partly on Loti's novel. Two years later, on March 5, 1900, a theatrical version of "Madame Butterfly" by American playwright and impresario David Belasco opened in New York City. This was followed by its most successful incarnation: Giacomo Puccini's operatic version. *Madama Butterfly*, Puccini's musical reworking of Belasco's play, opened at Milan's La Scala in 1904 and in New York, in English, at the Garden Theater in 1906. The following year, it opened in Italian at the Metropolitan Opera House, and was performed there every year until 1921. During the 1907–8 season alone, 300 performances of the opera were staged in 112 cities, amounting to the largest comprehensive tour of any opera up to that time.

As Klein observes, the narrative structure of "Madame Butterfly" relies on the "twin poles" of marriage and adoption to imagine U.S. relations with Asia. In Loti's novel, contact between the East and the West comes to an amicable end when both parties agree to dissolve the marriage. In the subsequent American texts, however, this ending, a literal end of contact, changes. East–West contact is refigured from amicable, childless divorce to "failed marriage and successful adoption."[47] Such a reconfiguration not only breathes new life, literally, into East–West relations, but constructs a particular model for how those relations should be managed. In this transformed narrative, American Naval Officer Benjamin Pinkerton abandons Butterfly, his Japanese wife, by returning to the States and marrying another woman. He and his new white American wife then go back to Japan, only to claim the child fathered by him and Butterfly. This story, culminating in Butterfly's tragic suicide, could be interpreted as a critique of Western imperialism, a parable of the West's greed and willingness to exploit others. Klein writes, however, that the adoption of the biracial child by Kate Pinkerton ensures the primacy of the white American mother, and thus transforms a narrative of imperialism to one of immigration. Kate is willing to adopt the child, whereas Butterfly must remain, and ultimately dies, in Asia. We see that maternal benevolence, as a sign of American benevolence, has its limits. Thus, "Butterfly's displacement by the American mother solves the problem of race that so disturbed Americans, who were at that moment cutting off Asian immigration: as long as the child can never return, or 'regress' back to the status of the mother, then he can be accepted as an American."[48]

In my view, however, the status of the Asian mother is much more overdetermined than such a resolution allows. Butterfly in Long's story, as opposed to being an unassimilable alien figure, "a typical Japanese woman," is "an American refinement of a Japanese product, an American improvement in a Japanese invention, and so on."[49] This figuration of Butterfly as an improved "Americanized" product or commodity, an economic motif that interestingly gets dropped in Puccini's subsequent operatic adaptation, suggests less a metaphorization as sexual object or conquest and more a literalization of U.S. market relations with Asia at this time. We will recall that at the turn of the century, within the context of the global expansion of capitalism, the restriction of Asian immigration to the United States was coextensive with U.S. expansion into Asia. With the conclusion of the Spanish–American War in 1898, the same year Long published his short story in *Century Magazine*, the United States emerged as a formal imperial power with the acquisition, among other territories, of the Philippines and Guam. American politicians prized these territorial conquests in the Pacific as stepping stones to the fabled

Chinese market. Thus, while the Madame Butterfly genre, as Klein suggests, can be read as a would-be narrative of imperialism ultimately covered over and recuperated as a narrative of immigration through the successful adoption of the biracial Asian child by the white mother, America's enduring desire for the Asian market and favorable trade relations are literalized by Long in "Madame Butterfly" through a curiously abiding concern with money matters.

Indeed, Pinkerton is proud to have struck a favorable bargain. His marriage to Butterfly is "brokered" by a marriage-broker, and he leases a house for 999 years. The length of this agreement is not because "he could hope for the felicity of residing there with her so long, but because, being a mere 'barbarian,' he could not make other terms." This suggestion that he was taken advantage of or hoodwinked in entering into such an absurdly long lease is ironic on a few levels. First, he "did not mention that the lease was terminable, nevertheless, at the end of any month, by the mere neglect to pay the rent."[50] Second, the "felicity" of penetrating the Japanese market and entering into something favorable like a 999-year trade arrangement, revocable at any time, was precisely what the United States had imagined between the mid- to late nineteenth century.[51] By the end of the story, Pinkerton does indeed terminate the lease, and thus his marriage to Butterfly, in the same manner in which he entered into it: through purchase. Just as he purchased Butterfly, he attempts to purchase or buy her off by giving her a large sum of money. Here again, he strikes a bargain, this time a two-for-one: he buys off Butterfly's title to him as his wife as well as her title to their child as his mother. This bargain turns out, ultimately, not to be a bargain at all but something even better: free, or the ultimate bargain, in which he pays nothing for that which he desires. For not only does Butterfly refuse the money, but she also returns to Pinkerton the money he had left her before abandoning her for America. Pinkerton's imperial excursion in Japan, then, generates a huge return for very little principal investment. The extraction of natural resources—a fundamental imperial injunction—is literally born in and through Pinkerton and Butterfly's child, who at the end of the story is extracted from the periphery and brought back to the metropole to be made into an "American refinement of a Japanese product." Unlike Hwang's Rene Gallimard (as we shall see in the following section), in this turn of the century fable, when Asia still exists as limitless possibility rather than complex loss, Pinkerton consummates America's imperial desire in Asia.

What Do Hula Hoops and Squirt Guns Have to Do with the Cold War?

By the time of David Henry Hwang's reinterpretation of the Madame Butterfly genre in his 1988 Tony Award winning Broadway play *M. Butterfly*,
almost a hundred years after Long's short story, it is indeed difficult, if not
laughable, to imagine an "American refinement of a Japanese product." Its
chiastic reverse—a Japanese refinement of an American product—is, however, all too imaginable and real. Japan is figured in Hwang's narrative through
metadramatic "asides" of reworked Pinkerton scenes from Puccini's opera as
the diplomat Rene Gallimard imagines them. Significantly, as I noted previously in tracing Butterfly's intertextuality, this economic valence is a crucial
feature of Long's short story but is dropped in Puccini's operatic rendition.
Thus, with the reappearance of this valence, Hwang's play, while a self-
described "deconstructivist" take on Puccini's opera, is in many ways much
closer to a "deconstructivist" version of Long's 1898 short story. On the surface, *M. Butterfly* itself is about a French diplomat assigned to China, Gallimard, who has an affair with a local woman, Song Liling, and fathers a son.
But Long's "Madame Butterfly" and Puccini's *Madama Butterfly* also figure
as a parodic play within the play. Read alongside the context of the United
States' trade deficit with Japan, most acute in the 1980s and coinciding with
M. Butterfly's successful Broadway run, Hwang's engagement with tropes of
economic exchange to figure Pinkerton's affair with Butterfly, with the balance of trade decidedly in America's favor, is highly ironic and betrays an
abiding nostalgia for a time when an "American refinement of a Japanese
product" was not only possible, but could be had at a great bargain.[52]

   While Butterfly's turn-of-the-century incarnations thus figure significantly
in Hwang's play, the immediate inspiration for his rendition is actually a
strange real-life espionage case. In his playwright's notes on the play, Hwang
writes that his play was "suggested" by newspaper accounts of a 1986 espionage trial in which a former French diplomat and Chinese opera singer
were convicted of spying for China and sentenced to six years in prison. This
trial drew international attention and parlor room chatter not because of
the charge of spying itself—such charges were not unheard of during the Cold
War—but, as indicated by the *New York Times* headline, its "odd" circumstances, amounting to a sensational tale of "clandestine love and mistaken
sexual identity."[53] Testimony during the trial revealed that Mr. Bouriscot, the
French diplomat, met and fell in love with Mr. Shi, an acclaimed Peking Opera
singer, when the former was stationed at the French Embassy in Peking as an

accountant in 1964. For twenty years, Mr. Bouriscot believed Mr. Shi to be a woman. During the course of their affair, he gave classified information on France to Mr. Shi, who was reputedly working for a then-existing Chinese Communist Party intelligence unit.[54] In his playwright's notes, Hwang cites a segment from the *New York Times* article and indicates, as a disclaimer, that while his play was "suggested" by this real-life case, it does not "purport to be a factual record of real events or real people."[55] Hwang's play, then, while not purporting to be a factual record of the Bouriscot/Shi espionage trial, is a dramatization of the historical grounds that made possible, frames, and sustains the case of "mistaken sexual identity" such that Bouriscot's mistake, far from being aberrant, is an amplification of how the West views the East. In other words, it is an allegory of the uneven geopolitical relations between the West and the East, rendered in gendered terms, in which a powerful imperial West, figured as masculine, dominates a weak emasculated East, figured as feminine. Indeed, writes Hwang in the afterword, "From my point of view, the 'impossible' story of a Frenchman duped by a Chinese man masquerading as a woman always seemed perfectly explicable; given the degree of misunderstanding between men and women and also between East and West, it seemed inevitable that a mistake of this magnitude would one day take place." He continues, "For this formula—good natives serve Whites, bad natives rebel—is consistent with the mentality of colonialism. Because they are submissive and obedient, good natives of both sexes necessarily take on 'feminine' characteristics in a colonialist world."[56]

Why did Hwang feel it necessary to write such an afterword, several months after the play's successful Broadway opening? Seeking to address the charge that *M. Butterfly* is an "anti-American play, a diatribe against the stereotyping of the East by the West," he insists that his play is rather "a plea to all sides to cut through our respective layers of cultural and sexual misperception, deal with one another truthfully for our mutual good, from the common and equal ground we share as human beings."[57] This humanist plea blunts the pointed political valence of the play, and what many had interpreted as a political parable of the pitfalls of Western imperialism is offered instead as a humanist parable of mutual misperception. The lesson to be derived, then, from this parable of East–West relations, is to transcend the world of "surfaces," "misperceptions," and "myths" in order to achieve "truthful contact." While Hwang begins his afterword with a critique of the intersection of race, sex, and imperialism and of U.S. foreign policy blunders in Asia, he curiously ends it with a plea to go beyond stereotypes and misperceptions. What is left uninterrogated is the complex relationship *between* imperialism and stereotypes. By thus shifting the critical register from imperialism to stereotypes, Hwang turns attention away from the material conditions that overdetermine and help give rise to such stereotypes in the first place and continue to fuel their generation, circulation, and effectivity. Similarly, critical writing on *M. Butterfly* has tended to either celebrate or deride the play's attempt to deconstruct essentialist and Orientalist tropes that rely on the gendering of Asia as feminine and weak.[58] Indeed, the play's epigraph thematizes this problematic. It is a line from a David Bowie/Iggy Pop song, called, appropriately enough, "China Girl": "I could escape this feeling/With my China girl . . ."[59] The problem Hwang grapples with, it seems, is the problem of Orientalist essentialism, read as a symptom of the West's imperialist attitude toward Asia.

While, as critics have rightly pointed out, tropes of gender and sexuality figure prominently in the play, a curiously parallel set of tropes concerning economic exchange, purchase, trade, worth, and money structures the play. In my analysis, I trace these tropes and argue that *M. Butterfly* can be read as a rehearsal and palimpsest of America's ongoing preoccupation with the Asian market and the Cold War loss of that market in 1949 to Mao's Communist victory in China. *M. Butterfly* reveals this preoccupation as an imperialist and gendered racial projection, and like Kingston's narrator, the play thematizes "Communism" as a complex problem of knowledge embedded within uneven relations of (geopolitical) power. Thus, instead of reading Orientalism as simply a problem of stereotypes or misperceptions, I link it to America's capitalist modernity and analyze Hwang's play not as an allegory of the facile consummation of America's imperial desires in Asia, but as a genealogy of their very limits. Indeed, Arif Dirlik argues that "it is insufficient to conceive of Orientalism simply in terms of Eurocentrism or nationalism. It is position [*sic*] in the capitalist structuring of the world that ultimately accounts for the changing relationships between discourse (Eurocentric or self-orientalizing) and power." He continues: "It seems to me to be more important to question the assumptions of capitalist modernity (not merely Eurocentrism) of which Orientalism is an integral expression. To the extent that they have assimilated the teleology of capitalism, recent challenges to Eurocentrism (such as with the Confucian revival) have promoted rather than dislodged Orientalism. What is necessary is to repudiate historical teleology in all its manifestations."[60]

I begin my analysis, then, by noting how *M. Butterfly* metadramatically stages the literal commodification of relations between two people, Pinkerton and Butterfly, in the sections that reimagine Long's short story and Puccini's opera. This parallels Marx's conception of commodity fetishism: relations between people taken as relations between things. In *Capital,* Marx writes that while a commodity appears upon first glance to be quite an obvious, even "trivial" thing, further analysis reveals it to be a very "strange thing, abounding in metaphysical subtleties and theological niceties." Why is the commodity a strange thing? Why indeed, is it "mystical" and "mysterious?" It is not because of its use-value, in the sense that its "raw" or natural properties satisfy human needs or that its natural properties are changed by human labor so as to become useful. Rather:

> The mysterious character of the commodity-form consists therefore simply in the fact that the commodity reflects the social characteristics of men's own labour as objective characteristics of the products of labour themselves, as the socio-natural properties of these things. . . . It is nothing but the definite *social relation* between men themselves which assumes here, for them, the fantastic form of a relation between things. . . . I call this the *fetishism* which attaches itself to the products of labour as soon as they are produced as commodities, and is therefore inseparable from the production of commodities.[61]

M. Butterfly elaborates and complicates the notion of commodity fetishism by staging it as a gendered racial projection. That is, what happens when the "social relation between men themselves" constitutes the relations between a Western man and an Asian woman? Within this relationality, the woman herself becomes the gendered racial fetish.[62]

In *M. Butterfly,* Pinkerton is introduced by Gallimard as "not very good-looking, not too bright, and pretty much a wimp."[63] He is, however, an excellent bargain hunter, and he takes great pride in this skill. Gallimard observes that Pinkerton has "closed on two great bargains: one on a house, the other on a woman—call it a package deal. Pinkerton purchased the rights to Butterfly for one hundred yen—in modern currency, equivalent to about . . . sixty-six cents. So, he's feeling pretty pleased with himself" (5). The parodic heights of Hwang's portrayal of Pinkerton hinge not on the character's caddishness, but on his stinginess. Butterfly, at sixty-six cents, is cheap, but it is in fact Pinkerton who is uber-cheap. Hwang lampoons this economy:

PINKERTON/GALLIMARD: Sharpless! How's it hangin'? It's a great day, just great. Between my house, my wife, and the rickshaw ride in from town, I've saved nineteen cents just his morning.

SHARPLESS (THE AMERICAN CONSUL): I can see the inscription on your tomb-
stone already: "I saved a dollar, here I lie." (5)

Pinkerton marries Butterfly, knowing that if he should leave for a month, the
marriage would be annulled. He intends, of course, to leave, and is ecstatic
over the "generous trade-in terms" (6) provided by an annulment. When he
leaves, he brags that Butterfly will have known what it is like to have loved
a real man, and that he'll "even buy her a few nylons" (6). He will not take
her to America with him; in fact, he finds such a notion ridiculous, citing as
his reason the absurdity of attempting to imagine her "trying to buy rice in
St. Louis" (7). Why this obsession with saving money, and why is the idea of
a Japanese woman trying to buy rice in St. Louis unfathomable? While the
"Asiatic" has historically been looked upon with much suspicion by the West
as the locus of "primitive accumulation" or secretive hoarding, in *M. Butterfly,* we see a reversal: the American turns out to be the hoarder par excellence. Moreover, Pinkerton's persistent preoccupation with saving money is
coupled with a desire to maintain a favorable balance of trade by keeping all
things Japanese in Japan. American nylon stockings are exported to Japan,
but Japanese imports (Butterfly herself as well as rice) should not find their
way into the American market. This, read against the actual ubiquity of Japanese imports in the United States at the time of Hwang's production, produces an all too obvious ironic disjuncture, and Pinkerton's obsession with
saving money and his attempt to keep all things Japanese in Japan betray
America's own fears about Japanese competitiveness in the 1980s. Japan, then,
is figured nostalgically as a ready market for American consumption and
American consumerables: cheaply available Japanese goods for American consumption and readily received American goods for Japanese consumption.
The Cold War economic success of Japan, underwritten militarily and finan-
cially in large part by the United States, comes ironically to haunt the sponsor.
The Soviet Union is doubly displaced: when Communist China becomes the
United States' principal ideological rival in the Cold War, and later again when
Japan becomes the United States' chief economic rival. Indeed, Bruce Cumings writes that it is Japan that has "truly proven to be a disease of the heart
(and communism a mere disease of the skin, sure to disappear if we allow it
do to so). . . . Japan is the active factor in East Asia. It is still today the sole
comprehensively industrialized Asian nation operating at a technologically
advanced level, and thus the only real rival to the Western powers."[64] More

recently, China's increasing openness to "free market" practices and rising competitiveness have complicated this formulation.

In revealing the palimpsest of the complex triangulation of the Cold War in Asia, Hwang juxtaposes Japan (in the Pinkerton scenes) with China (in the Gallimard scenes). Even as the Cold War necessitated the distinction between enemies and allies, the West has historically figured the East as an undifferentiated, homogenous mass, with one Asian nation fungible with another, and Hwang complicates this geopolitical imaginary. Indeed, he has stated in an interview that "the West looks at the 'East' as sort of a monolith. Whether we've been at war against Japan or Korea or Vietnam or in a Cold War with China, it's all 'oriental.' But of course the Asians see themselves as very different."[65] While the economic success of Japan provokes a nostalgic return to the days of America's perceived unrivaled economic hegemony, China is imagined as at once a nostalgic Cold War "loss," as unlimited future possibility, and as potential threat. The desire for the Chinese market, repressed during its Cold War "loss," returns through an imagining of a ripe postcommunist field of commodity production and consumption. This figuration of China is revealed in an exchange that Gallimard has with Renee, a young Danish student with whom he is having an affair:

GALLIMARD: And what do you do?

RENEE: I'm a student. My father exports a lot of useless stuff to the Third World.

GALLIMARD: How useless?

RENEE: You know. Squirt guns, confectioner's sugar, hula hoops . . .

GALLIMARD: I'm sure they appreciate the sugar.

RENEE: I'm here for two years to study Chinese.

GALLIMARD: Two years?

RENEE: That's what everybody says.

GALLIMARD: When did you arrive?

RENEE: Three weeks ago.

GALLIMARD: And?

RENEE: I like it. It's primitive, but . . . well, this is the place to learn Chinese, so here I am.

GALLIMARD: Why Chinese?

RENEE: I think it'll be important someday.

GALLIMARD: You do?

RENEE: Don't ask me when, but . . . that's what I think.

GALLIMARD: Well, I agree with you. One hundred percent. That's very farsighted.

RENEE: Yeah. Well of course, my father thinks I'm a complete weirdo.

GALLIMARD: He'll thank you someday.

RENEE: Like when the Chinese start buying hula hoops?

GALLIMARD: There're a *billion bellies* out there.

RENEE: And if they end up taking over the world—well, then I'll be lucky to know Chinese, too, right? (*Pause.*)

GALLIMARD: At this point, I don't see how the Chinese can possibly take—(52–53, emphasis added)

I quote this scene at length because it encapsulates the simultaneous imagining of China as loss, possibility, and threat. Hwang rehearses America's historical desire for the fabled Chinese market.[66] The Cold War closure of China's market, its "billion bellies," to Western capitalism is lamented. The Cold War, while thwarting America's desire to have access to these billion bellies and producing a profound paranoia about the communist enemy, particularly when this "red menace" merged with the historical "yellow peril" in China, also produced an apparently opposite yet related paranoia. It was that China, with its vast population and resources, would one day rival the United States not as a communist state, but a capitalist one. The temporality of America's desire for the Chinese market—a past of thwarted attempts, a present that is an interregnum on the eventual road to a market economy, and a future of unlimited possibilities—is both dream and nightmare. What should happen if the Chinese, as opposed to being passive consumers, also become active producers, as the Japanese example demonstrates? With its vast population, China's consumption power is also, after all, its labor power. The "useless" goods exported to other parts of the Third World—"squirt guns, confectioner's sugar, hula hoops"—would not be possible without the extraction and exploitation of Third World natural resources and cheap labor. This balance of trade will stay in place as long as the Third World remains just that, and would continue to remain so if China would somehow enter a postcommunist stage as a Third World country rather than a strong economic rival. The "Third World" moniker was created, as I discussed in the introductory chapter, at the 1955 Bandung Conference by nonaligned nations to signal their refusal to be drawn into the bipolar Cold War conflict between the capitalist and communist blocs (the first and second worlds, respectively). However, it has since come to mean something else. The denotation of nonalignment has come to connote underdevelopment, poverty, and backwardness. Indeed, the ideal of nonalignment has come to serve as an enabling fiction for the increasing globalization of capitalism, writ large by the super-exploitation of the "nonaligned" Third World.

In *M. Butterfly,* Hwang reveals how the West imagines and hopes that China, though still a "primitive" element of the communist bloc, will one day join the global economy in terms that are favorable to the United States. That is, by making available its "billion bellies" to hula hoops. In tracking this curious appearance of the hula hoop in the play, we are again reminded that the commodity and its value are neither trivial nor simple. Indeed, the peculiarity of this particular commodity form, the hula hoop, derives precisely from its overdetermined inception and reception during the height of the Cold War. The toy was first introduced by an American company, Wham-O-Manufacturing, in 1958.[67] Within a year, more than 100 million were sold worldwide. Japan, however, America's Cold War ally in Asia, banned the hoops, most probably because it deemed the hip movements of hooping to be sexually provocative. The Soviet Union, America's Cold War enemy, demonstrated a similar disdain, though for a seemingly unrelated reason: the hula hoop was viewed as an example of the emptiness of American culture. Perhaps this pronouncement was derived in part from the actual physical emptiness of the hula hoop—its empty middle and hollowness within its plastic tubing. We see, then, that the value—monetary, cultural, and indeed moral—of the hula hoop, a simple round piece of hollow plastic tubing, to quote Marx, "does not have its description branded on its forehead; it rather transforms every product of labour into a social hieroglyphic. Later on, men try to decipher the hieroglyphic, to get behind the secret of their own social product: for the characteristic which objects of utility have of being values is as much men's social product as is their language."[68] The hope that China will one day ascribe the hula hoop with value is hinted at in Gallimard's discussion with Renee. He applauds Renee for her "farsightedness" in choosing to learn Chinese. For once China opens its market to the world, it will be "important" to know the Chinese language. Renee remarks that she will in fact be "lucky" to know the language if China ends up "taking over the world." Here, Hwang signals the ambivalence of the desire for the Chinese market. The Communist Revolution in China is lamented as both a Cold War loss and celebrated as the postponement of inevitable Chinese domination of the world market. As opposed to being passive squirt-gun and hula-hoop *receptors,* what if China, with its vast population, should become hyper-competitive squirt-gun and hula-hoop *producers* for the world market? What if China should surpass Western productivity, as the example of Japan illustrates?

The ambivalence of America's imperial and gendered racial projection is further revealed in *M. Butterfly* through a play on the relationship between productivity and reproductivity. Like Pinkerton's Butterfly, Gallimard's Song Liling provides him with a son. We know, of course, that since Song is actually a man masquerading as a woman, he could not have given birth to the child himself. Instead, he asks the Communist Party, for whom he is working as a spy, to provide him with one, convinced that a child will cement his relationship with Gallimard and therefore allow him to continue his espionage activities indefinitely. Comrade Chin, the party member assigned to Song, initially remains unconvinced, exclaiming that "the trading of babies has to be a counterrevolutionary act!" Song responds, "Sometimes, a counterrevolutionary act is necessary to counter a counterrevolutionary act" (62). This logic ultimately works on Comrade Chin. Initially, however, she views Song's request as a "trading of babies," much like an illicit, illegal trade of contraband. By "trading" a baby for classified information, Song reverses the balance of trade. Chinese bellies, while figured by Gallimard and Renee as a future reservoir of passive consumers, turn out to be active agents of the Chinese Communist state. A billion Chinese bellies, while potent precisely because of their number, are also literally potent because of their productive and reproductive capability. The contraband baby, while not a product of Song in this instance, had, after all, to be reproduced from some Chinese belly. And while Pinkerton's "Japanese invention" commits herself to remaining in Japan by committing suicide, in *M. Butterfly,* Gallimard's Chinese invention follows him to the West, along with "their" baby. On the one hand, the balance of trade is reversed by strengthening Communist intelligence-gathering activities. On the other hand, *M. Butterfly* appears to anticipate the end of the Cultural Revolution, signaling the imminent ubiquity of hula hoops in China. As Song tells Gallimard, "Chinese are realists. We understand rice, gold and guns" (65).

The classified information for which the baby is traded renders America's simultaneous desire for and fear of the Chinese market all the more acute. This desire for the Asian market, as I stated previously, operates through an economy of the substitutability and fungibility of specific Asian nations. Or, to repeat Hwang's formulation, "it's all oriental." *M. Butterfly* disrupts this economy of fungibility further by critiquing French and U.S. imperialisms in Vietnam. We learn that the intelligence gathered by Song from Gallimard concerns U.S. involvement in Vietnam. Toulon, Gallimard's boss, reveals America's plans to secretly bomb North Vietnam and Laos, complaining, "What a bunch of jerks. Vietnam was our colony. Not only didn't the Americans help us fight to keep them, but now, seven years later, they've come back to grab the territory for themselves. It's very irritating" (44). In his analysis, Gallimard, much like the Americans fighting the war, miscalculates the situation. A swift American victory was not to be had. The attempt to contain or roll back communism in Asia, overdetermined by the historical desire for markets in Asia, relied on a template or geopolitical reading practice that did not take into account Asian agency and nationalism. Gallimard is dumbfounded: "And somehow the American war went wrong too. Four hundred thousand dollars were being spent for every Viet Cong killed; so General Westmoreland's remark that the Oriental does not value life the way Americans do was oddly accurate. Why weren't the Vietnamese people giving in? Why were they content instead to die and die and die again?" (68). That the Viet Cong will not surrender in the face of U.S. military might is unfathomable to Gallimard. The only way in which he can make sense of it is to reduce it to an economic equation: "Four hundred thousand dollars were being spent for every Viet Cong killed" (68). We see here again the peculiar compulsion to calculate human life and relations between people into a specific dollar figure. Hwang reveals the absurdity and perversity of Gallimard's logic. Gallimard concludes that America's willingness to spend four hundred thousand dollars to kill one Viet Cong demonstrates how highly Westerners value life, whereas the Viet Cong's willingness to let their own "die and die again" shows that they do not value life as highly. We know, rather, that the economic costs of America's war in Vietnam, along with the burgeoning space race and military industrial complex during the Cold War, were investments in capitalism and the protection and expansion of markets. The question of value, then, is strictly in an extra-moral sense. We speak not of moral values, but of use and exchange value. Gallimard can only read Asia in terms of its use and exchange value to the West, so the notion of a "useless" or "unexchangeable" Asia is oxymoronic to him. His grand miscalculations—symptomatic of U.S. Cold War policy in Asia—result in his transfer back to France. As Toulon points out, nothing that Gallimard predicted in Asia actually happened. China did not open itself to Western trade, nor did the Americans succeed in Indochina.

Just as Gallimard's miscalculations vis-à-vis Indochina as well as his ignorance of Song's true identity mark a problem of knowledge, a lack of revelatory knowledge, Hwang's parodic limning of Chinese communism during its Cultural Revolution phase is not meant to reveal "the truth" of Mao's rule, but rather to critique the logics of American anticommunism. Through Comrade Chin, Song's handler, Hwang lampoons the perceived absurd orthodoxy of the party. Comrade Chin notes that Song is always "in character," meaning wearing a dress, when they meet for debriefings. Calling actors "weirdos," she interrogates Song:

> CHIN: You're not gathering information in any way that violates Communist Party principles, are you?
> SONG: Why would I do that?
> CHIN: Just checking. Remember: when working for the Great Proletarian State, you represent our Chairman Mao in every position you take.
> SONG: I'll try to imagine the Chairman taking my positions.
> CHIN: We all think of him this way. Good-bye, comrade. (*She starts to exit*) Comrade?
> SONG: Yes?
> CHIN: Don't forget: there is no homosexuality in China! (48)

The last line of this exchange—"Don't forget: there is no homosexuality in China"—parallels the musings of Kingston's young Chinese American narrator, the epigraph from *China Men* with which I began this chapter. In a string of metaphors, Kingston's narrator speculates that "maybe [Communism] had to do with no sex." Her naïve interpretations of her family's narratives parallel Hwang's parodic send-up of the Cultural Revolution. As such, Kingston and Hwang both thematize Chinese communism as a problem of knowledge saturated by the related registers of American anticommunism, on the one hand, and America's imperial and gendered racial projections, on the other. The symptoms of this problem of knowledge are the metaphorics of "no homosexuality," "no sex," but "new songs" and "new dances."

By tracing these metaphorics, I hope to have shown in this chapter the critical *Cold War compositions* that reveal and give important form to how the U.S.–Soviet rivalry was triangulated in China. Insofar as Soviet Russia is already racialized as oriental, and China itself transmogrifies into the "red peril," such a triangulation witnesses imperialist and gendered racial metaphorics in America's Cold War imaginary that attempt to make sense of the "loss" of the "Eldorado of commerce." Yet as *M. Butterfly* reveals, this loss simultaneously generates fears of the inevitable awakening of a "sleeping giant." Indeed, recent media coverage of China, including that of the 2008 Summer Olympics in Beijing, has also put such fears on display. Furthermore, while China's rapid economic rise in the post–Cold War period has garnered much attention, its formidable military strength is also being analyzed. Notably, a 2005 cover article in the *Atlantic Monthly* entitled "The Next Cold War: How We Would Fight China" argues that the "center of gravity of American strategic concern is already the Pacific, not the Middle East," and that the competition between the United States and China constitutes a "second Cold War" that "may stretch over several generations."[69] In this second Cold War, the Chinese will not engage in conventional air and naval battles, but will approach the United States "asymmetrically, as terrorists do. In Iraq the insurgents have shown us the low end of asymmetry, with car bombs. But the Chinese are poised to show us the high end of the art. That is the threat."[70] This military contest in the Pacific, the article predicts, will define the twenty-first century, and China will be a "more formidable adversary than Russia ever was." Moreover, "Pulsing with consumer and martial energy, and boasting a peasantry that, unlike others in history, is overwhelmingly literate, China constitutes the principal conventional threat to America's liberal imperium."[71] As my analysis demonstrates, in *M. Butterfly* this "second Cold War" is already hinted at and anticipated.

From this discussion of China as America's principal *threat*, arguably already during the "first" Cold War, I turn in the next chapter to Japan, America's principal or junior Cold War *ally* in the Pacific. I show how in Japan, World War II bled into the Cold War, by analyzing how Japanese American cultural productions imagine the atomic bombings of Hiroshima and Nagasaki, the U.S. occupation of Japan, and Japanese American internment as linked projects of what I call gendered racial rehabilitation.

3

ASIAN AMERICA'S JAPAN

The Perils of Gendered Racial Rehabilitation

In the opening scenes of Alain Resnais's film *Hiroshima, Mon Amour,* the dialectic of remembering and forgetting is hauntingly captured through alternating images of the entwined bodies of a pair of lovers and significant sights in the city of Hiroshima—the hospital for the bomb victims and the Peace Museum.[1] Throughout, a voiceover in the form of a succession of assertions and the negation of those assertions, presumably in the voices of the two lovers, articulates the problematics of attempting to represent, see, know, and remember such a historical trauma. This verbal volley ensues thus:

MALE VOICE: You saw nothing in Hiroshima. Nothing.

FEMALE VOICE: I saw everything. I saw the hospital. I'm sure of it. The hospital in Hiroshima exists. How could I not have seen it?

MALE VOICE: You didn't see the hospital in Hiroshima. You saw nothing in Hiroshima.

FEMALE VOICE: Four times at the museum.

MALE VOICE: What museum in Hiroshima?

Even as viewers are given a measure of access to the museum through extreme close-ups of its displays, the voiceover (in the female voice) throws that access into question, reminding the viewer that the displays are mere reconstructions, "for lack of photographs," and that the "explanations" are there "for lack of anything else." Indeed, though the reconstructions are as "authentic as possible," and though she has seen the newsreels produced in the days immediately following America's World War II atomic bombing of

95

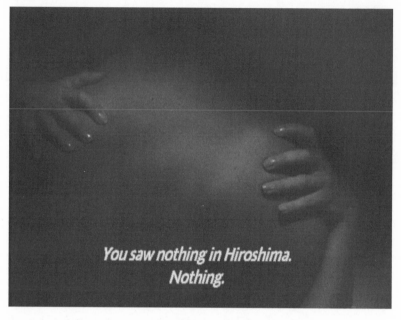

*You saw nothing in Hiroshima.
Nothing.*

The entwined, healthy bodies of the lovers in the film, who voice the complexities of witnessing and remembering such a historical trauma (from *Hiroshima, Mon Amour*, 1959).

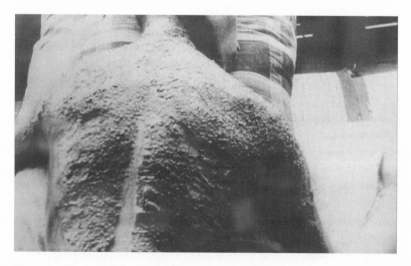

The scarred back of a bomb victim.

What was there for you to weep over?

Hiroshima's devastated landscape in the wake of the bomb.

Hiroshima (and thus goes from merely "seeing" to "knowing"), the conviction that she/we will "never forget it" is simply an illusion.

Hiroshima, Mon Amour suggests that just as we believe we will remember love, most ardently our first love, we believe we will remember an atrocity such as Hiroshima, yet we forget both. We find out later in the film that the female lover, a French woman who remains nameless, has indeed forgotten the (illicit) first love she had with a German soldier in occupied France during World War II. This intersection of personal and collective memories/histories is visualized in the film when ashes begin to fall on the entwined bodies of the lovers, and their skin is suddenly replaced with that of the burned bomb victims captured in newsreels. The insistence, moreover, that you/I/we "saw nothing in Hiroshima" contains multiple meanings. On the one hand, it voices the process of a willful historical amnesia or forgetting, that we "saw nothing" because we did not want to see, whether because of shame, the sheer horror, or the denial of collective accountability. We also "saw nothing" because gendered racial taxonomies deem some lives to be "human," and thus worth seeing and mourning, while other lives are differentially (de)valued as "nothing." On the other hand, in the aftermath of total atomic annihilation, there was literally nothing left to see except for that very annihilation, and thus you/I/we "saw nothing in Hiroshima."[2] Indeed, as captured in the subtitled voiceover of the image above, "What was there for you to weep over?" While the U.S. government has attempted to forget its act of atomic terror for obvious political reasons, insofar as a recollection of the bombings of Hiroshima and Nagasaki has been tethered to a concomitant recollection of Japan's own imperial militarism and perpetration of atrocities in World War II, even the Japanese government has been complicit in this willful historical amnesia.

Hiroshima, Mon Amour presents us with a conundrum: the inevitability of forgetting against the obvious necessity of remembering, or what I have referred to above as the dialectic of remembering and forgetting. By the end of the opening verbal volley between the two lovers, the opposing voices cleave together: "Listen to me. Like you, I know what it is to forget. . . . Like you, I forget." Because they/we forget, "It will begin again." And yet we are asked: "Why deny the obvious necessity of remembering?" The film also highlights how memory and historical knowledge are multiply-mediated and is self-conscious about its own participation in this process. Indeed, as I will be discussing later in this chapter, when Japanese American poet David Mura visits Hiroshima, even in the physical presence of the city itself, he can only apprehend and make sense of it through his experience of the film *Hiroshima, Mon Amour.*

In this chapter, I investigate the partially forgotten, partially remembered history of how in Japan, World War II led into the Cold War. By "partial," I mean to signal the word's two related senses as incomplete and prejudiced. I offer an analysis of how a group of Japanese American cultural texts— Steven Okazaki's documentary *Survivors,* David Mura's memoir *Turning Japanese: Memoirs of a Sansei,* and Ruth L. Ozeki's novel *My Year of Meats*—critically imagines and grasps the partially forgotten and partially remembered history of America's imperial and gendered racial encounter with Japan.[3] These works display the haunting and at times grotesque remainders and reminders of how World War II bled into the Cold War in Japan—from America's atomic bombings of Hiroshima and Nagasaki (August 1945) to its military occupation of Japan (1945–52). These cultural productions ask, moreover, why the atomic bombings of Hiroshima and Nagasaki can only be grasped in fragments, while U.S.–Japanese economic "cooperation" (what the British once called a "strange neo-imperialism of a mystical irrational kind") is ubiquitously and often grotesquely present.[4] In particular, I argue that Okazaki, Mura, and Ozeki give form to the atomic bombings of Hiro-shima and Nagasaki, the World War II internment and relocation of Japanese Americans in the United States, and the U.S. occupation of Japan as trans-nationally linked projects of what I call *gendered racial rehabilitation*. I demon-strate how gendered racial rehabilitation paternalistically attempts to produce properly assimilated and anticommunist liberal Japanese and Japanese Amer-ican citizen-subjects, on the one hand, and a tamed and demilitarized yet economically integrated Japanese nation-state that would serve as America's junior Cold War partner in Asia, on the other. That is, by gendered racial rehabilitation, I mean to suggest the complex ways in which Japanese and Japanese American subjects—formerly enemies and "enemy aliens," respec-tively—are transformed into a Cold War junior ally in Asia and a "model minority"[5] in America through their interpellation by and suturing to the protocols and logics of America's Cold War imperial project.

As I will go on to demonstrate, the specific racial contours of rehabilita-tion attempt to incorporate and assimilate Japanese and Japanese Americans into the U.S. Cold War projects of liberal democracy and capitalism, yet this process is not one of deracination. Rather, the Japanese American cultural texts I analyze thematize the transpacific and transnational logics of racial proximity, mimicry, and tightly circumscribed similarity. Japan is an ally, but still miniaturized and rendered a diminutive junior ally, and Japanese Amer-icans are a model, but still a minority. In other words, both are compelled to be, as Homi Bhabha has succinctly put it in his analysis of mimicry and the ambivalence of colonial discourse, "almost the same, *but not quite*," or "not quite/not white."[6] This logic of proximity and mimicry attempts to contain, tame, and "domesticate" racial hyper-competitiveness or superiority, of the kind that was putatively demonstrated by imperial Japan in World War II and by Japanese American farming communities on the West Coast of the United States. These racial contours are intimately linked, as I will elaborate throughout this chapter, to the specifically gendered valences of rehabilita-tion. We can track the gendered valences through the trope of "domestica-tion" and its related trope of "domesticity." Whether domesticating a former enemy *nation* by demilitarizing and feminizing it, or domesticating a former enemy *alien* by replacing the site of patriarchal authority from the male head of the household to the U.S. government's carceral War Relocation Author-ity and thereby producing a sense of diminished masculinity for (former) patriarchs, what we witness are the racial and gendered dynamics of rehabil-itation. Domestication simultaneously generates a preoccupation with the

cult of normative liberal capitalist capitalist domesticity and the construction of a
proper "Japanese womanhood" modeled on the white American heteronormative feminine bourgeois ideal.[7] This project of gendered racial rehabilitation, moreover, did not end with the release and relocation of Japanese
Americans at the close of World War II in 1945 nor with the occupation's
end in 1952, but persists in contemporary symptoms of the imperialism of
U.S.-led corporate globalization (what we could euphemistically call U.S.–
Japanese economic "cooperation") and its articulation with the gendered racial
formation of both Japanese and Japanese American subjects.

While providing a critical imagining of the perils of gendered racial rehabilitation, *Survivors, Turning Japanese,* and *My Year of Meats* also register the
failures and contradictions of this Cold War imperialist project. We meet
people and characters who remain decidedly *un*rehabilitated, and thus expose
how the U.S.–Japanese Cold War alliance that undergirds U.S. global capitalism and hegemony emerges out of a genealogy of a palimpsestic arrangement of gendered racial imperialisms. In this arrangement, U.S. gendered
racial imperialism is layered over the Japanese one, and we witness a double,
or twinned, burial of this very genealogy by both nations. These unrehabilitated bodies thus provide critical possibilities for arrangements—alternative identifications, desires, social formations, and geopolitics—that refuse
to be enframed and ensnared by America's Cold War "ends of empire."

"A Strange Neo-imperialism of a Mystical Irrational Kind"

I shall begin my analysis, then, with a brief historical accounting of how the
"ends" of World War II overlap with the beginnings of the Cold War in Japan.
In the aftermath of Japan's bombing of Pearl Harbor on December 7, 1941,
American public opinion, linked to a longer history of anti-Asian and anti-
Japanese agitation, reached virulently racist heights. This widespread popular structure of feeling was captured by *Time* magazine when it called the
attack "premeditated murder masked by a toothy smile."[8] A few months after
the bombing, on February 19, 1942, President Franklin D. Roosevelt signed
Executive Order 9066, authorizing the internment/incarceration of over
120,000 Japanese Americans (including U.S.-born citizens) living on the West
Coast. In 1944, as the Pacific War heated up, a Gallup Poll revealed that 13
percent of the American public favored "exterminating *all* Japanese" (emphasis added). In a June 1945 survey, one-third of the respondents called for the
summary execution of Emperor Hirohito, while most wanted him condemned
as a war criminal. Members of Congress echoed similar sentiments: Senator

Lister Hill (D-Alabama) urged the U.S. Army to "gut the heart of Japan with fire"; Senator Ernest McFarland (D-Arizona) argued that "the Japs [should] pay dearly through their blood and the ashes of their cities" for having the audacity to attack America; and Senator Theodore G. Bilbo (D-Mississippi) sent a letter to General Douglas MacArthur shortly after Japan's surrender calling for the sterilization of all Japanese. Doing Senator Bilbo one better, an advisor to the important State-War-Navy Coordinating Committee (SWNCC) proposed the "almost total elimination of the Japanese as a race," while other top government officials called for the near eradication of Japanese civilization as well as its civilian population. And perhaps not surprisingly, even the president expressed interest in a scheme to "crossbreed" the Japanese with "docile Pacific Islanders," telling a Smithsonian anthropologist that compulsory eugenics might eradicate the "primitive" brains and "barbarism" of the enemy race.[9] Indeed, Naoko Shibusawa argues that the "war in the Pacific unleashed a racial hatred that sometimes bordered on genocidal rage, which continued throughout the conflict."[10] Ironically, however, the United States had entered World War II's theater in the Atlantic putatively in order to counter Hitler's genocidal rage. As the war reached its last battles, Time-Life publisher Henry Luce made the frank observation that "Americans had to learn how to hate Germans, but hating Japs comes natural—as natural as fighting Indians once was."[11] While Luce was uncritically linking the "naturalness" of fighting two different races similarly racialized as savage, his remark unwittingly reveals America's genealogy of continental and extracontinental genocidal conquest.

Within the context of such viscerally felt and violently expressed racial logics, a decision was made, putatively to hasten Japan's surrender and end the war in the Pacific, by dropping atomic bombs on Hiroshima and Nagasaki in August 1945. As I noted in chapter 1, according to Nakajima Mineo, this decision was overdetermined by an already detectable Cold War between the United States and the Soviet Union. Although the United States already had knowledge at the time that Japan was sending out peace feelers through Moscow, the atomic bombs were used in large part as an attempt to keep the Soviet Union out of Japan, and thus to minimize its postwar claims and power there.[12] This "atomic diplomacy" becomes more apparent when examining the timing of the bombings. Significantly, the Hiroshima atomic raid, on August 6, came two days before the Soviet entry into the Pacific War. Moreover, Thomas J. McCormick observes that the "unseemly haste" with which the second atomic bomb was dropped on Nagasaki on August 9, just three days later, before the Japanese government had time to make sense of and respond to the first Hiroshima bombing, explains how the United States "wanted the war ended within days (not weeks or months) in order to limit the size and scope of Soviet involvement."[13]

After General MacArthur accepted Japan's formal surrender aboard the USS *Missouri* on September 2, 1945, he set about the task of "taming" a warrior race with enthusiasm and claimed for himself an unsurpassed knowledge of the "oriental mind."[14] In a similar vein, American GIs saw themselves as experts on "Babysan's world," referred disdainfully to Japanese women as "gook girls," and self-amusingly joked that their knowledge constituted a unique "slant" on Japan.[15] As these racial grammars and epistemologies suggest, the virulent anti-Japanese racism Americans expressed during World War II did not disappear or evaporate once this enemy group was vanquished, but rather transmogrified into a (still) white supremacist racist paternalism relying on and reinvigorating preexisting discourses of manifest destiny and the "white man's burden." Indeed, while these racial optics might have overdetermined the occupation of Japan as a racial *project*, the occupation of Germany did not witness parallel racial affects or effects. John W. Dower writes, "Unlike Germany, this vanquished enemy represented an exotic, alien society to its conquerors: nonwhite, non-Western, non-Christian. Yellow, Asian, pagan Japan, supine and vulnerable, provoked an ethnocentric missionary zeal inconceivable vis-à-vis Germany. Where Nazism was perceived as a cancer in a fundamentally mature 'Western' society, Japanese militarism and ultranationalism were construed as reflecting the essence of a feudalistic, Oriental culture that was cancerous in and of itself." As such, Dower continues, American reformers approached the occupation with "almost sensual excitement," and felt that they were "*denaturing* an Oriental adversary and turning it into at least an approximation of an acceptable, healthy, westernized nation."[16] Moreover, Yukiko Koshiro argues, "A strong racial awareness was deemed necessary as the United States battled what it thought was the legacy of Japan's racial conspiracy against whites. To American eyes, the worst Japanese war crime was the attempt to cripple the white man's prestige by sowing the seeds of racial pride under the banner of Pan-Asianism. Now it was up to the United States to salvage that prestige."[17]

As I will go on to demonstrate later in this chapter, the Japanese American cultural productions I analyze critically thematize how such an attempt to "salvage" America's "prestige" depends on the transformation and reconstitution of Japanese and Japanese American subjects from World War II enemies and "enemy aliens," respectively, to liberal capitalist consuming and productive subjects on the proper anticommunist side of the Cold War. Indeed, Lisa Yoneyama argues that America's Cold War perception of itself as the defender of world freedom and democracy (defined against the totalitarianism of the Soviet Union) is intimately connected to America's memories of the war against Japan (1941–45) during World War II as a "good war." According to this dominant memory, the war against Japan "not only liberated Asians, including Japanese themselves, from Japan's military fanaticism, but also rehabilitated them into free and prosperous citizens of the democratic world." In other words, she continues, "dominant American war memories are tied to what might be called an imperialist myth of 'liberation and rehabilitation' in which violence and recovery are enunciated simultaneously. According to this myth, the enemy population's liberation from the barbaric and the backward and its successful rehabilitation into an assimilated ally are both anticipated and explained as an outcome of the U.S. military interventions."[18] The gendered racial contours of this "imperialist myth of 'liberation and rehabilitation'" are partly constituted by what Dower, as I quoted above, describes as the project of "*denaturing* an Oriental adversary," or what I am calling gendered racial rehabilitation. Gendered racial rehabilitation emerges in the Japanese American cultural texts I discuss as paradoxically the precise antidote for Japanese "racial pride," or what was perceived to be "Japan's racial conspiracy against whites." That is, Japanese colonialism in Asia and the Pacific Islands and wartime atrocities were themselves informed by and thus not necessarily antithetical to Western white supremacy and racial taxonomies. The *perception*, however, that Japan was engaging in a "racial conspiracy against whites" involved a reassertion of white supremacy in the U.S. occupation of Japan and the gendered racial rehabilitation of Japanese subjects first as vanquished, demilitarized, and emasculated "Orientals" and later as "honorary whites" and partners of strategic value in the Cold War. This gendered racial economy relied on, even as it transformed, what Traise Yamamoto traces as the Western imagination's infantilization and feminization of Japan since the late nineteenth century.[19] Within such a context, the relationship between the "trans-Pacific" racisms of the United States and Japan, as Koshiro argues, can more accurately be described as one of "co-dependence" rather than mere "coexistence," and "the race issue was transformed from an instrument of wartime hatred into a negotiable part of a broader Japanese-American arrangement during the Occupation."[20]

Though formally called the Allied Occupation of Japan, it was in effect a

U.S. occupation. In what Dower calls a "neocolonial revolution from above" in the specific form of a "neocolonial military dictatorship," MacArthur and his command ruled Japan like colonial overlords who were beyond criticism and as inviolate as the emperor and his officials had been.[21] It is no wonder, then, that this attempt to create democracy by fiat was full of inherent contradictions. How does a neocolonial military dictatorship promote "freedom" within the context of unconditional surrender, and what do freedom and democracy mean when they become tethered to and synonymous with a policy of massive reeducation, strict demilitarization, and anticommunism? How, in other words, can democracy and strict authoritarian rule coexist? In this schizophrenic project of democracy-within-authoritarianism, the massive U.S. army of occupation, which created a colonial enclave, or segregated "little America" in the unbombed section of Tokyo's downtown, constituted and enjoyed the privileges of a separate caste, class, and race.[22] Such a "revolution from above," moreover, failed to extend democracy to Japan's former Asian colonies (Korea, Taiwan, Manchuria, Okinawa, and the Pacific Islands) and ignored their role in helping to bring about Japan's defeat in the Pacific theater of World War II. The contradictions of attempting to promote freedom within the space of military dictatorship and unconditional surrender played out concretely in occupation reform policies, which sought a wholesale gendered racial and economic rehabilitation of Japan. Reforms favored the expansion of U.S. global capitalism and shaped Japan into America's junior Cold War partner in Asia.[23] These efforts call to mind Kennan's preoccupation with national health and vigor as the necessary "immunities" against the disease of Soviet communism. Yet even as Japan's economy was being rehabilitated by the U.S. occupation authority, the gendered racial rehabilitation I speak of pointedly excluded the literal rehabilitation and treatment of atomic bomb victims. Indeed, survivors of the bombs were heavily censored by the U.S. government and prohibited from even grieving or speaking publicly about their traumatic experience.[24] Meanwhile, America's imperial vision came into sharper focus as the Cold War intensified with the Chinese civil war, and as I analyzed in the previous chapter, the "loss" of China in that war to Mao's Communist victory in 1949.

Historians generally periodize the occupation of Japan in two phases.[25] During the initial "reformist" phase, which lasted through early 1947, General MacArthur and his Supreme Commander for the Allied Powers (SCAP) office enjoyed greater control and were more in sync with Washington's vision, which, after the demilitarization of Japan, encouraged New Deal reforms, including representative government, free labor unions, anti-monopoly laws, and the enfranchisement of women. As such, Japan's new constitution, which took effect in May 1947 and was drafted and imposed by the American occupation authorities, preserved the emperor system (while stripping him of temporal political authority), reformed civil and criminal law, strengthened the Diet, broadened voting rights, increased the power of local government, redistributed land, purged left-leaning "communists" from government and civilian life,[26] eliminated ultranationalist philosophy from the educational system, and in Article 9 declared Japan's renunciation of "war as a sovereign right of the nation and the threat of force as means of settling international disputes."[27] Akira Iriye argues that because the emperor system was maintained, and because the United States enjoyed sole power in Japan, it was paradoxically "possible to carry out some far-reaching reforms of Japanese society."[28] As such, the subjects of the emperor were theoretically transformed into citizens, but as Dower observes, they became in effect "the subjects of the Occupation."[29]

In the second phase of the occupation, called a "reverse course" or undoing of the previous reformist phase of attempting to democratize Japan, we see an increasing split between MacArthur and the Truman administration. This "reverse course" away from democratic reforms and toward economic revitalization was shaped by the intensification of the Cold War after the 1949 Communist victory in China and the need to solve, as I elaborated in the introduction, the structural impasses or crises of Western capitalism. The United States was propelled by the desire to develop Japan as the hub of a regional Asian economic zone and as the model of capitalism in Asia, linked to and supporting the regional economies of the Western Hemisphere, which were headed by the United States and Western Europe. This triumvirate of economic zones would, of course, present a strong anticommunist challenge to the Soviet Union and the further spread of communism in Asia. Thus, liberal reforms, plans to try Emperor Hirohito as a war criminal, and the payment of war reparations to Japan's Asian conquests were eschewed in favor of building Japan's industry and developing a strong export-led economy, while at the same time expanding American military bases on the island. In this way, Japan's Asian neighbors were subjugated once again, this time as a "quasi-colonial source of raw materials"[30] for both Japan and its U.S. Cold War sponsor. Members of the British Parliament and Foreign Office would characterize this policy as a "strange neo-imperialism of a mystical irrational kind," a "drive for exports which has acquired a certain force of desperation."[31]

Increasingly, America's "strange neo-imperialism" relied on a reactionary containment of the "threat" of radical democracy, a certain degree of remilitarization, and the "Red Purge" as an instrument to discipline Japanese society away from left-leaning and communist strains. The purge was aggressively used to search out and eliminate left-wing and communist influences in all sectors of Japanese society, including communist leaders, radical intellectuals, and workers. By 1948 and 1949, SCAP (with Washington increasingly restricting its independence) passed revised labor legislation that drastically curtailed the political and economic power of organized labor, banned strikes by public workers, abolished collective bargaining, and severely restricted labor activity in the public sector. In 1950, after the outbreak of the Korean War, the purge was extended to the private sector, including the mass media. This "Red Purge" coincided with the "Depurge," which effectively pardoned "for all time" individuals who had previously been purged for actively abetting militarism and ultranationalism.[32]

George F. Kennan, believing that the stability and economic development of Japan were crucial in building a secure, U.S.-friendly Asia, helped abolish the antimonopoly and reparations programs, and he became instrumental in getting a recovery package passed by Congress. In June 1948 Congress funded the Economic Recovery in Occupied Areas (EROA) aid package (with $125 million in aid for Japan, Korea, and the Ryukyus) as part of the larger Government and Relief in Occupied Areas (GARIOA) program, which included another $422 million for Japan.[33] The U.S. government policy in Japan of privileging an export-driven economic recovery over and against a speedy peace settlement or social reform was formally drafted by Kennan and his staff as NSC 13 (amended as NSC 13/2). While Kennan, as I elaborated in chapter 1, would later distance himself from what became his famous doctrine of containment, he singled out his policies in Japan and the Marshall Plan as his most significant contributions. In thus shaping Japan into an industrial powerhouse, or the "Germany of the Orient,"[34] it is important to note that the United States relied on the collaboration of Japanese conservatives, for whom the paradigm of modernization theory held great promise.[35] Modernization theory's emphasis on the possibility of racialized nations developing or maturing into modernity—defined as liberal capitalist democracy—provided policy makers with a scheme that purported to disrupt global racial hierarchies by holding out the promise of modernity to all nations but actually worked to reinforce those hierarchies by defining "modernity" itself and controlling the terms under which nonwhite nations would have relative "access" to it.

On September 8, 1951, a Peace Treaty and U.S.–Japanese Mutual Security Pact were signed, formally reinstituting Japanese sovereignty while at the same time extending the United States' right to maintain armed forces and military bases in Japan and its vicinity. Japan did prohibit, however, the United States from stockpiling nuclear weapons on those bases. The United States found a solution to this by virtually annexing Okinawa, an island already annexed by Japan in the late nineteenth century.[36] Japanese prime minister Yoshida Shigeru was also pressured by the United States into signing a separate peace treaty with Chiang Kai-shek's Nationalist regime in Taiwan (the Republic of China). In mainland China, Foreign Minister Chou En-lai declared this two-China policy to be insane and argued that Japan's signing of peace treaties with the United States and Taiwan "showed that Japanese imperialism still dreamed of enslaving the Chinese and other Asians in collaboration with United States imperialism."[37] Hanson Baldwin, the military commentator for the *New York Times,* captured the contradictions of the U.S. occupation and the restoration of Japan's formal national sovereignty by pronouncing the inauguration of a "period when Japan is free, yet not free."[38] Moreover, in a poll conducted soon after the signing of the treaty, the Japanese were asked if Japan had now become an independent nation. Only 41 percent answered yes. Yoshida Shigeru later compared the U.S. occupation of Japan to the partition of Korea, describing how the occupation had left a "thirty-eighth parallel" running through the heart of the Japanese people because it had led to the emergence of a liberal, left-wing opposition that vocally critiqued the collusion of United States and Japanese conservative political and economic interests and the incorporation of Japan into the Pax Americana.[39]

In perhaps one of the many tragedies of the Cold War in Asia, Japan's continued and rapid economic development, and by extension that of U.S. global capitalism, was made possible by American military orders (called offshore procurements or Special Procurements Program) in the Korean and Vietnam wars. Virtually every sector of Japan's economy was enlisted in America's war efforts and proved to be a critical boom.[40] Indeed, the governor of the Bank of Japan encapsulated the significance of the Korean War to Japan's economic recovery by calling the U.S. government's procurement program "divine aid."[41] This "divine aid" or "gift from the gods" would continue throughout the protracted Vietnam War not only for Japan but also especially for Korea. While U.S. imperialist intervention in Vietnam was guided by Cold War efforts to maintain Southeast Asia as a regional market and source of raw materials for Japan, the intervention or war itself turned out to "aid" Japan. Michael Schaller concludes that "these expenditures cemented the relationship between Japanese recovery and American security policy throughout Asia."[42] In an interesting reversal of sorts, one of the legacies of America's Cold War logics and military architecture is that today, Japan pays the United States for this architecture. As of the late 1990s the Japanese government was paying the United States approximately $4 billion per year to help defray the costs of maintaining U.S. military bases in Japan, whose troops have no military functions and are held in reserve for deployment in other parts of Asia. As Chalmers Johnson notes, this makes Japan "perhaps the only country that pays another country to carry out espionage against itself"[43] and constitutes one manifestation of how Japan was transformed into the "richest prize in the American empire."[44]

In the following sections, I turn to how Japanese American cultural producers imagine, critique, and link this transformation of Japan to the World War II internment of Japanese Americans as related projects of gendered racial rehabilitation full of perils for Japanese and Japanese American subjects. Just as Japan undergoes a gendered racial rehabilitation or "domestication" from a former enemy to a proper Cold War junior ally, Japanese Americans undergo a similar process of gendered racial rehabilitation in the internment's attempt to domesticate the "enemy alien" into a "model minority." Internment was articulated and rationalized as the U.S. government's benevolent protection of Japanese Americans from racial violence during World War II. However, if we consider how Japanese American farmers had been figured and legislated against as improperly hyper-competitive farmers on the West Coast, we see how this rationalization occludes the ways in which internment functioned to protect white farming and property interests. Yet as imagined by Japanese American cultural producers, this linked transpacific project of gendered racial rehabilitation was rife with contradictions and full of perils for Japanese and Japanese American subjects. These contradictions and perils, and thereby the limitations and failures of gendered racial rehabilitation, are precisely and transnationally indexed by the Japanese American cultural productions I analyze. Such productions thus undermine Cold War imperial and gendered racial mandates.

Hiroshima's Future Anterior

Donald Pease argues that the governmentality of the United States as a "National Security State" derived from Hiroshima. The fear of nuclear holocaust, which the United States itself unleashed in the wake of Hiroshima but which got enfolded within the Manichaean logics of the Cold War, legitimated the National Security State and compelled the U.S. populace to submit to wartime discipline in a time of "peace." In other words, as Pease notes, "Hiroshima" in this symbolic economy refers not to the actual historical event—America's atomic bombing of the city on August 6, 1945, that resulted in over 140,000 Japanese military and civilian deaths in just a few months— but to the "*possible* fate of U.S. citizens if Soviet imperialism remained unchecked."[45] Hiroshima, then, functions as a purely symbolic Cold War referent, in which the United States evades responsibility, and displaces and projects its *actual* nuclear aggression as that of the *potential* nuclear aggression of the Soviet Union. This logic of the future anterior, or "what will have happened" had not the United States deterred or opposed the Soviet Union's nuclear capacity, displaces the historical reality and materiality that the "what will have happened" became possible as a legitimating narrative—and was simultaneously forestalled/foreclosed as an actual historical event or occurrence—through what the United States *had already done*. In this instance, then, the logic of the future anterior functions as an imperial temporality. Pease writes:

> As the no-place the United States might have become had it not proleptically opposed, as the precondition for the postwar settlement, the Soviet Union's nuclear capacity, Hiroshima also presignified the geopolitical fate of those nation-states which had not identified the paradigmatic event of the U.S. national archive ("liberation from [Soviet] imperial aggression") as the "political truth" of their nationhood. The name of the always already displaced event which every other cold war event at once deferred yet anticipated, Hiroshima held the place of what might be called the cold war's transcendental signifier.[46]

To some extent, this "transcendental signifier" transcends the Cold War itself, since in the "post–Cold War" extension of the National Security State via the "War on Terror," the notion of a "preemptive war" against Iraq relies on a metaleptic substitution in which Iraq comes to stand in for al-Qaeda and its actions and on a proleptic "preemption" of future attacks against the United States. Moreover, several months before the war against Iraq began, a *New York Times* article headlined "U.S. Has a Plan to Occupy Iraq, Officials Report" revealed that the Bush administration planned a postwar occupation of Iraq "modeled on the postwar occupation of Japan."[47] As Yoneyama suggests, this particular remembering of the occupation as a success anachronistically enabled the American public to foresee the success of the U.S. postwar occupation of Iraq prior to the war itself.[48] Still further, in the realm of popular culture, we have witnessed a biting critique of such logical and temporal obfuscations in *The Daily Show with Jon Stewart,* a "fake" news show on cable television's Comedy Central channel that satirizes both the content of actual or "real" news and the form in which it is covered by the media. On the May 6, 2004, episode, in the wake of the Abu Ghraib prison abuse scandal, the show's correspondent Rob Corddry explains to Jon Stewart, "Jon, there's no question what took place in that prison was horrible, but the Arab World has to realize that the U.S. shouldn't be judged on the actions of a . . . well, that we shouldn't be judged on actions, Jon. It's our *principles* that matter, our inspiring, abstract notions. Remember, remember Jon, just because torturing prisoners is something we *did* doesn't mean it's something we *would* do."[49] These dominant discursive constellations and memories, instantiated through a confounding marshaling of metalepses, prolepses, and anachronisms, serve as the *casus belli* of our times.

Working in the prolonged aftermath of Hiroshima, and in the protracted afterlife of the Cold War, Japanese American cultural producers Steven Okazaki, David Mura, and Ruth Ozeki write against this perverse temporal logic of Hiroshima as Cold War "transcendental signifier." They displace the future anterior of "what will have happened" with the past tense "it happened" and the interrogative "why did it happen?" Their intervention thus complicates not only U.S. imperial nationalist ontology and discourse, but also Japanese nationalist disavowals of its own imperial past and perpetration of World War II atrocities. In the following discussion, I would like to offer an analysis of how Okazaki, Mura, and Ozeki "return" us to the site(s) of Hiroshima, the subsequent U.S. occupation of Japan, and the internment of Japanese Americans not in order to render them wholly and transparently visible, but to grasp them in fragments that critically index what the United States *had already done.* These fragments reveal the constitutive link between American empire and American gendered racial formation (both in its domestic and overseas modalities) by thematizing Hiroshima, the occupation, and the internment of Japanese Americans as linked projects not only of gendered racial *formation,* but also specifically of gendered racial *rehabilitation.*

I begin, then, with Steven Okazaki's *Survivors,* a rare English language film on the Japanese *American* survivors of the atomic bombings of Hiroshima and Nagasaki.[50] Among the estimated one thousand atomic bomb survivors living in the United States at the time of the film's initial distribution in 1982 in anticipation of the fortieth anniversary of the bombings (later updated for the fiftieth anniversary), most are American citizens of Japanese ancestry who were working or studying in Japan during the war, and some immigrated to the United States after the war as wives of U.S. servicemen. The film focuses on the personal testimonials of these survivors, whose names remain unidentified in order to protect their privacy. Viewers are forced to contend not only with these painful memories and experiences, but also with graphic images of the suffering victims taken in the immediate aftermath of the bombings.[51] The largely neglected and invisible population of Japanese American survivors has a unique conundrum: of not only being the survivors of the first and only atomic bombings in history, but also of having survived the atomic atrocities of their *own* government. As such, the film allows the important voices of these survivors to be heard and highlights how they are in a uniquely qualified position to be the pedagogical witnesses and bearers of the lessons to be derived from the bombings. This powerful Japanese American witnessing thus complicates the assumption that wartime atrocities and acts of violence can only be committed against the people of an enemy nation, and like the incarceration of Japanese Americans, it signals the limits of Cold War productions of knowledge of who belongs to and will act as the "enemy race." In a poignant effort to make a gesture beyond such limits, the last frame of the film ends with this intertitle: "Five Decades After the first / And only atomic bombings in / History, the remaining survivors / Worry that their stories will / Be buried with them and that / The lessons of the past will / Be Forgotten." In this dialectic of forgetting and remembering, even as many survivors wish to forget and leave behind their trauma, they are haunted by flashbacks, dreams, and nightmares, and their bodies bear the knowledge, imprints, and lingering effects of radiation exposure. In *Survivors,* gendered racial rehabilitation emerges through the radical disjuncture between these scarred bodies that were denied mental and physical rehabilitation or treatment, and the very reason why they needed such rehabilitation and treatment in the first place. This reason is, of course, the atomic bombings as themselves a project of gendered racial rehabilitation that attempted to vanquish and properly rebuild and reform the enemy. Moreover, the gendered logics of rehabilitation are made visible through a consideration of how women have been disproportionately affected by illnesses caused by radiation exposure, and the gendered politics of what it means to have a scarred and disfigured face or body. The film also shows that while the pained constitution of those who managed to survive—the bearers of survival guilt, psychic and physical scars, and illnesses—is acutely overburdened precisely because it cannot forget the horror, this painful inability to forget is an important form of witnessing, testimony, and commemoration.

I begin my analysis of *Survivors* with a discussion of another radical disjuncture: that between the aesthetic beauty of the detonating bomb's light and the unimaginable ugliness of the death, pain, and suffering it produced. One survivor remembers the bombing as a "beautiful light," one she had never before seen in her life. That something aesthetically "beautiful" can cause such devastation is one of many paradoxes unleashed by the atomic bombings of Hiroshima and Nagasaki. A heretofore "unimaginable" horror was made imaginable through graphic images documenting the bombs' effects, yet the U.S. government's quick censorship of such images promoted a collective forgetting that would render nuclear annihilation again "unimaginable" and temporally and spatially abstract. A deafening explosion was followed by the deafening silence of shock, and the pain suffered by the grossly wounded who actually managed to survive led one witness and fellow survivor to ask why they couldn't die, because at that time, "death was the most kindest way of going." Another witness in *Survivors,* a Japanese American man born in Honolulu, remembers being angry at himself for not being able to ease his dying friend's pain and suffering instead of being angry at the United States, his own government, for dropping the bombs on such heavily populated cities. He says, "I've never felt any anger toward [the] United States because I am one of the United States' citizens. But I feel and I felt sad that, you know, our leaders had to drop the bomb on a populated area. I feel they should have been able to drop it on an unpopulated area, and even then the people of Japan and the leaders of Japan would have realized that it was no use in continuing to fight against the United States."

Through the witnessing of such survivors, the documentary also reverses and multiplies assumed trajectories of "guilt." While guilt in the aftermath of the atomic bombings commonly refers to the guilt felt by individual Americans for the actions of their government, *Survivors* meditates on the haunting legacies of what has been called "survivor guilt," or guilt felt by the survivors themselves for having survived while their family and friends did not. A few survivors recollect feeling certain that they would die, in fact believing that they were dead. And perhaps more poignantly, still others wished that they had died and wondered why they had been spared. A Los Angeles–born Japanese American woman who had gone to Japan with her grandparents in

1941, when she was only eight years old, remembers getting separated from her grandparents and brother during the bombing. She walks for three weeks straight looking for them. She finds her grandparents under some rubble, both dead, and musters the strength to dig them up and cremate them. But she does not find her brother. She testifies, "It was a feeling of really loneliness and looking at the devastation of the whole city wondering why God left me here alone, why he didn't take me too . . . at the time I wanted to go too. I thought I should have gone instead of being left alone." The haunting complexities of this cycle of what has been called survival guilt is captured eloquently by Robert J. Lifton, author of *Death in Life: Survivors of Hiroshima,* and a professor of psychiatry at Yale when interviewed for *Survivors:* "A survivor always asks himself or herself why did I survive while he, she, or they died? That's the beginning of what we call survivor guilt or sometimes guilt over survival priority. What priority did I have in living while he or she or they died? It's a haunting personal question. One never fully satisfactorily answers it. In fact, this feeling begins at the moment the bomb falls when one's ordinary self would have in some way tried to combat it or tried to save people. There was no opportunity to save people. People struggled desperately if they could to save their children or somebody in their family and they had great difficulty doing even that. They remained haunted by the cries of others around them." How does one give adequate expression to and represent such a "haunting personal question," one that can never "fully satisfactorily" be answered? As if to symptomize this representational conundrum and problem of knowledge, instead of remaining on Lifton's face in the mode of the talking-head style, *Survivors* couples his remarks with an animation segment that attempts to visualize the process he is describing. The simple cartoon can only gesture toward and approximate the haunting. While *Survivors* makes reference to the guilt felt by individual Americans about the bomb—one survivor expresses surprise that so many people feel guilt, "as if they personally dropped it themselves"—the documentary exposes the more troubling and lingering effects of survivor guilt.[52] Survivor guilt is a way of marking the fact of having survived the catastrophe amid the very erasure of the fact of that catastrophe's occurrence. The trauma of the event itself, and the trauma of having survived it, represents a "death in life" that ruptures the assumed or taken-for-granted radical discontinuity between life and death. Guilt in this context thus marks a mode of remembering, most achingly a form of remembering and memorializing the dead. While the dead have physically been buried, and while the United States and Japanese

governments have attempted to bury the memories of the horrific manner
of their death, survivor guilt articulates that which remains unburied, the
trauma that refuses to be completely buried even as its adequate representation presents a certain impossibility.

In addition to this complex meditation on psychic economies of guilt and
what it means to be a "survivor," Okazaki's documentary also conjures and
disrupts the racial optics governing the atomic bombings through an elaboration of what it means to "pass" as someone who is indeed *not* an atomic
survivor and why it might be desirable to do so. While the trope of passing
is usually used to describe racial passing, in which a racialized person attempts
to pass as white or is simply perceived as white, passing can take on a different valence. Japanese American (and Japanese) atomic bomb survivors who
have no external or visible physical manifestations of the experience can pass
as not having gone through such a horrific ordeal. On the other hand, as
Lifton explains in *Survivors,* if, for example, you have a scar formation, a
keloid scar, that is unavoidably visible, you cannot "pass" in that manner, and

"A survivor always asks himself or herself why did I survive while he, she, or they
died?" (from *Survivors,* 1982, updated 1994).

How does one give adequate expression to the complexities of "survivor guilt"?

"then you go through life something like the experience of a person with some deformation. It makes people uncomfortable to look at you, and you know that, so every single human encounter has a dimension of awkwardness and therefore a kind of mutual exchange of awkwardness, guilt, and shame. It's a heavy burden." The "deformation" that visibly marks the survivor over-determines every human interaction, in the same way that perceptions of racial phenotype might overdetermine every human interaction. Indeed, while Japanese and Japanese Americans were subjected to atomic bombings and mass incarceration precisely because of their racialization as an "enemy race" that could not pass as white, for atomic bomb survivors, passing conjures not only the specter of phenotypical difference, but also questions about what constitutes a whole, undamaged human body. This, too, is the trauma and burden of having survived—the twinned psychic and physical scars. As one visibly scarred Japanese immigrant survivor poignantly tells it, a mundane activity, like picking up her third-grade son from school, has the potential of setting into motion the "mutual exchange of awkwardness, guilt, and shame."

She recollects how, upon seeing her scars, her son's friend asked what had happened to his mother's face, to which her son replied, "You stupid, I told you not to mention in front of her, I told you what happened." She continues: "He felt I'm hurt. He so care about me. And one time he saying to his friend my mother's lucky she's alive. Many people died. So one thing I'm so grateful he doesn't feel he have looks strange mother. He doesn't feel ashamed of me." The poignancy of this mother's witnessing is compounded further when we consider the gendered dynamics of what it means to have a scarred face and body. In a global social formation where women are differentially prized, valued, and objectified for their beauty and physical appearance, indeed often defined solely by their beauty and physical appearance, what must it be like for this woman to have a scarred face and body, in addition to a racialized face and body that already fall outside the parameters of normative standards of beauty?

As painful and difficult as this visible scarring caused by the atomic bombings of Hiroshima and Nagasaki can be, *Survivors* reveals how such scarring can only scratch the surface of the deep psychological and physical infliction of pain and disease, including survivor guilt, what we would now call posttraumatic stress disorder, radiation sickness, and a host of short- and long-term ailments, including leukemia; cancers of the thyroid, breast, lung, and other organs; early menopause; coronary heart disease; stroke; and cataracts. Women have been disproportionately affected by these illnesses, and there have been genetic effects on subsequent generations. Close to a half million people have perished from the atomic bombings. Over 80 percent of people within one kilometer of each bomb's hypocenter died instantly or soon afterward, and many have died from the long-term effects of radiation exposure.[53]

While the U.S. government engaged in projects that I have conceptualized as gendered racial rehabilitation, those in actual need of physical and mental rehabilitation—the survivors of the U.S. government's atomic bombings—were denied it. Indeed, as I noted previously, the U.S. occupation government would not even allow the survivors to talk about their pain or grief publicly. That is to say, the U.S. government would not even acknowledge the survivors *as* survivors, as having survived, in other words, what the United States "had already done" in dropping the atomic bombs. These silenced survivors were thus rendered effects without a cause and lifted outside of time and history. In titling his documentary *Survivors,* then, Okazaki reverses this trajectory and inserts the survivors back into history.[54] He reveals, moreover, the disjuncture between the loyalty of Japanese American survivors to their country and their country's abandonment of them. One survivor recalls, "Coming back it was a thrill that you can't imagine, because this is my country. Even during the wartime you dream about your country, the streets you walked, the trees you climbed. Japan was a temporary place for me; it wasn't my country. I just stood there and cried. I knew I was home." Yet when a group of survivors formed the Committee of Atomic Bomb Survivors in the USA to lobby the U.S. federal government for medical benefits, the government refused to provide them. This is all they were asking for, "just a group of little old ladies, Japanese American ladies, trying to get some medical benefits before [they] all die." Similarly, in Japan, although the U.S. government established the Atomic Bomb Casualty Commission (ABCC) to study the effects of the bomb on humans, it prohibited the ABCC doctors from providing treatment to the Japanese subjects whom they were studying. Such treatment, argued the government, would be tantamount to an apology, an apology that it did not owe and did not wish to give. So in yet another instance of the Cold War as an epistemological and pedagogical formation, racialized Japanese subjects—the very targets of atomic violence—were to be used instrumentally as the U.S. government's objects of knowledge in ways that would benefit the United States.

In the following discussion, I turn to how Japanese American writers David Mura and Ruth Ozeki imagine the disruption of this instrumental knowledge and instruction by Japanese and Japanese American subjects who thwart interpellation as the objects of America's gendered racial rehabilitation. In a cruel irony of sorts, while wounded and dying atomic bomb victims were refused physical rehabilitative treatment by the U.S. government, in the more recent Cold War conjuncture, "healthy" Japanese and Japanese American subjects are being dosed with ideological rehabilitative treatment and poisoned food.

A New Japan

In *Turning Japanese: Memoirs of a Sansei*, poet David Mura, a third-generation Japanese American, writes of his year abroad in Japan as a 1984 U.S./Japan Creative Artist Exchange Fellow. We see how Mura encounters the traces of Hiroshima and the U.S. occupation of Japan, and how he articulates his own family history with Japanese American internment. The specific contours of what I have been calling gendered racial rehabilitation emerge in this text through Mura's meditations on his troubled racialized masculinity, which has been overdetermined, on the one hand, by his encounters with a gendered racism in the United States that has cast Asian American masculinity as deviant and nonnormative. On the other hand, as I will trace in my analysis, these meditations in turn generate a critique of Japanese American internment as a significant historical and familial source of his beleaguered and shame-inducing masculinity. Indeed, the incarceration of Japanese Americans during World War II as an attempt to racially rehabilitate and domesticate this "enemy alien" group into what later became America's "model minority" had the connected gendered register of transforming already unstable patriarchal formations within Japanese American communities. Such patriarchal formations were already unstable or precarious precisely because of gendered racism in the United States, which casts men of color as falling outside the parameters of normative (white) masculinity and patriarchal authority. Internment replaced the Japanese American figure of patriarchal authority with that of the U.S. carceral state, specifically the War Relocation Authority (WRA), which administered the internment.[55]

While I do not wish to rehearse here the well-known litany of racist and what might seem to contemporary ears absurd reasons that were marshaled for why Japanese Americans had to be interned, it is significant to note what Colleen Lye calls "racism's heterogeneity" in her analysis of the "uncomfortable tie" between internment and the liberalism of the New Deal. The privileged subject, beneficiary, or target of FDR's New Deal Program has been thought to be the poor white migrant laborer, who found a new visibility through such figurations as the Joads of John Steinbeck's *The Grapes of Wrath* (1939). Yet as Lye argues, that visibility "intersected with a prior discourse on Asiatic unassimilability."[56] The WRA sought to extend the Farm Security Administration's discourse and project of *rural* rehabilitation, realized in the 1930s through the building of government camps for white workers. This came in the wake of attempts to racially rehabilitate or curb Japanese American farmers, who had enjoyed a notable degree of success, by passing a string of Alien Land Laws that stripped "aliens ineligible for citizenship" (especially Japanese immigrants) of the right to own land.[57] The WRA explained internment as an act of conservation, claiming that Japanese American farming practices decreased the fertility of the soil. Therefore, Lye writes, "the perception of Japanese Americans as environmentally damaging—and damaged— pointed to another sense in which they would figure as the WRA's targets of reform." In a report entitled *A Story of Human Conservation* (1946), the WRA acknowledged that it had been unsuccessful in protecting "evacuee" property but had been successful in protecting the evacuees themselves from the "racial terrorism" of unreasonable West Coast politicians and business interests.[58]

By thus casting itself as the protective custodian of Japanese Americans, the WRA could claim not only a story of soil conservation, but also "a story of human conservation." Lye concludes that "in an important way, internment was part of a federal reconstruction of California, whose 'Asiatic problem' was joined to the enlargement of the nation's global stakes."[59] This would explain in part why Japanese Americans in Hawaii, the location of Japan's Pearl Harbor attack, were not interned. At the same time, internment was symptomatic of and dependent on, as Kandice Chuh argues, "the conversion of the threat of Japanese empire into Japanese (American) racial difference by governmental and legal apparatuses of U.S. nationalism through . . . a 'transnationalization' of Japaneseness. That conversion into a 'nikkei transnation' enabled the justification of internment as necessary to contain that threat."[60] Thus was produced the category of the Japanese immigrant and Japanese American "enemy alien." The WRA's project of "human conservation" was (also), I suggest, a project of gendered racial rehabilitation through which Japanese Americans could learn to be productive subjects without "damaging" the environment, becoming hyper-competitive in any field, or contributing to California's "maladjustments." As such, they were "relocated" or scattered from the West Coast to such remote locations as Jerome, Arkansas.

The New Deal liberalism of the internment paralleled in many ways the New Deal liberalism, as I have previously discussed, of the first "reformist" phase of the occupation. Indeed, Caroline Chung Simpson shows that "liberal anthropologists stationed in the internment camps to observe Japanese Americans were also instructed to use the opportunity to develop policies for administering the Japanese after the war." Specifically, interviews of internees were to be used to develop theories of "Japanese behavior" that would be useful in the occupation.[61] Just as the WRA saw its role as that of a protective custodian, MacArthur saw his role as that of a benevolent father figure who would reform his naughty children. According to his logic, the job of the occupation was the "job of rearing seventy million problem children." This racist paternalism, informed by anthropological theories of the childlike features of "Japanese character structure," made its way to a Senate subcommittee hearing. MacArthur testified that the Japanese "would be like a boy of twelve as compared with our development of forty-five years."[62] This developmentalist and reformist discourse mirrored similar arguments about the need to acculturate and assimilate Japanese Americans.

Indeed, a significant legacy of the internment has been the attempt by Japanese Americans themselves to assimilate and prove their "Americanness" such that a similar fate of being singled out as a racial group and incarcerated would not befall them again. Already during World War II, for example, we saw this process take shape with Japanese American men actively enlisting in the army to prove their loyalty to the United States, and since the war, we have seen high rates of outmarriage among Japanese Americans. With Mura's memoir, his very choice of title, *Turning Japanese*, already signals how his encounter with Japan is mediated by his Japanese *American* experience. "Turning Japanese" is the title of a song by a British band, the Vapors, that was a hit in the United States in the early 1980s. As a Sansei, or third-generation Japanese American, Mura identifies as *American*, and this identification is overdetermined by his family's internment experience. He admits that he applied for the fellowship because he needed time to write, and not because he had a burning desire to go to Japan. Indeed, growing up, Japan for him was either a "nonplace" where his grandparents lived but no one spoke about or an Orientalist phantasmatic space projected on American movie screens. He writes:

> Japan? That was where my grandparents came from, it didn't have much to do with my present life. But then Japan had never seemed that important to me, even in childhood. . . . I didn't notice that my grandfathers were in Japan, my grandmothers dead. No one spoke about them, just as no one spoke about Japan. We were American. It was the Fourth of July, Labor Day, Christmas. . . . For me Japan was cheap baseballs, Godzilla. . . . Then there were the endless hordes storming G.I.'s in war movies. Sometimes the Japanese hordes got mixed up in my mind with the Koreans, tiny Asians with squinty eyes mowed down in row after row by the steady shots of John Wayne or Richard Widmark. Before the television set, wearing my ever-present Cubs cap, I crouched near the sofa, saw the enemy surrounding me. I shouted to my men, hurled a grenade. I fired my gun. And the Japanese soldiers fell before me, one by one.[63]

As this passage reveals, if Mura had been interned during World War II and subjected to the loyalty questionnaire, it's quite possible that he would not have been a "no-no boy" but a "yes-yes boy": yes, he would have served in the U.S. armed forces wherever ordered, and yes, he would have sworn "unqualified allegiance" to the United States, "faithfully defend" it, and "forswear any form of allegiance to the Japanese Emperor" or any other foreign entities.[64] Yet even as Mura is distanced from and distances himself from Japan by taking on the gaze of and identifying with John Wayne, the hegemonic figure of white American masculinity, his "Americanness" is haunted and circumscribed by the World War II internment of his Issei (first-generation) grandparents and Nisei (second-generation) parents, by the history of American racism that structured this internment and continues to persist in various modalities, and by the silences surrounding the internment.[65]

This conundrum of what it means to be an *ethnic* American is captured by the titular "Turning Japanese," for in the hit song, "turning Japanese" turns out to be a euphemism for excessive masturbation, a problem that plagued Mura himself at one point in his life. He writes of this, and his addiction to pornography, as symptoms of the gendered racism that Asian American men have been subjected to, as well as of the gendered racial shame that it produces, in *Where the Body Meets Memory: An Odyssey of Race, Sexuality, and Identity* (1996). Cynthia Franklin notes that we see in the song an equation of "alienation, masturbation (and its overtones of deviant and shameful sexuality), and Japanese identity (and here the lack of distinction between Japanese and Japanese Americans is precisely the point—both are equally alien)."[66] Indeed, within the historical context of exclusionary immigration laws that effectively barred women from most Asian countries from migrating to the United States until after World War II, and the so-called Asian American "bachelor societies" that were formed as a result of such restrictive legislation, Asian men in the United States have been cast as embodying a deviant, alien masculinity and sexuality. In terms of masculinity, Asian American men have been figured either as overly or backwardly patriarchal and sexist or more often as emasculated houseboys, laundrymen, restaurant workers, and so forth. This association between Asian American men and "domestic" labor has functioned to domesticate, neuter, and feminize them. Similarly, in terms of sexuality, Asian American men have been cast either as sexually lascivious, and therefore threatening to white female chastity and domesticity, or more often as asexual, queer, or otherwise falling outside the bounds of proper heteronormativity. This race-gender-sexuality matrix that configures Asian American men as deviant, what David Eng calls "racial castration," overdetermines the gendered racial dynamics of Japanese American internment.[67] While Japanese Americans, unlike other Asian American groups, had been able to form families in greater numbers, familial patriarchal arrangements, which were already unstable because of gendered racism, get transferred, as I have noted, from the male head of the household to the carceral state, the War Relocation Authority.[68] While the formation of families and a less skewed gender ratio might thus have presumably exempted or relatively shielded Japanese American men from the trope of deviance, the gendered racial dynamics of internment come to shatter this presumption. Even as Japanese American men might have had opportunities to reassert their masculinity, in some cases by volunteering for the army or resisting as no-no boys, what ensued was not a restoration or bestowal of a proper masculinity. Rather, as Caroline Chung Simpson argues, debates about the no-no boys, for example, "cohered as part of more visible fears about the state of national masculinity in the postwar period," demonstrating how dominant narrative framings of the internment as a conflict between race and nationality "was coincident with the then current anxieties about gender and class, including in particular anxieties about American manhood."[69] Thus, even as Japanese American men were held at a distance from normative (white) American manhood in order to fortify it and keep it coherent, this very distancing worked to reveal its fractures and contradictions. These histories and arrangements complicate Mura's gendered racial identity and sexuality, and the trope of deviance in some ways gets recycled through his excessive masturbation and addiction to pornography. This dynamic also overdetermines his object choice, specifically his desire for white women, and his strong identification as American.

We get the sense that in professing how American he is, and in claiming that geopolitics does not have much to do with him because he is, after all, "a poet" (8), perhaps Mura is protesting too much. Indeed, his memoir is replete with political discussions and incidents, ranging from the treatment of Koreans in Japan, to the differences between American and Japanese feminisms, to the rights of farmers. Even as Mura often does not know how to make sense of these issues and refuses to get embroiled, he cannot help but write about them. Moreover, while in Japan, he cannot help but visit Hiroshima. He writes: "Perhaps naively, I felt I might somehow capture the Japanese perception of the event, but with an American eye. Still, I worried about seeming like a vulture, scraping away at the remains of the dead" (17). What he finds out, however, is that the "Japanese perception" and "American eye" are in many ways intricately entangled. While the United States would rather forget its atomic bombing of Hiroshima or at least, as Donald Pease suggests, enframe it symbolically in a way that displaces responsibility and the fact of its actual historical occurrence, one would expect that the Japanese, the victims, would have political investments in remembering it. Mura is told by Miura, a well-known novelist and head of the Bunkacho, the Cultural Affairs Department of the Japanese government, that it would not be a good idea to visit Hiroshima and Nagasaki. Miura insists that it's "best you forget about such things. We have gone on from there. This is the new Japan. We have forgotten such things. . . . There's so much else to see. I've read you're interested in visiting your grandfather's hometown. Where is that?" (19). In speaking of the willful forgetting of the bombings, Miura cannot even name that which he is forgetting and can only refer to it as "such things." What this collective amnesia cannot recognize is that "such things" and the subsequent U.S. occupation of Japan were the very conditions of possibility for the "new Japan." Yet the unintended effect of Miura's injunction to "forget about such things" is precisely a demonstration of the significance of "such things," the bombings, and of why such U.S. war atrocities and the "new Japan" cannot exist within the same space in the dominant nationalist memories of both countries. As Christine Hong argues, "At this point always already contextualized against the spectacular economic rise of Japan, as exemplary Cold War U.S. client-state, the spectacularity of the bombing of Hiroshima has been effectively canceled out."[70] When Miura says that "we have gone on from there," he claims for himself and the "new Japan" a properly rehabilitated, that is to say demilitarized and U.S.-friendly, state. Gendered racial rehabilitation transforms a "warrior race," an enemy race, into properly consuming and producing agents within U.S. global capitalism and into healthy citizen-subjects within an economically rehabilitated "new Japan" that is America's junior Cold War partner in Asia. Yet not all subjects are successfully rehabilitated.

Against Miura's advice, Mura does visit Hiroshima. As I noted at the beginning of this chapter, he can only experience and make sense of it through scenes from the film *Hiroshima, Mon Amour*. Hiroshima signifies many things—a city, a commemorative site, a movie, a historical event, a Cold War "transcendental signifier," a forgotten thing, even peace—and can only be apprehended through multiple mediations. Indeed, as Lisa Yoneyama writes, the commemorative city of Hiroshima is itself an American invention and construction:

> the Occupation authorities and U.S. officials determined that their interests would be furthered by connecting the atomic bomb to the idea of peace and, more important, by displaying that linkage to the world. The commemorative city of Hiroshima was, as it were, designed specifically to demonstrate the interchangeability of "the atomic bomb" and "peace." Remembering a link between the bomb and peace fostered the conviction that without use of the atomic weapon, peace in the Pacific could not have been achieved in a timely manner.

This is a historical narrative that stubbornly continues to form our assumptions even today, despite historians' efforts to show that such an argument—more specifically, that use of the bomb was unavoidable if the war was to end without enormous cost in human lives—was fabricated ex post facto.[71]

As I have noted previously, the decision to drop the atomic bombs on a racialized populace that many Americans wanted to see almost completely eradicated had much to do with American efforts to thwart potential Soviet power and influence in Japan. Put simply, the United States did not wish to "share" Japan with the Soviet Union. To this extent, then, the atomic bombings made Japan "America's Japan," as suggested in part by the title of this chapter. In writing about this horror, of what America *had already done* in Hiroshima, Mura reveals a profound ambivalence. Although he feels the burden of attempting to represent such a historical trauma, claiming that "not everything needs to be in a poem" (even though he had already written a poem about the *hibakusha*, the atomic bomb victims, before going to Japan), he cannot help but describe in graphic detail the museum displays at the Peace Museum (120). Even as he critiques the "lifeless wax art" for seeming to "mock the memory of the victims," he makes them come alive, so to speak, through the vividness of his description (19). Moreover, in his poem entitled "The *Hibakusha*'s Letter (1955)," Mura writes powerfully about the atomic bomb survivors, whose name, "*hibakusha*" (literally meaning "A-bomb received person"), comes to be associated with keloid scars, defects, disease, and disgrace. Though they physically survived, they live a living death, haunted by the ghosts of those who perished, and find themselves shameful ghosts in the eyes of Japanese society: "I can't conceive, and though Matsuo says / It doesn't matter, my empty belly haunts me: / Why call myself a woman, him a man, / If on our island only ghosts can gather? ... / ... Here / Fewer eyes shower us in shame."[72] We witness here a haunting articulation of the specific gendered effects of the violence unleashed by the bomb and a simultaneous overturning of gendered distinctions in the acknowledgment that all survivors, whether woman or man, are similarly shunned. As such, they are all "ghosts" who suffer a living death. Yet because the ghost is, as Avery Gordon compellingly argues, a "crucible for political mediation and historical memory," paying attention to its presence, its haunting, allows an "alternative diagnostics" that links the politics of accounting to "a potent imagination of what has been done and what is to be done otherwise."[73] Mura's ghosts, and the "survivors" of Okazaki's film discussed in the previous section, thus provide an "alternative diagnostics" of the atomic bombings as a project of gendered racial rehabilitation.

These ghostly presences haunt and complicate Mura's own racialized and gendered identity. Indeed, what interests me about Mura's decision to write about Hiroshima in this poem and in his memoir, and therefore to bear the burden of its historical weight, albeit ambivalently, is not only the question of the politics of commemoration (for every such attempt is ideologically overdetermined), but also more immediately the question of how Hiroshima allows an occasion for him to link the atomic bombing to his own politics of racial identification and to the unspoken past of his Nisei father's internment during World War II. He writes:

> I had bought some books in the museum and later, in a bookstore nearby, picked up a copy of Marguerite Duras's filmscript for *Hiroshima, Mon Amour*. I was caught by the conjunction of the images of destruction with the image of a Japanese man and a Caucasian woman. The city had somehow made me aware of our racial differences in a rather disturbing way; after all, I felt, it's partially because [my wife's] a white *gaijin* that the Japanese doctors like her so much. She's like a prize to them. Immediately a voice inside echoed: "And to you."
> (199)

That a white woman is "like a prize" to a Japanese American (and Japanese) man bespeaks the racialized and gendered hierarchies of power and desire that structure intimacies not only in the United States, but globally. For racialized subjects who are compelled to internalize this hegemonic economy, racial shame promotes a desire to be white and to be *with* a white person. The lovers in *Hiroshima, Mon Amour* mirror the race and gender matrix of Mura's own coupling with a white woman, and while Mura had been comforted by the fact that in Japan he looked just like everybody else, his encounter with Hiroshima via *Hiroshima, Mon Amour* produces an unexpected heightened self-consciousness about his race. While he tries to overcome his gendered racial shame through his white object choice, that same choice produces a racial "self-consciousness" in the context of Japan. This complex gendered racial shame, itself in part a legacy of the gendered racial shame produced by Japanese American internment, is intricately connected to the shame experienced by the "ghosts" of the bomb. Survivors of the bomb and Japanese American subjects like Mura are both constituted by and objects of gendered racial rehabilitation, which functions at once to heighten gendered racial shame and weaken it by holding Japanese and Japanese Americans at a certain, seemingly close proximity to whiteness. And while survivors might remain unrehabilitated because they have been denied medical treatment and their very survival is "living proof" of the United States' atomic atrocity, Mura remains unrehabilitated partly because he "dares" to have a white wife. Even as gendered racial taxonomies instigate a desire to be white or to have a white partner, such interracial desires have historically been heavily censured, legislated against, and violently attacked. While white men have historically enjoyed sexual license, interracial and otherwise, racialized subjects have been barred from crossing this particular color line through practices ranging from antimiscegenation laws to lynching.[74] Mura's experience of Hiroshima, particularly as mediated through the film *Hiroshima, Mon Amour,* threatens to unravel and further complicate an already fraught gendered racial identity and the identifications and desires that at once consolidate and destabilize such an identity. Thus, he attempts to manage and contain his experience "into certain neatly carved grooves—anti-nuclear politics, questions of racism and the dropping of the bomb, outrage at the militarism of the United States, the only nation that has used the bomb" (121).

Yet scenes from *Hiroshima, Mon Amour* persistently find their way back into Mura's thoughts, and they trigger or flare up memories about how his psychic discomfort with his skin color (and the racialized masculinity that is tethered to that skin color) would somatize as literal flare ups of his skin:

> Walking past the displays, I'd felt both moved and morally numbed, accused both by my response and my inability to respond. All the while, I kept flashing on the images from *Hiroshima, Mon Amour,* the skin of the lovers and the skin of the bomb victims. From adolescence on, I seem to have always been aware of my skin. But it was more than the color of my skin that occupied me. I also suffer from eczema, a condition that is both hereditary—my skin is abnormally dry—and psychological: my eczema flares up during times of stress. (121)

In juxtaposing the skin of the lovers in *Hiroshima, Mon Amour,* the skin of the bomb victims (who could very well have been relatives of his), and his own skin, Mura reveals in this passage what the passage itself attempts to deemphasize: the color of his skin. The source of his preoccupation with skin, what he deems to be "more than the color of [his] skin," turns out to be eczema, and his eczema "flares up during times of stress." However, this equation elides the fact that the color of Mura's skin is often the cause of his stress. Moreover, if we are to consider "skin" more generally, as that which seals in, contains, and demarcates discrete individual subjecthood, when it is "compromised" as such (whether through war injuries, scarring, lesions, dermatological ailments, and the like), it becomes a powerful metaphor for debilitation. Indeed, you literally cannot live in your own skin; your very body becomes uninhabitable.[75]

What Mura attempts to repress in the above passage, even as the passage itself reveals what is being repressed, returns right after his trip to Hiroshima. The trip causes Mura to think, "for the first time," about where his father might have been on the day the war ended, because by then he would have been released from the camp in Jerome, Arkansas. In wondering about this unspoken (family) history, Mura links the racial logics of what was done to the Japanese in Hiroshima and Nagasaki to what was done to the Japanese Americans on the West Coast of the United States. His rumination about his father's whereabouts is all the more poignant because it has to be imagined anew rather than recollected as stories his father has already told him. In the absence of such tellings, Mura fills the gaps and silences with the "*what could have been*":

> After we returned from Hiroshima, for the first time I started to think of where my father was on the day the war ended. By then he had been released from the camp in Jerome, Arkansas, for more than a year and was going to Western Michigan University in Kalamazoo, living with the family of a professor. *Probably* my father is both pleased and anxious about this precarious new freedom. *Perhaps* he has looked through the pages of *Life* or *Time*, has seen the cartoons depicting the Japanese: they are lice, vermin, tiny thoraxes with huge heads attached, a bucktooth smile and squinty eyes behind thick glasses; they are small, slant-eyed rats squirming under the huge boot of a G.I. giant smashing down with unfathomable power. *Perhaps* he has seen the way some of his classmates look at him, casting glances sideways in history or English or as he passes in the halls. *Perhaps* they whisper loud enough for him to hear. *Perhaps* not. (Is he imagining this? Or am I?) I know he does not date in college. There are no other Nisei, none of his kind. Does he admit to himself his desire for the white girls in his classes? Or is the sexual conflict inside him too dangerous to acknowledge? It is the year the war has ended, the summer between his freshman and sophomore years. August, a few days after Hiroshima and Nagasaki. A holiday has been declared, men sweep women up in their arms in the middle of streets and kiss them. . . . On August 15, 1945, my father is sitting on the steps of a

house in Kalamazoo, Michigan. . . . "It won't always be like this," he remembers his teacher in the camps saying. "After the war you will be free again and back in American society. But for your own sakes, try to be not one, but *two hundred percent American.* . . ." I am American, he says to himself. I am glad we won. He repeats his mantra over and over. He learns to believe it. (123–24, emphasis added)

In the face of his father's silence, Mura imaginatively (re)constructs *what "perhaps" could have been.* We might also interpret his imaginative recon- struction as actually a case of the son projecting onto his father his own issues and desires.[76] Mura himself asks parenthetically, "Is he imagining this? Or am I?" However, what remains significant is that traumas are passed down from one generation to the next. That is, the internment is a source of trans- generational haunting, or what Marianne Hirsch calls "postmemory."[77] If Mura is indeed projecting onto his father in the passage above, it might seem to reverse the trajectory of "postmemory," in which traumatic memories are passed down, rather than projected upward, to the next generation. Yet this unidirectional economy and trajectory get complicated when we consider that Mura's own projections (and the identifications and desires they reveal) are themselves overdetermined and haunted by his father's experience of the internment and his silence about it.

This silence is not unique to his father, but was a collective silence among Japanese Americans who had been interned. Just as Miura tells Mura in Japan that the Japanese have forgotten "such things," Japanese Americans attempted to forget (the shame of) the internment and tried to assimilate and integrate themselves into American society as "not one, but two hundred percent Amer- ican," or proper subjects of gendered racial rehabilitation.[78] Perhaps then a similar fate would not be repeated on them. Japanese Americans had been singled out for internment, while German and Italian Americans had not. Being "two hundred percent American" later transmogrifies as the so-called model minority—a model, but still a "minority." Mura's imagining of his father's life at the end of the war shows his father to be a proper subject of gendered racial rehabilitation, interpellated as "American." Yet the passage also shows the irony of this 200 percent Americanness, for as a 200 percent Japanese American, Mura's father cannot date the white classmate, or "sweep women up in [his] arms in the middle of streets and kiss them" to celebrate America's victory in World War II. Rather, he sees cartoons of "slant-eyed rats squirming under the huge boot of a G.I. giant smashing down with unfathomable power" or sits "on the steps of a house in Kalamazoo, Michigan." His "precarious new freedom" is at once pleasing and anxiety-inducing.

Through this irony and others, Mura's memoir registers "racism's heterogeneity" in connecting Hiroshima, internment, and occupation as linked projects of gendered racial rehabilitation. *Turning Japanese* also displays the heterogeneity of racism's *effects*. That is to say, it turns out that not all Japanese are grateful children; they remain racially unrehabilitated. Certainly, there are those who are rehabilitated and are grateful to MacArthur. Mura meets such a person in Okubo, the realtor who helps him find an apartment in Japan. Interpellated by America, Okubo has a favorite raincoat, because "it's like the T.V. detective Corombo." He declares: "I will always be grateful to America. After the war, we were starving, we thought the Americans would come and kill us. And the G.I.'s came and started handing out chocolate to the children. We are all so surprised. . . . I owe everything to MacArthur. When the Americans came, I got a job with them. I translated and helped distribute food. MacArthur saved my life" (29). Dumbfounded, Mura does not know how to respond to this. He has a different genealogy of America's Cold War in Asia, a different hermeneutic. He writes: "Influenced by thoughts of MacArthur and Korea, by the stereotypes of *Teahouse of the August Moon*, by the relocation camps and West Coast wartime hysteria, I didn't completely share this attitude toward postwar Japanese and American relations; still, I was glad Okubo seemed to like Americans so much" (29–30). Here, Mura names and connects the imperial and racial architecture of U.S. domestic politics and overseas exploits. The U.S. occupation of Japan, the Korean War, and the internment of Japanese Americans are linked to one another, as well as to the racial ideologies of popular culture as articulated in films such as *Teahouse of the August Moon* (a 1956 satire of U.S. occupation efforts in Okinawa) and of popular sentiment as expressed in the "wartime hysteria" that clamored for the elimination of the Japanese race and the internment of Japanese Americans.

Mura's alternative interpretive frame demonstrates that the coherence of U.S. popular memory and culture, while consolidated and made legible by the re-narrating of imperialism as democratization or internment as conservation or assimilation, is inherently unstable and cannot contain or predict all of its narrative effects. For example, in *Sayonara*, the companion piece to *Teahouse of the August Moon*, the U.S. occupation is allegorized as an interracial romance between an American air force major and a Japanese woman.[79] This relationship triumphs over what are deemed to be the mutual prejudices of Japanese tradition and American custom, and is cemented by the liberal discourse of tolerance and understanding. This liberal discourse elides how such interracial intimacies, and the sexual license of white men, are indeed the intimacies of empire. There is a curious moment in the film, however, when the presence of the U.S. military in Japan is made explicit as that of an occupying power. Major Lloyd "Ace" Gruver (played by Marlon Brando) encounters a group of Japanese bearing signs that read "Say Good By Yankee," "We Don't Want Yanks," "Go Home Yank," "Don't Date Our Girls," and "Orient for Orientals."

Major Ace Gruver, stationed in Japan during the U.S. occupation and the Korean War, embarks on an interracial love affair with Hana-ogi, a Japanese woman (from *Sayonara*, 1957).

The Japanese protest the "Yankee" presence in Japan.

Within the diegesis of the film, there is an attempt to contain this "sign-ing" of the U.S. occupation when Major Gruver's commanding officer (and one-time future father-in-law) General Webster explains to him that the "hoodlums" who attacked him were not all his Japanese neighbors, but were for the most part "professional troublemakers" sent to his street to create an incident "specifically" with him. Thus, while the movie as a whole relies on allegory, General Webster's explanation for the Japanese attack on Major Gru-ver attempts to go against an allegorical register. In other words, we are told specifically that Major Gruver should not be seen as a metonym of the U.S. occupation and that the "professional troublemakers" do not represent Japa-nese resistance to that occupation.[80] While this scene is thus constructed to heighten the resistance to Gruver's relationship with Hana-ogi (played by U.S.-born Miiko Taka), and therefore the need to put an end to it, it cannot help but exceed its diegetic function and containment with the signage of "Say Good By Yankee." Ultimately, the Yankee does say "Good By" or "Say-onara," but he does so along with his Japanese betrothed.

These fissures in U.S. popular culture and memory and Mura's critical genealogy and hermeneutic make room for the emergence of the ungrateful or racially unrehabilitated Japanese subject. We hear the story of Matsuo, a political activist who was only a child during the occupation years. He had been "fed on food from America served at his school" (238), so like Okubo, it would appear that he has reason to be "grateful to America." But one day, while still a young boy, he discovers that "the labels on the crates of food from America said, FOR ANIMALS ONLY: NOT FOR HUMAN CONSUMPTION" (239). This moment in Mura's memoir ruptures the dominant liberation and democracy tropes through which the U.S. occupation has been narrated. Indeed, Japanese writer Kawakami Tesutaro had cleverly mocked the contra-dictions of the occupation in October 1945 by describing U.S. policy as one of "rationed-out freedom," evoking the food-rationing program that the Japa-nese had been subjected to both during the war and the occupation.[81] The U.S. government's food rationing program had been so disastrous that a nationwide demonstration against it, dubbed "Food May Day," had occurred on May 19, 1946, ten years after the Japanese government had outlawed the celebration of "May Day" itself.[82]

In *Turning Japanese*, Matsuo's story also reveals U.S. complicity in bury-ing Japan's own wartime atrocities. He discovers that the food rationed out by America is "not for human consumption" soon after his uncle shares with him a harrowing story about his experiences as a Japanese soldier in the invasion of Manchuria. Ordered by his commander to kill a group of villagers, the uncle refuses, only to then be a witness to the mass execution perpetrated by the remaining soldiers of his unit. Haunted by memories of Japanese militarized state violence, and unable to participate in the postwar rebuilding, the uncle kills himself during the waning years of the U.S. occupation. Because he refuses to "forget such things," he cannot be a part of the "new Japan." As an adult, Matsuo remembers his uncle's suicide and what his uncle saw in Manchuria. He recognizes that the "new Japan" is the product of a densely colluded project of forgetting. The "new Japan," structured as and dependent on economic cooperation or partnership between Japan and the United States, emerges out of a genealogy of a palimpsest of racialized imperialisms in which the U.S. variety is layered over the Japanese one. The "new Japan" also emerges through a twinned or double burial of this very genealogy by both the United States and Japan. In other words, Matsuo's childhood diet (the U.S. occupation) and the cause of his uncle's suicide (Japanese atrocities in World War II) also constitute the "such things" that must be collectively erased and cannot even be named. And though the "new Japan" is deemed to be a thoroughly demilitarized one, Matsuo names the violence the Japanese state continues to inflict. He tells Mura and their friends that the Japanese government has won a suit supporting its banning of a text stating that the Manchurian invasion was in fact an "invasion" and not an "incursion." He says, "The government wants to wipe out that history, keep the people from remembering. And it's succeeding. That's what kind of violence the state does" (239). "Violence" here signifies not only the violence of the Manchurian invasion itself, but the violence of wiping it out of official nationalist history and ontology. It is the psychic, epistemic violence of a state-compelled forgetting.

"Not for Human Consumption"

If Mura narratively regurgitates the literal and ideological diet of the "new Japan" as "NOT FOR HUMAN CONSUMPTION," then Ruth Ozeki also demonstrates the perils of such consumption practices. Her novel *My Year of Meats* links the U.S. occupation's food distribution program to what could be called the food distribution program of the contemporary moment of U.S. global capitalism: a scheme to market unhealthy hormone-injected beef to Japan, a historically non–beef consuming nation. In order for this economic imperialism to be successful, it must be coupled with the cultural imperialism of selling and teaching good old-fashioned American values, coded as white, heteronormative, and middle-class, to Japanese housewives. *My Year of Meats* depicts this conjoining of imperialisms through a show called *My American Wife!*, a "day-in-the-life" documentary series commissioned by the Beef Export and Trade Syndicate (BEEF-EX) as a vehicle to market the "wholesomeness" of beef and American values to Japanese consumers. Just as Hiroshima, the occupation, and Japanese American internment were projects of gendered racial rehabilitation, Ozeki shows how a more recent instance of American imperialism—the aggressive exporting and marketing of beef—requires gendered racial rehabilitation of Japanese consuming subjects. Indeed, such trade agreements between the United States and Japan have their genealogy in the U.S. occupation, or what, as I have noted, the British called a "strange neo-imperialism of a mystical irrational kind." Except in the contemporary conjuncture, the trade imbalance with Japan that the United States itself caused with its occupation reforms of creating an export-led economy must be reversed. As I discussed in the previous chapter, America's junior Cold War partner in Asia comes to haunt and challenge its imperial sponsor with its economic hyper-competitiveness, a process that finds a historical antecedent in the perceived agricultural hyper-competitiveness of Japanese Americans on the West Coast of the United States in the years leading to the World War II incarceration of Japanese Americans. In the late and post Cold War, since such American-made products as automobiles are not competitive, unwholesome American beef, packaged as embodying wholesome American values, is exported instead. *My Year of Meats* tells the tale of the grotesque dangers of this hormone-fattened meat, of how it too, like the cans of food distributed by the American army during the occupation, is "NOT (FIT) FOR HUMAN CONSUMPTION." We see the monstrous ironies of American largesse. This literal largesse/largeness is revealed to be barren on two levels: it is a gift of poison and it can cause barrenness in the women who consume it. The specific contours of gendered racial rehabilitation are thematized in Ozeki's novel through this disjuncture among rehabilitation, reproduction, and poisoning, as well as a biting critique of the attempt to mold "Japanese womanhood" and domesticity modeled on what we can link together as the white-American-heteronormative-feminine-bourgeois-nuclear-family ideal.

My Year of Meats is constructed as a metadocumentary of sorts. This novel about the making of a fictive documentary series called *My American Wife!* itself contains a series of actual "Documentary Interludes" explaining the dangers of consuming American beef injected with growth hormones, detailing how such beef was banned in Europe and needed to find a new market in Asia. It is worth quoting one especially revealing "Documentary Interlude" at length:

> DES, or diethylstilbestrol, is a man-made estrogen that was first synthesized in 1938. Soon afterward, a professor of poultry husbandry at the University of California discovered that if you inject DES into male chickens, it chemically castrates them. Instant capons. The males develop female characteristics—plump breasts and succulent meats—desirable assets for one's dinner. After that, subcutaneous DES implants became pretty much de rigueur in the poultry industry, at least until 1959, when the FDA banned them. Apparently, someone discovered that dogs and males from low-income families in the south were developing signs of feminization after eating cheap chicken parts and waste from processing plants. . . . But by then DES was also being widely used in beef production, and oddly enough, the FDA did nothing to stop that. DES changed the face of meat in America . . . this was an economy of scale. . . . Researchers and doctors were prescribing it for pregnant women in the belief that DES would prevent miscarriages and premature births. . . . Then, in 1971, a team of Boston doctors discovered that DES caused a rare form of cancer, called clear cell adenocarcinoma, in the vaginas of young women whose mothers had taken the drug during pregnancy. And as if that wasn't bad enough, DES was finally exposed as a complete sham. That was the real tragedy. It was all hype. As early as 1952, researchers had found that DES did absolutely nothing to prevent miscarriages. . . . Today, although DES is illegal, 95 percent of feedlot cattle in the U.S. still receive some form of growth-promoting hormone or pharmaceutical in feed supplements. The residues are present in the finished cuts of beef sold in the local supermarket or hanging off your plate. . . . In 1989, Europe banned the import of U.S. meat because of the use of hormones in production. BEEF-EX started looking for a new market. In 1990, as a result of pressure by the U.S. government, the New Beef Agreement was signed with Japan, relaxing import quotas and increasing the American share of Japan's red-meat market.[83]

Here again, we see a resurgence of America's abiding desire for the Asian market. As imagined in *My Year of Meats,* the exported product turns out to be unfit for human consumption. Such "documentary interludes" function beyond the force of evidentiary value or facticity, and like Okazaki's *Survivors,* are a crucial form or site of critical remembering. They disarticulate the fictions of U.S. benevolence and alternatively articulate the perils of gendered racial rehabilitation and its link to market logics.

The sordid tale is told from the alternating perspectives of Jane Takagi-Little, the hapa (mixed-race) American production coordinator and later director of *My American Wife!*, and Akiko Ueno, the Japanese housewife who represents the show's target viewing audience. It would appear that Jane and Akiko are the purveyor and recipient, respectively, of the gendered racial rehabilitation that *My American Wife!* promises and promotes. Indeed, as the novel opens, Jane nabs the job as production coordinator with this convincing pitch:

> Meat is the Message. Each weekly half-hour episode of *My American Wife!* must culminate in the celebration of a featured meat, climaxing in its glorious consumption. It's the meat (not the Mrs.) who's the star of our show! Of course, the "wife of the week" is important too. She must be attractive, appetizing, and all-American. She is the meat made manifest: ample, robust, yet never tough or hard to digest. Through her, Japanese housewives will feel the hearty sense of warmth, of comfort, of hearth and home—the traditional family values symbolized by red meat in rural America. (8)

As this pitch captures, *My American Wife!* is a commercial pedagogy whose function is to sell meat by selling and teaching the ethos of traditional family values, abstracted as "American" but as it will soon become clear, particularized as white heteronormative middle-class domesticity. For consumers in Japan, then, the ingesting of each featured meat recipe is an ingestion of American "traditional family values," or an induction into gendered racial rehabilitation. As production coordinator, it is Jane's job to scout out and procure the "wife of the week" and to act as a liaison between the wife, her family, and the Japanese crew sent to shoot the series. In Jane's words, she is a "go-between, a cultural pimp" (as both a hyphenated Japanese American and mixed-race woman) who sells off "the vast illusion of America to a cramped population" in Japan (9). She persuades the targeted "wife of the week" that it is her patriotic duty to appear in the program and "promote American meat abroad and thereby help rectify the trade imbalance with Japan" (35). Since BEEF-EX is the show's sole sponsor, the entire series itself functions as a long commercial for beef: "Each episode of *My American Wife!* carried four attractive commercial spots for BEEF-EX. The strategy was 'to develop a powerful synergy between the commercials and the documentary vehicles, in order to stimulate consumer purchase motivation.' In other words, the commercials were to bleed into the documentaries, and documentaries were to function as commercials" (41).

Relieved to have a job at last, Jane finds herself in the position of having to apologize for and explain the white heteronormative middle-class directives for the show sent from the Tokyo office to her American research staff. The list of "Desirable Things" includes such things as attractiveness, wholesomeness, obedient children, a docile husband, and a clean house. "Undesirable Things" include physical imperfection, obesity, squalor, and "second class peoples" (10–11). Jane explains that "second class peoples" does not refer to race or class, and that Kato, the Japanese head of production, does not want the American staff to "think that Japanese people are racist" (13). Rather, she suggests, Japanese market studies show that the average Japanese housewife finds a middle- to upper-middle-class white American wife with two to three children "sufficiently exotic yet reassuringly familiar" (13). Why would such a demographic configuration be "reassuringly familiar"? Here, Ozeki traces the past out of which the contemporary moment emerges. She reminds her readers of the U.S. presence in Japan, a presence that long precedes the introduction of *My American Wife!* into Japanese homes. As Yoneyama writes, the postwar demilitarization and occupation of Japan were a "highly gendered process."[84] MacArthur ranked the enfranchisement of women at the top of his so-called Five Great Reforms, and the new constitution's granting of full civil rights to women as a marker of the political liberation of Japanese women was deployed as a measure through which to assess the overall success of the occupation. Yet, as Yoneyama argues, this putative "liberation" was constrained by the contexts within which it took place: first, the space of military occupation, which is a space of unfreedom and nonrights, is ruled by the "state of exception," and is simultaneously violent and benevolent; and second, "cold war feminism," an anticommunist liberal, white bourgeois feminism that "proceeded to marginalize and subordinate a number of other diverse feminist modalities and aspirations."[85] In a similar vein, Mire Koikari contends that "rather than an unprecedented moment of liberation for Japanese women, gender reform in occupied Japan was intimately connected on the one hand to prewar nationalist and imperialist politics, and on the other to emerging Cold War cultural dynamics. . . . [I]t is an extraordinarily complex and problematic instance of Cold War imperial feminism in the Far East."[86] Japanese women were thus encouraged to look upon American women, who had themselves been disciplined and contained (as Elaine Tyler May and others have shown) within the confines of a heteronormative bourgeois domesticity, as their role models.[87] Indeed, MacArthur's own wife, who lived with him in Japan during the occupation, was touted as a model because she chose to remain a housewife. This Japanese modeling of American women predated the postwar period but took on new urgency within the context of occupation reforms.[88] In turn, American women needed Japanese and other racialized women to constitute and consolidate their own self-identity as the practitioners of a true "cold war feminism" and embodiments of that which is modern and progressive. The supposed liberation of Japanese women, reported in *Newsweek* as "Free Butterfly," represented a sudden and strategic reversal or amnesia of wartime figurations of Japanese women warriors, paralleling what we could call the "callback" of American women from wartime jobs back into bourgeois domesticity, or the transformation of Rosie the Riveter into Rosie the Homemaker.[89] The global ramifications of these gendered racial logics of Cold War politics were famously expressed in what has been dubbed "The Kitchen Debate" between Vice President Richard Nixon and Premier Nikita Khrushchev, in which Nixon argued that modern kitchen and household appliances found in American homes demonstrated liberal democracy's superiority over communism.

My Year of Meats reveals the contemporary manifestation of this project of gendered racial rehabilitation. What are the legacies of such a paradoxical and constrained "liberation" of Japanese women? In unpacking the appeal of "all-American values" to the research staff, Jane argues that the American wife of the 1990s is much like her World War II–era predecessor: both are role models for Japanese women. The difference in the 1990s is that given Japan's "economic miracle," the Japanese woman is no longer impressed with modern gadgetry. In fact, she is more familiar with such consumer items than her American counterpart. Therefore, the point is not to sell American consumerism, but good old-fashioned American values and nourishment as congealed in a good meat dish. The appeal of *My American Wife!*, then, depends upon the "American wife" already having an iconic presence in the Japanese cultural imagination. She is "reassuringly familiar" as the normative feminine ideal that Japanese women have been told to emulate and aspire to since World War II and the U.S. occupation. As such, we may ask, precisely whose wife is the *My American Wife!* of the show's title? It is the Japanese man's wife, who becomes and is interpellated as "American" without having to set foot outside of Japan. It is precisely because of this racialized and gendered imperial genealogy that *My American Wife!* is legible to Japanese housewives. Indeed, the introduction of beef itself to Japan in large quantities was part and parcel of the U.S. occupation. Before this period, dating back to the sixth century, beef had been forbidden by Japanese Buddhism, in accordance with the Buddhist doctrine of mercy for all living beings. After contact with the Western world, the Japanese disparaged beef as Western and barbaric. In the wake of the U.S. occupation, however, disparagement turned into praise, such that a dish dubbed "a civilized bowl of rice" meant that it contained beef or pork slices.[90]

In the novel, this U.S. imperial genealogy intersects with Jane's own family genealogy. While she plays up the stereotypes of American–Asian romances by joking that her mother was a prostitute on the streets of Tokyo and her father a GI, it turns out that her father's presence in Japan was indeed a part of America's imperial mission. Jane explains, "Dad was a botanist in the army. They sent him to Japan as part of a team of scientists doing research in Hiroshima. They were kind of checking up on their handiwork—you know, looking at people and monstrose [*sic*] plant mutations—to see if we should drop an A-bomb on Korea. Dad died of cancer and I've always wondered whether there's some connection" (235). While scouring the country in search of possible "wives of the week," Jane learns that the traces and victims of the atomic bombings of Hiroshima and Nagasaki can also be found on American soil:

> On the way to Fly, Oregon, driving through southwest Washington state, we had unwittingly stumbled across the border of the U.S. Department of Energy's Hanford site . . . when we came to the barbed wire and a sign said "Department of Energy—Keep Out," how was I supposed to know that we'd reached the perimeter of the 570-mile nuclear city that produced the plutonium for "Fat Man," the bomb that leveled Nagasaki? Later, as we were passing through the adjacent town of Sunnyside, I happened to ask our waitress at a diner about the facility, and she raised her eyes and whistled.
>
> "You went in there?" she said. "Ooh, that's a no-no." Hanford was one of three atomic cities hastily constructed in 1943 to produce plutonium for the Manhattan Project. Over the next twenty-five years, massive clouds of radioactive iodine, ruthenium, caesium, and other materials were routinely released over people, animals, food, and water for hundreds of miles. In the 1950s, it was discovered that the radioactive iodine had contaminated local dairy cattle, their milk, and all the children who drank it. As the incidence of thyroid cancer grew, the farmers in the surrounding areas—"downwinders," they're called—began to wear turtlenecks to hide their scars. It was the fashion, the waitress told me. (246)

Ozeki transnationally connects and makes visible the Japanese and American victims of the bomb, both groups that have been forgotten by the nationalist narratives of the United States and Japan. Through Jane's role as "go-between" or "cultural pimp" emerges the critical capaciousness of being *in*-between national(ist) frames, and having the vision to see beyond those frames.

Indeed, while Jane had started out her job composing apologetics for the race, gender, and class bias of her Japanese employer, she soon finds herself subverting the white-bourgeois-heteronormative-feminine-nuclear-family-ideal matrix by seeking out wives and families who decidedly fall outside this rubric and can be seen as critically indexing the enabling contradictions of "American values" and American imperial logics. She also starts featuring "lesser meats" like pork and lamb as well as vegetarian(!) dishes. We meet the Beaudroux family, white Southerners who opt to adopt babies of color. They adopt not black American babies, but twelve "little oriental babies from Korea and Vietnam who don't have anyone to care for them or buy them toys or educations" (69). The first of these, Joy, is picked from a Christian adoption catalog and is the abandoned "Amerasian" daughter of a GI and a Korean prostitute. We also meet Helen and Purcell Dawes, a poor black couple with nine children who eat chitterlings and hog maws, and Laura and Dyann, an interracial vegetarian lesbian couple, as well as the Martinezes, a Mexican immigrant family in Texas with a father who has lost his hand to a hay baler. Finally, we meet the Dunn family, who run a cattle feedlot. While at the feedlot, Jane and her crew learn a horrible, grotesque truth about the meat business: that the growth hormone DES, while illegal, is still being used by many in the beef industry. The cowboys at the Dunn feedlot inject the cows with "boss's special formula," not knowing that it is DES. One of them remarks that "these cows here's goin' straight to Japan. . . . Straight to Japan, Taiwan, and Korea. You ask me, it's a darn shame, wasting all that good American meat on a bunch of gooks" (266–67). The dramatic irony of the cowboy's reference to DES-poisoned beef as "good American meat" is heightened by his racist conjuring of "gooks." He is unaware that far from wasting "good American meat on a bunch of gooks," he is (again) engaged in a project of poisoning a "bunch of gooks." As I discussed in the opening of this book, the etymology of "gook" and its "pan-racist" usage bespeak America's history of racialized imperialist aggression and war-making. *My Year of Meats* links this imperial aggression and war-making with the peculiar "American value" called frontier culture and justice, composed of a violent alchemy of "guns, race, meat, and manifest destiny" (89), and shows how this linkage allows the ongoing poisoning of "gooks." It also allows a white man in Louisiana to be acquitted in a criminal trial of shooting dead a sixteen-year-old Japanese exchange student who knocked on his door to ask for directions.[91] He was acquitted on the grounds that "he had acted in a reasonable manner to defend his home" (88). Jane has no excuses or explanations to offer her Japanese crew. Simply put, she says that "We are a grisly nation" (89). As the production coordinator and later director of *My American Wife!* Jane thus thwarts the project of gendered racial rehabilitation that she was initially hired to promote.[92]

Similarly, back in Japan, we see that Akiko, who is unhappily married to the advertising executive whose firm has been hired by BEEF-EX to promote its mandate of "foster[ing] among Japanese housewives a proper understanding of the wholesomeness of U.S. meats" (10), initially dutifully watches the show her husband's firm has created. She painstakingly makes each featured weekly meat recipe and ranks each episode in terms of its "Authenticity," "Deliciousness of Meats," and "Wholesomeness." Instead of identifying with the white middle-class heteronormative feminine ideal, however, she cathects to Laura and Dyann, the interracial vegetarian lesbian couple with children. While watching their episode, she sheds "tears of admiration for the strong women so determined to have their family against all odds. And tears of pity for herself, for the trepidation she felt in place of desire . . ." (181). Something Dyann had said about "impossibility and desire, or lack of it" (181) resonates with Akiko, and she comes to the realization that "she wanted a child; she'd never wanted John; once she became pregnant, she wouldn't need him ever again" (181). So when she does become pregnant, she leaves him. In thus refusing to be his "American wife," and questioning her assumed heterosexuality, she refuses to be the object of gendered racial rehabilitation.

Ozeki's Akiko and Jane in *My Year of Meats* and the other voices in Okazaki's *Survivors* and Mura's *Turning Japanese* thus imagine the critical possibilities offered by the multiple failures of gendered racial rehabilitation. Through my analysis of these cultural works, I have tracked in this chapter the imperial and gendered racial contours of America's encounter with Japan and demonstrated how Japanese American cultural producers reveal and critically reimagine these encounters. While we are much familiar with the domino theory or analogy of the Cold War, *Saturday Evening Post* journalist Stewart Alsop, in a March 11, 1950, article entitled "We Are Losing Asia Fast," offered a bowling analogy, recalling the "ten pin theory," to demonstrate the importance of Japan. Lamenting that the "loss of China" made Southeast Asia— "the greatest reservoir of untapped natural wealth"—ever vulnerable, and arguing that the Kremlin had designs to organize an "infinitely vaster Asiatic

Co-Prosperity sphere" than Japan's previous one, he predicted a certain pattern of Soviet penetration into Asia, and claimed that it had an analogy with bowling. China, the head pin, was down already, and if Burma and Indochina, the two pins in the second row toppled, so would Siam, Malaysia, and Indonesia, the three pins in the third row, and this would almost certainly knock down the four pins of the pivotal fourth row: India, Pakistan, Japan, and the Philippines.[93] Published just a few months before the Korean War, the matrix sketched in this article does not include the small peninsula. In the next chapter, I turn to how the Korean peninsula, forgotten in Alsop's Asian pyramid scheme, becomes the violent site of a still "Forgotten War."

4

THE FORGOTTEN WAR

Korean America's Conditions of Possibility

What most Americans know about Korea has been told from the point of view of a U.S. military member or a missionary, about prostitutes, beggars, and orphans, many of them mixed race children, never speaking but always spoken for and about, souls being saved by the civilizing missions of neocolonialism and evangelism. No doubt they would have found it difficult to imagine that one day the voice of the native, having returned to the imperial center, might speak back—in English—from its very different positionality.

ELAINE H. KIM, "Myth, Memory, and Desire: Homeland
and History in Contemporary Korean American Writing and
Visual Art"

In her poem "Fragments of the Forgotten War," Korean American poet Suji Kwock Kim "speak[s] back—in English—" to American empire from a "very different positionality." The positionality expressed by the poem encompasses multiple generations of a Korean family divided and scattered by the Korean War: a Korean American daughter who dedicates the poem to her father and writes in his voice, and the father who in turn addresses in the poem the parent(s) he had to leave behind when fleeing south during the war. Indeed, the poem opens with his address: "You whom I could not protect / . . . when will I forget the NKPA soldiers who took you away for questioning, / so we never saw you again? / We three sons fled south in January 1951 / without you . . ."[1] As one "note" in a collection entitled *Notes from the Divided Country,* this poem captures the ironic disjuncture of remembering in graphic detail a war that, as the very title of the poem suggests, has been "forgotten." While the Korean War (1950–53) has been dubbed the "Forgotten War" or "Unknown War" by Americans, it remains for Koreans and the global Korean diaspora it engendered a defining moment of family and national history. The interrogative "when will I forget" that opens Kim's poem transforms later into a declarative "I'll never forget." The subject of the poem declares that he will "never forget" the horrors of war: "the smell of burning flesh"; the "smell of people rotting who hadn't died yet"; a "boy sinking his teeth into his arm" in order to take his mind off the wound in his stomach.[2] Yet this firsthand witnessing, experiencing, and knowledge of such suffering exist in sharp contrast to, and cannot fill in for, that which he does not know: *how* the parents he was forced to leave behind must have suffered. In the poem, the recollected horrors produce a simultaneous knowing and unknowing: "I know you suffered, but I'll never know *how*."[3]

Similarly "speak[ing] back—in English—from [a] very different positionality," in an untitled multimedia work by artist Ji-Young Yoo, one hundred shallow relief faces made of white clay and juxtaposed like tiles act as a screen for the projection of digitized archival footage of the Korean War as well as textual excerpts from an oral history of Korean American memories of the war. One such remembrance, by second-generation Korean American Orson Moon, reads: "Why hold on to the past? For me, it is not the past. The fear and terror of this time period have carried forward into my dad's life. . . . It's carried forward to my sisters' lives, my life, as a hole, a silence."[4] This piece is part of a unique interactive multimedia exhibit entitled "Still Present Pasts: Korean Americans and the 'Forgotten War.'" Ramsay Liem, the exhibit's project director, sees the exhibit as "a space of Korean American memory" that "lifts the silence shrouding the Korean War."[5] Orson Moon speaks to how the silent memories of the Korean War are carried transgenerationally, passed from father to children as "a hole, a silence." As such, "it is not the past," and the Korean War thus remains, as the exhibition title suggests, a "still present past."

I begin with "Fragments of the Forgotten War" and "Still Present Pasts" because they encapsulate this chapter's focus on how Korean American cultural producers offer multiple "fragments" and "notes from a divided country" that critically index an occluded history: the link between America's imperial presence over "there" in Korea and the gendered racial "return" of the Korean subject over "here" to the imperial center. In contrast to the proliferation of knowledge, albeit a certain kind of knowledge, about the "losses" of China and Vietnam, the Korean War represents a curious lacuna. Even as the war has not technically come to an end (since an armistice, and not a peace treaty, was signed in 1953), the war's very existence has been "forgotten." And even as North Korea remains a sensational fixture in the U.S. news media, what gets ignored is America's Cold War intervention in creating a North Korea in the first place. Indeed, as one historian writes, "Korea would not prove a great national war of unifying singular purpose, as World War II had been, nor would it, like Vietnam a generation later, divide and thus haunt the nation. It was simply a puzzling, gray, very distant conflict, a war that went on and on and on, seemingly without hope or resolution, about which most Americans, save the men who fought there and their immediate families, preferred to know as little as possible.... Korea was a war that sometimes seemed to have been orphaned by history."[6] Yet every willful forgetting leaves its symptoms and traces, and to label an event a "Forgotten War" paradoxically inaugurates an attempt to retrieve that which has been forgotten. Post-1945, and especially post-1965, Korean migration to the United States, then, is at once a significant trace of the erasure and its retrieval. The contemporary Korean American cultural productions I analyze in this chapter make visible the imperial and gendered racial formations of this migration, but like Suji Kwock Kim's poem, they do so in "fragments." For the Korean War signals more than the traumatic and violent separations of (and from) self, family, and country that complicate the politics of individual and collective memory. It also signals a broader problem of Cold War knowledge that saturates both American nationalist discourse and Korean America's public or "admitted" knowledge about the conditions of possibility for its very formation in the post-1945 conjuncture.

In the discussion that follows, I examine how Susan Choi's haunting novel *The Foreign Student,* Heinz Insu Fenkl's autobiographical novel *Memories of My Ghost Brother,* and Deann Borshay Liem's highly personal documentary *First Person Plural* offer an unsettling hermeneutic of the Korean War that does not posit naïve or wholesale retrieval as the desired or even possible corrective to historical and narrative erasure, but rather attends to the war as a complex problem of knowledge production.[7] In other words, the Korean War appears not simply as a congealed historical episode that is given narrative form after-the-event, but also as a Cold War epistemology in the making. Such a figuring reveals how the Korean War is not only an epistemological *object* of historical investigation, but also how it was—and continues to be— itself an epistemological *project* generating a certain Cold War knowledge that attempts to foreclose alternative or "nonaligned" knowledges. These works ask what it means to want to represent or "remember" a war that has been forgotten and erased in the American popular imaginary, but has been transgenerationally seared into the memories of Koreans and Korean Americans, and is experienced anew every day in a still-divided Korea. As Korean immigrants in the United States, the narrators of these cultural productions are subjected to a double injunction: to forget (as assimilated Americans) and to remember (as gendered racial Korean immigrants and postimperial "exiles"). They reveal how the gendered racial stakes of this double injunction become even more fraught when even the act of remembering the war inaugurates in turn its own forgettings and risks revealing a long-standing "dirty secret": that the majority of Korean America's post-1945 formation can be attributed to chain migrations set into motion by Korean military brides who sponsored (extended) family members but who were shunned for marrying "foreigners," especially when those foreigners were black Americans. In this instance, Cold War epistemology intersects in troubling ways with Korean America's own self-knowledge about its very formation.

"A War between Gods Who Weren't Gods"

I would like to begin my analysis with a brief discussion of the Korean War's multiple "beginnings" as a way of demonstrating how what began essentially as a local civil conflict and decolonization project in a small nation got ensnared within the global Cold War superpower rivalry between the United States and Soviet Union.[8] In the poem I analyzed above, Suji Kwock Kim calls this "a war between gods who weren't gods,"[9] and a Korean aphorism describes Korea's positionality in what Americans call the Korean War as a "shrimp caught in a fight between two whales." Because the Korean peninsula (which had been colonized by Japan formally since 1910) had been unilaterally divided in August 1945 by the United States into a Soviet occupation zone in the North and an American one in the South,[10] Korean attempts to reunify their country preceded by many years the U.S. designation of the official start of the war as June 25, 1950, when the North "attacked" the South. While left-wing Koreans in the North (led by Kim Il Sung) and right-wing Koreans in the South (led by Syngman Rhee) might have appealed to their respective occupying superpowers for military aid at different points, each group sought to reunify their country on their terms and saw superpower aid simply as a means to this ultimate end of reunification and independence.[11] As such, before 1950, a bloody civil conflict had already ensued, with heavy fighting along the 38th parallel and guerilla war on both sides claiming a hundred thousand lives after 1946 and *before* the formal beginning of America's Korean war in 1950.[12]

Political tensions in Korea, themselves a legacy of the long period of Japanese colonial occupation and rule, were exacerbated when the U.S. occupation forces in the South immediately went about forming a "governing commission" of "several hundred conservatives" who had collaborated with the Japanese colonial administration. This formation of a pro-American elite coincided with the targeting and repression of "leftists, anticolonial resisters, populists, and advocates of land reform" as "Communists" within the context of a rapidly bipolarizing Cold War rivalry.[13] Leading up to the formation of this parallel or "double bipolarity," one within Korea itself and the other between the superpowers, there were radical Korean nationalists and communists who were both anti-Soviet *and* anti-American, and before U.S. intervention in 1950, Koreans themselves were more welcoming of armed efforts at reunification than either superpower.[14] Seen in such a light, in can be said that the Korean civil conflict, which then erupted into and was superseded by America's Korean War as a "proxy" or "hot war" in the bipolarizing Cold War between the superpowers, was also a project of decolonization. This project of decolonization had historical roots dating back to the Japanese colonial period and was set into motion and exacerbated by the Soviet and American division and occupation of Korea. Moreover, this division and occupation were themselves made necessary by Japanese colonialism, for the Soviet Union and the United States reasoned that the long period of Japanese colonial rule and government had rendered Korea unfit or unprepared for self-government. Indeed, the U.S. occupation of Korea south of the 38th parallel from 1945 to 1948 involved the full operation of a military government commanded by General John R. Hodge, and even after the last U.S. troops pulled out in 1949, they left behind over five hundred military advisors.[15] The Korean civil conflict materialized from these successive occupations and rather arbitrary division at the 38th parallel by outside forces, and can thus be seen as an arrested project of decolonization. For many Koreans and the Korean diaspora, then, the 38th parallel is a wound that awaits suturing.

Within the context of Cold War geopolitics and logics that were rapidly congealing as the dominant structure of feeling and knowledge, Washington policy makers and President Truman could not and did not interpret the North's "attack" on the South on June 25, 1950, as part of a continuum in Korea's own local efforts at reunification and decolonization. These efforts, as previously noted, had been well underway ever since the country's division at the end of World War II. Although by 1949 both Soviet and American occupation forces had pulled out, and although North Korea (Democratic People's Republic of Korea) and South Korea (Republic of Korea) had each declared itself to be the sole legitimate government of all of Korea, the Cold

War "scene of persuasion"[16] convinced the United States that the North's
incursion on the South was Soviet inspired and sponsored.[17] Thus, Truman
saw the North's offensive as a direct Soviet challenge to and test of American
power not only in Asia but in Europe and the rest of the world. His reasoning relied on an operation of substitution and metonymy: Korea itself was
not significant, but Korea as a Cold War proxy and metonymic example of
what could happen to the rest of the world was of vital significance. As such,
Truman quickly decided to intervene in the war by aiding South Korea, and
was able to do so only two days later on June 27 by circumventing a formal
declaration of war (which would require the approval of Congress) via a UN
resolution for a "police action" that turned into a de facto U.S. operation in
Korea.[18] This "war by executive decision" would later become the rule rather
than the exception, as it set the pattern for later interventions in Vietnam
and the Persian Gulf.

Within the first three months, the UN/U.S. forces, led by General Mac-
Arthur, were able to drive the North Koreans back up to the 38th parallel.
But not quite satisfied with successful "containment," the United States decided
to "roll back" what it perceived to be Soviet-led communism and reunify Korea
under South Korea's right-wing, procapitalist, U.S.-dependent regime. The
directive allowing MacArthur to cross the 38th parallel was signed by Truman on September 11, 1950. This fateful decision led directly to Chinese entry
into the war on the side of North Korea, and soon the UN/U.S. forces were
driven back to Seoul, South Korea's capital. After Stalin's sudden death in
March 1953, with a prolonged stalemate along the 38th parallel since the UN/
U.S. forces had been forced back south in 1951, an armistice was signed on
July 27, 1953, returning to the status quo before the war.[19] American troops
sardonically termed this stalemate "die for a tie."[20] To this day, the two Koreas
remain hostilely divided.

One of the many tragedies of this "limited war" is that Washington introduced what it called "weapons of mass destruction" (atomic, chemical, and
biological weapons), and though atomic weapons were ultimately not used,
relentless aerial bombing and the dropping of a new weapon called napalm
almost completely leveled northern and central Korea, resulting in a stagger-
ing *civilian* death toll throughout the peninsula of 3 million and forcing those
who survived underground into caves. Bruce Cumings notes that this was
"unrestrained air war," a form of psychological and social warfare, and offers
as an epitaph the revealing reasoning of its architect, General Curtis LeMay:

We slipped a note kind of under the door into the Pentagon and said, "Look, let us go up there . . . and burn down five of the biggest towns in North Korea— and they're not very big—and that ought to stop it." Well, the answer to that was four or five screams—"You'll kill a lot of non-combatants," and "it's too horrible." Yet over a period of three years or so . . . we burned down every town in North Korea and South Korea, too. Now, over a period of three years this is palatable, but to kill a few people to stop this from happening—a lot of people can't stomach it.[21]

While the war ended literally where it had begun—at the 38th parallel—its legacies are significant. The containment doctrine was extended to an attempt at rollback or "liberation," albeit a failed one in this case. Significantly, the war set into motion a neoimperial relationship between the United States and South Korea. Following the war, the United States poured $4 billion of aid into South Korea in one decade alone and supported a string of auto-cratic and military-controlled regimes, beginning with Rhee's. Today, the United States continues to maintain a strong military presence in South Korea, making South Korea's efforts toward a peaceful reunification with North Korea much more difficult.[22] The massive military spending inaugurated by the war transformed not only Japan's economy (as explained in the intro-duction and in the previous chapter), but justified NSC 68's call for massive military spending to rearm Europe and the United States and to help the French maintain colonial control over Indochina.[23] This produced a war boom with global effects that alleviated the structural impasses in the world econ-omy. Domestically, military spending constituted increasing percentages of America's GNP, shifting resources away from domestic programs while cur-tailing civil liberties.[24] The war also significantly witnessed a further severing of relations between the United States and China when the United States' decision to cross the 38th parallel triggered Chinese entry into the war. Thus, it further triangulated the bipolar rivalry between the United States and the Soviet Union not only because it was fought on Asian soil, but also because it brought into active contention the possibility of Communist China becom-ing America's chief Cold War threat. A war that had been thought to be inspired by the Soviet Union actually turned out to be fought literally by the Chinese Red Army. Indeed, as noted by one observer, "700 million potential customers had turned into the apparition of 700 million dangerous adver-saries."[25] China's Red Army represented an "apparition" of the yellow peril combined with the red menace, a different "Agent Orange," if you will. This

severing of relations between the United States and China also coincided
with the early stages of detectable disagreements and tensions between China
and the Soviet Union, which erupted by 1960 into the so-called Sino–Soviet
split. Indeed, leading up to the war, Stalin was more cautious and less in control of events than the United States believed, and he himself came to be suspicious of Mao and Mao's relationship with Kim Il Sung, to the extent that
it complicated the talks between Mao and Stalin that led to the signing of the
Sino–Soviet Treaty in February 1950.[26] Additionally, the Korean War played
an important role in congealing Cold War logics, catalyzing a "Cold War
consensus" and setting a precedent for how the United States would interpret and intervene in subsequent civil wars and anticolonial nationalist movements in Asia and elsewhere. Finally, the war set off the significant, hitherto
unprecedented, migration and scattering of Koreans internally within Korea
itself and across the globe, especially to the United States. It is this Cold War
constitution of Korean migration to the United States—the constitution of
Korean America as an imperial and gendered racial formation—that Korean
American cultural workers reveal, and it is to this rich body of work that I
now turn. In what follows, I will show how Korean American cultural non-
alignments critically account for what is left out of detailed diplomatic histories of the Korean War, dominant Cold War knowledge projects, and U.S.
national memory.

"I'm Not Here, If This Doesn't Happen": The Foreign Student

Susan Choi's haunting novel *The Foreign Student* excavates the link between
the Korean War and Korean migration to the United States. Rendered largely
in flashback and through the recurring dreams of its title character, Chang
"Chuck" Ahn, who flees Korea by becoming a "foreign student" at the University of the South in Sewanee, Tennessee, the Korean War emerges in the novel
as a persistent problem of memory, knowledge, and narration. Unlike the subject of Suji Kwock Kim's "Fragments of the Forgotten War," we know precisely
how Chang suffered when he was captured, interrogated, and tortured by
the South Korean government on suspicion of being a North Korean spy, but
the war itself is thematized as requiring various acts of translation, approximation, and sometimes narrative fabrication in order to be made legible or
scrutable to its multiple audiences during and after its occurrence. Thus, *The
Foreign Student* reveals how the Korean War constitutes as much an active
production of Cold War knowledge and ideology as it does an event or set
of military strategies, battles, and engagements. That is to say, the historical

event and epistemological *object* we have come to name and know as the "Korean War" was itself (and continues to be) an epistemological and pedagogical *project*. The novel suggests that it is precisely because this foreign war—much like the foreign student himself—is an inscrutable object requiring constant translation or production of knowledge about itself that it remains a largely "Forgotten War" in the American popular imaginary.

In the novel, Chang functions as the bearer and embodiment of the Korean War, even as he attempts to repress its painful and traumatic imprints on his body and psyche. Chang is at once the victim, survivor, refugee, teacher/instructor, translator, and at times even fabulist of the war. At the war's end, he tries to flee South Korea by applying for college scholarship sponsors in the United States. Soon enough, he is given a full scholarship by the Episcopal Church Council to attend the University of the South as a foreign student. This arrangement itself indexes the long history of U.S. Christian missionary activity in Korea, a significant project of U.S. cultural imperialism that long precedes and later articulates with the project of U.S. military imperialism and occupation. In exchange for his scholarship, Chang agrees to give periodic talks on Korea to member churches of the council. On one occasion, he is accompanied by Katherine, a local Sewanee resident with whom he begins a tentative friendship and later a romantic relationship. She admits her ignorance about the war: "I don't know anything about the war. . . . I've always wondered what a war really looks like. There's no way to tell, reading the papers"; Chang nonchalantly responds, "There is not much to know."[27] His nonchalance is at once fitting and ironic. On the one hand, what can he say about a war that he himself would like to forget and that does not seem of immediate interest to everyday Americans? On the other hand, as the novel progresses, we find out that there is all too much to know, yet also much that will never be known, that defies simple explanations and representations. Even as Chang attempts to make the war transparent to the American audience in the novel just a couple years after the 1953 armistice—to literally show what a "war really looks like"—through a prepared slide presentation, the multiply and strategically mediated logics of his pedagogy renders the war opaque to us, the reading audience of the novel. *The Foreign Student*, both the novel and the character, thus present the Korean War as an epistemological conundrum, a problem of knowledge production and comprehension overdetermined by and saturated with the imperial and gendered racial optics of the Cold War military intervention and its aftermaths.

Chang carefully and strategically constructs his slide lectures to conform to the expectations of his audience members and to "translate" a foreign and inscrutable Korea for them. He realizes that Korea, if known at all to his audience, exists primarily through racialized and primitivist tropes. Indeed, when Katherine attempts to educate herself by conducting some library research, the sole book she finds is one that is principally on the Japanese empire and thirty years out of date. A short section on Korea reads:

> *Korean ideas of hygiene are as negligible as those of a Hottentot. The average Korean well is little short of a pest-hole. The average Korean man is 5 ft. 4 in. tall, of good physique, well formed, with not unhandsome Mongoloid features, oblique dark brown eyes, high cheek-bones, and noncurling hair that shades from a russet to a sloe black. The olive bronze complexions in certain instances show a tint as light as that of a quadroon.* (44)

Within this epistemological context, it is no wonder that Chang receives questions such as whether "Koreans live in trees" (39) or that he therefore provides a pat, canned history of the war, coupled with generic statements that "Koreans were farmers, that they enjoyed celebrating their holidays clad in bright costumes, that they were fond of flowers and children—that they were unremarkable, hardly worth the trouble of a lecture" (39).

Feeling hopeless against the expectation that he "deliver a clear explanation of the war" when it "defied explanation" (51), he attempts to make the war legible and interesting to his churchgoing audience by skipping over the causes of the war in his presentations and starts by simply comparing the shape of Korea to that of Florida and "groundlessly" comparing the 38th parallel to the Mason-Dixon line. He explains the North Korean communist advance south to the city of Pusan at the beginning stages of the war: "This is like if the war is all over Florida, and our side are trapped in Miami" (52). Indeed, his narratives of the war become increasingly elaborate ruses that he begins to believe in himself:

> He genuinely liked talking about the landing, and MacArthur. It all made for such an exciting, simple minded, morally unambiguous story. Each time he told it, the plot was reduced and the number of details increased, and *the whole claimed more of his memory for itself and left less room for everything else.* He punched the slide-changer now, and Korea After 1945 was replaced by the U.S. Infantry coming out of the Seoul Railway Station, a soap-scrubbed and smiling platoon marching into the clean, level street. This image made a much better

illustration of the *idea* of MacArthur than any actual picture of the Korean war could have. People were often surprised by the vaulted dome of the train station, and the European-looking avenue of trees. "That's Seoul?" a woman asked, vaguely disappointed. The file of troops looked confident and happy, because the picture had not been taken during the Korean conflict at all, but in September 1945, after the Japanese defeat. The photo's original caption had read, "Liberation feels fine! U.S. and their Soviet Allies arrive to clean house in Korea." (52, emphasis added)

Chang follows this ruse with another, showing slides titled "Water Buffalo in Rice Paddy" and "Village Farmers Squatting Down to Smoke," which mends the epistemological rupture experienced by the woman who seemed disappointed that the Seoul Railway Station looked so modern and thus familiar. Chang sees that "Everyone murmured with pleasure at the image of the farmers, in their year-round pajamas and inscrutable Eskimos' faces" (52). We are reminded of the gap between MacArthur and the *idea* of MacArthur, between the Korean War and the *idea* of the Korean War, between Koreans and the *idea* of Koreans. In Chang's lectures, as in the minds of his American audience, the idea of the thing comes to supplant the thing itself. Hence, Chang ends his lectures without mentioning how MacArthur, despite the "genius" that he was, was essentially fired by President Truman later in the war, and how despite the general's famous "Inchon Landing," the war failed to reunify Korea and ended literally right where it had begun—at the 38th parallel.

Even as Chang is captivated by his own "revisionist" history of the Korean War, and even as it "claimed more of his memory for itself and left less room for everything else," the "everything else" begins to erupt in his lectures and through protracted flashbacks throughout the novel. The "Korea After 1945" slide that appears repeatedly throughout Chang's lecture literally maps a still-divided Korea, a Korea that is never the same "after 1945." The war fails to change or eradicate the dividing line, so there is no need for a "Korea After 1953" (after the war) slide in Chang's slide tray. *The Foreign Student* makes visible this historical and literal rupture of Korea into a North and a South, for what remains unchallenged amid Chang's poetic license is that we are left with two Koreas, or "Korea After 1945." Korea must still be grammatically qualified, either through this periodization (after 1945) or through geographic specification (North or South). Paralleling this national severing, Chang himself experiences a doubling or splitting:

He could not remember the pain he had felt, as if all that had happened to him had been enacted on another. Although he had witnessed every detail, the pain was as distant from him as the distance between two bodies; the other may be there, in your arms, their length matched against yours, but whatever they feel is darkness. It could be another universe, it could not exist at all. He could not imagine what the other body felt, and so he became another to himself; and after this happened, how could he be close to someone, when he was two people? (317–18)

Despite this splitting of the self, Chang is haunted by recurring dreams of Korea, and Choi reveals through flashbacks why and how it is that Chang became the figure of "the foreign student." We find out that his skills at literal and figurative translation did not start with his church slide lectures in the United States. Indeed, having been raised in a privileged family with a professor father trained at a Japanese university, Chang knew the English language before coming to Sewanee. Immediately after graduating from high school, he is thus able to get a job as a translator for the South Korean government's new Ministry of Public Information. But because South Korea is militarily occupied by the United States, with the operation of a full military government commanded by John Hodge, Chang finds himself taking orders from him. By thus including actual historical figures, and having their lives intersect with that of Chang, her protagonist, Choi meticulously imagines and narrates what it might have been like for a young Korean man such as Chang to experience the American occupation, the war, and subsequent migration to the United States. As such, *The Foreign Student* can be approached as a historical novel of the Korean War that offers a critical perspective that is largely absent in academic and oral histories. While we certainly have access to histories told from the Korean perspective in Korean and histories told from the U.S. perspective in English, what is rare is a narrative told from the perspective of a Korean who experienced the war and migrated to the United States soon thereafter.

The Foreign Student attempts to fill this lacuna but is mindful of the limits of such an attempt. Indeed, in translating and making visible the American occupation and Korean War through Chang, the novel highlights translation's very failings, especially in a Cold War context in which nuance, complexity, and contradiction are eschewed in favor of simple Manichaean binaries. This inadequacy is shown through Chang's actual job as a translator:

And so Hodge decided to build the Republic of Korea its own army. Almost immediately he ran into a problem with words. Korea had its own language for weapons and warfare and soldiers, but the words were attached to Korean ideas, and these were of no use to Hodge. He wanted only the American idea of expedient slaughter, the American idea of order. He didn't know any Korean. . . . Hodge told Chang not to bother him with nuance. Hodge only wanted the Korean soldiers to be taught to give and receive orders, as if they were really American. "Make it work and don't tell me about it," he said. In the end it was probably wise. Chang had done enough translation already to know that there weren't ever even exchanges. You wanted one thing to equal another, to slide neatly into its place, but somehow this very desire made the project impossible. In the end there was always a third thing, that hadn't existed before. For Hodge there could never be third things. Hodge meant to imagine an American-style army out of the materials at hand, and what did not fit would be altered by force. In this spirit, Chang didn't adjust things to the names that existed, but adjusted new names to the things. The result was that Hodge's Republic of Korea Army was inarguably American apart from the fact that it consisted entirely of Koreans in oversized uniforms running around yelling things like, "Grab your mechanical-gun-that-shoots-fast and get into the car-with-no-top!" (66–67)

This passage highlights translation's limits and the impossibility of formal equivalence. Yet in the context of a Korea militarily occupied by the United States, it is this very failure of translation, of "adjust[ing] new names to the things," that successfully conjoins linguistic and cultural imperialism to military imperialism. If translation, as Naoki Sakai writes, is a social relation, then the impossibility of formal equivalence—highlighted in the above passage by "mechanical-gun-that-shoots-fast" and "the car-with-no-top"—signals a broader unequal or nonequivalent social relation between Korea and the United States.[28]

The repression of the "third thing," the "unnatural by-product" (84) that is the trace or symptom of translation's failure, allows America's binary Cold War logics to uniform, literally in this case, South Korean bodies. Such a critique of the Cold War in Korea through the trope of translation calls to mind Theresa Hak Kyung Cha's experimental text *Dictee*.[29] In Cha's confounding nonlinear assemblage of pieces (ranging from historical documents, personal poems, and letters to photos and film stills without captions), imperfectly transcribed and translated dictation and translation exercises serve to, as Lisa Lowe has written, show how the subject of *Dictee* is "unfaithful to the original."[30]

As such, she refuses to submit to any one ruling ideology or influence, whether that is French Catholicism, Japanese colonialism in Korea, or Cold War geopolitics. Moreover, what Choi's linking of the trope of translation to the Korean War also calls to mind is Walter Benjamin's observation that translation is a mode that necessitates a twinned "fidelity and license—the freedom of faithful reproduction and, in its service, fidelity to the word." He argues, however, that "meaning is served far better . . . by the unrestrained license of bad translators" than by faithful literal translation.[31] In revealing, then, both this failure or impossibility built into every act of translation as well as the very repression of such failure, *The Foreign Student* demonstrates how the Korean War gets "translated" through the dominant Manichaean schema of the Cold War rivalry between the superpowers. That is, what might have begun as a local civil conflict and attempt to reunify Korea—in the aftermath first of Japanese colonialism and then of American and Soviet division and occupation—through a nonaligned "third way" gets derailed, interpellated, and superseded by the bipolar Cold War rivalry between the two superpowers, and later with China added to the constellation. As such, as I have noted, the Korean War can be interpreted as an arrested project of decolonization. Indeed, Choi's novel critically limns the uninterrupted chain of colonial and imperial succession in Korea. In the fall of 1945, "everywhere the Japanese disappeared from their buildings," and a "surreal flood of American things"—"Coca-Cola arrived, and Budweiser, and American trash became the stuff that held the city together" (69). *The Foreign Student* is thus a "bad translator," as it were, of the Korean War. In other words, its (re)translation of the Korean War takes license with and lacks a fidelity to the dominant Manichaean ways it has been represented. The war thus emerges as a complex problem and production of knowledge rather than a congealed, "untranslatable" event. Indeed, as I will elaborate further in my discussion of *Surname Viet Given Name Nam* in the next chapter, this is what I have called the protracted afterlife of the Cold War, its epistemological valence that continues to generate "new" knowledge or translations after the end of its historical life or eventness.

Although commanded to ignore the "third thing," and thus to preserve the dominant translation of the Korean War, Chang is himself a third thing "that people like Hodge both despised and required" (84). Realizing that he had no true place in South Korea—like his father, who had been jailed by the South Korean government as a Japanese collaborator—Chang "crosses over" and becomes a translator for the U.S. State Department's United States

Information Service (USIS), the "overseas purveyor of American news and American culture" (84). "The prospect of selling the U.S. to South Korea suddenly seemed much more attractive than that of selling South Korea to the U.S." (84). Chang is christened by Petersfield, his USIS boss, as "Chuck," an act that later provokes a British journalist to declare that "American imperialism is nothing if not redundant" (90), for the monosyllabic "Chang" is an unusually easy name for Westerners to remember and pronounce. Chang as "Chuck" not only decides how to translate things, but also *what* should be translated and passed on to the South Korean media in the first place. As "the arbiter, the censor," Chang spends his days "culling and embroidering and shaping" the "raw material of a world at his disposal" (86). This incessant production, fabrication, and omission of (mis)information by both the American and South Korean sides demonstrate the extent to which the Cold War militarization of South Korea went hand in hand with a "public information" or knowledge industry that performed the symbolic labor of Cold War logics. Within such an epistemological and pedagogical economy, local South Korean guerilla movements that oppose the U.S. military occupation and division of Korea are "translated" as the acts of either "docile, misled peasants" (84) or communist infiltrators from the North.

Chang's decision to "cross over" to the USIS from the South Korean Ministry of Public Information is less a pledge of loyalty or allegiance to the occupation government, which euphemistically calls itself a "facilitating presence" during South Korea's period of "transition" (164), than it is a rejection and critique of the corrupt and brutal excesses of Rhee's Republic of Korea. He sees that it is a "government that only seemed to exist in order that it not be a Communist government," that his father had been jailed, and that while his family's land north of the 38th parallel had been confiscated by the Communists so that it could be redistributed, the land south of the parallel, within the Republic, "had simply been confiscated for the sake of confiscation, and not put to any use" (164). Neither aligning formally with the Communist Party nor supporting Rhee's (and America's) Republic of Korea, Chang thus fashions a "philosophy" of nonalignment in the interest of pragmatic survival:

> It occurred to him that his dislike of the southern government was a perfectly sufficient underpinning for whatever he might do. He could come up with philosophy later. His father had never been loyal to the Japanese, but he had recognized that they could be used. Chang felt that his recognition was the same: the Americans could be used, but the Republic of Korea was useless. He would

be loyal to nobody but himself. Then Petersfield had abandoned him in Seoul, and he knew that in spite of his resolve his loyalty had attached itself to Petersfield like an indiscriminate, compulsive tentacle, expecting loyalty and love in return. He regrouped, declared himself a small principality, and pledged his undivided allegiance again. The Committee for the Preservation and Welfare of Himself convened its first meeting and passed a resolution excising agitators from his heart, and these included Petersfield. The resolution might have been only the product of his injured feelings, but once it was made, he found it had the power to dictate each decision that followed, as if he'd come up with philosophy after all. (164–65)

This resolution of affective and political nonalignment is a pragmatic philosophy of survival in a war-torn, occupied, and corrupt country, where active efforts at reunification on either side of the 38th parallel could only be interpreted and punished through the Cold War lens of being pro-Soviet or pro-American, but never simply pro–Korean reunification. Chang finds himself at odds with the governing forces in South Korea, but ironically, his "Committee for the Preservation and Welfare of Himself" could very well have taken shape as the "Committee for the Preservation and Welfare of a Reunified Korea" before the Cold War overdetermined and derailed Korea's efforts at national reunification and independence. Even Kim, a childhood friend and schoolmate of Chang's who joins the communist guerilla movement in South Korea, recognizes that nonalignment might be the only path to freedom. When Chang thinks about joining the Communist Party, Kim warns, "hang on to your freedom. You don't need to affiliate yourself with the party or anything else. Keep clear of that, whatever happens" (89). In yet another irony, however, freedom—the kind of freedom that Chang's class privilege allows—is precisely why Kim had joined the party, only to be disillusioned about freedom's possibility as Cold War geopolitics intervened in Korean politics.

Within this context, from "crossing over" to USIS, Chang comes over to the USA. I conclude my discussion of *The Foreign Student*, then, by returning us to this American context, the setting with which I began my analysis of the novel. Chang's migration is not a chasing after the "American Dream," but a running away from the nightmare that is Cold War South Korea. It is a further nonalignment achieved through a physical detachment and departure from the peninsula's shores. Indeed, echoing the postcolonial mantra that "We are here because you were there," Chang finds himself declaring in his slide lectures for the Episcopal Church Council's members, "I'm not here, if this doesn't happen" (50). By "this," he is referring to MacArthur's Inchon Landing (or, more broadly, U.S. military intervention during the Korean War), and he begins his addresses by saying that "his presence before them was the direct result" of it (50).[32] Chang's attempt at nonalignment thus indexes the link between America's Korean War and the migration of Koreans to the United States, as well as the racial logics that subtend this connection. While he attempts a detachment from Cold War geopolitics and logics, their racial registers follow him from Korea and reattach to his racialized body in the United States. On a bus ride from Tennessee to Chicago, he learns that gooks "over there" are still (called) gooks "over here." A child's observation on this ride that "you can't tell the difference between gooks and chinks" (232) turns out to be a foreshadowing of the racial profiling that Chang is subjected to toward the end of the novel. Arriving in New Orleans to meet Katherine, he is detained and interrogated by a "Port Security Program" official: "Are you a Chinese national? . . . Are you familiar with the Port Security Program? Are you an able-bodied seaman? . . . Are you a member of the Communist Party? . . . Are you or have you ever been associated with a known member of the Communist Party?" (275). This racial profiling, enacted and justified in the attempt to address the putative "problem [of] Chinese Communist agents infiltrating American harbors" (278), bespeaks the racialized economy of Cold War logics and the increasing significance that China would play in the triangulation of the Cold War in Asia. How might the Port Security Program have singled out a possible *Soviet* communist attempting to "infiltrate American harbors"?

In the next section, I elaborate on this imperial and gendered racial formation of Korean migration to the United States in an analysis of Heinz Insu Fenkl's novel *Memories of My Ghost Brother*. While Susan Choi's Chang comes to the United States as a foreign student, Fenkl's lyrical narrative introduces us to a different yet related mode of migration impelled by the persistence of the U.S. military presence in Korea. Fenkl offers an unsparing look at the desperate worlds, economies, hopes, and desires created by U.S. military camptowns in Korea and the military brides who have come to see America as the Promised Land.[33]

A Matter of Endurance

Historian Ji-Yeon Yuh writes, "The study of Korean migration has long been a stepchild constrained by the nationalist visions of larger and more powerful fields."[34] Departing from nationalist and nation-bound research agendas, Yuh provides an analysis of the powerful extent to which post-1945 Korean migration has been constituted by the division and militarization of the Korean peninsula, and in particular by the Korean War. She argues that the Korean War led to an expanded exodus of Koreans who sought security in Europe, Latin America, and the United States. She calls this development "refuge migration" and notes that it is "hidden in other categories, such as the marriage migration of military brides and the labor and professional migration of miners, doctors, and nurses. Although ostensibly migrants or immigrants rather than refugees fleeing from an immediate danger, their life narratives demonstrate that flight from war and its consequences is a crucial factor in their migration." Expanding the limited scope of the United Nations designation of "*refugee* migration," Yuh posits that "*refuge* migrants" are "fleeing perceived danger and seeking peace of mind," as well as a "stable environment that doesn't feel like it's always threatening to explode."[35] Since the armistice of 1953, the threat of war has been ever present. Motivated by a psychological need to leave behind the chaos, insecurity, and trauma triggered by the Korean War, refuge migrants are thus significantly different from immigrants who leave their countries in search of better economic, educational, and life opportunities. Yet this refuge migration has not been recognized as such, because it has been legally classified as labor, family, or economic migration.

Military brides constitute a significant part of the "refuge migrant" category.[36] More than one hundred thousand military brides have immigrated to the United States since 1950, and due to the continued presence of the U.S. military in South Korea, this migration has not abated. Because military brides sponsored multiple and extended family members and became the first link in long chain migrations, they enabled the majority of Korean migration to the United States during the 1970s and early 1980s. Indeed, military brides are directly and indirectly responsible for an estimated 40 to 50 percent of all Korean immigration to the United States since 1965.[37] As such, military brides can be seen as the pioneers of post–World War II Korean immigration to the United States. Why, then, have they not received widespread public acknowledgment as such, especially by Korean America itself? Why has this knowledge been disavowed? Yuh writes that "as women who have married non-Koreans and as women who—regardless of their social background—are stained by presumed association with U.S. military camptowns and prostitution simply because they married an American soldier, they are left standing outside the bounds of both respectable Korean womanhood and authentic Koreanness."[38] Whether military brides, military sex workers, or, as I will discuss in the next section, transnational adoptees, these are gendered racial bodies that emerge out of the Korean War. Indeed, as Grace M. Cho observes, "Women's bodies are not only subjected to practices of war; they are constituted by these very practices. Out of the ruins of war, new bodies emerge. They are stigmatized bodies that are reminders of collective trauma . . . and they are embodiments of a disrupted social order in which women are exposed to a wider range of both freedoms and dangers."[39]

In grappling with this vexed constitution, I turn in this section of my chapter to Heinz Insu Fenkl's 1996 novel *Memories of My Ghost Brother.* Fenkl's narrative of camptown life, at once moving and disturbing, reveals the unsettling intersection between Cold War epistemology and Korean America's own admitted knowledge about the conditions of possibility for its post-1945 formation. Within American Cold War logics, military brides and their mixed-race children, especially those who immigrate to the United States, are the undesired index, reminder, and literal offspring of America's protracted military presence in South Korea. Such militarist imperialism contradicts the Manichaean narrative of American benevolence. Within Korean nationalist and patriarchal protocols, military brides are figured as traitors who consort with foreigners, are largely presumed to have been camptown prostitutes or sex workers, and serve as unwanted reminders to the Korean nation-state that its sovereignty is circumscribed by U.S. military authority on Korean soil. Thus, they are often shunned by larger Korean society. *Memories of My Ghost Brother* gives names, faces, and histories to these women pioneers and critically exposes the desperate, circumscribed camptown terrain within which they live and make difficult choices. While it would be easy to judge and condemn such choices as morally questionable or bankrupt, the novel interrogates and complicates such a facile economy of moral absolutism. That is to say, Fenkl shows how individual decisions that appear to be perverse or pathological are themselves symptomatic of a perversely imperialistic and militarized collective social architecture undergirded by racialized and gendered taxonomies of domination.[40]

Set in Pupyong, near the Taegu base in South Korea, and told from the recollected perspective of Insu/Heinz, who is the product of a Korean mother and a German American GI father stationed at Camp Casey during the Vietnam War, *Memories of My Ghost Brother* provides a palimpsest of U.S. militarism in Korea and other parts of Asia. Indeed, Elaine H. Kim writes that "Pupyong is a metonym for Korea, and there Insu must negotiate a complex and often shifting hierarchy of race, gender, class, and culture that emerges in the shadow of the American empire."[41] The lingering ghosts of Japanese colonialism, the U.S. atomic bombings of Hiroshima and Nagasaki, and the Korean War populate the novel against the backdrop of the Vietnam War in the years surrounding the Tet Offensive of 1968 and the ongoing presence of the American military in South Korea. The house into which young Insu's family moves at the beginning of the novel contains the ghosts, memories, and survivors of this traumatic history. Once belonging to a Japanese colonel, the house becomes a haven for refugees during the Korean War and is later rented by a few families, including Insu and his mother, his aunt and uncle and cousins, and a couple who moved back to Korea from Nagasaki with their crippled son. Young Insu often hears whispers, which he knows are "the lamentations of the refugees who had died [in the house] during the war."[42]

Insu's mother and growing members of her family represent a large population of rural Korean farmers who have been displaced by the Korean War and have been forced to migrate to cities and the camptowns surrounding the many U.S. military bases in South Korea. In one of many tragic ironies, the residents of the camptowns, forced to reside there because they have been displaced by U.S. military intervention during the Korean War and the transformation of South Korea's economy through a U.S.-supported and sponsored export driven model, now find themselves economically dependent on the very forces that displaced and impoverished them in the first place. Insu's mother is followed by her sister and brother-in-law and their children, and later a niece named Gannan sent by another sister from the family's historical residence in the countryside. Insu's *Emo* (Aunt) laments, "Before the war we all lived well there. . . . If there were only as many plots of rice as there used to be, [Gannan] could stay in the country" (14). Both Insu's mother and his cousin Gannan support the extended family by working within the precarious and hyper-competitive camptown economy. Insu's mother sells products she purchases from the PX on the black market (an activity she keeps secret from her German American GI husband Heinz), and Gannan works at the club in ASCOM, the American army post. Young Insu, interpellated by the camptown world, the only world he knows, harbors naïve hopes of one day contributing to the household income (and thus to his family's happiness) as well by becoming a GI like his father:

> *Emo*'s sadness made my heart feel heavy. I promised to myself that when I grew
> up and became a dark-haired GI, I would make lots of money and buy everyone

everything they wanted so they would be happy always. We would have servants so *Emo* wouldn't have to work in the kitchen; Mahmi [Mommy] could stop going to the PX to buy things for other people; *Hyongbu* [mother's brother-in-law] would have his American cigarettes and whiskey. And my father, by then, would surely be a great general with white hair and a beard instead of only his short yellow hair.... I would be a GI. I could go to America to see the many, many PX's, NCO clubs, and all the tall people in green with their sharp, pulled-out noses. (19)

By imagining himself as a "dark-haired GI," Insu phenotypically and racially disidentifies with yellow-haired GI's like his very own father and marks the "tall people in green with their sharp, pulled-out noses," among other odd features, as a decidedly foreign presence in Korea. Ironically, however, his imagination can only stretch so far, because he can still only imagine himself *as* a GI. Within the circumscribed world of Pupyong, he has no other role models; he does not yet realize that the presence of the GI, the privileged figure of deliverance in his fantasy of escape from unhappiness and impoverishment, is in many ways the index of—rather than the solution to—his family's losses.

Indeed, through the figure of the GI, as represented by Insu's father, the novel lays bare the charged racial logics through which America's military occupation of and violence in Korea and other parts of Asia materialize. Though he marries a Korean woman, Insu's father derides Korean culture as heathen, barbaric, and pagan, and is ashamed to be seen in public—especially in front of his men—with his Korean wife and son. While stationed at Camp Casey in between active duty (sometimes voluntarily) in Vietnam, he is "not at all happy" to see his son and wife when they visit him, telling his wife that "having his men see his Korean wife undermined his authority" (131). Insu recollects that the aftermath of the Viet Cong's Tet Offensive in 1968 prompted a significant change:

The mood among the GIs in Korea became thick and black, full of hate for Asian people and tense with the fear that the North Koreans might invade. The GIs were afraid to stay in Korea, but even more afraid that they might be shipped to Cam Ranh Bay to join some counteroffensive against the North Vietnamese. Houseboys and prostitutes were beaten more frequently, there were more fights in the clubs. The Korean army stayed on alert and continued to mobilize more men to send to Vietnam. There was constant news about the White Horse Division, the Tiger Division, and the Blue Dragon Brigade. (131–32)

Here, we see anti-Asian "hate" structuring and saturating America's triangulation of the Cold War in Asia, producing violence and the beating of Asian bodies belonging to allied South Korea. Even as *geopolitical* distinctions are made between allies and enemies—between South and North Korea and between the South Vietnamese and the Viet Cong—*racial* distinctions between a group taxonomized as similarly "oriental" or "gook" cannot and will not be made.

To mark yet another ironic disjuncture, even as Korean bodies—"houseboys and prostitutes" and many others—are beaten more frequently, the Republic of Korea's army is itself interpellated and inducted into America's imperial violence, including atrocities committed against civilians, in Vietnam. Indeed, in an article entitled "America's Korea, Korea's Vietnam," Charles Armstrong writes of the "ambiguous legacy" of the Vietnam War for South Korea.[43] Dispatching troops far exceeding the number sent by all other Allied nations combined, South Korea reaped huge financial rewards through the Vietnam War. Armstrong writes that "Vietnam was a goldmine for Korea," "responsible in no small measure, for the economic 'miracle' of the 1960s to the 1990s."[44] Just as the Korean War had been "divine aid" or "a gift from the gods" for Japan, the Vietnam War was Korea's divine goldmine. More disturbing than this financial economy, however, is the racial economy of the conduct of South Korea's army in Vietnam. As the above passage from *Memories of My Ghost Brother* reveals, hatred toward and suspicion of the Viet Cong get displaced onto the bodies of Koreans by American soldiers stationed in Korea. At the same time, however, as Armstrong argues in his analysis of the "ferocity" of Korean atrocities in Vietnam, "the ambiguous racial—one might even say semi-colonial—position of the Korean soldiers placed between the Americans and the Vietnamese" played a significant role. "The Koreans 'looked like' the enemy and therefore had to doubly prove themselves as effective fighters in the eyes of the Americans. . . . Just as Koreans in Manchuria were often seen by the Japanese as superior to the local Chinese but inferior to their Japanese masters in the 1930s, so Koreans could become more than 'gook,' if not quite 'white,' in the eyes of the Americans in Vietnam." It is a case of "yellow skin, white masks."[45] Such a desire to gain favor with white American soldiers, tethered to an already existing indigenous Korean sense of superiority vis-à-vis Southeast Asians, comes to overdetermine "Korea's Vietnam." We see the layered, multiple ironies of this racial logic. Gooks are atrociously killing (other) gooks in order to be less gook-like, but because they are gooks nonetheless, they are getting beaten back at home in Korea by their "allied"

American soldiers. Indeed, as Jinim Park writes in her comparative analysis of American and Korean narratives of the Vietnam War, "Koreans vacillated between two conflicting views of themselves: one as American allies, and one as the same Asian 'gooks' as the Vietnamese, a combination that frequently resulted in a sense of loss as 'in-between' beings."[46] Though formally American allies, it has been observed that Koreans, along with the Filipino and Thai soldiers who served in Vietnam, were in effect American "mercenaries."[47] Park demonstrates how this contradiction and liminality find expression in Korean representations of the Vietnam War, such as Hwang Suk-young's *The Shadow of Arms*. In this novel, a Vietnamese character named Toi points out the racial proximity between Koreans and Vietnamese, which makes these groups more similar to each other than to their white American allies:

> "You and I, Ahn, we're both gooks, slopeheads."
> "In the eyes of the Americans I suppose so."
> "In our own eyes, too. It's nothing to feel bad about."[48]

Despite American GI violence, the GI is still figured as the object of desire and means of escape in *Memories of My Ghost Brother*. Like Insu, his cousin Gannan also hopes to help her family and escape the cycle of sadness and poverty. However, while Insu wishes to accomplish this by becoming a GI, Gannan wishes to have or marry one. Through Gannan and the other women in Pupyong, *Memories of My Ghost Brother* juxtaposes longing and desire against inevitable loss and disillusionment. When Gannan becomes pregnant by her white American GI boyfriend, she kills herself in shame and despair. Even when some of Insu's mixed-race friends and their mothers do manage to escape to the mythic America, the cycle persists. When Jani's GI father dies in Vietnam and his widowed mother finally finds another yellow-haired GI to marry her, they make it to Minnesota in the summer of 1970. But Jani dies of leukemia just before his twenty-second birthday. When Changmi's mother finds herself a black GI, he turns out to be impotent. When James, whose father is a black American GI, dies mysteriously, and his mother manages to find herself a white American GI and goes to America, she heads straight back to Korea when her husband is stationed again at Taegu. Indeed, when Insu eventually leaves for America with his family, because his father does not want him to be raised and educated improperly among "heathens," "barbarism," and "pagan ceremonies" (239), he is breaking the odds.

As an adult who has become deeply disillusioned with the mythic lure of

America, Insu reflects back on his childhood in Pupyong, and attempts to make some sense of the cruel fates experienced by so many of his childhood friends, especially James. Looking back, he realizes the following:

> For the longest time, I had not realized what it meant that James was black. I had seen it, of course. I had chanted the chocolate rhyme at him, compared the tones of our flesh, called him a *kkombungi*. And he had chanted the chocolate rhyme himself, singing about the Negro men from Africa and their kindness. He did not seem to notice, any more than I, that his difference went further than simply being of mixed blood. To both of us, I think his blackness was lost under the labels we heard—*ainoko, cahpjing, t'wigi*—and that commonness obscured the fact that when people looked at us oddly, they looked at him more oddly than at me. Even a decade later, I could not look back and see that James's tragedy was in the fact that his father was black. The irony and the symmetry of what his mother and Changmi's mother had done never struck me until twenty years later. How pragmatic was that balancing act: James's mother destroying her half-black son to find a white husband, Changmi's mother plotting to bear a half-black son to keep her new black husband. Bartering sons for their own welfare. It was unfortunate that the rules of blood would not permit one mother simply to hand her son to the other, to keep the balance sheet in the world of the living and not in the sad realms of ghosts and memory. I would learn that women—even seemingly devoted mothers—will traffic in children for the mythic promise of America. And they would all look back in regret from the shores of the westward land. (232)

Here, we see the perversity of America's racial taxonomies as they travel overseas in military uniform, taxonomies that are at once historically persistent and newly transformed. Yet the perversity that often *is* America is disguised as a "mythic promise," whose proportions are so grotesquely twisted as to lead one mother to kill her half-black son and another to bear one at any cost. It is a promise that leads mothers to "traffic in children," something we later find out that Insu's own mother did to marry his father. The "ghost brother" of the novel's title is the son whom Insu's mother gave up for adoption as a precondition to marrying his father, who did not want to raise another man's child and who is ashamed even of his own mixed-race son. Within this context, many of the children of Pupyong are relegated to the "sad realms of ghosts and memory." Indeed, Pupyong's biopolitics are such that death is an everyday occurrence, whether you are drowned by your mother or killed by a truck or train. As a node in America's imperialist and global militarized order, the camptown's material, racial, and gendered economies upturn normative moral economies and preservation of life.

The adult Insu recognizes that within Pupyong's precarious world, there is a certain "balance" and "symmetry" in the "bartering" of children, whether given up for adoption, "disappeared," or conceived out of wedlock in order to stay "in" wedlock. This bartering is a pragmatic logic of survival and endurance. Insu neither lambastes nor excuses the unthinkable crime that James's mother has committed:

> To say I hated James's mother would be inadequate. Somewhere, running through my tangled emotions there might have been a single thread of hate, but my feelings were too incoherent and too frayed for me to examine so concisely. Looking back—or even now—it would be easier for me to feel vengeful, to wish her ill, and be done with it; but what I felt in my heart then, and what I feel now, is a great emptiness. It is a profound sadness, a fatalism, a knowledge that the world is the way it is, and that the path of blame is not an arrow's flight, but the mad scatter of raindrops in a storm. I could have blamed James's mother, but that would have been too simple to do her justice. In the end there is no blame, only endurance. (232)

Similar to Chang's formation of the "Committee for the Preservation and Welfare of Himself" in *The Foreign Student,* the military brides of Pupyong enact a biopolitcs of their own in order to survive and escape the economic and physical precariousness of their world and reach the mythic shores of America. In this way, *Memories of My Ghost Brother* meditates on the lives that have been lost, bartered, and disavowed to make post–World War II Korean migration to the United States possible. They are the lives that have been bartered to give birth to contemporary Korean America.

In the next, concluding section of this chapter, I turn to Deann Borshay Liem's documentary *First Person Plural.* If the brother of *Memories of My Ghost Brother* can only remain a banished and later spectral presence in Insu's family's psychic economy and memory, then Borshay Liem's fraught, personal narrative of her transnational and transracial adoption by a white American family invites her audience to reckon with what might have happened—and indeed did happen—to the lives of such "orphaned" children in the prolonged aftermath of the Korean War and the lingering U.S. military presence in Korea. Yet again, in one of many tragic ironies, while Insu's mother had to give up her son Kuristo to an orphanage—and presumably leave him behind in Korea—in order to then marry an America GI and go to the fabled United States, in all likelihood Kuristo might himself have made it to the United States as a transnational, transracial adoptee.

An "Orphan" with Two Mothers: The Production of "Social Orphans" and the Social Death of Birth Mothers

Recent high profile transnational, transracial adoptions by white U.S. uber-celebrities like Angelina Jolie and Brad Pitt, coupled with dramatic increases in the numbers of such adoptions in the last decade, have made what Toby Alice Volkman calls these "new geographies of kinship" highly visible.[49] Yet this "new" visibility and relative "popularity" of transnational adoption obscure the long-standing history of the practice, a history whose modern origins we can trace back to the end of World War II and one that intersects in complex ways with America's imperialist Cold War geopolitics and gendered racial logics in Asia.[50] Indeed, America's protracted Cold War military interventions in Korea and Vietnam have witnessed the significant migration of Koreans and Vietnamese to the United States not only as immigrants, military brides, and "refugees," but also as transnational and *transracial* adoptees.[51] The adoption of Korean babies after the end of the Korean War inaugurated what ultimately developed into the world's largest and longest-lasting transnational adoption program, and, as I will elaborate in the next chapter, the adoption of Vietnamese babies was made possible in the final days of the Vietnam War when the American government launched a controversial "campaign" called Operation Babylift to airlift over two thousand "orphans" out of Vietnam.[52] This intersection, or conjoined genealogies of Cold War imperialisms in Asia and transracial adoptions out of Asia, impels us to reckon with the complex politics and affects of transnational, transracial adoption as not simply or solely an individual, private choice and practice motivated by benevolent or altruistic desires to form new kinships and to provide "better lives" for orphaned and abandoned children. It is also a highly racialized and gendered process implicated in the United States' imperialist, capitalist modernity and indeed its foundational or constitutive projects of racial formation and "nation-building" both domestically and internationally.[53] As such, I seek to highlight the Cold War relations between the United States and Asia as a particularly charged, protracted, and significant condition of possibility and locus for a practice whose disturbing intersections with imperialist violence witnesses a proliferation of locations.

In the following discussion, I grapple with these complex intersections, politics, and affects by analyzing Deann Borshay Liem's *First Person Plural*, a fraught autoethnographic documentary on Borshay Liem's experience of being a transracial Korean adoptee. Her film displays the complexities of adoptions that are not only transnational, but also *transracial* and gendered. I argue that *First Person Plural* is an important site of knowledge production and representation that offers an unsettling hermeneutic of the imperialist and gendered racial logics of the Cold War in Asia. I analyze how this film, a cultural work produced by a transracial adoptee herself, critically indexes the conditions of possibility for a practice we have come to call transracial adoption, and a subject we have come to name transracial adoptee. These conditions of possibility, as *First Person Plural* makes visible, surface at the disturbing nexus of the successive forced migrations engineered by American and Western capitalist modernity, American Cold War imperialism in Asia, the gendered racial logics subtending America's white heteronormative bourgeois nuclear family ideal, and the enduring imperialist sentimental desire to "save" the world. More specifically, within the context of the Cold War in Asia, American military intervention and war produced the conditions—the birth of GI babies, increasing numbers of orphaned and abandoned children, devastation of local economies, and unequal economic and neoimperial dependencies, to name just a few—that led to the availability of children for adoption. This increased availability of potential adoptees coincided with the demand to "rescue" Asian girls from a more putatively pernicious Asian patriarchy,[54] and, more recently, with the maternal desires, nontraditional (re)productive possibilities, and middle-class material privileges afforded by liberal feminism.[55]

Moreover, to the extent that the adoptee of *First Person Plural* has, like many other orphans, at least one living birth parent, these orphans are not biological but rather what are called "visa" or "social orphans" who are legally produced and made available for adoption as such. Given this, I argue that a particularly elided yet significant condition of possibility for transracial adoption is the conjoined "social death" of the adoptee and the birth mother.[56] The very production of the adoptee as a legal orphan, which severs the adoptee from any kinship ties and makes her an exceptional state subject, renders her the barest of social identities and strips her of her social personhood.[57] This social death is paradoxically produced precisely so that the legal orphan can become an adoptee, a process that presumably negates her social death through a formal reattachment to kinship and thus a restoration of social identity and personhood. Yet this "temporary" social death that is contradictorily a condition of possibility for its very (presumably permanent and complete) negation indexes the lingering displacements, irrecoverable losses, and un-healed wounds that come to overdetermine adoptee subjectivity and affec-tive economies. "Successful" placement and adoption cannot fully account for or resolve these residues. Similarly, the disparate conditions and circum-stances that make it disproportionately difficult or unlikely for racialized birth mothers to keep or *parent* their children produce a kind of social death for such mothers, and by extension, for their families and communities. This is not to reify and naturalize motherhood by presuming that mothers should always mother, or want to mother, their children. Rather, it is to index the multiple dislocations, in this instance the exigencies and violences of the Cold War in Asia, as significant forces that would compel a birth mother to give up her child. Within this context, birth mothers are biologically alive, but such profound natal alienation, the capacity to give life but the severing of rights to claim and parent that life, radically circumscribes the quality of their lives such that they undergo what has been called a death-in-life, or social death. That is, if we are to adopt an expanded notion of reproductive justice, one that includes the right of birth mothers to parent their children, then the denial of that right—and of the material conditions that make it possible to exercise that right—constitutes a biopolitical regime generating and contributing to the social death of a growing body of poor, racialized, and gendered birth mothers throughout the world, including the United States.[58] Yet still, such an expanded conceptualization of transnational repro-ductive justice, even as it would seek to recognize the right of birth mothers to parent their children, would situate that right within a broader and wide-ranging framework of reproductive autonomy, one that does not necessarily privilege the biological. Within this framework, reproductive autonomy would also recognize a birth mother's active choice or ability *not* to parent.

Thus, I depart from studies of adoption that have focused largely on med-ical, legal, and social services issues and on clinical assessments or "outcomes" of the pathologized adoptee's adjustment and assimilation. Such quantita-tive studies buttress fantasies of U.S. liberal multiculturalism and tend to elide enduring racial hierarchies by plotting a linear, developmentalist tele-ology of arrival, settlement, and assimilation without interrogating why the adoptee is impelled to be "here" in the United States in the first place.[59] In-stead, I build on work coalescing as an emergent interdisciplinary field of crit-ical adoption studies. For example, while the modern origins of transnational adoption in the United States date back to the immediate post–World War II period, Pauline Turner Strong's analysis sheds light on how the history of this practice intersects with the very formation of the U.S. nation-state from a white settler colony. Strong writes within the context of a protracted history of generations of Native American children being forcibly removed from their homes, relatives, and communities by government officials, missionaries, and service workers who believed that assimilation into the dominant society via adoption, foster care, or education in off-reservation boarding schools served the children's best interest. She poignantly captures the complex, irreconcilable contradictions of adoptions that are not only transracial, but also transnational or nation-to-nation interactions between a colonial settler state and putatively sovereign "domestic dependent" indigenous nations. She writes, "Adoption across political and cultural borders may simultaneously be an act of violence and an act of love, an excruciating rupture and a generous incorporation, an appropriation of valued resources and a constitution of personal ties."[60] Similarly, in a study of America's more recent transnational adoptions of Chinese babies, Sara K. Dorow writes of "the joyful intimacy of making family next to the unjust history that it might recall." For her, this disjunctive juxtaposition materializes as three "impossible contradictions": the "uneasy relationship between commodification and care"; the "demands of dislocation and relocation," of biological origins and culturally chosen kinship; and "fixed and flexible racialized imaginaries."[61] In this section of my chapter and the chapter that follows, I build on such work, coalescing as an emergent interdisciplinary field of adoption studies, and analyze recent cultural works of Asian American transnational, transracial adoptees (a critical mass of whom have come of age as adults) as a heretofore largely untapped source of knowledge and cultural articulation.[62]

Deann Borshay Liem's highly personal documentary *First Person Plural* is an emotionally charged account of a transnational, transracial Korean adoptee's attempt to remember and reckon with her lost Korean origins, and as the title suggests, her plural identities. Borshay Liem's story is especially complex, for in her search what comes to light is that she was not an orphan at all, but had been given up for adoption by her poor, widowed, and still surviving Korean mother who could not feed all five of her children in the aftermath of the Korean War and her husband's death. Moreover, she discovers that the orphanage in Korea forged her adoption papers and passed her off as another girl who was scheduled to be adopted by the Borshays in California, but who was reclaimed by her birth father. Afraid that Borshay Liem's Korean mother would change her mind, the orphanage passed Borshay Liem off as this other girl, told her to be silent about her true identity, and sent her to the Borshays. This case of a forced "mistaken identity," and the proliferation of identities it sets into motion, reveal the complex gendered racial psychic and material economies of transracial adoptions.[63] While the contemporary popularity of transracial adoptions might suggest that it is a relatively recent phenomenon, *First Person Plural* uncovers a long-standing post–World War II genealogy. Indeed, transracial adoptees like Borshay Liem constitute, along-side the military brides of Fenkl's Pupyong camptown, a gendered, "privileged"[64] form of Cold War Asian migration to the United States. Such adoptees also index the displacements precipitated by the Korean War and the protracted presence of the U.S. military in Korea as well as the ontological and epistemological conundrum of discovering and knowing who you "really" are if you are a "first person plural." I argue that as a particularly vexed gendered racial Cold War subject, the transracial Asian (American) adoptee produces her own knowledge project, an attempt to get to know and negotiate her own complex subjectivity vis-à-vis multiple filiations and affiliations, whether familial, cultural, racial, or national. This negotiation is overdetermined by

Deann Borshay Liem (from *First Person Plural*, 2000).

fantasies of return, projections of loss, and desires for reunion, and as *First Person Plural* shows, it is a fraught process that at once enables and disables a coherent narrative of self and kinship.

First Person Plural opens with Borshay Liem's face shot from different angles with different lighting effects, including an unsettling solarized silhouette, coupled with this voiceover: "My name is Kang Ok Jin. I was born on June 14, 1957. I feel like I've been several different people in one life. My name is Cha Jung Hee. I was born November 5, 1956. I've had three names, three different sets of histories. My name is Deann Borshay. I was born on March 3, 1966, the moment I stepped off the airplane in San Francisco. I've spoken

Cha Jung Hee.

Kang Ok Jin (Deann
Borshay Liem).

different languages and I've had different families." This triplicate of names and identities—the person she was literally born as, the person she was passed off as, the person she was figuratively (re)born as when she landed in San Francisco as the adopted daughter of Alveen and Arnold Borshay—bespeaks not only a complex transnational and transracial adoptee subjectivity, but also the material conditions of possibility for such a triangulated and entangled personal history.

Such a proliferation of identities and histories produces an affective and cognitive dissonance for Borshay Liem. How is she to feel and know who or what she "really" is, and who or what her "real" family is? This problem of knowledge, and the project of knowledge acquisition it inaugurates in terms of personal identity, family history, and adoptee ontology, form a significant part, then, of the epistemological valence of the Cold War that I have been attending to throughout this book. One way to grapple with the complex questions and knowledge projects raised by *First Person Plural* is to situate the transnational adoptee as a particular kind of Asian American immigrant. If, as David Eng suggests, the "transnational adoptee is, in fact, an Asian American immigrant, what kind of labor is she performing for the family, and for the nation?"[65] Eng argues that the ideological labor the adoptee performs is, on the one hand, the shoring up of the white American heterosexual nuclear family ideal, and a mediation of domestic white–black racial binaries as yet again the "model minority," on the other hand. I focus in my analysis on the ways in which she also reveals the problematic fictions, repressions, and denials through which such a family gathers its seeming coherence and the Cold War logics within which such labors—ideological, (re)productive, and consumptive—are undertaken.

I begin, then, by asking why a white American family—already an ideal nuclear family unit with a mother, father, and a son as well as a daughter—would seek to adopt a child from a foreign country in the early 1960s. And how might the very knowledge of such adoptions as a possibility have been disseminated? In the opening moments of *First Person Plural*, amid a structured montage of voiceovers, on-camera interviews, and 8-millimeter old home movies shot by Arnold, Alveen explains why they decided to adopt "Cha Jung Hee," whom they renamed Deann, and whom they later find out is actually Kang Ok Jin. Inspired and moved by an NBC television segment called a "Foster Parents' Plan" for the "thousands of needy children in Europe and Asia," and made possible by the family's middle-class economic ascendance, Alveen decides to "sponsor" a child for fifteen dollars a month, and after about two and a half years of sponsorship and correspondence, adopts the eight-year-old girl from South Korea. This 1960s television segment, complete with pathos-generating footage of suffering orphans in South Korea, constitutes what Laura Briggs calls a "visual iconography of rescue."[66] It participates in and builds on what Lisa Cartwright writes is a "long history of a Western gaze riveted on distant human suffering." She considers the contemporary "visual classification and management of the global social orphan in terms of a transnational politics of pity at the end of the twentieth century."[67]

But as *First Person Plural* and the segment that so moved Alveen Borshay reveal, such visual classification and the "transnational politics of pity" at the end of the twentieth century have an earlier Cold War genealogy. Indeed, in the aftermath of the World War II atomic bombings of Hiroshima and Nagasaki, Norman Cousins, the editor of the *Saturday Review,* conducted two sponsorship or "adoption" programs: the Hiroshima Maidens Project, through which women disfigured by the bomb were brought to the United States for reconstructive surgery and housed by "host" families, and the Moral Adoptions Program, through which Americans "adopted" four hundred Japanese children orphaned by the Hiroshima bombing. As Christina Klein notes, these adoptions were virtual (consisting of the donation of money and the exchange of letters) because U.S. policy barred the actual immigration of Japanese people.[68] Cousins was likely inspired by the Christian Children's Fund (founded originally in 1938 as the China Children's Fund), which by 1955 had successfully appealed to American donors to sponsor children in fifteen Asian countries, many of whom were Chinese and North Korean refugees. The Christian Children's Fund grew and expanded in step with the Cold War in Asia, and by yoking the "politics of pity" to a politics of fear and figuring sponsorship as "adoption" in its ads, it constituted one important site of Cold War ideological and epistemological formation. Indeed, as one of their typical advertisements in the 1950s reads: "[T]he communists care enough to make very successful capital of democracy's failures and with the strong conviction that we Americans can not close our eyes or stop our ears to the cry of a hungry child anywhere in the world—black, brown, yellow or white. The hungry children of the world are more dangerous to us than the atom bomb." Another advertisement, with the sensational title "This Picture is as Dangerous as it is Pitiful!" and a picture of a bony, emaciated naked South Korean child, claims: "The ominous significance of this picture is that it threatens to take from us all that we hold most dear—life, liberty and the pursuit of happiness. Not only in South Korea, where this picture was taken, but in India and other democratic countries, millions awoke this morning hungry. . . . The road to communism is paved with hunger, ignorance and lack of hope. What does a man, woman or child, without a roof over their heads, with no personal belongings whatever—what do such have to lose if they listen to communist propaganda? Their resentment may any day ignite the spark that will explode the hydrogen bomb."[69] The trope of adoption, as Klein observes, symbolically "solved" even as it obscured the problem of racist immigration exclusion laws, and through a logic of consumption, the advertisements made it possible for Americans to "purchase a child, [get] protection from communism, and [achieve] relief from a sense of political helplessness"—all for the sponsorship cost of $10 a month.[70] Moreover, these print ads allowed Americans to engage in and alleviate at once a politics of pity, fear, and salvation, but also presented an educational or pedagogical opportunity to learn more and gain more knowledge about Asia through the charged anticommunist and Manichaean rhetorics of the Cold War. These affective politics and politics of affect strategically attempted to displace and obscure the Cold War militarist and imperialist politics of the United States in Asia, but are themselves part and parcel of the imperialist project. Indeed, such affective labors, or sentimental affects, desires, and narratives of "saving" unfortunate souls, have a long-standing history, constituting what Briggs calls a "secular salvation theology," often working alongside a sometimes *not* so secular theology.[71] Evangelical Christian organizations and adoption agencies, particularly Holt International, played significant roles in spearheading the transnational, transracial adoption of children from countries such as China and Korea as well as in efforts to liberalize restrictive immigration laws that prevented such adoptions.

By the 1960s, when Borshay Liem was adopted at the age of eight, it was possible to go from virtual adoption or sponsorship to actual legal adoption, enabling the immigration of the Asian adoptee to the United States. On the one hand, while the "privileged" gendered immigration of Asian females to the United States—as military or war brides, mail-order brides, and transracial adoptees—might be seen to reverse the gendered racial exclusion of Asian immigration to the United States dating back to 1875, Borshay Liem's searing personal trauma forces us to reckon with the violent terms, historical catastrophes, multiple losses, and costs under and through which such a "reversal" takes place. Indeed, perhaps some of the most troubling aspects of transracial adoption and its attendant discourse, then and now, are their saturation within the logic of consumption, the marketplace, and an uneven global political economy that compels poor countries that cannot provide for their own children to send them to wealthier, usually Western nations. As Toby Alice Volkman asks, "Even when there appears to be no evidence of corruption or trafficking in children, does the very existence of the transracial adoption as a practice create a demand and hence a supply of children?" Moreover, she notes, the fact that potential adoptive parents are presented with "choice" makes it a "topic in adoption discourse that is fraught to the degree that it implicates the possibility of the child as commodity."[72] This becomes more fraught when we consider that many orphanages require the adoptive parent(s) to make a substantial donation to the orphanage in addition to paying the processing fees, and many intermediaries (private adoption agencies, lawyers, etc.) profit handsomely. Given this context, Eng argues that "the transnational adoptee is a form of embodied value, a special type of property uneasily straddling both subjecthood and objecthood."[73]

Indeed, what is striking in *First Person Plural* is that the racialized hierarchy between Borshay Liem and her white adoptive family is most tellingly displayed by the racialized logic of consumption, possession, and ownership through which the Borshay family figures its relationship to Deann. The Borshays reveal a "possessive investment in (their own) whiteness."[74] Denise is Deann's adoptive sister, and in a film otherwise weighed with emotionally overwrought episodes, her affect on camera could best be characterized as oddly flippant. She recalls the day the family picked up Deann from the airport: "I think mother went up to the wrong person. Yeah. I think we didn't know until we checked her name tag or somebody told us who you were. It didn't matter. I mean one of them was *ours*." She also recounts how she had to take an upset Deann home early on her first day of school: "I carried you kind of like a little monkey, your little arms and legs just kind of wrapped around me and we just started walking home." Though Denise repeats throughout the interview segments that Deann is her family, her sister, despite differences in appearance or "nationality or whatever," even remembering how one person asked if they were sisters because they looked "just alike," there are moments when consumerist and racial logics—"one of them was ours" and "like a little monkey"—erupt and ultimately exceed the rhetorics of kinship. The racial complexities, contradictions, and ironies of the multiracial Borshay family are further revealed in a home movie of them enjoying breakfast at a restaurant called Aunt Jemima's Kitchen. Moreover, Duncan, Deann's adoptive brother, also insists that "color and look doesn't make any difference," and that Deann is just as much his sister as Denise is. But in a telling grammatical slippage, he reveals, "You didn't come from *my* mommy's womb but I don't care." Why would he say "*my* mommy's womb" to his sister? Wouldn't this normally be articulated between siblings as "*our* mommy's" or simply "mommy's"? For him, "color and look doesn't make any difference," yet at the same time, he betrays a profoundly imperialist attitude: "Of course I can't help as a red-blooded American boy only knowing America and this culture, I think it's superior to everywhere else in the world in every way. That may be arrogant and condescending of me but I can't help it."

Even Alveen, Deann's adoptive mother, participates in this discursive economy of ownership, saying, "I didn't care that they had switched a child on us.... You were Deann and you were *mine*." And interestingly, when Deann *qua* Cha Jung Hee arrives in the United States, Alveen does not notice that the girl with the stricken expression on her face standing in front of her, née Kang Ok Jin, does not resemble the picture of Cha Jung Hee sent to her by the orphanage. Moreover, when she and Arnold make a trip with Deann to

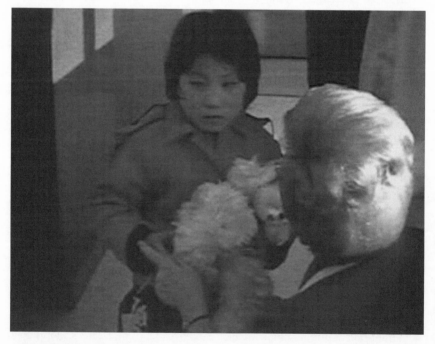

Deann Borshay Liem as she steps off the plane from Korea.

The Borshay family enjoys breakfast at Aunt Jemima's Kitchen.

Korea for a "reunion" with the long lost Korean family, she cannot "equate" Deann with Korea at all. When asked by Deann why not, she answers, "You belong *to* us, at home. It's almost like we're just visitors and so are you." While the last part of this statement—that they are visitors to Korea—might be true, what is revealing is the first part, that Deann does not simply belong *with* her adoptive parents in America, but that she belongs *to* them. In a further denial of Deann's Korean identity and history, even while they are in Korea on their way to meet Deann's biological family, we see this exchange:

DEANN: You can call my brothers and sisters by their first name.
ALVEEN: Ok Jin.
DEANN: I'm Ok Jin.
ALVEEN: You're Deann.
ARNOLD: Ok Jin is your brother.
DEANN: Ok Jin is meeeee. . . .
ARNOLD: . . . skip that part of this tape . . .

In discussing these contradictions, my point is not to question the sincerity of Alveen and Arnold's motivations or their love for Deann. Rather, my aim is to highlight the messy affective economies that such an adoption, not only transnational but also transracial, can engender, as well as the uneven geopolitical terrain giving rise to such a practice.

For social orphans like Borshay Liem, having multiple sets of parents complicates an already fraught transnational geography of kinship, instantiating a cognitive and affective economy that is at once one of excess and one of lack. Once Borshay Liem travels back to Korea and meets her Korean birth mother, she finds it difficult to have room in her mind for two mothers. Yet this excess of mothers also signals a lack. Borshay Liem has two mothers, yet she is differently estranged from both of them, precisely because there are *two* of them. Borshay Liem articulates this multiplicity of mothers as a confused and confusing tautology: "I didn't know how to talk to my mother about my mother because she was my mother." As a presumed orphan who actually turns out to have not only one but two mothers, Borshay Liem's tautological conundrum is also an oxymoronic one. Such tautologies and oxymoron's signify some of the painfully "impossible contradictions" engendered by transracial adoptions.

While Borshay Liem's estrangement from her birth mother results from the effects of their physical separation, her estrangement from her adoptive mother, Alveen, is specifically racial. She confesses tearfully:

> There's a way in which I see my parents as my parents, but sometimes I look at them, and I see two white American people that are so different from me that I can't fathom how we are related to each other and how it could be possible that these two people could be my parents. When they adopted me they really accepted me as their child, and I really became a part of their family. Even though I wasn't related to them by blood it was as if I had been born to them somehow. As a child I accepted them as my parents because I depended on them for survival. But as an adult I think that I haven't accepted them as my parents, and I think that's part of the distance I've been feeling with them for a lot of years.

Because of their racial difference, Borshay Liem cannot "fathom" how she could be "related" to "two white American people." This tear-filled admission conjures the repressed specter of racial difference and complicates facile and idealistic attempts to reconfigure kinship beyond the ties of blood. Indeed, because of such racial estrangements, there is in transracial adoption, as Dorow observes, "an oblique return of biologism to the racialization of 'different types of human bodies' . . . because . . . race doubles as an expression of biological difference between parent and child."[75] This biological difference, made visible as racial difference, also signals different racialized experiences, treatment, identifications, and hierarchies for parent(s) and child.

In giving voice to and displaying the ruptures of racial estrangement, what Borshay Liem calls a "distance," *First Person Plural* interrogates the ideological labor—of reproducing the white heteronormative nuclear family ideal and mediating domestic black-white race relations—that the transracial adoptee presumably provides. As an adult, Borshay Liem refuses to be sutured to and to enable the social reproduction of the white heteronormative nuclear family ideal. Through this refusal, and indeed through the very making of her documentary, she explodes this ideal rather than consolidating it. She refuses to perform the ideological labor prescribed for her. Stereotypes of Asian female filial piety (even as the Asian child's very adoption removes her from the culture that presumably inculcates such piety), the related trope of Asian Americans as the "model minority" in the United States, and patriarchal protocols in Asia overdetermine the desirability and availability of Asian female babies.[76] Such a high demand for Asian female babies is linked to the gross overrepresentation of African American children within the child protective system, in foster care, or waiting to be adopted. On the one hand, this is a result of racism in the child welfare system, a racism that denies, in many instances, the right of African American parents to *parent* their children. Yet as Dorothy Roberts observes, the debate over domestic transracial adoption obscures this reason, the reason why there are so many African American children waiting to be adopted in the first place.[77] On the other hand, the National Association of Black Social Workers' controversial 1972 position against whites adopting black children was never enacted as law, and the federal 1994 Multiethnic Placement Act and its 1996 amendment the Interethnic Adoption Provisions provide against the consideration of race in domestic adoption practices. That is, the acts render "race-matching" illegal and thus in effect promote transracial adoption. African American children are not "model minority" transracial adoptees in the way that Asian babies are. Indeed, in recent high-profile cases such as those of Madonna and Angelina Jolie, when black babies have been adopted, they have been from Africa. African *American* children are being adopted abroad because of a shortage of adoptive parents in the United States willing to adopt them.[78]

The social reproduction of the white heteronormative bourgeois nuclear family ideal was especially prescriptive before the advent of more recent practices of "open adoption" and the "politically correct" attentiveness to the child's different national, racial, and cultural background. For social orphans like Borshay Liem who were adopted in this previous period, their forced migration to America also meant a forced cultural Americanization. This rapid assimilation, and the denial and repression of her true family history and identity, produce an unmourned, indeed an unmournable, loss for Borshay Liem. It is a loss that cannot be mourned precisely because her adoptive family not only refuses to acknowledge or even simply investigate her true family history and identity (and the fraud committed by the adoption agency), but also because the Borshays cannot fathom that their affective *gain* derived through the joys of having Deann as their daughter and raising her, and the material comforts that Deann herself gains by joining a middle-class American family, come at the price of a great affective or psychic *loss* for Deann. Deann confesses:

> I think being adopted into my family in some ways brought a lot of happiness both for me and for my parents, my American family. But there was also something that was ... [t]here was also a lot of sadness that I think that we couldn't deal with as a family. And a lot of that sadness had to do with loss. I was never able to mourn what I had lost with my American parents.

It is precisely this conundrum, this repression of her loss, that causes her such pain: "I *belonged only* to my American parents. It meant that I didn't have a Korean history or a Korean identity. For a long time I couldn't talk to my American parents about my Korean family because I felt like I was somehow being disloyal to them." Upon arriving in America, while she vows never to forget Korea, she ultimately forgets everything, including her real name. While she confesses her true identity to Alveen as soon as she learns enough English, Alveen dismisses the story as "just bad dreams" that will soon go away. This denial, the "unspoken contract" that Deann was an "orphan with no family ties to Korea," along with rapid assimilation or Americanization (complete with a plethora of white dolls, becoming a cheerleader, and being elected class president as well as prom queen in high school), relegates her memories of Korea to the "category of dreams."

Korea thus becomes the site of denial and repression, and not surprisingly, what Borshay Liem has repressed returns to her when she moves away from home. Ghosts visit, and dreams return. Borshay Liem experiences a period of what she calls depression, and gradually realizes that her dreams must actually be memories of Korea coming back to her. Thus, she tells her viewers, "I was beginning to unravel the mysteries of my past." A significant part of this unraveling constitutes a contextualization of her personal past within Korea's national past. Indeed, what ensues immediately after her revelation that she was beginning to unravel the mysteries of her past is a voiceover (paired with archival film footage of the Korean War and its aftermath) providing an abridged historicization of the conditions of possibility for her adoption. It is worth quoting at length:

> The Korean War ended in 1953, leaving the country devastated. A huge international relief effort began, aimed at helping thousands of destitute families and orphans. In 1955, Harry Holt began a small rescue operation of children orphaned by the war. Tens of thousands of orphans were subsequently sent overseas for adoption by American and European families. As the years passed, the South Korean government began rebuilding the country, but there was no plan to deal with widespread poverty, orphans, or families in need. Even though the war was long over, the number of orphans and orphanages continued to multiply. The more children orphanages had, the more money they received from abroad. By the 1960s when I was adopted, the government was expediting overseas adoptions at an unprecedented rate. What Harry Holt began as a humanitarian gesture right after the war became big business in the decades that followed. South Korea became the largest supplier of children to developed countries in the world, causing some to argue that the country's economic miracle was due in part to the export of its most precious natural resource—its children. In 1965, the adoption procedure for Cha Jung Hee was completed. My [adoptive] parents signed the papers and sent money to the adoption agency in Korea. One month before Cha Jung Hee was scheduled to go to the U.S., her father found her at the Sun Duck orphanage and took her home. Cha Jung Hee was no longer available for adoption. Assuming no one would notice, the adoption agency falsified her paperwork, and I was sent in her place. I had been given a history and an identity that didn't belong to me.

Significantly, the first wave of South Korean transracial adoptions was of abandoned mixed-race GI babies, many of whom were adopted by American military families. The American military, then, at once gives birth to, abandons, and adopts its Korean offspring. Just as we saw in *Memories of My*

Ghost Brother with the formation of military brides being critically linked to the U.S. military presence in South Korea, here we see in *First Person Plural* transracial adoption being critically linked to the Korean War and the political economy of the Cold War. This global economy, spearheaded by the United States, shaped South Korea into an export-led economy that left no room for social services and produced a modernization project with a host of brutal contradictions.[79] Within this economy, children became one of Korea's many exports, and Kang Ok Jin, passed off as Cha Jung Hee and renamed Deann Borshay, became one of them. Indeed, as articulated by Borshay Liem in the voiceover above, "South Korea became the largest supplier of children to developed countries in the world," and its "economic miracle" was underwritten significantly by "the export of its most precious natural resource— its children." We see again, as we saw in *Memories of My Ghost Brother,* a "bartering" of children, this time as a form of natural resource extraction and exportation. Within this nation-to-nation bartering of children, we also see multiple complicities at work, complicities that make visible the manifold role of the state in producing, on the one hand, the *social* orphan through brutal economic and social welfare policies with uneven gendered effects, and the *legal* orphan through juridical procedures, on the other.[80] These layered complicities include: U.S. global capitalism, Korean cooperation and collaboration with that capitalism, and in more recent decades, the shifting politics of gender, motherhood, and reproduction in the United States that have led to such developments as the legalization of abortion, delayed motherhood for professional women, and a broadening of reproductive and

In the wake of the Korean War, "orphaned" Korean children board a plane for adoption in America and Europe.

Korea's "precious natural resource."

parenting possibilities (including single motherhood, same-sex parenting, etc.). As I discussed earlier, these complicities are further implicated with domestic racial politics in the United States.

By providing this critical context, *First Person Plural* allows us to see transnational, transracial adoption as a type of forced migration, one among a succession of forced migrations of people from the global, postcolonial South and East to the dominant North and West. In the past fifty years, transracial adoption has been responsible for the migration of almost half a million children to Western countries.[81] The geopolitics of the Korean War and subsequent Cold War policies impelled Borshay Liem's Korean birth mother to give her up for adoption, entering Borshay Liem into the growing ranks of "social orphans" where at least one biological parent is alive but cannot bear the burden of continuing to care for the child's precarious life. Indeed, the term "orphan," precisely because it is so rhetorically powerful, acts as a legal fiction that obscures the material reasons why so many children in regions throughout the world—particularly those facing a U.S. military or missionary presence—are socially orphaned or made available for adoption

in the first place. In countries such as Korea, the "production of the legal
orphan" involves removing the orphan from the family registry, placing her
into an orphan registry, and stripping her of Korean citizenship. Eleana Kim
writes that through "[t]his disembedding of the child from a normative kinship structure and its legal reinscription as a peculiar and exceptional state
subject," the orphan "becomes a person with the barest of social identities,
and in the context of Korean cultural norms, she lacks the basic requirements
of social personhood—namely, family lineage and genealogical history."[82]
As such, we can say that the legal production of the orphan renders a social
death to the orphan, whose formal adoption into the United States—which
itself engenders more irreconcilable contradictions and losses—does not necessarily constitute or lead to a complete reversal of this social death.

Moreover, as Christine Ward Gailey notes, through this legal sleight of
hand, birth parents also become "socially dead" or rendered invisible and
nonexistent, allaying the fears of adoptive parents that birth parents might
reclaim their child or that adult adoptees might later "reclaim" their birth
parents.[83] While Gailey thus registers social death at the level of recognition,
especially in terms of the law, I would also stress that this necessary social
death of the birth parents also functions to cover over—even as it is intricately linked to—the material conditions of possibility for the making of the
"social orphan" who is transnationally and transracially adopted into the
United States. That is, the confluence of forces that makes it disproportionately difficult for racialized birth mothers to exercise the right to keep or
parent their children and to then give up their children to strangers (as opposed to their extended kin or friends) itself constitutes a social death for
such mothers. These forces include, but are not limited to, the multiple dislocations related to imperialism, war, poverty, sexual and gendered violence,
racism, sexism, disruption of local social networks, resources, and institutions,
and so forth. Today, such imperialist violences and uneven global economies
continue to produce a "supply" of children, especially female babies of color,
for "consumption" by the West and privileged classes worldwide, thus constituting a biopolitical regime of global proportions. Indeed, China's one-
child policy, for example, which has tragically resulted in a great number of
abandoned girls who are transnationally and transracially adopted out of
China, has produced social death for many Chinese mothers. Within this
context, Jane Jeong Trenka, Julia Chinyere Oparah, and Sun Yung Shin argue
for an expanded definition of reproductive justice, one that goes beyond issues
relating to abortion, contraception, and sterilization. They write, "we must

work to create and sustain a world in which low-income women of color do not have to send away their children so that the family that remains bequeaths power to some mothers but not to others. . . . It is critical . . . that a real transnational feminist solidarity be created, one that leads women to fight for each others' most basic human rights to parent their own children and that rejects transactions that pit (birth) mother against (adoptive) mother."[84]

I point to the social death of racialized and poor birth mothers, then, not to privilege or reify biological kinship, nor to argue that all mothers should (or should want to) parent their children. Rather, I am indexing a biopolitical regime that disproportionately works against the desires and abilities of birth mothers who *do* wish to parent their children, or *would* wish to do so if their material circumstances were different. This call for transnational reproductive justice is particularly urgent in the contemporary context of greater numbers of babies being, as reported in a November/December 2008 *Foreign Policy* article, "systematically bought, coerced, and stolen away from their birth families." Indeed, "Westerners have been sold the myth of a world orphan crisis . . . [but] many of the infants and toddlers being adopted by Western parents today are not orphans at all. . . . There are simply not enough healthy, adoptable infants to meet Western demand—and there's too much Western money in search of children. As a result, many international adoption agencies work not to find homes for needy children but to find children for Western homes." Entitled "The Lie We Love," the article goes on to report how astoundingly easy it is to "manufacture an orphan," to produce "'paper orphans' for lucrative export" by separating children from vulnerable birth mothers who are often "poor, young, unmarried, divorced, or otherwise lacking family protection."[85]

First Person Plural at once works against and reveals the social death of the birth mother. The film gives visibility to the figure of the birth mother, whom we see when Borshay Liem returns to Korea to meet her birth family.[86] If we consider how she has been rendered "socially dead" through the mechanics of erasure and invisibility, and the legal denial of her rights as a mother (whether she has actually relinquished those rights or not), her appearance in the film and Borshay Liem's reclaiming of her function to work against this social death. If, however, we also see her social death as constituted by the material conditions, geopolitical mandates, and biopolitical regimes that make it insurmountably difficult for her to parent her child, her visibility and voice in the film function to explain, critically unpack, and give embodied form to such social death. When Borshay Liem and her adoptive parents visit her birth mother in Korea, she acknowledges her natal alienation from her daughter, explaining to Borshay Liem that although she is Borshay Liem's mother, she only gave birth to her. As such, Borshay Liem should really love and do everything she can for her adoptive parents. Indeed, Borshay Liem's birth mother's emotional pain and regret are visceral and searing as she tearfully explains why she had to take Borshay Liem to an orphanage, and why she finally consented to giving her up. She explains, "If she had lived with me, she wouldn't have been educated. She would have just suffered. At that time, we were very poor. We had to send her to be educated and to have a worthwhile life. Instead, she is filled with endless heartache. So my own heart aches." She goes on to confess the details of the circumstances that compelled her to give up Ok Jin:

> For five years after her father died, I made just enough to feed my children but not enough to send them to school. Next door there was this man who worked at an orphanage. And he said to me, "You can barely feed these five children. . . . Why don't you put the three youngest into the orphanage where I work." I had no idea about such things. So I just followed his suggestion . . . and sent them to the orphanage. After a while the orphanage asked me to give up Ok Jin for adoption. They asked me on three separate occasions, and each time I refused. At the time, I was going to church, and deacons at the church said since I already have three daughters, I should send one to the U.S. to get a better life. . . . I have no words to describe the agonizing years after that . . .

Deann Borshay Liem and her birth mother hug tearfully.

Although mother and daughter were supposed to meet one last time, the adoption agency feared that the mother would change her mind. So Ok Jin/ Deann was sent away ahead of schedule as Cha Jung Hee.

Borshay Liem's critical historical and personal reckoning in *First Person Plural* thus reveals not only the complex racialized and gendered economy of what it means to be a female transracial adoptee from Korea, but it also offers a critical genealogy of what has been observed in the contemporary moment to be the gendered international division of labor and the commodification of racialized and gendered Third World bodies. Increasingly, Third World women and women of color (even in so-called developed economies such as South Korea) are not only forced to provide productive labor, but as birth mothers living in countries that can make it extremely difficult for them to feed and parent their children, they are also providing crucial reproductive labor (literally, in this case) to First World nations. In making this observation, I am not reifying the dichotomy between First and Third Worlds or positing them as internally homogenous, undifferentiated sites. Rather, I am indexing relative levels of geopolitical, economic, and racial power, which have historically condensed and congealed in the United States and (Western) Europe. Within this context, we can speak of a transnational politics of motherhood and care that disrupt normative economies and taken-for-granted familial arrangements. We can speak not only of birth mothers who are compelled to give up their children, but also, for example, of great numbers of Filipinas, many with children, who must go far overseas to places like the Middle East to work as domestics and nannies. In this case, mothers do not

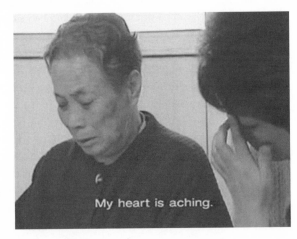

Deann's birth mother.

My heart is aching.

formally give up their children, but must in effect give up their right to parent or raise them directly and seek employment caring for and raising other people's children, precisely so that the remittances they send home will allow them to "keep" their children (alive). *First Person Plural* allows us to connect these contemporary arrangements of labor and care to one another, and to the longer historical genealogies out of which they arise. The figure of the birth mother, hitherto largely absent in adoption discourses, is given voice in the film, and the reproductive labor that she provided back in the 1950s is linked to what Eng argues is the "consumptive labor" provided by her daughter, the transracial adoptee Deann Borshay Liem, whose labor is not exploited as wage labor following Marx, but "serves to produce and organize social community as supplement to capital" in the shift to globalization.[87] On the one hand, she is positioned as the body that is "consumed" in the service of ideologically reproducing the social relations of the white heteronormative nuclear family ideal. On the other hand, she is also now legally incorporated by the South Korean government into the "global family" of Korea and increasingly showcased as a privileged overseas Korean who can act as a cultural and economic bridge and mediator of global capital.[88] However, Borshay Liem attempts to resist such a positioning and appropriation, and reveals the gendered racial excesses and Cold War imperialist histories upon which this consumption and incorporation depend but must be repressed and denied in order for them to maintain their fiction of coherence. One of these enabling fictions, so painfully shattered by *First Person Plural*, is that transracial adoptees are in fact orphans without living parents, and thus need to be "saved" and reconstituted within a normative nuclear family structure. In the following chapter, I discuss another Cold War staging of America's imperialist rescue fantasy: the Vietnam War's Operation Babylift.

In my foregoing analysis of *First Person Plural*, I have made my observations as a means of gesturing toward some of the disturbing links that the current visibility of transnational and transracial adoption actually renders invisible. The forces that compelled Deann Borshay Liem's mother in 1960s Korea to give up her daughter for adoption are intimately linked to the forces that compel an African American mother in twenty-first century America to surrender her child to the "protective" services of the government. And these forces are in turn also linked to the historical reification, emulation, protection, and rewarding of (white) middle-class motherhood. Mothers (and fathers) of color everywhere, here in the United States and the global South, are disproportionately denied their reproductive rights to *parent* their children, and this denial, this social death, constitutes the conditions of possibility for transnational and transracial adoption as a project that attempts to socially reproduce the white heteronormative bourgeois nuclear family ideal.

I have sought in this chapter to show how Korean American cultural productions offer an unsettling hermeneutic of the "balancing acts" of Choi's foreign student, the women of Fenkl's Pupyong camptown, and those of Borshay Liem and her birth mother, by exposing the imperialism and gendered racial formation that have necessitated such acts. From this discussion of America's "Forgotten War" in Korea, I turn in the next chapter to America's hypervisible war in Vietnam. I interrogate the contours of the war's masculinist hypervisibility and analyze how Vietnamese American cultural productions make visible the problematics of representations of America over "there" in Vietnam that fail to reckon with Vietnamese Americans over "here" in the United States.

5

The War-Surplus of Our New Imperialism

Vietnam, Masculinist Hypervisibility, and the Politics of (Af)filiation

It should not surprise anyone that Vietnamese Americans would want to remember amidst all that forgetting. One does not become recognizably human until one acts in one's history. And for that, one needs to have history.... For us, remembering in mourning, in commemoration, in symbolic local politics, is not a symptom of an incessant, pathological return to be cured with assimilationist remedies, but a way in which we can recover our histories which intersect, rather than coincide, with American nationalist history.

> NGUYÊN-VO THU-HUONG, "Forking Paths: How Shall We Mourn the Dead?"

From Hollywood to Hanoi, a personal documentary made by Vietnamese American actress and filmmaker Tiana (Thi Thanh Nga), opens with the following epigraph:

I am neither a communist
nor a nationalist:
I am Vietnamese.
Is it not enough?
For thousands of years
that's what I've been:
Don't you think that's enough?
WHO AM I? by Tru Vu[1]

This articulation of what we could call a poetics of nonalignment rejects the ideologies of both communism and nationalism, and embraces instead a third term—"Vietnamese"—as identity and ontology. In declaring "I am

Vietnamese" and asking "Is it not enough? . . . Don't you think that's enough?" Tru Vu questions the ideologically saturated historical process through which being Vietnamese has precisely been deemed *not* to be enough. That is, "Vietnamese" as sign has been transformed from an unqualified noun into a qualifying adjective, as either Vietnamese communist or Vietnamese nationalist. Vietnamese as such literally cannot stand alone, but must be conjoined with and serve as the predicate for communist or nationalist. Against such logics, Tru Vu remains (simply) "Vietnamese," and has been "For thousands of years." This long genealogy of being Vietnamese signals the relative recentness of communist and nationalist as ideological identifications, identities, and cleaving alignments in Vietnam, and while they have been deemed to be essential or necessary, Tru Vu exposes them as superfluous or excessive. Rather than an ontological lack or incompleteness, being Vietnamese for him signals a long-standing plenitude; it is "enough."

Indeed, following this on-screen epigraph, *From Hollywood to Hanoi* embarks on a cinematic journey of what it means to be Vietnamese through the literal journey of Tiana's first trip(s), starting in 1988, back to Vietnam since leaving for the United States as a young child in 1966. Billed as the first post–Vietnam War American film shot in Vietnam, this "video diary" comments on and makes critical interventions in America's images of the war during and after the event, of how these images have not only overdetermined the event, but have become *the* event. Along the way, to note just some of the film's many interwoven interventions, Tiana makes fun of her acting career playing mostly Orientalist caricatures; questions the absurdity of having to choose between being "Vietnamese" or "American"; satirizes the arrival of American GIs in Vietnam (calling them "saviors" and "red-faced big noses"); reveals the penetration of American capitalism and the dollar—the "real magic weapon"—in Vietnam; dramatizes the pain of family separation and fleeting reunion; shows the pernicious effects of Agent Orange; interviews survivors of the My Lai Massacre; and questions General Westmoreland on camera about his claim that "the Oriental doesn't put the same high price on life as the Westerner."[2] Through these and other interludes, viewers are challenged to see what has previously only existed as the exotic backdrop or inscrutable enemy in shadows: Vietnam and the Vietnamese. The dislocations, dissonances, and profound contradictions wrought by America's protracted imperialist war in Vietnam and its ever more protracted legacies are thus finally filmically captured from the perspective of a Vietnamese American in the late 1980s and early '90s.

Vietnamese American cultural productions such as *From Hollywood to Hanoi* critically display the problematics of what I am calling the masculinist hypervisibility of American representations of the Vietnam War. The Vietnam War or so-called "conflict" is perhaps America's most debated and protracted Cold War project of empire and gendered racial formation in Asia. It is a war that the United States would like to forget but by which it is persistently haunted. Since the war, Americans have been obsessively representing it in a variety of sites as an attempt to make sense of, or repress, the defeat of America's military and technological superiority by a small, poor nation. Yet in the end, what is actually revealed about this defeat, the defeated, and the defeaters? And is the defeat even acknowledged as such? Indeed, America's repetition compulsion symptomizes an inability to come to terms with its protracted war in Vietnam. Rick Berg and John Carlos Rowe write:

> We are obsessed with the trauma and injury we have suffered, as if the United States, not Vietnam and Kampuchea [Cambodia], were the country to suffer the bombings, the napalm air strikes, the search-and-destroy mission, the systematic deforestation, the "hamlet resettlement" programs. The cultural and economic means by which we have commodified Vietnam have been our means of keeping silent about the political and historical realities of our involvement in western imperialism. And yet these same means of imagining Vietnam as the mirror we hold up to ourselves, as the searching, critical "self-image" of our collective failure as a democratic people, are themselves the essence of the new brand of imperialism that we continue to sell in the furthest reaches of the world. . . . When we failed to sell America to the Vietnamese, we tried to sell Vietnam to America. *That* Vietnam is the war-surplus of our new imperialism, and it should hardly surprise us that it has virtually nothing to tell us of Vietnamese history, culture, and politics.[3]

More recently, this repetition compulsion in the terrain of culture, this "new brand of imperialism," has exploded in a repetition compulsion in the literal geographic terrain of nations such as Iraq, who are experiencing similar and tragically uncanny acts of U.S. military aggression.

In this chapter, I argue that Vietnamese American cultural productions critically disarticulate the masculinist hypervisibility of the Vietnam War, the "war-surplus of our new imperialism," in America's popular imaginary, imperial memory, and Cold War epistemology. They challenge that masculinist hypervisibility and production of knowledge, most (in)famously conjured in such films as *Platoon* and the Rambo series,[4] by displaying the complicated "return" of Vietnamese subjects (whether as "refugees" or adopted "orphans") to the American metropole, and by privileging the heretofore displaced subjectivity of Vietnamese people. In particular, I examine the PBS documentary *Daughter from Danang,* Aimee Phan's short story collection *We Should Never Meet,* and Trinh T. Minh-ha's experimental feature-length film *Surname Viet Given Name Nam.*[5] I analyze the complex ways in which these cultural forms show a Vietnam that is different from America's Vietnam. Moreover, these works ask how the masculinist hypervisibility of representations of America over "there" in Vietnam fails to reckon with Vietnamese Americans over "here" in the United States. In this instance, then, visibility is neither some teleological endpoint of political recognition or empowerment nor transparent access to "knowledge" about the Vietnam War, but a persistent problematic and preoccupying symptom that reveals America's anxieties about its defeat. The imperialist, masculinist, and racist thrust of that very war, defeat, and knowledge project might at times erupt in these anxieties, but are not adequately accounted for, acknowledged, or resolved. In the following section, I situate my analysis of Vietnamese American cultural productions in this chapter with a discussion of the imperialist and gendered racial logics that figure not only the cultural or representational terrain of America's Vietnam, but the driving force of such logics in the war or military intervention itself. How do "Vietnam" and the "Vietnamese" get produced as a discursive imperialist and gendered racial formation, and how does this production get "militarized" through and during the war?

"Kill Them All! Let God Sort Them Out!"

Beginning in early 1950, with a financial commitment to the French in its war to keep its Indochinese colonial territory,[6] and a rejection of the North Vietnamese offer to negotiate in August 1964, by the time Saigon fell to North Vietnamese forces on April 30, 1975, America's Vietnam War had escalated to one ton of bombs dropped for every minute Nixon was in office, $150 billion spent between 1954 and 1975, a deployment of 2.7 million servicemen, and the dropping a total of 10 million tons of bombs.[7] Such figures, while astonishing in and of themselves, cannot of course account for the great many lives lost and the even greater number of lives displaced and irreparably altered, on all sides.[8] Nor can such figures, beyond their sheer enormity, tell us how America's Vietnam War, given unique visibility as the nation's first "televised" war, was not unprecedented in its imperialist and gendered racial logics. Indeed, such logics find a long-standing genealogy coeval with the very formation of the United States through continental and extracontinental conquest.

I shall begin, then, with America's other notorious war in Asia, notorious but, unlike Vietnam, an object of enduring historical amnesia until recently. I speak of a notable moment in the strange career of American imperialism: the onset and conclusion in 1898 of the Spanish–American War, which resulted in the United States seizing Guam, Puerto Rico, and the Philippines, and gaining great control over Cuba. The United States waged a genocidal war of conquest in the Philippines, deploying tactics carried over from the so-called Indian Wars or conquest of Native Americans. The ensuing period of U.S. colonization of the Philippines, which lasted until the end of World War II, would prefigure American perceptions of the Vietnamese and provide the positive example against which the United States would critique the ineffectiveness of French colonial rule in Indochina. Indeed, on many occasions during World War II, President Roosevelt evoked the Philippine analogy as a telos of both successful, effective colonial administration and eventual independence. For example, in a November 1942 radio address on American policy vis-à-vis colonial territories, he argued: "I like to think that the history of the Philippine islands . . . provides . . . a pattern for the future of other small nations and peoples of the world. It is a pattern of what men of good-will look forward to in the future—a pattern of global civilization."[9] American colonization of the Philippines informed in particular Roosevelt's vision for a postwar trusteeship in Vietnam and its timetable. Within his teleological scheme, a protracted period of colonization and trusteeship are held out as the necessary preconditions and preparations for eventual independence. On his return trip from the Yalta Conference in 1945, he told a group of accompanying reporters, "The situation there [in Indochina] is a good deal like the Philippines were in 1898. It took fifty years for us to . . . educate them for self-government."[10] In interpreting the Indochinese situation via the imperialist and racialized patronizing logic through which Filipinos, America's "little brown brothers," had been "benevolently assimilated" into the universality of American democratic ideals, Roosevelt exhumes America's imperialist past in order to rewrite it as a telos of Asian independence.

Although Vietnam and Southeast Asia would take on new *strategic* importance for the United States as Cold War geopolitics became triangulated in Asia and played out in ways that were at once acute and chronic, the imperialist, gendered racial, and cultural logics that would play a key role in America's

conduct of the Vietnam War long predated that war. Indeed, Roosevelt's repeated use of the Philippine analogy during World War II is determined not
only by the contours of America's long period of colonial rule in the Philippines, but is overdetermined and prefigured by (and also articulated with) a
long-standing French and European Orientalist discourse of Indochinese/
Vietnamese primitivism and immutability. This discourse gained visibility
in the United States and would inform U.S. accounts of the Vietnamese in
the years between the two world wars. In these accounts, the Vietnamese are
commonly described as "lazy," "primitive," "liars," "effeminate," lacking in
"ambition," and their country as a fossilized "little China." In notably gendered terms, Vietnamese men are seen as weak, possessing a "puerile vanity,"
and Vietnamese literature is noted for its "conspicuous absence of epic viril-
ity."[11] Within the logics of such a discursive scheme, Air Force General Curtis
LeMay's famous injunction during the Vietnam War that "We should bomb
them into the Stone Age" is at once disturbingly unsurprising and oddly
anachronistic or redundant, for wasn't "primitive" Vietnam deemed to be
already in the Stone Age, or some age close to it?[12] Thus, while geopolitical
and strategic considerations were certainly significant in driving American
military intervention in Vietnam, this imperialist and gendered racial cultural logic also helped to shape American policy in crucial ways.

In the years immediately leading up to and during the Vietnam War, this
cultural imaginary lent shape to an unfortunate series of conflations made
by the United States that effaced Vietnamese agency and resulted in the killing
of so many Vietnamese, including civilians, during the war. First, we see how
Vietnam is conflated with China, recalling the previous designation of Vietnam as a fossilized "little China." A member of the Policy Planning Research
Staff, for example, when asked if the Vietnamese had resisted French colonial rule, replied, "These areas had been protectorates of China and it was . . .
from the Chinese that the main objections had come."[13] As China increasingly displaced the Soviet Union as America's principal Cold War enemy in
Asia, American policy makers tended to conflate Vietnamese and Chinese
communists. Indeed, as the war in Vietnam escalated with "Rolling Thun-
der" (the systematic, long-term bombing campaign against North Vietnam)
and with the official introduction of ground combat troops in 1965, President Johnson explained in a speech at Johns Hopkins University that "over
this war—and all Asia—is another reality: the deepening shadow of Communist China."[14] This prompted LeMay to then propose that the United States

solve the problem by "nuking the Chinks."[15] The United States had already, of course, "nuked" the Japanese, and the possibility of dropping another atomic bomb on an Asian nation had also been brought up by Truman during the Korean War. At the same time, however, we also see a distinction being made between the Chinese and Vietnamese communists. While there was a shift in the perception of Chinese communists—from "unaggressive, nonmechanical, and unmartial" "comic opera warriors" to "excellent soldiers"—in the wake of their participation in the Korean War, a similar shift in the assessment of Vietnamese communists does not take place, despite much evidence suggesting their military strength and strategic sophistication.[16] Whether differentiated or conflated, though, what remains constant is a denial of Vietnamese agency. In another disturbing conflation, this denial of agency and full humanity would extend during the war to the South Vietnamese, the United States' ostensible allies and for whom the United States putatively fought the war. Novelist and veteran Philip Caputo explains, "Our mission was not to win terrain or seize positions, but simply to kill: to kill Communists [ideally, but] . . . '[i]f it's dead and Vietnamese, it's VC,' was a rule of thumb in the bush."[17] This fatal conflation, and the perception that all Vietnamese (and all Asians, for that matter) are "gooks," began in basic training, and American soldiers were also taught that in a guerilla war, women and children were also potential enemy "gooks" and should be engaged as such. In a further conflation, "gooks" also included Asian *Americans,* some of whom fought in the war. Scott Shimabakuro, a Japanese American GI, recalls his sergeant telling him not to marry his Vietnamese girlfriend "because she was a gook, which struck [him] as kind of funny because [he] was a gook also."[18] Thomas Borstelmann writes, "There was increasing slippage between 'Americans' and 'gooks': the former mostly killed, but sometimes married and sometimes even *were,* the latter."[19]

In analyzing how "race remained to the very end a powerful yet ambiguous category for American thinking and behavior in Vietnam," structuring not only U.S.–Vietnam relations but interracial relations among differently racialized American GIs, Borstelmann interrogates the "quagmire" metaphor, noting how this troping of Vietnam itself, its land(scape), revealed and furthered a conflation of Vietnamese allies and enemies. He writes:

> Reimagining American forces as bogged down in some form of quicksand allowed the land of Vietnam itself to be seen as the treacherous aggressor and the Americans there as its victims. In this construction, not only the real American

role in the war but also the actual Vietnamese people disappeared from the story. There was a parallel here to Africa, where the indigenous people were equally obscure to most Americans, and the landscape stood out as dark and perilous jungle—or, in the words of Undersecretary of State George Ball, "the African swamp" that the United States "should not get bogged down in."[20]

Within this racialized terrain—the metaphor of the quagmire, coupled with the image of the "gook" and its other meaning as liquid slime—there was a growing tendency to see all Vietnamese, and not just the North Vietnamese army, as the enemy. This was made startlingly clear in such incidents as the My Lai Massacre of civilians, largely women and children. It was also made startlingly clear on a T-shirt favored by some American troops: "Kill Them All! Let God Sort Them Out!"[21]

Such a genocidal injunction to "Kill Them All!" was not unique to the Vietnam War. As I have noted, the racial logics of the Vietnam War find a long-standing genealogy, for example, in Roosevelt's World War II ruminations on the links between a colonized Southeast Asia and U.S. colonialism in the Philippines. Indeed, the U.S. colonial conquest of the Philippines had itself been informed by and conducted through a racialized dichotomy between "civilized and savage war."[22] According to this dichotomy, Filipinos engaged in guerilla warfare and flouted the civilized laws of war not because of ignorance or strategic considerations, but because they were a savage race. Paul A. Kramer writes that race, the racialization of guerilla warfare in particular, "became the sanction for exterminist war, the means by which earlier distinctions between combatants and noncombatants—already fragile—eroded or collapsed."[23] This logic was repeated in Vietnam, with the racialization of guerilla warfare serving yet again as the rationale for the genocidal injunction to "Kill Them All!" Moreover, the tactics of nineteenth-century "Indian Removal" in the United States, which had also informed the U.S. conquest of the Philippines at the turn of the twentieth century, would get projected onto another Asian site, this time at the latter half of the twentieth century. Indeed, as Thomas J. McCormick observes, the "Strategic Hamlet" program in South Vietnam, which removed peasant families and even whole villages and resettled them in "larger, more defendable arrangements sometimes little better than concentration camps," was "reminiscent of nineteenth-century Indian removal and reservation resettlement." This program, carried out in the name of village protection, was actually a means of separating "rebels" from their potential peasant support.[24] The mantra, then, that "We had to destroy the village in order to save it," echoed, as David Trask notes, the logic of late nineteenth-century "Friends of the Indian," who argued that off-reservation Indian education was effective in creating citizens out of the "nation's wards." The mantra guiding their program was the need to "Kill the Indian to save the man." In Vietnam, "the soldiers themselves conjured the spirit of the nineteenth century when they labeled the areas beyond fortified compounds as 'Indian Country.'"[25] Military operations were called "Daniel Boone," "Cochise," and "Crazy Horse," while going on patrol was "playing cowboys and Indians."[26] Yet in recent years, following the normalization of relations between the United States and Vietnam and within the context of a signed 2006 agreement between these nations formerly at war with one another to "increase military contacts" and "defense cooperation," this logic of racial and developmental equivalence finds an apparent rupture. On his first trip to Hanoi as Secretary of Defense, Donald Rumsfeld extolled Vietnam's cultural heritage and its economic success, claiming upon visiting the Temple of Literature that when it was built in the eleventh century, "American Indians were still living in 'mud huts.'"[27] This comment might seem to "take back" or reverse the previous wartime designation of Vietnam as "Indian Country." However, it actually resuscitates the designation, and displays the extent to which U.S. imperial logics and temporalities rely on a racialized civilizational and developmental narrative. While in this recent articulation Rumsfeld holds Vietnam in opposition to "Indians," what remains the same is that they are still compared to each other along a developmental continuum.

The invisibility of the North and South Vietnamese—even as so many enemies and allies alike were being killed in free fire and friendly fire zones—configured not only how the Vietnam War was conducted, but would later be represented in various cultural sites. This erasure and displacement of Vietnamese agency, subjectivity, and presence can be traced through the reigning tropes of American images of the Vietnam War. Katherine Kinney, for example, contends that solipsistic narratives of friendly fire—Americans killing Americans, or the idea that Americans fought themselves—is "virtually the only story that has been told by Americans about the Vietnam War . . . the image of friendly fire, the death of one American at the hands of another, structures the plotting of both realist gestures toward 'what really happened' in Vietnam and symbolic expressions of what Vietnam meant. . . . Americans are portrayed as the victims of their own ideals, practices, and beliefs."[28] In a similar vein, Susan Jeffords argues that such representations are only topically about the war. The driving narrative is really the masculine response to changing gender relations in which the "feminine" is cast as the "enemy" to be conquered and overpowered.[29] Milton J. Bates argues, moreover, that the "sex war" is only one among "the wars we took to Vietnam," which also include the domestic frontier, race, class, and generational wars.[30] Marita Sturken discusses how America remembers the Vietnam War, particularly through sites such as the Vietnam Veterans Memorial. She emphasizes the dialectics of memory and argues that remembering and forgetting are not opposites but rather "co-constitutive processes; each is essential to the other's existence." Indeed, "[a]ll memories are 'created' in tandem with forgetting; to remember everything would amount to being overwhelmed by memory. Forgetting is a necessary component in the construction of memory. Yet the forgetting of the past in a culture is often highly organized and strategic."[31] This construction of memory, actually enabled by an organized and strategic forgetting, allows an active scripting and rescripting of the war. Attempts to "heal" through such sites as the Vietnam Veterans Memorial and the discussions surrounding them are structured by the forgetting of the Vietnamese people. Sturken notes that "they cannot even be mentioned," for the memorial is not a memorial to *their* loss.[32] Furthermore, such (re)scriptings of the war transform the healing process into a spectacle and commodity, contributing to and constituting what she calls a "Vietnam War nostalgia industry,"[33] or what Berg and Rowe index as the "war-surplus of our new imperialism" in the passage I cited earlier. I call this representational matrix, so complexly analyzed by the scholars I have noted, the masculinist hypervisibility of the Vietnam War in America's imperialist and gendered racial imaginary, and ask in this chapter how Vietnamese Americans—the very population produced by the war—show different ways of imagining.

"I Just Don't Know"

I shall begin my analysis, then, with a pair of works that gives visibility to transnational and transracial Vietnamese adoptees in the United States, a population largely invisible within both hegemonic American Vietnam War images and Vietnamese American discourses. The PBS documentary *Daughter from Danang* and Aimee Phan's short story collection *We Should Never Meet* offer an unsparing and unsettling hermeneutic of America's war in Vietnam by focusing on Operation Babylift, launched by the U.S. government in 1975 to fly more than two thousand Vietnamese (mostly mixed-race or "Amerasian") orphans out of Vietnam for adoption by American families. What became of these children? *Daughter from Danang* and *We Should Never*

Meet reveal the troubling pasts and presents of what, as I cited in the previous chapter, Toby Alice Volkman calls "new geographies of kinship" that are formed through transnational adoption.[34] These works compel us to recognize that such "new" transnational and transracial geographies of kinship find an "old" genealogy in America's Cold War in Asia, dating back to the aftermath of the atomic bombings of Hiroshima and Nagasaki, heightened during the Korean War, and continuing in Vietnam and its aftermath. While *First Person Plural* displays the formation of a "new geography of kinship" and the subsequent disidentification with that kinship by Deann Borshay Liem, *Daughter from Danang* and *We Should Never Meet* display how a newly reconfigured kinship might be foreclosed altogether, and might not thus be a formation that results from or is guaranteed by transnational adoption.

On April 2, 1975, President Ford announced that $2 million would be directed from the Special Foreign Aid Children's Fund to fly two thousand South Vietnamese orphans as soon as possible to the United States for adoption by American families. Many critiqued what came to be called Operation Babylift as one last desperate publicity ploy or photo opportunity to gain sympathy and thus more funding for the war.[35] Indeed, Ford flew from Washington, D.C., to San Francisco to meet one of the planes from Vietnam and was photographed carrying a baby off the plane. Tragically, the first U.S. government plane (actually a cargo plane) flying the babies out of Saigon crashed within minutes after take-off due to equipment malfunction, killing 134 of the 330 on board.[36] In the ensuing four weeks, more than two thousand children boarded nineteen flights bound mostly for the United States, but also for Europe and Australia. It was later discovered that many of the children were not orphans at all, and about two hundred were later reclaimed by their Vietnamese families, who had subsequently immigrated to the United States. Operation Babylift represents, then, at once a special campaign in the Vietnam War, a militarized case of transnational adoption, a tragic plane crash, and to some a mass kidnapping of Vietnamese babies by the U.S. government—what could be called "Operation Babysteal." It provokes the mantra that "First you destroy our country, and then you rescue our children."[37] While Operation Babylift was very much a public or *overt* campaign in the closing days of the Vietnam War, such a Cold War "operation" involving the coordinated transfer of children finds a *covert* antecedent in the CIA-backed Operation Peter Pan, a clandestine scheme through which fourteen thousand unaccompanied Cuban children were brought to Miami between 1960 and 1962. Cuban parents were pressured to send their children through such tactics as CIA-sponsored propaganda that the new Cuban revolutionary government would strip parents of their parental rights and "nationalize" Cuba's children. Horrific rumors led parents to believe that their children would be sent to the Soviet Union for indoctrination or harsh labor, or that they would be eaten (!). As Cold War tensions heightened between the United States and Cuba, these parents and children could not be reunited. Many of the children, placed in long-term foster care and orphanages throughout the United States, spent their childhoods "as miniature icons of anticommunism, appearing at American Legions and Catholic church functions, for example, to narrate their story as an anti-Castro parable."[38] Forty years later, one of these "Peter Pan" children, Republican Mel Martinez of Florida, became a U.S. Senator, and not surprisingly he used his story of the "escape from communism" to link the Cold War to the "War on Terror" in Iraq and Afghanistan.

The critically acclaimed documentary *Daughter from Danang* offers an unsparing and unsettling hermeneutic of America's war in Vietnam by focusing on Operation Babylift.[39] While *First Person Plural*, as I discussed in the

Operation Babylift babies onboard a U.S. government cargo plane (from *Daughter from Danang*, 2002).

Visibly upset Operation Babylift children on plane.

previous chapter, displays the formation of a new geography of kinship and the subsequent disidentification with that kinship by Deann Borshay Liem, *Daughter from Danang* displays how a newly reconfigured kinship might be foreclosed altogether. If, as I have been arguing throughout this book, the Cold War is a knowledge project saturated with America's imperial and gendered racial projections of Asia, this project dialectically generates in turn the Cold War subject's—in this case the mixed-race or "Amerasian" Vietnamese transnational adoptee's—own formations of knowing and unknowing. This process is overdetermined by psychic economies of loss and yearning, and it is precisely this overdetermination that emerges in *Daughter from Danang* as an epistemological conundrum or problem of knowledge. As her trip (back) to Vietnam shatters all her expectations, Heidi Bub (née Mai Thi Hiep) experiences an emotional breakdown, yet that breakdown, and the decisions she makes thereafter, can only be explained through a discursive economy of distinguishing what she "knows" from what she "doesn't know." Indeed, in a film bursting with affect and emotion—literally overflowing with tears—

President Ford carries an Operation Babylift baby off a plane in San Francisco.

this recourse to "rational" knowing and unknowing is painfully disjunctive, but is mobilized by Bub to contain her emotions and rationalize her actions. Thus, while the film's directors Gail Dolgin and Vicente Franco have been rightly criticized by Gregory Paul Choy and Catherine Ceniza Choy for turning what could have been a critical collective history of the "political, social, and economic contexts of international adoption" into "an individual West-meets-East story of culture clash," and for compromising Bub's "integrity" in the process, my analysis reads against the grain of the film's trope of "culture clash" as a problem of individual naiveté or selfishness on Bub's part.[40] Rather, I argue that the irreconcilable collisions (which cannot be reduced to "culture clash") and limits of knowledge (which cannot be reduced to "naiveté") in the film symptomize the uneven, indeed disparate, geopolitical and racial economies and terrains traversed by Bub and her Vietnamese birth mother, Mai Thi Kim. While Bub's experience is singular, and while the film attempts to frame her story through the reigning trope of "culture clash" as an individuated, privatized family melodrama, *Daughter from Danang* also reveals how a transnational and transracial adoption such as Bub's is a kind of lingering collective imperial violence that refuses to be assimilated within or sutured to contemporary discourses of "healing" and reconciliation in the prolonged aftermath of America's war in Vietnam.

Daughter from Danang begins with a layered montage that situates Mai Thi Kim's difficult decision to give up her daughter, and Bub's vivid memories of her separation from her mother, within the context of the Vietnam War. The voices and images of mother and daughter are intertwined with documentary footage of the war and specifically of Operation Babylift. What is soon revealed is that Operation Babylift was not solely or necessarily a humanitarian mission representing a departure from an otherwise bloody, imperialist war, but rather a convergence of a variety of racialized and militarized imperialisms driving America's (and Europe's) multiple campaigns in Vietnam. In giving visibility to the birth mother, Mai Thi Kim, *Daughter from Danang* intervenes in a discursive and representational field in which birth mothers are often invisible or only spectrally visible, since adoptees, after all, are presumed to be "orphans." As with the appearance of Deann Borshay Liem's birth mother in *First Person Plural,* Mai Thi Kim's appearance works at once against her social death and makes it visible. Instead of appearing in the film at the moment when Bub meets her in Vietnam, Mai appears in the very opening sequence of the film, before Bub does, and lingers beyond Bub's departure from Vietnam. Throughout, the film provides alternating perspectives of mother and daughter. As such, it suggests that the story of the "daughter from Danang" cannot be told without also simultaneously privileging the story of the "mother from Danang," the mother who was compelled to give up her daughter. Indeed, the film opens with stock footage of the war, but immediately following this is Mai's on camera testimonial. She explains, "There were so many rumors, I was so frightened. If I didn't send my child away both she and I would die." This anticipates and responds to what follows it, Bub's question: "How could you give up a child like that?" Such a reversal, of posing the answer before the question, is one of many reversals shown in the film. Mai goes on to reveal that after her Vietnamese husband left to join the North Vietnamese Army, she was compelled to work at a U.S. military base, where she met the white American GI with whom she would have an extramarital relationship. He leaves four months after Mai becomes pregnant with Bub. Struggling to feed her family within the precarious confines of a wartime economy, subsisting in effect as a single mother in the absence of both her Vietnamese husband and Bub's biological father, and scared by rumors that the Viet Cong would burn mixed-race babies, Mai decides to give her daughter Mai Thi Hiep up to Operation Babylift.

If I didn't send my child away, both she and I would die.

Mai Thi Kim, Heidi Bub's birth mother, explains why she had to give Heidi up for adoption.

In these opening scenes, directors Dolgin and Franco critically account for the militarized, imperialist, and gendered racial Cold War conditions of possibility for such transnational and transracial adoptions as that of Heidi Bub. In what could be described as a sentimental imperialism articulated with and taking place amid a militarized imperialism, we see America's long-standing history of what, as I cited in the previous chapter, Laura Briggs calls a "secular salvation theology" condensing around the figure of the Vietnamese "war orphan."[41] In one particularly disturbing interlude, we see a white American female volunteer social worker, who represents a U.S. adoption agency, attempting to persuade and pressure a young Vietnamese mother into giving up her toddler son for adoption. She insists, "You can help me if you know people who are poor, who cannot take care of their children, their mixed children. I would like to help them. I'm not taking [the babies] away from [the parents]. . . . I'm sending them to good families. Tell them, because I can take their children and send them to America and it's better for everyone. . . . Can I take him, can I take him [to the] United States?" When the

how could I find my child in the future?

An American volunteer worker convinces a Vietnamese mother to send her child to the United States.

Vietnamese mother responds in the negative, the volunteer worker says, "Oh ... you think, you think about it because he saw me take other boy, other boy very happy, very happy." Ultimately, the Vietnamese mother relents, and is told that she has done a "good thing" for her son and should be "proud." Like many other Vietnamese mothers, she relented without necessarily signing official documents, and only after being told that the Americans would come back, and that her baby would be returned to her. Indeed, as recounted in the film by Tom Miller, an American attorney, the U.S. government never had a complete list of the children, even as the children were literally being "dumped" on the plane. He and his wife, Tran Tuong Nhu, a Vietnamese American journalist who helps Bub find her family in Vietnam and accompanies her there, recall how they met one of the Babylift planes in San Francisco, and heard many of the children talking about their families. Tom immediately notified the adoption agencies and the U.S. government that many of the babies were not in fact orphans. He was met with "zero response," because, as he explains, Vietnam had become the site of an adoption "industry" for American adoptive parents wishing to adopt "cute" Vietnamese children from families that had been "induced" to give them up. Indeed, as with Deann Borshay Liem's adoptive father's home videos, in the footage of the children's arrival in the United States, there cannot be a wider disjuncture between the tearful, stricken, and frightened expressions on the Vietnamese children's faces and the smiling, elated, and joyful expressions on the faces of the white American social workers and adoptive parents.

One of these frightened, tearful faces belonged to Heidi Bub. Born to a white American GI father (whom she never meets or knows) and a Vietnamese mother in 1968, at age seven Bub was airlifted out of Vietnam in April 1975 as a part of Operation Babylift and adopted by a single white American woman. Like Deann Borshay Liem in Fremont, California, she undergoes a process of rapid assimilation in Pulaski, Tennessee. In the film, Bub comments that her adoptive mother tried to make her as "American as possible," while a Girl Scout leader and family friend recall respectively that they "made a Southerner out of her real quick as far as that goes," and she became "strictly all American." And just as Borshay Liem's Korean past was erased, Bub's Vietnamese side is kept hidden. Unlike Borshay Liem, however, because Bub is mixed-race, she is able to pass as white American. The family friend observes that she was "like an American with a suntan," "not much Oriental in her." Indeed, her adoptive mother tells her not to tell anyone that she is Vietnamese, and chooses a fictive birthplace, Columbia, South Carolina, for her. However, Bub's attempt at passing, by all accounts successful, is as much an effort to "Americanize" or assimilate as it is to evade the racism of Pulaski, a Southern town where the Ku Klux Klan originated. When she later tells John Bub, her husband (who, like her biological father, is a white American military man), that her mother had forbidden her from revealing her Vietnamese background, he understands, because he is aware of Pulaski's racist past and present. He remarks, "The racism there, they keep it hidden," but every year, the KKK marches on the anniversary of the day of its founding with Confederate flags raised.

Heidi Bub's experience disrupts the presumed teleology from orphan to adoptee to formation of "new geographies of kinship." The summer after her sophomore year in college, she has a falling out with her mother, one that ends their relationship and kinship altogether. When she is ten minutes late coming home from a date one night, Bub explains that her adoptive mother, Ann, "dead bolted the door . . . she told me she felt like I owed her for the life she had given me," and that "[because I] live under her roof, [I should] go by her rules, or leave. . . . I've tried contacting her over the years after that. She told everyone she doesn't have a daughter." After this, Bub enters a period of depression, wondering why she has lost two mothers, why one gave her up and one didn't want her. She can't help but feel that she must be a "horrible person." In a poignant segment, Bub explains: "I've always wanted the feeling, you know, that someone would love me no matter what when I never had that with Ann. . . . She was a single parent. I had everything growing up. I just never had a loving parent. . . . She hardly ever told me she loved me, never hugged . . ." Her adoptive uncle, Ann's brother, reveals, "Basically, mother was a disciplinarian, a screamer and hitter. . . . I hope Ann didn't raise Heidi the way we were raised . . . [you] would go to jail now." Bub then qualifies this, saying "I don't want to portray her as a child batterer . . . she had no control over what she was doing." Bub explains that as she started dating more, Ann's anger grew: "I was going to be all of hers or none at all." As with *First Person Plural*, we see the logics of possession and ownership. Disowned by her adoptive mother, and bereft of unconditional parental love, Bub decides to find her Vietnamese mother. She expects that a reunion will be "so healing" for both of them, "make all bad memories go away," and make "all those lost years not matter." She successfully locates her mother with Tran's help and makes a trip to Vietnam (with Tran, who acts as a translator) to be reunited with her.

Ann's severing of her kinship ties with her adopted daughter reverses the dominant salvation narrative, where adoption is figured as an act of salvation in which the adoptive parents "save" the orphan child from a life of misery and suffering. This reversal takes greater effect when Bub reveals that she feels like she is the figure of salvation for her birth mother and siblings. Such a trajectory and affective economy complicate what Karen Dubinsky identifies as the "two main narratives of adoption in the West: 'rescue' versus 'kidnap.'"[42] Mai explains that the daughter who went away prospered, while the one who stayed behind, Bub's older sister, leads a miserable life. She asks Bub to help out the sister who stayed behind. Bub does give her sister some money, but is "insulted" when she is asked for more, and explains, "I don't want them to put me on the pedestal and say, you know, this is the one that's going to save us, [be]cause I didn't come here to be anybody's salvation. I came here to be reunited." We then see Bub paying for a family meal at a restaurant, and proclaiming that she is broke. Yet, as the film itself explains through the voice of Tran Tuong Nhu, it is common knowledge in Vietnam that the overseas relative is "the benefactor . . . who's going to save the family

... [be the] lifeline." However, in Bub's case, she is a specific kind of relative, a child who was given up for adoption, and her situation complicates this literal economy of relations. So when asked by her brother if she could take their mother to America and sponsor her immigration, or to support her with a monthly stipend, Bub breaks down emotionally. Visibly upset as well, her mother explains that they don't speak the same language, "so it's not clear. What does she [Bub] know about the Vietnamese notion of love and emotion? She's used to living a different way. She doesn't understand it. It's not good to force her. . . . Poor thing, she sees me and thinks I'm asking for money. And all I know is how much I love her."

Daughter from Danang not only makes visible the reversal of the salvation narrative, but complicates the notion that the adopted child is a "freely given gift." In this gift exchange, it is presumed that a selfless mother freely and selflessly gives her child away in order to give the child a better life. But as Barbara Yngvesson observes, the discourse of freedom in the concept of the adopted child as gift elides the "enchainments of adoptive kinship." That is, "imagining placement [of the child] to be a consequence of the voluntarism by a birth mother or of 'choice' by prospective adoptive parents obscure[s] the dependencies and inequalities that compel some of us to give birth to and give up our children, while constituting others as 'free' to adopt them. . . . However freestanding the child is 'made' by adoption law, he or she can *never* be free of the 'implicate field of persons' in which he or she was constituted as legally adoptable."[43] Indeed, as I argued in the previous chapter, the "dependencies and inequalities" that compel a birth mother to give up—as opposed to "freely give"—her child constitute her social death. Moreover, the juridical apparatus that produces the "freestanding" legal orphan as a "peculiar and exceptional state subject" with the "barest of social identities" and personhood by formally severing her from a normative kinship structure renders the social death of the adoptee as well.[44] In *Daughter from Danang*, Mai's "freedom" in giving up her daughter was radically circumscribed by the exigencies of the Vietnam War. The "gift child" she gives to Bub's American adoptive mother is in a sense "returned" when Bub is effectively disowned by her adoptive mother. The gift of a better life that Mai gives Bub by giving her up does not free Bub, but ultimately enchains her to her Vietnamese relatives when they expect her to repay them by sponsoring Mai's immigration to the United States and literally through a "monthly stipend." The economic and geopolitical inequalities that compelled Mai to give up Bub continue to enchain their (newfound) relationship. These complex enchainments, as we shall see, become too suffocating and heavy for Bub to bear.

In a further reversal, Bub comments that the parent-child roles have switched, where she is expected to be the parent. She begins to feel smothered by her mother's attention and affection, complaining of too much "touchy touchy feel feel" and admitting to feeling homesick, even at the risk of sounding selfish. She confesses:

> Since we've been here it's definitely put me in a different world, another planet, away from my husband and two little girls. I'm feeling homesick . . . setting in really hard. I know this is going to sound so selfish of me but I just cannot wait to get out of here. I want to go home and escape this world and go back to the one *I know* and is comfortable to me, that's sane almost. Sometimes I wish I could turn back the clock and *not know* any of this.

Already regretting her trip, Bub wishes to reverse the trajectory she has embarked upon by "turning back the clock" and returning to her previous state

Heidi and her birth mother reunite.

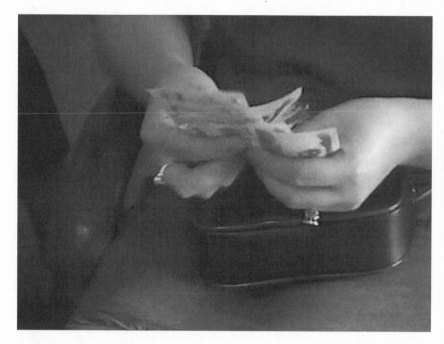

Her Vietnamese family's request for financial assistance later becomes too much for Heidi to bear.

of proverbially blissful ignorance/innocence. While she had made the trip so that she *could know* her mother, in an ironic reversal, she wants to erase that which she has *come to know* and go back to what she *had already known*— the American world of her two girls and husband. Her Vietnamese family's poverty and their expectations of her, someone who describes herself as "110% Americanized," later become too much to bear. Bub's "110%" Americanization is significantly colored by what Fiona I. B. Ngô calls "militarized orientalisms" in her analysis of the film. Militarized orientalisms range from Bub's imaginings of Asian women (particularly her birth mother) as "soft-spoken, kind, loving, caring," to misgivings about her own birth being the result of an extramarital affair on the part of her birth mother.[45] Thus, the misunderstanding between Bub and her Vietnamese family is not simply a linguistic barrier, or a problem of literal translation from one language to another. Rather, it is a broader problem of cultural translation, and as such, Bub cannot know the "Vietnamese notion of love and emotion." It is a problem not simply of cognition, but of feeling and embodiment.

In displaying this reunion gone awry, and framing and highlighting the differences between Bub and her Vietnamese family, *Daughter from Danang* is on one significant level a melodramatic "culture clash" narrative. As Choy and Choy argue, although the critical contextualizations of the uneven geopolitical hierarchies governing transnational adoption that are made in the beginning of the film challenge "the popular conceptualization of this phenomenon as primarily humanitarian rescue and colorblind love, these critical interventions become lost as the film continues."[46] The film devolves into an individuated culture clash narrative that ultimately overshadows the critical interventions and possibilities suggested by the opening scenes. Indeed, both Bub and Mai are portrayed in rather unsympathetic ways. Bub is cast as a typically naïve "ugly American" figure, scripted "as a simpleton who is not a historical agent of her own life, but rather someone who is acted upon."[47] Her birth mother, Mai, can appear to be disingenuous, and as some might see it, instrumental in her newfound relationship with Bub. She is in fact asking Bub for money, but insists that all she knows is how much she loves her. Moreover, she asks for money from a daughter she gave up, and upon this daughter's very first trip of reunion back to Vietnam. While some might wonder how Bub could have been so ignorant as to be surprised and offended by the request, others might similarly wonder, given the fraught circumstances, how Mai and the rest of the family would even "dare" to make such a substantive request (a monthly stipend and/or immigration sponsorship) in the first place. Thus, in interrogating the "not-so-innocent politics of [documentary] filmmaking," Choy and Choy contend that the filmmakers, despite their best intentions, "inadvertently perpetuate a key aspect of the violence of war—specifically, the objectification, infantilization, and dehumanization of Asian adoptees in the United States—through the film."[48]

However, what interests me about the film is that there are moments that exceed its generic containment as a West-meets-East story of "culture clash." This reading against the grain is not an attempt to rehabilitate the film or its directors. Rather, it is an attempt to highlight how the film's very problematics, failings, and lost critical interventions display the "impossible contradictions" constituted and engendered by transnational, transracial adoption. Such impossible contradictions are precisely those that erupt in such vexed and disturbing ways in the film: how to reckon with a perhaps unrecoverable loss, and how to show that reckoning in ways that do not contribute further to the adoptee's and birth mother's abjection and conjoined social death. Instead of faulting Bub for not being able to handle her family's request for money, or wondering why and how it is that she could have been so naïve as to feel blindsided and overwhelmed by the request, I would like to ask why the request was made in the first place. As I have observed, despite what Bub's birth mother says (that all she knows is how much she loves Bub), she is in fact asking Bub for money. Because of Vietnam's relative lack of economic and political power vis-à-vis the United States, Mai's love for and relationship to her daughter is necessarily overdetermined by material and ideological exigencies. This overdetermination was set into place long before Bub made her trip back to Vietnam. Indeed, it is the very reason why Bub had to leave Vietnam in the first place. That is to say, Mai had to give up Bub because of material exigencies, because of the violence of war, and because Bub is the product of an interracial and extramarital affair. The persistence of those exigencies mediates and ultimately ruptures their reunion. Bub and her mother are severed from one another and remain so because of U.S. imperial and economic dominance over Vietnam (despite Vietnam's formal war victory) as well as the racial taxonomies and conventions governing both nations. Rather than solely displaying a case of "culture clash," what *Daughter from Danang* makes visible, then, is also a clash of uneven geopolitical hierarchies, economies, and power. It is this clash that so discombobulates Bub, and her psychic economy—her acute longing for "unconditional love," healing, and reconnection with lost origins—cannot make room for her mother's literal "Third World" economy precisely because her psychic losses are so excessive. Moreover, these psychic losses are themselves conditioned by Bub's geographically and temporally specific ideology, indeed her romance, of what constitutes desired mother–daughter relations and her acute need for such relations in the wake of her abuse and disownment by her adoptive mother, Ann.

In tears, Bub repeats, "I don't know what to do. I just don't know anymore. I just don't know." This refrain is again used when she returns to the United States and explains why she hasn't touched the self-addressed envelope given to her by her mother so that she could write to her family: "I *wouldn't know* what to say." This lack of knowledge is heightened by its contrast to what Bub affirms she does know in a sequence in which she visits her adoptive grandmother with her daughters and husband two years after returning from the Vietnam trip: "That's still to me still a fuzzy dream that happened. This is *what I know* and this is what I grew up with." Flipping through Bub's Vietnam photo album with the two girls, Bub's grandmother tells her that she's glad Bub went to Vietnam and took many photos. Bub's response is, "But you're *who I know*." Continuing with her epistemological conundrum, she says, "The few contacts I've had with them, every letter they wrote was a plea for money. I felt like I couldn't do this anymore. It was just too hard for me emotionally, and now it's . . . I hardly hear from them, and of course they don't hear from me at all. . . . Looking back I just feel really bad the way I handled it. But you know, *I don't know them.* I mean I . . . they're strangers to me. I guess I have closed the door on 'em. But I didn't lock the door. [Giggles] It's closed but it's not locked." Why, then, does Bub repeatedly emphasize what she knows, in contrast to what she doesn't know? As she herself suggests, the situation was too difficult for her emotionally. By containing her emotions, and categorizing knowns and unknowns, Bub rationalizes her decision to "close the door" on her Vietnamese blood relatives. Whereas she had begun her journey to "heal" both herself and her mother so that "all those lost years [would] not matter," the messy tangledness of the politics and affects of transnational adoption, and the economic exigencies of a post-war Vietnam, intersect to shatter Bub's phantasmatic desires as well as her sense of reality. The trauma of the original separation is eclipsed by the trauma of the failed attempt at reunion. Bub must then contain the threat of affective and cognitive breakdowns by retreating back to "what she knows"—her (af)filiative kinship with her adoptive grandmother—and relegating her filial kin to the category of "strangers" whom she does *not* know. *Daughter from Danang* thus exposes the painful crossings of "new geographies of kinship" that are at once filiative and affiliative, and the multiple losses engendered when the fictions and fantasies through which the "adoption triad" of birth mothers, adoptive mothers, and adopted daughters manage and imagine their own subjectivities, lives, and relationships with one another refuse to be reconciled.

In the next section, I turn to another Operation Babylift narrative, Aimee Phan's short story collection *We Should Never Meet*. Phan's powerful stories display how the "adoption triad" can itself be a fiction. That is to say, not all orphans are "successfully" adopted, and not all orphans can meet or reunite with their birth mothers.

A Politics of Compassion

In Aimee Phan's *We Should Never Meet,* a collection of linked short stories inspired by Operation Babylift, we are introduced to the babies themselves, their adoptive and foster parents, their birth parents, and the Vietnamese and American workers, nuns, and volunteers who took care of them. Through these characters, Phan shows how the American presence in Vietnam produced a

Vietnamese presence in America. Against the uniform portrayal of the Viet-namese who sought refuge in the United States as desperate and pitiable "refugees" or "boat people," Phan highlights the heterogeneity to be witnessed even among the babies of Operation Babylift, who constitute only a very small fragment of the large numbers of Vietnamese who have migrated to the United States as a result of the war's displacements. Moreover, she works against the sentimentalist tropes saturating dominant representations of both refugees and transnational adoptees. As such, *We Should Never Meet* offers what Kim Park Nelson argues is a significant and much-needed analytic in discussions of transnational adoption, an "unsentimental critique."[49]

In the first story, "Miss Lien," we are compelled to confront an unspoken truth: that among the many mixed-race GI babies of Babylift, some were the product of American servicemen raping Vietnamese women. We meet Lien, a teenage girl in the Delta who is displaced by the war and must search for work in the nearest city to support her once prosperous family. While there, she gives birth to a baby at a midwife's house. The text hints at why Lien can-not keep the baby:

> It's all right, the girl said after the servant left. I wasn't sure about looking at my first either, knowing I had to give it up.
>
> Lien rolled her head to the side and looked at her. Where did you take it?
>
> There's this orphanage run by some catholic nuns. The girl shifted the infant so she could sit up more easily. They take every child in, no questions.
>
> How far is that from here?
>
> Just outside of Vinh Long. About fifteen kilometers north. The girl smiled sympathetically. You know, this baby could help you, if the father's an Ameri-can. That's why I'm keeping this one.
>
> Lien didn't say anything.
>
> Unless you don't want to see the father. Once again the girl's eyes traveled the length of Lien's face and body, as if she could tell just by looking at her. *Unless it was bad.* Then no one can blame you for getting rid of it.
>
> Lien twisted in her sheets until she found a comfortable position facing the wall. I can't keep it.[50]

By hinting at the rape, instead of engaging in a graphic portrayal of it, Phan powerfully alludes to the unspeakability of such a crime on multiple registers. Rapes committed by U.S. servicemen—in many ways a form of institution-alized, militarized, gendered racial violence—is at once ignored, condoned, and not spoken of by the U.S. military apparatus for all too obvious political reasons. For Lien, the survivor of such violence, the crime also remains unspeakable, indeed narratively unrepresentable, but for reasons that are at once intensely psychic and pragmatic. On the one hand, the trauma of the rape exceeds representation. On the other hand, Lien does not have the "luxury" of dwelling on her trauma; she must move on in order to survive and ensure the survival of her family.

In her portrayal of Lien and the baby she gives up, whom we encounter in subsequent stories, Phan disrupts a politics of pity and gestures instead toward what we might call a politics of compassion. While a transnational politics of pity might have moved well-intentioned Americans to adopt Vietnamese orphans, the presumed teleology from orphan to adoptee to formation of a "new geography of kinship" obscures the many instances in which Babylift children and the "unaccompanied minor" children who came after them on boats were not "successfully" adopted. Indeed, for these children, if a new geography of kinship is formed at all, it is with one another, often as abused foster children whom social services does not successfully place or protect.

In the story "We Should Never Meet," we meet Kim, a mixed-race Vietnamese American who came to the United States when she was three as a part of Operation Babylift and is now a young adult living in the "Little Saigon" of Southern California's Orange County. We also meet her foster sister Mai and foster brother and ex-boyfriend Vinh, who arrived later as "unaccompanied minors" with the boat refugees. Mai, who eventually stays with one stable set of foster parents for several years, compares her situation to Kim's upon her "emancipation" when she turns eighteen: "Though Mai eventually found a home with the Reynoldses, Kim never found hers. She never stayed in one place longer than two years. It wasn't supposed to be that way. Kim was meant to be luckier. She came over to the states as part of the Babylift evacuation and was promptly adopted by an American family. But the family had given her back, something about not realizing how difficult it would be to raise a foreign child. Social services put Kim in a foster home, which is where Mai had met her" (151). Yet throughout the years and even as a young adult, Kim blames herself for having been "returned" by the family who adopted her: "She'd only been three years old. But she must have done something wrong. It was too long ago to remember what" (48). Arriving from Vietnam with no identification but her name, never really knowing whether her biological parents were alive or not, and eventually realizing that "the adults who were supposed to look after her . . . screwed everything up" (45) instead, Kim forms a new geography of kinship with her foster sisters and brothers. The adults in her life consist of a string of foster fathers who molest and rape her and the incompetent social worker who repeatedly places her in the most inappropriate foster homes. Kim's already fragile kinship structure fissures as she and her foster siblings get older. Mai leaves for Wellesley College on a scholarship, Vinh gets increasingly enmeshed with his gang Brookhurst 354, and though Kim is a high school dropout, she tries to better her situation and keep things together by not allowing herself to be dependent on Vinh or to get sucked back into the gang. When her foster parents essentially kick her out of the house with an old suitcase and fifty dollars the day she turns eighteen, she finds herself having to stay at the apartment that Vinh shares with his gang brothers until she can save enough money for her own apartment. Yet she experiences a setback when she lets Vinh "fuck her out of gratitude" and must use her paycheck for an abortion. "But she still needed to get away from Vinh" (48). She strikes up a tentative friendship, possibly a new kinship, with a Vietnamese woman who owns a gift shop, and asks to borrow some money so that she can get away from Vinh and the gang. When the woman refuses, Kim is disappointed and hurt, and asks Vinh's gang to rob the store. This possible kinship is aborted, yet at the same time, Kim realizes that the kinship provided by a gang and a life of petty theft might have made sense in high school, but they are no longer options that she wants for herself. She knows she needs to get "a real job" (41). From toiling at a fast food restaurant, she applies for a secretarial job to earn a better income. While Phan suggests that Kim is thus able to escape the cycle of abuse and petty crime, the kind of lasting kinship that she so craves eludes her. Scarred by her experience, she "didn't like to be touched" by anyone (45). Her situation disrupts the facile assumption made by both the Americans and the Vietnamese at the time of the Babylift that life in the United States would necessarily have been better for such "orphans."

In an exposure of the different gendered effects of being an unadopted, parentless Vietnamese youth in the United States, we see that Vinh, unlike Kim, has his gang to turn to as an alternative new geography of kinship. Eschewing a politics of pity or of judgment, Phan offers instead a politics of compassion, creating in Vinh a thoughtful, complex character with a critical political diagnosis of the American war in Vietnam and the contradictions of the so-called American Dream. Instead of dismissing, judging, criminalizing, or indeed pitying Vinh as a gang member, Phan shows how he is a complex embodiment and index of the persisting legacies of the Vietnam War. On the lookout for Brookhurst 354's next home-invasion victim, Vinh allows himself to get drawn into helping out and walking home an old man, Bac Nguyen, whom he was simply supposed to follow surreptitiously instead. Accepting Bac Nguyen's offer of tea once they get to his house, Vinh engages in a conversation about the war:

> They've taken so much from us, the boy said.
>
> Yes, the Communists were heartless. Bac Nguyen still couldn't control the rush of blood to his head remembering that Communist sniper who gunned [his son] Anh down that day so long ago on the beach in Vung Tau.
>
> You misunderstand Bac, the boy said. I wasn't meaning the Communists.
>
> Oh, Bac Nguyen said, slightly confused, I just assumed—
>
> I was talking about the Americans. (94)

When Bac Nguyen concedes that "it's a complicated issue," Vinh replies, "Not for me. They destroyed our country, then they left. To ease their guilty conscience, they took some of us in. It's really simple" (96). While some might dismiss Vinh's political diagnosis—that the war was really a simple case of American imperialism—as itself rather simplistic, within the context of a post–World War II pax Americana and post–Cold War neoliberal triumphalism, his critique articulates what Christopher Connery calls the "continuing necessity of anti-Americanism" as a counterhegemonic project. Connery observes that "the years since the end of the Cold War have practically erased the memory that the US was ever anything but the unchallenged supreme power. In President Clinton's visit to Vietnam, toward the end of his presidency, no mention was made of Vietnamese victory and US defeat, suggesting that even the concept of defeat is alien to the current American reality."[51] How does defeat get conjured and rescripted as victory? Yen Le Espiritu argues that the U.S. media has "deployed the refugee figure, the purported grateful beneficiary of U.S.-style freedom, to remake the Vietnam War into a just and successful war." Within this representational matrix, Vietnam veterans and Vietnamese refugees, "as the purported rescuers and rescued, respectively . . . *together* reposition the United States and its (white male) citizens as savior of Vietnam's 'runaways,' and thus as the ultimate victor of the Vietnam War."[52] In *We Should Never Meet,* Vinh complicates the politics of defeat and victory by highlighting how much the ultimately "defeated" Americans destroyed

Vietnam and how much they took from there. He points instead to a dialectical notion of defeat *within* victory, or victory *within* defeat. Yes, Vietnam "won" the war, but at what cost? Part of the burden of this cost, Vinh suggests, is the loss of Vietnamese children to America, a displacement of Vietnam by America, or a "selling out." While Vinh had been angry for a long time about the children who were "left behind, unwanted, and forgotten," he comes to realize that such children were better off because "they knew where they stood with the Americans," whereas the "golden child" did not (103). Vinh's privileging of clarity is a productive unambiguity, a clearing away of the obfuscations and dissimulations that are passed off as "nuanced" or more "sophisticated" analyses of a "complicated issue."

While Vinh's anti-Americanism leads him to form a new kinship with his gang, it is also an index of the fissuring of the former kinship he shared with his foster sisters Kim and Mai. According to Vinh's logics, someone like Mai, "with her American dream family," is a sellout (165). In the story that focuses on her, entitled "Emancipation," the contradictions of what it means to "sell out" within this precarious economy of kinship is self-consciously explored through Mai's feelings about her college application essay, which wins her a five-hundred-dollar scholarship as her high school's best such essay. Mindful of the audience to which she is writing, and "remembering all the sympathies people had projected on her all her life" (147), Mai strategically engages in a politics of pity, embellishing her hardships as an orphaned refugee boat child under foster care. She had actually been "allowed a childhood" after moving in with the Reynoldses (with whom she would stay until she is emancipated at eighteen), so she "play[s] it up," "realizing her life had to be worse to count for something" (147). Phan makes it clear to her readers that this is a strategic deployment of what could be called refugee performativity, or "playing" the refugee by "playing it up." While Mai is successful in her refugee performativity and wins the award, she makes certain things clear:

> Principal Baldwin patted her shoulder . . . declaring her such a lucky girl with fortunate opportunities. He probably meant to be complimentary, but the words bristled her ego. Lucky. Fortunate. Had he talked to the school counselor? Did he know that Mai was still waiting on Wellesley? Did he think she was being ungrateful? It wasn't luck. Yes, she was once the poor orphan child, but she had earned this. Since middle school, she had worked to ensure a future other children already inherited. (147)

Put simply, Mai makes it clear that she is no charity case, no "poor orphan child" to be pitied. Even as she strategically uses the trope of the "pathetic refugee" in her college essay, she makes it clear that she has "earned" her promising future, a future that most children simply inherit. In this way, *We Should Never Meet* works against the reification of childhood innocence, or the social construction of childhood *as* innocence. Its representational strategy refuses what's been called the "sacralized" child, and departs from the familiar figuration of children as "objects of sentiment."[53]

Through the resilience of such characters and the alternative "new geographies of kinship" that they attempt to imagine and create, but that are often thwarted, Phan's stories thus resist a transnational politics of pity and inspire instead a politics of compassion and an "unsentimental critique." Indeed, cultural works such as *We Should Never Meet, Daughter from Danang,* and *First Person Plural* are potent sites where the fraught politics and affects of transnational, transracial adoption are not resolved, but complexly displayed as profound losses that cannot be regained and as multiple violences that cannot be mended. These losses and violences, and the unfulfilled yearning to overturn them, index America's Cold War in Asia as an imperialist and gendered racial project. In my analysis, I hope to have shown how transnational, transracial adoption has a long genealogy that intersects with America's protracted episodes of empire-building and war-making. In the contemporary moment, as we see in ever starker ways how some lives are valued more than others, indeed of how some lives are deemed to be "redundant" or disposable, the high "demand" in the United States for babies of color from abroad would seem to address and pose a challenge to such social and often physical death for racialized and gendered subjects. Yet the peculiar overvaluing and fetishizing of transnational, transracial adoptees, taking place within the context of a relative paucity of white babies available for domestic adoption, lead us to ask how such adoptees are positioned within, and what kinds of labor they provide for, the white heteronormative bourgeois nuclear family ideal. Moreover, as I have suggested, it is precisely in and through the parallel social death of birth mothers, and indeed the social death of the adoptee through her very production as a legal orphan, that the conditions of possibility for transnational, transracial adoption materialize. By making this visible, the cultural productions I have analyzed help us to imagine and form alternative kinships, those that resist the seductions of normative family ideals and do not exacerbate or depend on the differential valuing, protection, and "making possible" of some lives over others.

In the following section, I continue with my focus on how Vietnamese American cultural productions display the complicated "return" of Vietnamese to the imperial center by examining *Surname Viet Given Name Nam*'s politics of translation and what I call a ghostly genealogy of womanhood. Just as *We Should Never Meet* and *Daughter from Danang* are stories about the limits of narrative, physical, and affective reconciliation, *Surname Viet Given Name Nam* is a story about the limits of "translation."

"Translation" and the Afterlife of the Cold War

Trinh T. Minh-ha's experimental feature-length film *Surname Viet Given Name Nam* disrupts the conventions of narrative form to highlight the multiply mediated nature of representation. Polyvocal, nonlinear, abstract, nonsynchronous, fragmented, multilayered, and transgeneric, it alternately captures and confounds the attention of its viewers. And yet even as its formal aesthetics can elude complete elucidation, its political project, at once aligned with and resistant to its aesthetic project, could not in various moments be more lucid. This ambivalence toward the apparatuses of representation in *Surname Viet Given Name Nam* is rendered through a gendered meditation on the politics of "translation" in its various registers, whether that involves literal translation from one language to another or larger interpretive acts such as "translating" a historical event and knowledge formation like the Cold War. In privileging how Vietnamese and Vietnamese immigrant women critically provide a nonaligned translation of the Cold War and its afterlife, and conjuring what I call a ghostly genealogy of womanhood, the film exposes the masculinisms structuring both communist and capitalist states.

By giving voice, through interview testimonials, to the women of postwar Vietnam, *Surname Viet Given Name Nam* appears to be a documentary in the classic "talking heads" style. As the film unfolds, however, the viewer's expectations are not fulfilled, and what we see is not a documentary per se, but an anatomy of a documentary. The first part of the film is composed of interviews with Vietnamese women commenting on the challenges facing them in postwar Vietnam. Though they are speaking in English, we are provided with "subtitles" of various parts of their speech. Temporally and spatially, these words, either transcribed exactly or with a few "mistakes," alternately complement or compete with the voices and images of the women. Appearing either before, during, or after each woman's testimonial, and inserted unobtrusively on one part of the screen or obtrusively occupying the whole screen and obscuring the image of the woman, these subtitles, intertitles, and supertitles perform various functions at different points. This purposeful nonsynchrony, along with devices like extreme, lingering close-ups of parts of the women's body (such as the hands, neck, and feet), and having the women suddenly pace back and forth and at times outside of the frame, increase the viewer's awareness of the staged nature of the interviews. Then, in the second part of the film, we are shown that the interviews are indeed staged reenactments acted out by Vietnamese women living in California, none of whom is a professional actor. The staged interviews are translated "adaptations" of actual interviews that were conducted by Mai Thu Van in Vietnam in Vietnamese, then translated into French and published as a book in France.[54] This revelation comes yet again in the form of interviews, but this time it is one of the women as "themselves" in their everyday lives, whether that involves participation in a relative's wedding, cooking, attending a beauty pageant, expressing views on politics, or an explanation of why they chose to participate in the film. As noted by Amy Lawrence, however, the cinema verité style in this section "cannot be read as a simple relapse into documentary realism."[55] Indeed, in her voiceover narration, Trinh herself reveals a suspicion toward cinematic technologies. She notes, "By choosing the most direct and spontaneous form of voicing and documenting, I find myself closer to fiction" (78).[56] While the fiction film purports to "imitate" life and while the documentary form is seen to simply "duplicate" it, both forms are complicit in the "myth of cinematic 'naturalness.'"[57]

Throughout the film, Trinh also inserts black-and-white documentary stock footage (or rephotography) without explication or context, Vietnam War newsreels, Vietnamese folk songs sung in Vietnamese, translated Vietnamese poetry read in unaccented English, readings of personal letters, and multiple voiceover narrations. The documentary stock footage includes still photos and moving images of both historically dramatic events, such as the internal North–South migration of people, the Vietnam War, as well as pastoral scenes of everyday life. We also see what appear to be dramatic reenactments of the martyring of nationalist female figures. This layered montage, at times lyrically beautiful and nostalgic, graphically violent and tragic, visceral then abstract, opaque then seemingly transparent, displays both documentary desire and a self-conscious problematizing of that desire. On the one hand, in her voiceover narration, Trinh claims, "Life seems suddenly fragile and vulnerable. . . . The past resurfaces and what is almost forgotten reappears from the ruins" (56). On the other hand, "Of course, the image can neither prove what it says nor why it is worth saying it; the impotence of proofs, the impossibility of a single truth in witnessing, remembering, recording, rereading" (83). Focusing on this structuring ambivalence, one critic, Bill Nichols, while lauding *Surname Viet Given Name Nam*'s formal critique of cinematic, ethnographic, and documentary technologies and their modes of representation, chides the film for "flattening" issues of magnitude, most pressingly the continuing oppression of Vietnamese women, by failing to provide adequate explanations.[58] He thus reduces the film's political responsibility to a question of its explanatory power. Yet as Trinh herself, and women of color from diverse nations who have seen the film have identified, the "question of women" is not unique to socialist Vietnam. Trinh states, "That socialist Viet Nam is still caught in the patriarchal system is nothing particular to Viet Nam. The criticism of the film is therefore not directed toward Socialist Viet Nam per se; it is directed toward the condition of women—whether in socialist or capitalist context. . . . In forgetting this, I feel that the tendency is always to *obscure* the question of gender by reverting it to a question of communism versus capitalism and salvaging it in a binary system of thinking."[59] It is with

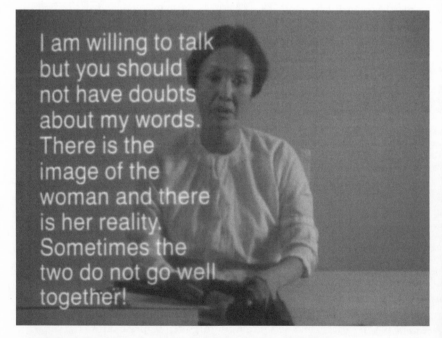

Khien Lai as Thu Van (from *Surname Viet Given Name Nam*, 1989).

this in mind, Trinh claims, that she chose particular representational strategies and content for the film. As such, *Surname Viet Given Name Nam*'s political responsibility is embedded within, and not eclipsed by, the film's critique of the apparatuses of representation. So political responsibility here constitutes not only the oppression of women, but how that oppression, and women as such, are to be represented.[60]

Even as Trinh is critical of documentary desire, this desire leaves certain residues, which are themselves linked to the residues of documentary history, poetry, and personal testimony. In my own tracing of these traces or residues, I turn here to *Surname Viet Given Name Nam*'s arguably central topos: the question or problem of translation. Let us begin, then, with Walter Benjamin's "The Task of the Translator." In this important essay, Benjamin notes the following:

> Just as the manifestations of life are intimately connected with the phenomenon of life without being of importance to it, a translation issues from the original, not so much from its life as from its *afterlife*. For a translation comes later than

Khien Lai as Khien (herself).

the original, and since the important works of world literature never find their chosen translators at the time of their origin, their translation marks their stage of *continued life.*[61]

Benjamin marks the temporal dimensions of translation. The task of the translator is to "echo" the original by finding and capturing the "intended effect" of the use of language in the original.[62] This echoing, as opposed to simply replicating the original in a different language, contributes to the "continued life" or "afterlife" of the original, and every act of translation can then be said to be an act of interpretation as well. I wish to extend this notion of translation to what I have been calling the protracted afterlife of the Cold War and its articulation or "translation" in *Surname Viet Given Name Nam*. Just as works of art or literature are translated, so are historical periods and events like the Cold War. That is to say, they are interpreted, whether in the same or different languages, and this interpretation "marks their stage of continued life." How, then, does *Surname Viet Given Name Nam* translate the Cold War?

By literally translating between and among languages (English, French, Vietnamese) and different forms of expression (speaking, writing, and imaging), *Surname Viet Given Name Nam* highlights the very difficulties of attempting such translations, especially within the context of postcolonial, gendered, racial, and nationalist concerns and their attendant uneven hierarchies of power. Trinh's voiceover narration asserts, "Do you translate by eye or by ear? Translation seeks faithfulness and accuracy and ends up always betraying either the letter of the text, its spirit, or its aesthetics" (80). She continues, "Grafting several languages, cultures and realities onto a single body. The problem of translation, after all, is a problem of reading and of identity" (89). Indeed, critical attention on the film is largely focused on this problematic.[63] The central question underpinning these readings is an echoing of the title of Gayatri Spivak's important article "Can the Subaltern Speak?"[64] Grappling with this, the film negotiates between the two poles of the Cold War Manichaean dyad, communism and capitalism. Indeed, it critiques the very logics, the formal Manichaeism, underpinning Cold War politics, suggesting how each pole purports to speak on behalf of "woman" but instead appropriates her voice and expropriates her labor. In the following discussion, I will elaborate on what mode this critique takes in the film and how it "translates" the Cold War.

On the one hand, *Surname Viet Given Name Nam*'s politics of suspicion vis-à-vis the "fictions" of documentary is certainly not an attempt at ideological or representational closure. On the other hand, its translation, I would like to argue, does not, as Lawrence suggests, recuperate a traditional Cold War axis "with 'the commies' as the bad guys."[65] What, then, is the status of the "bad commie," which by now is a familiar trope in American popular culture and political discourse? This figure has come to occupy a privileged place in what I have called the "form of politics" of the Cold War. Indeed, the "bad commie" is a constitutive feature of this form, for the "bad commie" is the "good cappie's" (the good capitalist's) self-consolidating Other. In *Surname Viet Given Name Nam,* the "bad commie" refuses to play this pre-scripted and prescriptive role. This does not mean, however, that this figure transmogrifies somehow into the "good commie." Rather, Trinh's film resists the reinscription of these Manichaean figures within these terms. It thereby translates or retranslates the "form of politics" of the Cold War by attempting to draw a new path for its "continued life."

First, and most obviously, "commies" are not the "bad guys," but "bad gals" in the film. That is, strictly speaking, as members of the Vietnamese Communist Party, and of the Vietnamese nation in general, it could be said that the women who were actually interviewed by Mai Thu Van and "played" by the nonprofessional "actresses" in Trinh's film are "bad commies." If, however, we examine their refusal to tow the orthodox party line at all costs, the "bad" signifier gets resignified to mean inadequate, unsatisfactory, or following Althusser, badly interpellated subjects.[66] Consider, for example, the following testimonial by Thu Van, a thirty-five-year-old health technical cadre in 1982:

[When I first met the women of the South,] we looked at each other with distrust, if not with hostility. Slowly we started talking to each other. From distrust, we have come to dialogue. And this was a radical turn that changed my political understanding. Before, I learnt in the political courses that capitalism was the exploitation of man by man. Period . . .

I ignore how a capitalist society functions, I ignore its diseases. (Thu Van smiles). . . . *Between two modes of exploitation of man by man, it is difficult for me to choose!* In spite of all the years of resistance and of revolution, the same hierarchical principles exist. . . .

Socialist Vietnam venerates the mothers and the wives. The woman does not exist, she is only a laborer. The liberation of women is understood here as a double exploitation.

The men want to keep the better share of the cake. They hold the key positions of power, women only get the leftovers. . . . There is not a single woman at the Political Bureau. . . . The men are the only ones to discuss problems that concern us.

[As for the Women's Union], the Mother-in-Laws' Union, they have made of us heroic workers, virtuous women. We are good mothers, good wives, heroic fighters. *Ghost women, with no humanity*. . . . The very idea of heroism is monstrous! (51, 56, 60, emphasis added)

In accounting her first experience of meeting women from the South, Thu Van reveals the shedding of her communist-indoctrinated ideological rigidity. Through mutual "dialogue," she undergoes a "radical political understanding," a shift in her rigid notions concerning both communism and capitalism. She comes to realize that both systems are "modes of exploitation of man by man," and the patriarchal exploitation of woman by man. In socialist Vietnam, "the same hierarchical principles exist" in which women, though valorized in their roles as wives, mothers, and laborers, do not hold positions of power. Men speak and make decisions about and for them. As such, women are not real flesh and blood, complicated people, but "ghosts." These spectral figures can only be recognized and valued for the functions they perform for the family and the nation. This resonant critique of patriarchy is one that could also, of course, be applied to capitalist societies. Indeed, in a letter written by Mai Thu Van, which Trinh reads in the film, we hear that "in France . . . in spite of the *Mouvement de Liberation de la Femme*, maternalism remains the cornerstone of the dominant ideology" (83). What makes Thu Van's articulation here so poignant, however, is the context from which she is speaking, that "In spite of all the years of resistance and of revolution, the same hierarchical principles exist." And yet even as she considers capitalism a possible alternative by "ignoring" its "diseases," ultimately she cannot, and refuses to, choose. This is articulated by many of the women in the interviews; they are not, as Trinh comments, "just aspiring for capitalism in criticizing socialism."[67] Thu Van's refusal to choose, then, registers a politics of nonalignment, and she refuses to be a "native informant" for a Western capitalist audience eager to hear denunciations of both communism and Confucian patriarchy. Her choice, moreover, is actually a nonchoice. For women, choosing between capitalism and communism is not a choice between "good" and "evil," but two evils, between "two modes of exploitation." Neither system, neither ideology, is free of gender hierarchies. Anh, a sixty-year-old doctor who was also interviewed, states, "If only men reread their history books, they would never dare send their people killing each other for ideologies. The

Vietnamese people fought to [throw off] the yoke of domination. They didn't fight for some ideological principles. One should never forget this essential point" (70).

The ghostliness of actual living women in the film is juxtaposed with the spectrality of legendary feminist nationalist heroines in Vietnamese history, such as the story of the early nineteenth-century poet Ho Xuan, whose poems "were notorious for the scandal they caused and they continue today to defy the principles of right speech and good manner of womanhood. So some men went as far as affirming that poems signed under her name might not even be hers; they might, of course, be written by a man. Who was then, we may ask, this feminine man . . . who wrote feminist poetry on free love, on single mothers, and *labia minora* and *labia majora* desire; who attacked polygamy and double standards of morality, who ridiculed empty male authority and religiosity, and who challenged all the norms of Confucian patriarchy?" (56–57). Ho Xuan's spectrality, paired with the ghostliness of actual living women in contemporary Vietnam, traces a ghostly genealogy of womanhood. In her provocative study *Ghostly Matters: Haunting and the Sociological Imagination,* Avery Gordon writes:

> The ghost is not simply a dead or a missing person, but a social figure, and investigating it can lead to that dense site where history and subjectivity make social life. The ghost or the apparition is one form by which something lost, or barely visible, or seemingly not there to our supposedly well-trained eyes, makes itself known or apparent to us, in its own way, of course. The way of the ghost is haunting, and haunting is a very particular way of knowing what has happened or is happening. Being haunted draws us . . . in the structure of a feeling of a reality we come to experience, not as cold knowledge, but as a transformative recognition.[68]

Taking seriously Gordon's contention that the ghost is a "social figure," I would like to observe that in *Surname Viet Given Name Nam* the ghost is a social figure who not only comes to haunt us from the past, but also, as I have stated previously, exists in the present and speaks to the present. Ghost women in the film are not only historical figures such as Ho Xuan, but also living breathing women like Thu Van, both rendered ghostly by official state nationalist discourses and by the mediated nature of their "conjuring" in Trinh's film through voiceover narration, rephotography, and reenacted interviews. As such, Trinh's film provides a "potent imagination" not only of "what *has been* done and what is *to be* done otherwise," but also of what *is being* done. The film's "alternative diagnostics" of the Cold War is a "transformative recognition" from the perspective of these ghostly women speaking in the present.[69]

The nineteenth-century figuration of womanhood embodied by Ho Xuan, Trinh illustrates, is hardly outdated. Rather, it enjoys a continued life and persists stubbornly beyond years of revolution and resistance. The construction of "womanhood" remains fundamentally functionalist: a "woman" can only exist and be legible as such through her conjoined functions as mother, wife, daughter, nationalist martyr, and laborer, and to the extent that she complies with the feminine four virtues and three submissions of Confucianism.[70] Indeed, the title of the film, itself taken from a Vietnamese proverb, evokes this. Articulating the woman's literal marriage to the nation through her various functions, the proverb goes like this: When a man asks a young woman if she's married, she wittily replies, "Yes, I am with husband, his surname is Viet and his given name is Nam" (51). This functionalism, however, takes an interesting turn in the translation of Confucian patriarchy in the twentieth-century Cold War context. Alongside the critique of Confucian gender roles, the film also offers a less predictable and more complicated meditation on the vexed relationship among women, nation, and the imperial imaginary. Inserted in the first part of the film, among the reenacted interviews, is an American newsreel produced and aired during the Vietnam War: "When the smoke clears, the inevitable roundup of prisoners, many of them seriously wounded. Among the captured a large group of women, traditionally used by the enemy as ammunition bearers, village infiltrators, and informers" (67). This newsreel sound, in a film often at pains to produce nonsynchrony, is synchronized with film footage of the "roundup" of Vietnamese women. Here again, we see the trope of woman in terms of, and made legible by, her functionality. Yet this time, she is not mother, wife, or daughter, but "an ammunition bearer, village infiltrator, and informer," and her perceived function is narrated from an American, Western perspective. Beyond the question of whether "the enemy," the Viet Cong, in fact "used" women in this manner, I would like to pay particular attention to how the figuration of woman's functionality in this newsreel itself functions. Put otherwise, what function does the depiction of the Vietnamese woman's use-value as ammunition bearer, village infiltrator, and informer serve? Women have historically been figured as civilians or noncombatants in war. As such, at least according to the international conventions of warfare, they have remained immune from capture and attack. So in the American newsreel, the assumption that

Viet Cong women were "used" in the war effort serves a few significant conjoined functions. First, there is an implication that the "enemy" is flouting
the conventions of warfare by "using" its women in the war effort. Second,
this figuration of women justifies their "roundup" as "prisoners" of war by
the American soldiers. Further, the word "used" in the phrasing "used by the
enemy as ammunition bearers" vacates any volition or agency the Viet Cong
women might have had. That is, instead of choosing or acting, they were
"used" or compelled by their male compatriots. Paradoxically, though this
purported function of Viet Cong women makes them the "enemy" as well,
and hence the justification for their capture as prisoners, the grammatical
split between "a large group of women" and "the enemy" in the language of
the newsreel belies this. Overall, the newsreel also relies on historical Orientalist constructions of the Asian, whether man or woman, as sneaky and
inscrutable.

Surname Viet Given Name Nam provides a further elaboration of the ap-
propriative malleability of the trope of woman in nationalist, colonial, and

Self-immolation and nationalist female martyrs.

American newsreels depict Vietnamese women as "ammunition bearers, village infiltrators, and informers."

anticolonial narratives. It traces the translatability, as it were, of Vietnam's national epic poem, *The Tale of Kieu,* in different historical and political contexts. This account of the tragic life of Kieu, "a perfect model of Confucian feminine loyalty and piety, [who] was forced by circumstances to sacrifice her life to save her father and brother from disgrace and humiliation, and to sell herself to become a prostitute, then a concubine, a servant, and a nun, before she was able to come back to her first lover," is read as a national allegory (59–60). First, it was celebrated as a denunciation of feudal oppression. Then, it was taken as a metaphor for Vietnam's tragically long period of colonial domination. More recently, in the celebration of its two hundredth anniversary, Trinh's voiceover notes that "it was highly praised by the government's male official writers for its revolutionary yearning for freedom and justice in the context of the war against American imperialism." And finally, "For the Vietnamese exiled, it speaks for the exodus or silent popular movement of resistance that continues to raise problems of conscience to the international community" (91). Like the Cold War, *The Tale of Kieu* enjoys a continued afterlife.

By thus tracing this afterlife of *The Tale of Kieu*, and "translating" the Cold War through a ghostly genealogy of womanhood and the voices of Vietnamese and Vietnamese diasporic women, *Surname Viet Given Name Nam* offers a powerful gendered critique of the masculinist hypervisibility of the Manichaean "form of politics" of the Cold War. This attentiveness to the ghostly, and to the afterlives of people and events, invokes a set of questions posed by Nguyên-Vo Thu-Huong on the politics and ethics of such a project:

> How shall we remember rather than just appropriate the dead for our own agendas, precluding what the dead can tell us? Thus we must ask: Whom among the dead shall we mourn? How do we retrieve our histories containing events that had passed, with the dead, into accomplished fates? Finally, how shall we speak to those who survived, who now remember various histories amongst us? How we remember will either open or foreclose our paths to our various presents and futures.[71]

I opened this chapter with an epigraph by Nguyên-Vo in which she articulates the necessity of remembering and mourning, and I conclude it now by returning to her. This time, she powerfully and eloquently asks how precisely the remembering and mourning should be carried out, and how precisely we should "speak to those who survived." As I hope to have shown in this chapter, such a remembering, mourning, and speaking neither cannibalizes the dead (as Nguyên-Vo cautions against),[72] nor abets what we could call America's self-cathexis in the masculinist hypervisibility of the representations it continues to generate about the Vietnam War. Rather, the Vietnamese American cultural productions I have analyzed seek to open paths to "our various presents and futures," and to our Cold War pasts.

EPILOGUE

Imagining an End to Empire

In this book, I have analyzed how Asian American critique and cultural politics imagine America's imperial pasts and presents in Asia by reframing the Cold War as at once a geopolitical, cultural, and epistemological project of imperialism and gendered racial formation undergirding U.S. global hegemony. In doing so, I have privileged culture as a potent site of knowledge, one that offers discombobulating diagnostics and analytics, what I have called an unsettling hermeneutic, of America's exceptionalist (inter)national "identity politics" in the latter half of the twentieth century and beyond. While Asian American cultural texts have been literally and figuratively domesticated as "ethnic minority literature" within the corrals of U.S. liberal multiculturalism, I hope to have shown how such a domestication elides a global genealogy that intersects critically with the Cold War. I have thus, on the one hand, sought to provide an alternative conceptualization and reading of the Cold War, and, on the other, to advance an expansive way of situating and reading Asian American cultural texts. This conjoined reframing, moreover, allows us to rethink post–World War II Asian migration to the United States. The conventions of Asian American studies, migration studies, immigration history, and other related fields have largely viewed this migration through the schema and lens of "push" and "pull" factors, such as economic uncertainty in Asia and economic opportunity in the United States. What this lens tends to leave uninterrogated, however, is the significant extent to which the Cold War, as a project of imperialism and gendered racial formation in Asia, itself constitutes the "push" and "pull" factors. By critically centering the Cold War, we begin to see what, as I cited in chapter 4, historian Ji-Yeon Yuh calls "*refuge* migration," a category that expands the limited scope of the official

United Nations designation of "*refugee* migration."[1] Reconceptualizing post–World War II Asian migration to the United States as "refuge migration" disrupts the ways in which "immigration" has been figured as a reigning trope in teleological emplotments of the mythos of the American Dream, indeed the mythos that *is* "America." This reconceptualization also highlights the contradictions of seeking "refuge" in a country that created, in the first place, the very conditions from which you are seeking refuge. This is to articulate the mantra that "We are here because you were there," that "First you destroy our country, and then you rescue [us and] our children." Or, from the perspective of America, "We had to destroy the village in order to save it."

Such mantras distill American imperial violence, a violence that lingers long after America's putative Cold War victory in 1989. While neoliberal articulations of a facile Cold War triumphalism, most notably Francis Fukuyama's (in)famous declaration that the Cold War victory constitutes "the end of history" not as apocalyptic terminus but as teleological arrival, would suggest that imperialist war-making is no longer necessary in the "post"–Cold War era, the imperial mandate is alive and well.[2] Indeed, in the "War on Terror," we have witnessed an uncanny repetition or protracted afterlife of Cold War Manichaean logics. Consider, for example, director Jonathan Demme's 2004 remake of the 1962 classic Cold War film *The Manchurian Candidate* (which I discussed in chapter 2). In the remake, the Korean War (1950–53) of the original is updated with the first Persian Gulf War (1991), and the "red menace" embodied by Russian and Chinese communist conspirators is replaced with the capitalist menace of Manchurian Global, a corporation that bears a striking resemblance to Halliburton or the Carlyle Group.[3] What does it mean that a Cold War conspiracy film par excellence could be so compellingly remade in the beginning of the twenty-first century drawing on events of a much more recent past? After all, according to the logics and rhetorics of a post–Cold War neoliberal triumphalism, the first Persian Gulf War was a project of the "New World Order." This triumphalism assumes and marks the capitalist Cold War "victory" of 1989 as a radical historical break or rupture. Yet Demme's remake of *The Manchurian Candidate* and the narratives framing the post-9/11 eruption of the 2003 Iraq War (also called the Second Persian Gulf War) suggest that the Cold War as a structure of feeling and production of knowledge for interpreting and acting upon new geopolitical configurations in the "post"–Cold War era hardly seems to be residual, but (newly) dominant. Indeed, in light of these developments, a curious scene in the original 1962 film takes on a new meaning. In this scene, a brainwashed army intelligence officer who had served in the Korean War (played by Frank Sinatra) and a production assistant (played by Janet Leigh) meet on a train and ask one another if they are "Arabic" as a shorthand or racial screening for determining whether they want to continue speaking with one another. The odd prescience, as it were, of this scene in the original film and Demme's remake show how the logics of the Cold War continue to enjoy a protracted afterlife even as the fall of the Berlin Wall in 1989 and the aftermath of 9/11 have brought about new geopolitical, economic, and cultural constellations, and thus the necessity of new hermeneutics for apprehending and understanding those constellations.[4]

In the days immediately following 9/11, it seemed that the ideological currency of what Americans had historically come to know as an "evil" Other, namely the "evil empire" of the Soviet Union, was challenged because it lacked a traditionally identifiable locus. George W. Bush provided that much-needed locus in his State of the Union Address in January 2002. Deploying the Manichaean rhetorics of the Cold War, he named and instantiated the evil, this time not as an empire, but as an axis—the "axis of evil" formed by Iran, Iraq, and North Korea. Six months later, on June 6, 2002, in a presidential address to the American nation, he announced the formation of a permanent Department of Homeland Security, calling it "the most extensive reorganization of the federal government since the 1940s," and explaining that the War on Terror's "homeland security" state is an extension of the Cold War's national security state. Bush remarked, "During his presidency, Harry Truman recognized that our nation's fragmented defenses had to be reorganized to win the Cold War. He proposed uniting our military forces under a single Department of Defense, and creating the National Security Council to bring together defense, intelligence, and diplomacy. Truman's reforms are still helping us to fight terror abroad, and now we need *similar* dramatic reforms to secure our people at home."[5] And in late 2002, in a reprise of the battle waged on the cultural terrain during the inaugural height of the Cold War when artists and writers were called upon to extol the virtues of American democracy abroad, the Bush administration recruited prominent American writers, including the Pulitzer Prize–winner Michael Chabon, Poet Laureate Billy Collins, and Arab American Naomi Shihab, to act as cultural ambassadors. Asked to write about "what it means to be an American writer," they gave readings around the world and contributed to a State Department anthology that would be disseminated as part of a global pro-American public relations campaign.[6] Next, in signing the $87.5 billion aid package for Iraq and

Afghanistan on November 6, 2003, Bush likened it to the Marshall Plan and
the long Cold War struggle for "democracy." Then, on October 6, 2005, in a
speech sponsored by the National Endowment for Democracy, he effected a
rhetorical equivalence between the War on Terror and the Cold War: "Like
the ideology of communism, our new enemy pursues totalitarian aims. . . .
Like the ideology of communism, our new enemy is dismissive of free peoples,
claiming that men and women who live in liberty are weak and decadent."
Echoing the Cold War fear of communist infiltration and world domination
by an "evil empire," he claimed further that "[t]he militants believe that controlling one country will rally the Muslim masses, enabling them to over-
throw all moderate governments in the region and establish a radical *Islamic
empire* that spans from Spain to Indonesia." Finally, Bush called the campaign
against terrorism, like the Cold War, "the unfolding of a global ideological
struggle."[7] Indeed, in providing an alternative interpretation of 9/11, Mahmood Mamdani argues that rather than demonstrating a deep-rooted "clash
of civilizations," 9/11 "needs to be understood first and foremost as the unfinished business of the Cold War," the result of a previous Cold War alliance
between the United States and al-Qaeda (and the Taliban) in Afghanistan
"gone sour."[8]

Some disturbing continuities in the discursive and geopolitical matrices
of the Cold War and the more recent War on Terror are also indexed in representations of North Korea, a country that is itself a Cold War creation.
North Korea is a sensational fixture not only in the news and in government
pronouncements, but also in popular culture. Recent cinematic works such
as *Die Another Day* (2002) and *Team America: World Police* (2004) are but a
couple of examples. If North Korea is a Cold War remnant that the putatively victorious end of the Cold War did not "solve" but repressed, it returns,
with violent force in this instance, as the post–Cold War "rogue state" and
later as part of the War on Terror's "axis of evil." Indeed, North Korea and
Asia figure curiously and persistently in such "returns." In the days following
9/11, one of President Bush's errant analogies included a comparison of himself to FDR, calling 9/11 *his* Pearl Harbor. The Cold War genealogy of the
North Korean "problem" is elided in the political demonology of the "axis of
evil," an invention that fixates on North Korea as a problem even as it obscures
America's Cold War role in literally giving birth to that "problem" in the first
place. In a critique of the U.S. occupation of Korea at the end of World War
II in 1945, and America's refusal to recognize Kim Il Sung when he came to
power in the North in 1946, Bruce Cumings observes that in the first decade

of the twenty-first century, this nonrecognition policy has entered its seventh decade. Noting the two Septembers—September 8, 1945, when American troops landed in Korea and September 11, 2001, when the twin towers were attacked—he writes, "the leadership of North Korea was a problem for the United States sixty years ago, and sixty Septembers later it remains so."[9] Moreover, recent pronouncements of a "new cold war," this time with China, suggest that the triangulation of the "old" Cold War in Asia did not come to an end with the developments in Europe—the fall of the Berlin Wall in 1989 and the failed Soviet coup in 1991—that have been used to mark the official termination of the Cold War.

In this concluding discussion, I have linked our present imperial mandate, the War on Terror, to our "past" imperial mandate, the Cold War. I have done so with the hope that the critical siting of such links into our contemporary moment extends our reach closer to a "history of the future," a conjuring of "what could be" despite, and precisely because of, what has been and what is. The stakes and implications, then, of *Ends of Empire* as a book in its critical tracing of the multiple temporal, spatial, functional, material, and narrative "ends of empire" proceed immediately from the linked contexts and knowledge projects of the Cold War, Asian American cultural politics, and Asian migration to the United States. But what I hope my critical tracing gestures to is a broader interrogation of the intersecting genealogies that have produced our contemporary moment of neoliberal globalization, imperial mandate, and enduring gendered racial regimes of domination. I have endeavored to elaborate America's imperial pasts and presents by showing how Asian American cultural texts imagine anew the "what was," "what could have been," and "what is," with the belief that such an imagining helps us chart and invent anew not only "what could be," or the world's futures, but also *how* it is to be. The urgent project of writing a "history of the future," what Andrea Smith calls a "prolineal genealogy,"[10] would call into being geopolitical, social, cultural, and epistemological formations that do not take recourse to tired Cold War Manichaean binaries, the physical, social, and what Ruth Wilson Gilmore sees as the "premature" death of people of color everywhere, nor to the unrelenting teleology of capital.[11] Indeed, this is to call for(th) a radically post–Cold War globality, epistemology, and ontology. In these times of what Dylan Rodríguez marks as the "'multiculturalization' of white supremacy," the "discursive and material expansion of civil society's normative whiteness, to the extent that 'nonwhites' or 'people of color' have increasingly invested in the protection of this sanctified property interest," the pitfalls of inclusion, incorporation, and cooptation are numerous and all too often fatal.[12] Against this particular fatality, the critical Cold War compositions—as at once a geopolitical structuring, ideological writing, and cultural imagining—that I have examined in this book yearn for another fatality altogether. They diagnose the *ends of* empire and imagine an as yet unrealized singular *end to*, or termination of, empire. Asian American critique and cultural politics articulate a longing for a death of empire that has yet to be but can be imagined.

ACKNOWLEDGMENTS

I owe many debts to many people for transforming the writing of this book from a condition of seeming impossibility to a condition of sustained possibility. The project began as a dissertation at the University of California, Berkeley. I thank the members of my dissertation committee, Elaine H. Kim, Sau-ling C. Wong, and Colleen Lye. I am especially grateful to Elaine Kim for chairing the committee; she is not only a model advisor but also a model human being, and her unwavering patience, commitment, generosity, and good heart are unrivaled. It is rare to know a person so accomplished and yet so humble, and even rarer to have the fortune of counting that person among your chosen kin. Colleen Lye is a model not only of how to produce rigorous scholarship but also of how to provide steadfast and detailed guidance. Sau-ling Wong knows how to ask the tough, but necessary, questions. I acknowledge UC Berkeley's Graduate Division for its generous support through the Chancellor's Predoctoral, Foreign Language and Area Studies, UC President's Dissertation Year, and Summer Research fellowships. I thank Michael Omi, Anne Cheng, Marie Lo, Dian Million, and Anna Leong for their important encouragement and support. I am grateful to Lisa Lowe for her significant contributions to the field and for providing important guidance and mentorship at key moments. My deep thanks also go to Iyko Day and David Hernández for being such wonderful friends, interlocutors, and travel companions. Iyko's generous ear, constructive advice, and sushi parties have nourished me over the course of many years. Profound thanks go as well to So Yeon Park for seeing me through many difficult moments.

My friends and colleagues at the University of California, Riverside, and beyond are an ideal collective. I thank in particular Setsu Shigematsu and

Dylan Rodríguez, my co-conspirators. They have been key in creating a strong intellectual formation, community, and kinship. Setsu generously and tirelessly read multiple drafts of my manuscript, offering invaluable critical engagement and rigorous feedback at every turn, and our many conversations provided crucial encouragement, inspiration, and clarity. I could not have written this book without her, and I am forever grateful for her brilliant insights and broader life-sustaining practices. Dylan gave energetic and disciplined advice and mentorship in all matters great and small, from how to be productive and still have a life, to how to publish a book, to how to fish. I thank him for that and for indefatigably engaging in the collective work of shaping spaces that generate and recognize new intellectual and political projects. I thank the wonderful women in my UC Riverside writing group, Amalia Cabezas, Michelle Raheja, and Tamara Ho, whose big hearts, generous engagement with my work, and patience made it possible for me to complete my book without losing too much hair. My deep gratitude goes to Mariam B. Lam for her good cheer and warm friendship, to Vorris Nunley for being one of the best listeners I know, and to Stephen Cullenberg for being a supportive friend, colleague, and dean. I also express thanks to Keith Harris, Freya Schiwy, Alessandro Fornazzari, Traise Yamamoto, Ofelia Cuevas, Randall Williams, and Stephen Wu for their encouragement, and I must not forget Andy Smith, who blew into UCR at precisely the right moment. UCR's Center for Ideas and Society, directed by the late Emory Elliot, offered fellowship support that allowed me to make significant progress in writing this book. Profound thanks as well to Hector Dio Mendoza, who nurtured my life with his loving patience, creative spirit, and incredible kindness.

In Southern California, the fabulous women in the LOUD Collective (the academics formerly known as the So Cal Women of Color Writing Group) dazzle me with their important work and critical interventions. I thank Grace Kyungwon Hong, Christine Balance, Maylei Blackwell, Jayna Brown, Erica Edwards, Aisha Finch, Yogita Goyal, Kara Keeling, Arlene Keizer, Mignon Moore, Deborah Vargas, and Tiffany Willoughby-Herard. I am especially grateful to Grace for her incredible and untiring generosity, committed brilliance, and sinfully delightful baked treats. The monthly meetings of our writing and support collective (spanning Los Angeles, Orange County, the Inland Empire, and all points in between) have challenged, inspired, and sustained me, and I continue to learn from our ongoing projects and conversations.

At the University of Minnesota Press, I thank Richard Morrison, an ideal editor, and the fabulous editorial assistant Adam Brunner. Sue Breckenridge provided wonderful copyediting, and Douglas Easton skillfully produced the index. I thank George Lipsitz, series editor of Critical American Studies, as well as Lisa Yoneyama, who both generously provided invaluable comments and suggestions that improved my book immeasurably.

Finally, I thank my family. Thanks to Kelly Lee, who goes beyond the call of sisterly duty; to my brother-in-law, Jason Lee; and to my nephews Matthew, Andrew, and Colby, who are some of the funniest people I know. I thank my father, Hee Shick Kim, and my incredible aunts, who have survived many wars.

Notes

Introduction

1. Chang-rae Lee, *Native Speaker* (New York: Riverhead Books, 1995), 225.

2. The uncapitalized "cold war" and capitalized "Cold War" are both accepted forms of usage. Since the Cold War is one of the central critical terms of my study, I will use its capitalized form as a way of highlighting it. In cited passages I have retained the original form used by the author. For the term "communist," I will generally use the lowercase form and capitalize it only when it is a proper noun that designates a particular party, e.g., "Chinese Communist(s)" (meaning the Chinese Communist Party).

3. Lee, *Native Speaker,* 225.

4. Ibid., 225–26.

5. Kramer offers two plausible explanations for gook: 1. The term came from a Tagalog word pronounced *gu-gu,* a slippery coconut oil shampoo, and might have been used to note the Philippine enemy's "slipperiness" or elusiveness; 2. The term might also have been derived from a minstrel tune sung by U.S. troops on the voyage over to the Philippines containing the line "Just because she made them goo-goo eyes" in the chorus. This line was applied to Filipina women upon the soldiers' arrival in the Philippines, and when the soldiers learned that Filipino men considered it an insult, they used it to taunt the men. See Paul A. Kramer, *The Blood of Government: Race, Empire, the United States, and the Philippines* (Chapel Hill: University of North Carolina Press, 2006), 127.

6. Roediger tracks the term back to 1920, when it appeared in the *Nation.* Herbert J. Seligman wrote, "The Haitians, in whose service United States Marines are presumably restoring peace and order in Haiti, are nicknamed 'Gooks' and have been treated with every variety of contempt, insult, and bestiality" (quoted in David Roediger, "Gook: The Short History of an Americanism," *Monthly Review* 43 [March 1992]: 50). Roediger also notes that according to the 1989 *Oxford English Dictionary,* "gook" is an Americanism but its actual origins are unknown, and it is defined as "a term of contempt for a foreigner; a coloured inhabitant of (south-) east Asia" (50). Its application

in 1935 to Filipinos is offered as a first usage, and its use by U.S. troops in Korea and Vietnam is noted. The troops, however, were the foreigners, and those designated by them as "gooks" (foreigner) were actually in their native land. If the term did originate in the Philippines, it probably did so during the Philippine–American War (1899–1902) and not in 1935. An interesting point of usage in the varied history of the term is its gendered application in a 1893 citation from *Slang and Its Analogues,* in which gooks are defined as "tarts," particularly camp-following prostitutes (51). Then, during World War II, in 1943, we find its usage by Marines to designate "natives everywhere," especially Arabs (52).

7. The actual title of Churchill's speech, delivered on March 5, 1946, at Westminster College in Fulton, Missouri, is "The Sinews of Peace." The speech is reprinted in Walter LaFeber, ed., *The Origins of the Cold War, 1941–1947: A Historical Problem with Interpretations and Documents* (New York: John Wiley and Sons, 1971), 136–39. For an analysis of the speech as "great art" but "failed rhetoric," see Michael J. Hostetler's "The Enigmatic Ends of Rhetoric: Churchill's Fulton Address as Great Art and Failed Persuasion," *Quarterly Journal of Speech* 83 (1997): 416–28.

8. There have also been debates about when the Cold War began. The years 1917, 1945, and 1948 have been variously cited. This prehistory can be dated as far back as the 1890s, when the United States tried to contain Russian expansion, especially in Manchuria and northern China, sometimes by ambivalently supporting Japan. Michael Hardt and Antonio Negri write: "In retrospect, in those first decades of the October Revolution we can already recognize the roots of the Cold War—the bipolar division of the territories of the globe and the frantic competition between the two systems. The New Deal legislation itself, along with the construction of comparable welfare systems in Western Europe, might be cast as a response to the threat conjured up by the Soviet experience, that is, to the increasing power of workers' movements both at home and abroad. The United States found itself increasingly driven by the need to placate class antagonism, and thus anticommunism became the overriding imperative" (*Empire* [Cambridge, Mass.: Harvard University Press, 2000], 176).

9. Tobin Siebers, *Cold War Criticism and the Politics of Skepticism* (New York: Oxford University Press, 1993), 29. There is a growing literature on the Cold War's false endings. See, for example, Donald Pease, "Hiroshima, the Vietnam Veteran's Memorial, and the Gulf War: Post-National Spectacles," in *Cultures of United States Imperialism,* ed. Amy Kaplan and Donald E. Pease, 557–80 (Durham: Duke University Press, 1993). Pease observes that "with the end of the cold war in 1990, the Bush administration had lost the national other against which and through which Reaganism had articulated its 'deterrence' hegemony. As a consequence, Bush was faced with the task of reconfiguring the iconography of cold war rule within the objectives of a New World Order. To accomplish this task, the Bush administration staged a military victory in Iraq to celebrate the end of the cold war and [paradoxically] resuscitate its power to rule" (559). Similarly, Nikhil Pal Singh writes that the Cold War may have been "won" but has not "ended." See his "Culture/Wars: Recoding Empire in an Age of Democracy," *American Quarterly* 50.3 (1998): 471–522. Also, Tony Jackson writes that the Cold War's own "sense of an ending" (the title of Frank Kermode's influential study on narratives of apocalypse) is historically unprecedented for three reasons: first,

nuclear annihilation would be a final, absolute destruction; second, should such a destruction occur, it would be as a result of human action, as opposed to a natural disaster or the will of God; and third, this nuclear end might not occur at all. Thus, with nuclear war, the great certainty is what form the destruction will take, while paradoxically, the great uncertainty is whether the great destruction will take place at all. This is unlike traditional narratives of the end, whether Christian or Marxist, in which the certainty is that the end will take place while the uncertainty is exactly when and in what form. See Tony Jackson, "Postmodernism, Narrative, and the Cold War Sense of an Ending," *Narrative* 8.3 (2000): 332.

10. I would like to thank Iyko Day for suggesting that I elaborate on the multiple senses of "ends." For a discussion of "imperial debris," or "ruins of empire," see Ann Laura Stoler, "Imperial Debris: Reflections on Ruins and Ruination," *Cultural Anthropology* 23.2 (2008): 191–219.

11. Sherry B. Ortner, "Resistance and the Problem of Ethnographic Refusal," *Comparative Studies in Society and History* 37.1 (1995): 173–93.

12. Audra Simpson, "On Ethnographic Refusal: Indigeneity, 'Voice,' and Colonial Citizenship," *Junctures* 9 (December 2007): 78.

13. Lisa Lowe writes, "Let us stress that the force of Asian American Studies is not the restoration of a cultural heritage to an identity formation, but rather the history of Asian alterity to the modern nation-state highlights the convergence of nationalism with racial exclusion, gendered social stratification, and labor exploitation" ("The International within the National: American Studies and Asian American Critique," *Cultural Critique* 40 [Fall 1998]: 30).

14. Kandice Chuh argues for a deconstructive understanding of the category "Asian American." She writes, "*Imagine Otherwise* argues that current conditions call for conceiving Asian American studies as a subjectless discourse. I mean *subjectlessness* to create the conceptual space to prioritize difference by foregrounding the discursive constructedness of subjectivity." She continues, "Subjectlessness, as a conceptual tool, points to the need to manufacture 'Asian American' situationally. It serves as the ethical grounds for the political practice of what I would describe as a strategic *anti-essentialism*" (*Imagine Otherwise: On Asian Americanist Critique* [Durham: Duke University Press, 2003], 9, 10). My project explicitly interrogates American empire in Asia as at once the discursive and material conditions of possibility for the constitution and disarticulation of "Asian America" and the "Asian American subject."

15. Lionel Trilling's *The Liberal Imagination* is considered to be exemplary of a "liberal consensus" formation enabled by a reading of modernist form as subversive in terms that are not specifically anticapitalist. See Lionel Trilling, *The Liberal Imagination: Essays on Culture and Society* (New York: Viking, 1950). For an incisive study of the extent to which the Cold War has powerfully influenced the form of academic criticism that has come to be identified as "modern," see Siebers, *Cold War Criticism*. See also David Suchoff, who observes, "Trilling's cultural position dovetailed with the work of 'consensus' historians like Richard Hofstadter, and with the pluralist premise of 'American exceptionalism' that shaped books such as Louis Harz's *The Liberal Tradition in America* (1955) and Daniel Boorstin's *The Genius of American Politics* (1953). Hofstadter, in a review of pluralist approaches written in 1968, argued as

did Trilling for the 'complexity' of anti-ideological modernism and its criticism of culture. The 'consensus' approach which Hofstadter represented offered an alternative to the economic analysis of the progressives, seeing pluralism and status competition as replacing divisive social conflict. Daniel Bell argued that ideology in America had come to an end (*The End of Ideology*)" ("New Historicism and Containment: Toward a Post–Cold War Cultural Theory," *Arizona Quarterly* 48 [Spring 1992]: 140). Suchoff argues further that Fredric Jameson was appropriated by New Historicists as a "containment" critic when his work argued for "an oppositional cultural criticism.... But if the return of historicism, after its Cold War suspension, made Jameson's inaugural injunction in that book *The Political Unconscious*—'always historicize'—quotable in New Historicist work even without attribution, that injunction also appeared without the argument for the explicitly Marxist cultural criticism it implied" (150). Suchoff continues that Frankfurt School approaches to cultural critique offer the greatest potential for shaping a post–Cold War cultural criticism, one that is dialectical and takes into account the critical potential of mass culture. Indeed, Theodor Adorno and Max Horkheimer's 1969 preface to *The Dialectic of Enlightenment*, he cites, "argued that the Cold War, with its 'political divisions into immense powerblocks set objectively upon collision,' was itself the paradigm of containment, dependent on false opposition, since the conflict itself only served to continue a 'sinister trend' toward an administered world" (155).

16. Andrew Hammond writes, "The privileging of Western experience has not only taken place in the spheres of political rhetoric and Cold War historiography. In that strand of Western scholarship that examines the literary response to the international crisis of 1945 to 1989, there is a similar tendency to define 'Cold War' by the conditions where war was coldest, and to take American and Western European writing as the proper ground of study" ("From Rhetoric to Rollback: Introductory Thoughts on Cold War Writing," in *Cold War Literature: Writing the Global Conflict*, ed. Andrew Hammond [London: Routledge, 2006], 3).

17. In a critique of triumphalist neoliberal rhetoric celebrating the "end" of the Cold War, Jacques Derrida writes that "this neo-liberal rhetoric, but jubilant and worried, manic and bereaved, often obscene in its euphoria, obliges us, then, to interrogate an event-ness inscribed in the gap between the moment in which the ineluctable of a certain end was heralded and the actual collapse of those totalitarian States or societies that gave themselves the figure of Marxism.... This latency period ... is not just a temporal medium.... A set of transformations of all sorts ... exceeds both the traditional givens of the Marxist discourse and those of the liberal discourse opposed to it.... [T]hese mutations ... disturb political philosophies and the common concepts of democracy, and oblige us to reconsider all relations between State and nation, man and citizen, the private and the public, and so forth" (*Specters of Marx: The State of the Debt, the Work of Mourning, and the New International* [New York: Routledge, 1994], 70).

18. Donald E. Pease, "Moby Dick and the Cold War," in *The American Renaissance Reconsidered*, ed. Walter Benn Michaels and Donald E. Pease (Baltimore: Johns Hopkins University Press, 1985), 113.

19. Amy Kaplan and Donald E. Pease's coedited anthology, *Cultures of United*

States Imperialism, is an important early example of work that seeks to center American empire as an object of critique in cultural studies, and thus to bring various fields into conversation with one another. In her introduction, "'Left Alone with America': The Absence of Empire in the Study of American Culture," Kaplan notes "three salient absences which contribute to this ongoing pattern of denial [of American empire] across several disciplines: the absence of culture from the history of U.S. imperialism; the absence of empire from the study of American culture; and the absence of the United States from the postcolonial study of imperialism" (11). Increasingly, scholars are bringing together these lines of inquiry and making these absences visible. For example, Asian Americanist cultural critiques of U.S. imperialism in the Philippines include Victor Bascara's *Model-Minority Imperialism* (Minneapolis: University of Minnesota Press, 2006), and Allan Punzalan Isaac's *American Tropics: Articulating Filipino America* (Minneapolis: University of Minnesota Press, 2006). In American studies, John R. Eperjesi's *The Imperialist Imaginary: Visions of Asia and the Pacific in American Culture* (Hanover: University Press of New England, 2005) devotes much of its attention to such canonical American writers as Jack London, but the book does include an analysis of a couple of Asian American works.

20. Lisa Lowe writes: "The material legacy of the repressed history of U.S. imperialism in Asia is borne out in the 'return' of Asian immigrants to the imperial center. In this sense, these Asian Americans are determined by the history of U.S. imperialism in Asia *and* the historical racialization of Asians in the United States" (*Immigrant Acts: On Asian American Cultural Politics* [Durham: Duke University Press, 1996], 16).

21. In psychoanalytic discourse, identification is the process that simultaneously instantiates and destabilizes identity. Diana Fuss writes: "Identification is the psychical mechanism that produces self-recognition. Identification inhabits, organizes, instantiates identity. It operates as a mark of self-difference, opening up a space for the self to relate to itself as a self, a self that is perpetually other. Identification, understood throughout this book as the play of difference and similitude in self-other relations, does not, strictly speaking, stand against identity but structurally aids and abets it. Yet, at the very same time that identification sets into motion the complicated dynamic of recognition and misrecognition that brings a sense of identity into being, it also immediately calls that identity into question . . . identification is a process that keeps identity at a distance, that prevents identity from ever approximating the status of an ontological given, even as it makes possible the formation of an illusion of identity as immediate, secure, and totalizable. It is one of the central claims of this book that it is precisely identity that becomes problematic in and through the work of identification" (*Identification Papers* [New York: Routledge, 1995], 2).

22. Grace Kyungwon Hong, *The Ruptures of American Capital: Women of Color Feminism and the Culture of Immigrant Labor* (Minneapolis: University of Minnesota Press, 2006), xvi, xx.

23. Andrea Smith, *Native Americans and the Christian Right: The Gendered Politics of Unlikely Alliances* (Durham: Duke University Press, 2008), xxvi.

24. See, for example, John Lewis Gaddis, *The United States and the Origins of the Cold War, 1941–1947* (New York: Columbia University Press, 1972, repr. 2000); Lloyd C. Gardner, *Architects of Illusion: Men and Ideas in American Foreign Policy 1941–1949*

(Chicago: Quadrangle Books, 1970); Akira Iriye, *The Cold War in Asia: A Historical Introduction* (Englewood Cliffs, N.J.: Prentice-Hall, 1974); Walter LaFeber, *America, Russia, and the Cold War 1945–1992*, 7th ed. (New York: McGraw-Hill, 1993); David S. Painter, *The Cold War: An International History* (London: Routledge, 1999); Ronnie D. Lipschutz, *Cold War Fantasies: Film, Fiction, and Foreign Policy* (Lanham: Rowman and Littlefield Publishers, 2001); Christina Klein, *Cold War Orientalism: Asia in the Middlebrow Imagination, 1945–1961* (Berkeley: University of California Press, 2003); Matthew Frye Jacobson and Gaspar González, *What Have They Built You to Do? The Manchurian Candidate and Cold War America* (Minneapolis: University of Minnesota Press, 2006); Elaine Tyler May, *Homeward Bound: American Families in the Cold War Era* (New York: Basic Books, 1988); David Seed, *American Science Fiction and the Cold War: Literature and Film* (Chicago: Fitzroy Dearborn Publishers, 1999); Thomas Hill Schaub, *American Fiction in the Cold War* (Madison: University of Wisconsin Press, 1991); Siebers, *Cold War Criticism;* Stephen J. Whitfield, *The Culture of the Cold War*, 2nd ed. (Baltimore: Johns Hopkins University Press, 1996); Lary May, ed., *Recasting America: Culture and Politics in the Age of Cold War* (Chicago: University of Chicago Press, 1989); Alan Nadel, *Containment Culture: American Narratives, Postmodernism, and the Atomic Age* (Durham: Duke University Press, 1995); Patrick O'Donnell, *Latent Destinies: Cultural Paranoia and Contemporary U.S. Narrative* (Durham: Duke University Press, 2000); and Marcel Cornis-Pope, *Narrative Innovation and Cultural Rewriting in the Cold War and After* (New York: Palgrave, 2001). Such accounts, while valuable, have yet to link critically the Cold War in Asia to racial formation and empire, nor to privilege Asian American hermeneutics and cultural productions.

25. Lowe, "The International within the National," 30.

26. While I thus conceptualize Cold War compositions in the plural, Ann Douglas demonstrates the importance of the Cold War context in understanding the American Century by arguing that postmodernism and postcolonialism, both as periodizations of the second half of the twentieth century and their attendant critical discourses, cannot be understood outside of the Cold War context and thus group together as a "cold war composition." See Ann Douglas, "Periodizing the American Century: Modernism, Postmodernism, and Postcolonialism in the Cold War Context," *Modernism/Modernity* 5.3 (1998): 71–98.

27. Michael Rogin, *Ronald Reagan, the Movie, and Other Episodes in Political Demonology* (Berkeley: University of California Press, 1987). He writes, "American demonology has both a form and a content. The demonologist splits the world in two, attributing magical, pervasive power to a conspiratorial center of evil. Fearing chaos and secret penetration, the countersubversive interprets local initiatives as signs of alien power. Discrete individuals and groups become, in the countersubversive imagination, members of a single political body directed by its head. The countersubversive needs monsters to give shape to his anxieties and to permit him to indulge his forbidden desires. Demonization allows the countersubversive, in the name of battling the subversive, to imitate his enemy" (xiii). The American Cold War state, then, is a countersubversive state par excellence.

28. Laura Hyun Yi Kang, *Compositional Subjects: Enfiguring Asian/American Women* (Durham: Duke University Press, 2002), 17.

29. That is, they constitute a "composition" in Deleuze and Guatarri's sense of holding together and accounting for multiple elements and articulations not through a linear "arboreal" or binary (Manichaean) reductionism, but through a "rhizomatic" schema that transversally registers the Cold War's manifold layers and meanings. For their discussion of "composition" (or "consistency"), see Gilles Deleuze and Felix Guattari, *A Thousand Plateaus: Capitalism and Schizophrenia* (Minneapolis: University of Minnesota Press, 1987), 327–50.

30. This rallying cry or reminder was first used in the British context, with the "return" of immigrants from Britain's former colonies to the imperial center of England.

31. Bascara, *Model-Minority Imperialism*, 8.

32. Singh notes the following similarities between the culture wars and the Cold War: "Both have been defined around a set of general intellectual processes, including 1) anxiety-ridden efforts to establish the legitimacy of the 'liberal' state in the face of presumed threats from an irresponsible, unAmerican left, and a potentially xenophobic right; 2) crisis-driven processes of normalizing (or universalizing) state procedures governing intranational differences, specifically with respect to race and citizenship structures; and 3) the deepening imbrication and increasing confusion of identities and differences within and beyond U.S. national borders, requiring persistent, and frequently violent adjudication of what it means to be responsible for, or to in fact be, the world" ("Culture/Wars," 472).

33. Denise Ferreira da Silva, *Toward a Global Idea of Race* (Minneapolis: University of Minnesota Press, 2007), xxxii, emphasis added.

34. Penny M. Von Eschen, "Who's the Real Ambassador? Exploding Cold War Racial Ideology," in *Cold War Constructions: The Political Culture of United States Imperialism, 1945–1966*, ed. Christian G. Appy, 110–32 (Amherst: University of Massachusetts Press, 2000).

35. Lowe, "The International within the National."

36. The conference took place April 18–25, 1955, in Bandung, Indonesia, with five sponsoring nations: India, Pakistan, Ceylon (now Sri Lanka), Burma (now Myanmar), and Indonesia. The United States and Soviet Union were not invited. See Nikhil Pal Singh, *Black Is a Country: Race and the Unfinished Struggle for Democracy* (Cambridge, Mass.: Harvard University Press, 2004), 176. Although Latin American nations were not present at this conference (since for the most part they had formally decolonized before this period), they too would become the terrain for U.S. Cold War interventions.

37. Twenty-five countries participated in this first conference, including India, Indonesia, Egypt, Ghana, Yugoslavia, and Algeria. By the second conference, held at Cairo in 1964, the number of participating nations had almost doubled. See Odd Arne Westad, *The Global Cold War: Third World Interventions and the Making of Our Times* (Cambridge: Cambridge University Press, 2005), 107.

38. David Harvey, *The New Imperialism* (New York: Oxford University Press, 2003), 45.

39. Cedric J. Robinson, *Black Movements in America* (New York: Routledge, 1997), 134. I would like to thank Grace Kyungwon Hong for pointing me to this text.

40. Thomas Borstelmann, *The Cold War and the Color Line: American Race Relations in the Global Arena* (Cambridge, Mass.: Harvard University Press, 2001), 6.

41. Penny M. Von Eschen writes that while the Cold War climate of the early 1950s "effectively severed the black American struggle for civil rights from the issues of anticolonialism and racism abroad," the Bandung Conference broadened the horizon of political discussion to include once again a global vision that linked domestic civil rights struggles to anticolonialism and the fight against racism abroad. See her *Race against Empire: Black Americans and Anticolonialism, 1937–1957* (Ithaca: Cornell University Press, 1997), 3, 168. Singh argues that though the rigid East–West orientation of the Cold War rescripted the question of freedom and slavery as one of communist tyranny and dictatorship and occluded North–South discussions of racism and colonialism that had concerned African Americans during World War II, by the time of the Vietnam War, we see a return of the repressed. He writes, "Considered from this vantage point, the capitulation of selected black leaders to the discourse of the Cold War might appear as the aberration. From Martin Luther King's embrace of Gandhi's principles of nonviolence (*satayagraha*) to the revolutionary nationalism of Malcolm X, Robert Williams, Harold Cruse, and Huey Newton that looked toward Cuba, Africa, China, and Vietnam, antiracism and anti-imperialism remained powerfully fused with the black political imagination" (Singh, *Black Is a Country*, 168, 173).

42. Cynthia A. Young, *Soul Power: Culture, Radicalism, and the Making of a U.S. Third World Left* (Durham: Duke University Press, 2006), 2.

43. Arturo Escobar, "Imagining a Post-Development Era? Critical Thought, Development, and Social Movements," *Social Text* 31/32 (1992): 20–56.

44. Sucheta Mazumdar, "Asian American Studies and Asian Studies: Rethinking Roots," in *Asian Americans: Comparative and Global Perspectives,* ed. Shirley Hune, Hyung-chan Kim, Stephen S. Fugita, and Amy Ling, 29–44 (Pullman: Washington State University Press, 1991).

45. Borstelmann, *The Cold War and the Color Line,* 46.

46. I would like to thank Setsu Shigematsu for helping me emphasize this point.

47. Quoted in Douglas, "Periodizing the American Century," 76.

48. Quoted in Seed, *American Science Fiction and the Cold War,* 1. The National Security Act of July 26, 1947, was preceded by the establishment—effective May 5, 1947, but announced two days later on May 7—of a new Policy Planning Staff in the State Department. This new body, responsible for the formulation of long-range policies, provided a central bureaucratic apparatus for implementing what George C. Kennan had called in his famous telegram "our political general staff work." Not surprisingly, it would be headed by Kennan himself, who had previously been serving as the Deputy for Foreign Affairs at the National War College. Secretary of the Navy Forrestal, extremely impressed with Kennan's "Long Telegram" from Moscow in February 1946, had had Kennan recalled from his diplomatic post there for duty at the new National War College.

49. Chalmers Johnson explains the Cold War and post–Cold War proliferation of intelligence agencies, all operating on unpublished or secret "black" budgets: "With the onset of the Cold War, the Pentagon became addicted to a black-budget way of life. After passage in 1949 of the Central Intelligence Act, all funds for the CIA were

(and still are) secretly contained in the Department of Defense's published budget under camouflaged names. As the President, the Pentagon, and the CIA created new intelligence agencies, the black budget expanded exponentially. In 1952, President Truman signed a still-secret seven-page charter creating the National Security Agency, which is devoted to signals and communications espionage; in 1960, President Eisenhower set up the even more secret National Reconnaissance Office, which runs our spy satellites; in 1961, President Kennedy launched the Defense Intelligence Agency, the personal intelligence organization of the Joint Chiefs of Staff and the Secretary of Defense; and in 1996, President Clinton combined several agencies into the National Imagery and Mapping Agency. The budgets of these ever-proliferating intelligence organizations are all unpublished, but estimates of their size are possible. In August 1994, an internal Pentagon memorandum was accidentally leaked to and published in *Defense Week*, a weapons-trade magazine. According to this memo, the NSA at that time spent $3.5 billion per year, the DIA $621 million, and the NRO $122 million (the CIA was not included)." Johnson continues: "The official name for the black budget is 'Special Access Programs' (SAPs), which are classified well above 'top secret.' ('SAP' may be a subtle or unintentional bureaucratic reference to the taxpayer)" (*The Sorrows of Empire: Militarism, Secrecy, and the End of the Republic* [New York: Metropolitan Books, 2004], 117–18). Between 1948 and 1953, after passage of the National Security Act, Pentagon expenditures quadrupled.

50. Philip Kuberski, "Hardcopy: The Remains of the Cold War," *Arizona Quarterly* 46.2 (1990): 56.

51. Douglas, "Periodizing the American Century," 76.

52. Hammond, "From Rhetoric to Rollback," 1, emphasis added.

53. The "domino theory" was explicitly articulated and explained by President Eisenhower in an April 1954 news conference to justify increasing U.S. involvement in Southeast Asia. Previously, Truman had used the same logics in his famous 1947 Truman Doctrine speech calling for U.S. interventions to contain communism in Greece and Turkey. In recent history, the domino theory has had many uncanny returns. In a critique of the Bush administration's eagerness to go to war against Iraq, Tony Judt, director of the Remarque Institute at New York University, writes: "The domino theory is back, this time in reverse. First we remake Iraq in our own image, then others will follow: Damascus, Beirut, Riyadh, perhaps even Cairo" ("The Wrong War at the Wrong Time," *New York Times*, Op-Ed, October 20, 2002). Such uncanny returns, I suspect, occur perhaps because the domino theory never went away.

54. Singh, *Black Is a Country*, 161–62.

55. Indeed, by 1958 even the U.S. Information Agency (USIA) made this admission: "We don't see the Russian fleet in Oriental waters. We see only the American fleet. We don't see the Russian Army in mainland China but we see a good deal of the American Army in Formosa, and Japan, and Korea, and Okinawa, and the Philippines." Quoted in Borstelmann, *The Cold War and the Color Line*, 113.

56. The quota for the Eastern Hemisphere was 170,000 per year (with a maximum of 20,000 per country), and the Western Hemisphere annual quota was 120,000 (with no country ceilings). The spouses, unmarried minor children, and parents of U.S. citizens were allowed entry as nonquota immigrants. Before the passage of the 1965

Immigration Act, Asians were allowed entry in small trickles through the 1943 Chinese Repealer, the 1945 War Brides Act, and the 1952 McCarran-Walter Act. See Sucheng Chan, *Asian Americans: An Interpretive History* (New York: Twayne Publishers, 1991), 140, 145.

57. Quoted in Harvey, *The New Imperialism,* 50–51.

58. Singh, *Black Is a Country,* 137–38.

59. Christopher L. Connery, "Pacific Rim Discourse: The U.S. Global Imaginary in the Late Cold War Years," *boundary 2* 21.1 (1994): 30–56. Connery argues that Pacific Rim Discourse is "post-Orientalist" because it is a non-othering discourse, one that "presumes a kind of metonymic equivalence instead" (32).

60. Kramer, *The Blood of Government,* 2, 3.

61. John W. Dower, *War without Mercy: Race and Power in the Pacific War* (New York: Pantheon Books, 1986), 14.

62. Observed by then secretary of the navy James Forrestal, quoted in L. Gardner, *Architects of Illusion,* 273.

63. Singh, *Black Is a Country,* 7.

64. Mary L. Dudziak, *Cold War Civil Rights: Race and the Image of American Democracy* (Princeton: Princeton University Press, 2000), 13.

65. Jodi Melamed, "The Spirit of Neoliberalism: From Racial Liberalism to Neoliberal Multiculturalism," *Social Text* 89 (Winter 2006): 5. I would like to thank Grace Kyungwon Hong for pointing me to Melamed's article.

66. Susan Koshy, "From Cold War to Trade War: Neocolonialism and Human Rights," *Social Text* 58 (Spring 1999): 16.

67. Francis Fukuyama, *The End of History and the Last Man* (New York: The Free Press, 1992).

68. Oswaldo de Rivero argues that the triumph of the capitalist side does not mean that we are "entering a new ethical order and have overcome depredation. On the contrary, we are today facing world hegemony in its most predatory, most individualistic version. This brutal version of capitalism pursues happiness as never before, to be achieved by the highest degree of material accumulation. It spreads environmentally unsustainable patterns of consumption, and uses the market and technology to plunder persons, enterprises and nations. Now that the fear of communism has faded, the only interest lies in higher profits, quick and easy money, with no thought for the environmental and social costs" (*The Myth of Development: Non-Viable Economies of the 21st Century,* trans. Claudia Encinas and Janet Herrick Encinas [London: Zed Books, 2001], 139–40).

69. Ibid., 138, emphasis added.

70. Westad, *The Global Cold War,* 4–5.

71. Giovanni Arrighi, *The Long Twentieth Century: Money, Power, and the Origins of Our Times* (London: Verso, 1994), 295–97, emphasis added.

72. William S. Borden, *The Pacific Alliance: United States Foreign Economic Policy and Japanese Trade Recovery, 1947–1955* (Madison: University of Wisconsin Press, 1984), 5–6.

73. Ibid., 11, 12.

74. Ibid., 197.

75. Ibid., 22.

76. Ibid., 50, 51. The war sparked a huge speculative buying boom by business and resulted in windfall profits for raw materials producers. From July 1950 to July 1951, world gold and dollar reserves increased by $5 billion.

77. Ibid., 51, 56.

78. Ibid., 168. Through 1955 the cumulative dollar gap between Japan and the United States had been $6.2 billion, balanced by $2 billion in economic aid and $4 billion in military expenditures. By 1964 military procurement had increased to $7.2 billion, and by 1970, with the Vietnam War, it was nearly $10 billion. Over the course of twenty-five years, the U.S. government transfer of dollars to Japan averaged $500 million per year, and by the 1970s, Japan had become the dominant power in Asia. Japan had granted $400 million in aid to Korea, the Philippines, Indonesia, and India, and over $150 million to Taiwan, Burma, Thailand, and Pakistan. See Borden, *The Pacific Alliance*, 218–20.

79. Thomas J. McCormick, *America's Half-Century: United States Foreign Policy in the Cold War and After*, 2nd ed. (Baltimore: Johns Hopkins University Press, 1995), 99, 157.

80. Ibid., 110.

81. Ibid., 149.

82. Writing in the British context at the turn of the twentieth century, J. A. Hobson observed the following: "The fallacy of the *supposed inevitability* of imperial expansion as a necessary outlet for progressive industry is now manifest. It is not industrial progress that demands the opening up of new markets and areas of investment, but *mal-distribution of consuming power* which prevents the absorption of commodities and capital within the country." He continues, "If, by some *economic readjustment*, the products which flow from the surplus saving of the rich to swell the overflow streams could be diverted so as to raise the incomes, and the standard of consumption of this inefficient fourth, there would be no need for pushful Imperialism, and the cause of *social reform* would have won its greatest victory. It is *not inherent* in the nature of things that we should spend our natural resources on militarism, war, and risky, unscrupulous diplomacy, in order to find markets for our goods and surplus capital. . . . Where the *distribution of incomes* is such as to enable all classes of the nation to convert their felt wants into an effective demand for commodities, there can be no overproduction, no underemployment of capital and labour, and no necessity to fight for foreign markets" (*Imperialism: A Study* [1902; Ann Arbor: University of Michigan Press, 1965], 85–87, emphasis added).

83. Robinson, *Black Movements in America*, 135, 134.

84. Ann Laura Stoler, "Intimations of Empire: Predicaments of the Tactile and Unseen," in *Haunted by Empire: Geographies of Intimacy in North American History*, ed. Ann Laura Stoler (Durham: Duke University Press, 2006), 9–10.

85. Amy Kaplan, *The Anarchy of Empire in the Making of U.S. Culture* (Cambridge, Mass.: Harvard University Press, 2002).

86. Hardt and Negri, *Empire*, xv.

87. Singh, "Culture/Wars," 488. In *Black Is a Country*, Singh argues further that anticommunism "gave Cold War liberalism a stability that had always eluded New Deal liberalism" (162).

88. Hobson, *Imperialism,* 85–87.

89. Elaine H. Kim, *Asian American Literature: An Introduction to the Writings and Their Social Context* (Philadelphia: Temple University Press, 1982).

90. Stoler, "Imperial Debris," 192.

1. Cold War Logics, Cold War Poetics

1. Lee, *Native Speaker,* 225.

2. Ibid.

3. Ibid.

4. George F. Kennan, "Long Telegram," in *Foreign Relations of the United States (FRUS), 1946,* 696–709 (Washington, D.C.: Government Printing Office, 1969); George F. Kennan (as "X"), "The Sources of Soviet Conduct," *Foreign Affairs* 25.4 (1947): 566–82; "NSC 68: United States Objectives and Programs for National Security (April 14, 1950)," in *American Cold War Strategy: Interpreting NSC 68,* ed. Ernest R. May, 23–82 (Boston: Bedford Books of St. Martin's Press, 1993); "NSC 48/1: The Position of the United States with Respect to Asia," in *United States-Vietnam Relations, 1945–1967,* 226–64 (Washington, D.C.: Government Printing Office, 1971).

5. Pease, "Moby Dick and the Cold War," 116.

6. William Pietz, "The 'Post-Colonialism' of Cold War Discourse," *Social Text* 19/20 (Fall 1988): 55–83.

7. George F. Kennan, *Memoirs: 1925–1950* (Boston: Little, Brown and Company, 1967), 294.

8. Yonosuke Nagai, "The Roots of Cold War Doctrine," in *The Origins of the Cold War in Asia,* ed. Yonosuke Nagai and Akira Iriye (New York: Columbia University Press, 1977), 19.

9. Kennan, *Memoirs,* 293, emphasis added. The five parts of the telegram are: (1) "The Basic Features of the Soviet Post-war Outlook"; (2) "The Background of That Outlook"; (3) "Its Projection on the Level of Official Policy"; (4) "Its Projection on the Level of Unofficial Policy, i.e. Policy Implemented Through 'Front' Organizations and Stooges of All Sorts"; (5) "The Implications of All This for American Policy."

10. Ibid.

11. Ibid., 294–95, emphasis added.

12. Quoted in Frank Costigliola, "'Unceasing Pressure for Penetration': Gender, Pathology, and Emotion in George Kennan's Formation of the Cold War," *Journal of American History* 83.4 (1997): 1336.

13. Kennan, *Memoirs,* 9.

14. I take this from the title of John Lewis Gaddis's book *Strategies of Containment: A Critical Appraisal of Postwar American National Security Policy* (Oxford: Oxford University Press, 1982).

15. Kennan, "Long Telegram," 699; further citations to this work will appear in the text.

16. L. Gardner, *Architects of Illusion,* 273–74, emphasis added. He writes: "As parody on parody, Forrestal's demeanor resembled Ichabod Crane's terrified flight in Sleepy Hollow—were it not for the fact these views soon were not considered unusual at all."

17. Quoted in Borstelmann, *The Cold War and the Color Line*, 22.

18. Quoted in ibid., 50.

19. L. Gardner, *Architects of Illusion*, 273.

20. I take this from the title of Christina Klein's *Cold War Orientalism*.

21. The word "penetration/penetrate" appears no fewer than six times throughout the telegram. See Kennan, "Long Telegram," 702, 704, 705, 706.

22. Quoted in Costigliola, "'Unceasing Pressure for Penetration,'" 1310; George F. Kennan, "The Background of Current Russian Diplomatic Moves," December 10, 1946, in *Measures Short of War: The George F. Kennan Lectures at the National War College, 1946–47*, ed. Giles D. Harlow and George C. Maerz (Washington, D.C.: National Defense University Press, 1991), 85.

23. Costigliola, "'Unceasing Pressure for Penetration,'" 1310.

24. For an analysis of the gendered and sexually charged exploits of the American embassy in Russia, of which Kennan was a part, see Costigliola, "'Unceasing Pressure for Penetration.'"

25. See, for example, Nyan Shah's *Contagious Divides: Epidemics and Race in San Francisco's Chinatown* (Berkeley: University of California Press, 2001). In this excellent study, he observes that epidemics, such as the smallpox epidemic that struck San Francisco in the summer of 1876, were often blamed on the Chinese, whose presumed "excesses" were thought to carry lethal contagion and presented a menace to white bourgeois norms.

26. Nagai observes that Kennan's epidemiological logics are not unique. Historical examples include: "the disease of liberty" (Thomas Jefferson), "the scourge of war" (Abraham Lincoln), and, probably, the most famous of all, "quarantine" (Frankin D. Roosevelt). See Nagai, "The Roots of Cold War Doctrine," 23–24.

27. Kennan, "The Sources of Soviet Conduct," 566; further citations to this work will appear in the text. Costigliola writes: "Kennan, who sought out Anna Freud in London in 1944, found that the discourse of psychology buttressed his claim to special insights, offering knowledge that was 'objective' even if not discernible by others" ("'Unceasing Pressure for Penetration,'" 1323).

28. Costigliola writes: "When Kennan wrote the LT [Long Telegram], in February 1946, Americans were searching for a clear-cut, simple explanation of Soviet foreign policy. Joseph Stalin's government, however, displayed a confusing mixture of caution and self-aggrandizement. The Soviets angered the United States by their continued occupation of northern Iran and Manchuria, by their pressure on Turkey for base rights in the Dardanelles, and by their defense of Soviet spies caught in Canada. Yet they evacuated northern Norway and the Danish island of Bornholm in the Baltic sea, discouraged revolution in Western Europe, offered no leadership to communist revolutionaries in Southeast Asia, and played to both sides in the Chinese civil war; further, they went on to allow free elections in Hungary, Czechoslovakia, and Finland. What was the pattern to these events? Americans wondered. Was it possible and desirable to extend wartime cooperation into the postwar era? There was 'great confusion' in Washington, observed Dwight D. Eisenhower" ("'Unceasing Pressure for Penetration,'" 1312–13).

29. Douglas Field, Introduction to *American Cold War Culture*, ed. Douglas Field (Edinburgh: Edinburgh University Press, 2005), 6–7.

30. Quoted in Costigliola, "'Unceasing Pressure for Penetration,'" 1324.

31. Ibid.

32. Quoted in ibid., 1325.

33. Alan Nadel, *Containment Culture: American Narrratives, Postmodernism, and the Atomic Age* (Durham: Duke University Press, 1995), 17.

34. Quoted in Nagai, "The Roots of Cold War Doctrine," 23.

35. The full text of Truman's speech is printed in *The Origins of the Cold War, 1941–1947: A Historical Problem with Interpretations and Documents*, ed. Walter LaFeber, 151–56 (New York: John Wiley and Sons, Inc., 1971).

36. LaFeber, *America, Russia, and the Cold War 1945–1992*, 52–53.

37. Lee, *Native Speaker*, 225.

38. Quoted in *The Origins of the Cold War, 1941–1947*, 151.

39. LaFeber, *America, Russia, and the Cold War 1945–1992*, 55–56.

40. Ibid., 62–63.

41. Ibid., 58.

42. Ibid., 96.

43. Lloyd Gardner writes: "At the heart of these differences between Kennan and the authors of NSC-68 was a simple inversion of intellectual procedure: where Kennan tended to look at the Soviet threat in terms of an independently established concept of irreducible interests, NSC-68 derived its view of American interests primarily from its perception of the Soviet threat. Kennan's insistence on the need to deter hostile combinations of industrial-military power could have applied as well to the adversaries of World Wars I and II as to the Soviet Union. No comparably general statement of fundamental interests appeared in NSC-68. The document paid obeisance to the balance of power, diversity, and freedom, but nowhere did it set out the minimum requirements necessary to secure those interests. Instead it found in the simple presence of Soviet threat sufficient cause to deem the interest threatened vital" (*Architects of Illusion*, 98).

44. LaFaber, *America, Russia, and the Cold War 1945–1992*, 98.

45. Nagai, "The Roots of Cold War Doctrine," 36.

46. Walter LaFeber, "American Policy-Makers, Public Opinion, and the Outbreak of the Cold War, 1945–50," in Nagai and Iriye, *The Origins of the Cold War in Asia*, 62.

47. Nakajima Mineo, "The Sino–Soviet Confrontation in Historical Perspective," in Nagai and Iriye, *The Origins of the Cold War in Asia*, 207.

48. In 1950 the NSC had existed only three years. This cabinet-level committee, created to advise the president on issues that crossed foreign and defense policy lines, had a small staff and did not yet have a "National Security Advisor" position. The position, officially titled Assistant to the President for National Security Affairs, would later become significant, filled by the likes of Henry Kissinger and, more recently, Condoleezza Rice. An NSC paper normally came from the State Department or from one of the military services via the Joint Chiefs of Staff. It was then assigned a number as an NSC paper by the Council Secretariat. See Ernest R. May, *American Cold War Strategy*, 1.

49. It was distributed to the president, the vice president, the secretaries of state and defense, the statutory members and advisors of the National Security Council,

the chairman of the National Security Resources Board, the chairman of the Joint Chiefs of Staff, and the director of the CIA. See Ernest R. May, *American Cold War Strategy*, 2.

50. Kennan was the director of the Policy Planning Staff until December 1949, at which point he came counselor.

51. Ernest R. May, *American Cold War Strategy*, 9.

52. Quoted in ibid., 9.

53. See "NSC 68," 23–82; specific citations to this work will appear in the text. Although NSC 68 was presented to President Truman on April 7, 1950, he did not fully endorse the paper until September 30—three months into the Korean War. Alonzo L. Hamby argues that while Truman initially approved of the document's "conceptual framework of a long-term struggle between American freedom and Soviet totalitarianism," he was reluctant to implement the expansive policy recommendations contained in it. So he "instituted a process of having them studied and debated to death within the administration. . . . Truman was a cold warrior and a hard-eyed realist about the uses of military power; what most likely gave him pause were the domestic consequences of implementation." Hamby quoted in Ernest R. May, *American Cold War Strategy*, 153.

54. Ernest R. May, *American Cold War Strategy*, vii.

55. A later document in the series, NSC 48/5 (dated May 17, 1951), extends NSC 48/1's notion of the containment of communism in Asia as a project of "collective security," but is much more explicit about the United States' desire for and interest in the rich natural resources of Asia. See "NSC 48/5: United States Objectives, Policies, and Courses of Action in Asia (May 17, 1951)," in *Foreign Relations of the United States (FRUS), 1951*, 33–63 (Washington, D.C.: Government Printing Office, 1977).

56. "NSC 48/1," 226; further citations to this work will appear in the text.

2. The El Dorado of Commerce

1. Maxine Hong Kingston, *China Men* (New York: Vintage International, 1980), 276.

2. John Frankenheimer, dir., *The Manchurian Candidate* (United Artists, 1962), 129 minutes; David Henry Hwang, *M. Butterfly* (New York: Plume, 1989).

3. Quoted in Teemu Ruskola, "Canton Is Not Boston: The Invention of American Imperial Sovereignty," in "Legal Borderlands: Law and the Construction of American Borders," ed. Mary L. Dudziak and Leti Volpp, special issue, *American Quarterly* 57.3 (2005): 873–74, 880.

4. Ibid., 861.

5. Quoted in LaFeber, *America, Russia, and the Cold War 1945–1992*, 3.

6. Annex 4, *United States Relations with China: With Special Reference to the Period 1944–1949/Based on the files of the Department of State* (Washington, D.C.: Government Printing Office, 1949), 414–16.

7. Thomas J. McCormick, *China Market: America's Quest for Informal Empire 1893–1901* (Chicago: Quadrangle Books, 1967), 128.

8. Delber McKee, *Chinese Exclusion versus the Open Door Policy, 1900–1906* (Detroit: Wayne State University Press, 1977), 16–17.

9. William Appleman Williams, *The Tragedy of American Diplomacy* (1959; New York: W. W. Norton, 1972), 46.

10. Quoted in Iriye, *Cold War in Asia,* 117.

11. Ibid., 117–18. The Yalta Agreement of February 1945, signed by the leaders of Great Britain, the United States, and the Soviet Union, laid out plans for the postwar international order. Nakajima Mineo argues that the "biggest flaw in the Yalta Agreement was that it made a sacrificial object of China, which, although one of the victorious powers, suffered most from the war. The Agreement also miscalculated the future of China and made no provisions for responding to the rise of Chinese nationalism. The first American to recognize the dangers inherent in this secret agreement was the Ambassador to China, Patrick Hurley. However, Hurley failed in his attempts to revise the Yalta Agreement, and when the Kuomintang government discovered what the secret agreement was about, they hurriedly dispatched T. V. Soong to Moscow for discussions with the Soviets" ("The Sino–Soviet Confrontation," 207–8).

12. Iriye, *Cold War in Asia,* 119.

13. Most notably, in the key battle over Manchuria in the autumn of 1945, occupied by Japan since 1931, as Russian soldiers moved in to disarm the Japanese, and Chiang and Mao raced for control over this important region, Truman attempted to aid Chiang by keeping Japanese troops in place to fight the Communists until Chiang's army could move into position. Truman also dispatched as many as a hundred thousand soldiers to aid the Nationalists. Chiang's position, however, soon weakened, so Truman then attempted a diplomatic solution by sending General George Marshall on a famous(ly) failed yearlong diplomatic mission to mend the rift between Chiang and Mao. Marshall concluded that saving Chiang would involve a virtual U.S. takeover of the Chinese government, a long-term commitment from which it would be impossible to withdraw. Hoping, then, that the revolution would not be completed "for a long time," Truman retreated somewhat from China but continued to send economic and military aid to Chiang. Quoted in LaFeber, *America, Russia, and the Cold War 1945–1992,* 34.

14. Iriye, *Cold War in Asia,* 143.

15. Ibid.

16. Ibid., 155.

17. Ibid.

18. Painter, *The Cold War,* 27.

19. LaFeber, *America, Russia, and the Cold War 1945–1992,* 87.

20. Dean Acheson, "Letter of Transmittal," *United States Relations with China,* xiv–xvii, emphasis added.

21. Ibid., xvi.

22. Pease, "Moby Dick and the Cold War," 113.

23. Iriye, *Cold War in Asia,* 170.

24. Acheson, "Letter of Transmittal," xvi.

25. Iriye, *Cold War in Asia,* 167.

26. Ibid., 184.

27. LaFeber, *America, Russia, and the Cold War 1945–1992,* 174–75.

28. Ibid., 252.

29. Aruga Tadashi, "The United States and the Cold War: The Cold War Era in American History," in Nagai and Iriye, *The Origins of the Cold War in Asia*, 82.

30. Allen S. Whiting, "Mao, China, and the Cold War," in Nagai and Iriye, *The Origins of the Cold War in Asia*, 252.

31. Karen Leong argues that before 1949, and beginning in the 1930s, a new image of China took hold in the American imagination. She calls this the "China mystique": a romanticized, progressive, and gendered image of China as a "New China." See Karen J. Leong, *The China Mystique: Pearl S. Buck, Anna May Wong, Mayling Soong, and the Transformation of American Orientalism* (Berkeley: University of California Press, 2005), 1.

32. For a useful book-length analysis of this important film, see Jacobson and González, *What Have They Built You to Do?*

33. Dr. Yen Lo is played by actor Khigh Dhiegh (birth name Kenneth Dickerson), who is best known for his role playing another villainous Chinese Communist agent, Wo Fat, in the long-running television series *Hawaii Five-O*. Although he often played such Asian roles, he was actually of Anglo, Egyptian, and Sudanese ancestry.

34. Fears of Chinese Communist infiltration and possible takeover of the U.S. government saw a heated reprisal during the so-called Asian Donorgate controversy, in which the Democratic National Committee (and Vice President Al Gore and President Bill Clinton in particular) were accused of soliciting and accepting campaign donations from foreign Asian sources. The March 24, 1997, front cover of the *National Review*, entitled "The Manchurian Candidates," was a political cartoon of Al Gore, Bill Clinton, and Hilary Clinton in yellowface, as a Buddhist monk, a servant in a coolie hat, and a Chinese Red Army cadre, respectively. Many, especially members of the Asian American community, derided this cartoon as stereotypical and racist, and were further angered when interrogating phone calls were made to donors of the DNC with Asian surnames, including American citizens.

35. For a rigorous genealogy of American Orientalism, particularly of the "yellow peril" as "Asiatic racial form," see Colleen Lye's *America's Asia: American Literature and Racial Form, 1882–1943* (Princeton: Princeton University Press, 2004).

36. Rohmer enjoyed commercial success through the publication of thirteen Fu Manchu novels, which sold more than 20 million copies during his lifetime. In 1923 the first of these novels, *The Mystery of Dr. Fu-Manchu* (1913), was adapted into a movie in England by the Stoll Production Company. In the 1930s America's Hollywood took over the production of Fu Manchu films, and Rohmer himself made contributions to scripts and screenplays even as he churned out new novels. Then, during World War II, he further popularized his Fu Manchu narratives through radio broadcasts, and in the 1950s he participated in the creation of a series of half-hour television shows called *The Adventures of Dr. Fu-Manchu*. Urmila Seshagiri argues that Rohmer's Fu Manchu novels forge an "intimate connection between racial identity and the various promises of twentieth-century modernity," and that the figure of Fu Manchu "has cast a long shadow: not only was Fu-Manchu a progenitor of Flash Gordon's villain Ming the Merciless and James Bond's evil Dr. No, but his imprimatur has been stamped on comic books, board games, candies, mustaches, playing cards, cocktails,

and rock bands." See Urmila Seshagiri, "Modernity's (Yellow) Perils," *Cultural Critique* 62 (Winter 2006): 164.

37. Quoted in David Seed, "The Yellow Peril in the Cold War: Fu Manchu and *The Manchurian Candidate*," in Hammond, *Cold War Literature*, 18.

38. Quoted in ibid.

39. This term was coined by Philip Wylie in his 1942 book *A Generation of Vipers*. Within the context of popular psychoanalytic theories of sexual development, he argued that "momism" was particularly dangerous to sons, and by extension, to American masculinity as such. For an analysis of this trope in *The Manchurian Candidate*, see Michael Rogin, *Ronald Reagan, the Movie, and Other Episodes in Political Demonology*, 252–54. For an analysis of gender in the film, see Tony Jackson, "*The Manchurian Candidate* and the Gender of the Cold War," *Literature/Film Quarterly* 28.1 (2000): 34–40. Jared Gardner writes that the "the entire struggle [in the film] is exposed as a repressed Oedipal drama. What if the pleasures taken in telling and retelling the stories of the Cold War were shown to be Oedipal pleasure? And what if the paranoid style of American politics was itself revealed to be an elaborate transference: from the desire to expose our origins (to see Mother naked) to the desire to expose the origins of a great conspiracy—a transference from Mother Dearest to Mother Russia?" ("Bringing the Cold War Home: Reprogramming American Culture in *The Manchurian Candidate*," in *Proceedings of the Conference on Film and American Culture* [Williamsburg, Va.: Roy R. Charles Center, College of William and Mary, 1994], 28).

40. Hunter wrote a series of books on this topic, with titles such as *Brain-washing in Red China: The Calculated Destruction of Men's Minds* (1951), *Brainwashing: From Pavlov to Powers* (1956), and *Brainwashing: The Story of Men Who Defied It* (1956). For an analysis of brainwashing in *The Manchurian Candidate*, see Susan L. Carruthers, "*The Manchurian Candidate* (1962) and the Cold War Brainwashing Scare," *Historical Journal of Film, Radio and Television* 18.1 (1998): 75–95.

41. Edward Hunter, *Brain-washing in Red China: The Calculated Destruction of Men's Minds* (New York: Vanguard Press, 1951), 4.

42. Ibid., 301–2.

43. Jared Gardner writes: "Before the first evidence of widespread American collaboration became the central concern of the day, the public had already been taught to worry about brainwashing. . . . When the prisoner exchange took place in 1953, the press and the public knew what to look for in their returning sons: they would not be who they once were, somehow transformed into enemies of god, country, and family. In one of the great self-fulfilling prophecies of recent history, the military intelligence began investigating returning POWs utilizing the same executive order that had authorized McCarthy's House Un-American Activities Committee. Although there was initial sympathy for the fate of the brainwashed POWs, once the court martial trials began in 1955 the emphasis of the story shifted importantly away from the horrors and techniques of brainwashing, and towards the alarming fact of collaboration on the part of American soldiers. No longer was the primary question what have they done to our boys; by 1955 the question had been reformulated to ask why our boys had allowed them to do it? . . . Overshadowing the concern as to whether

the nation was bringing spies back into the family was this new anxiety that potential spies were being bred in the American family itself, vipers conditioned at home even before they had been sent overseas" ("Bringing the Cold War Home," 24).

44. Chunjin is played by actor Henry Silva.

45. See Carruthers, "*The Manchurian Candidate* (1962)."

46. Christina Klein, "Cold War Orientalism: Musicals, Travel Narratives, and Middlebrow Culture in Postwar America" (PhD diss., Yale University, 1997), 140.

47. Ibid., 143.

48. Ibid., 147.

49. John Luther Long, "Madame Butterfly," *Century Magazine,* January 1898: 377.

50. Ibid., 375.

51. American naval officer Commodore Matthew Perry, we might recall, "opened" Japan to the West in 1853 when he sailed into Edo (later Tokyo) Bay. In terms of the absurd length of the lease, the number, 999, resonates with the British "leasing" of the New Territories (part of Hong Kong) in 1898 for 99 years. Hong Kong Island and the Kowloon Peninsula, the other parts of Hong Kong, became a permanent colony in 1841. The then-impending expiration of the New Territories lease in 1997 led to the 1984 Sino-British Declaration, signed by Margaret Thatcher and Zhao Jiyang, the Chinese premier. Hong Kong was then granted special status as a "Special Administrative Region" of China for 50 years after 1997.

52. The post–World War II economic success of Japan, writes Bruce Cumings, "has been marked by strong state protection for nascent industries, adoption of foreign technologies, and comparative advantages deriving from cheap labor costs, technological innovation, and 'lateness' in world time. Each phase involved a bursting forth into the world market that has always struck foreign observers as abrupt and unexpected, thus inspiring fear and loathing, awe and admiration" ("The Origins and Development of the Northeast Asian Political Economy: Industrial Sectors, Product Cycles, and Political Consequences," in *The Political Economy of the New Asian Industrialization,* ed. Frederic C. Deyo [Ithaca: Cornell University Press, 1987], 45). In the United States, the backlash to Japanese economic success, especially in the auto industry, took a tragically violent turn in 1982, when Vincent Chin, a twenty-seven-year-old Chinese American draftsman, was beaten to death by two white unemployed auto workers in Detroit, because they thought he was Japanese.

53. Richard Bernstein, "France Jails 2 in Odd Case of Espionage," *New York Times,* May 11, 1986, K7.

54. Ibid.

55. Hwang, playwright's notes to *M. Butterfly,* unpag.

56. Hwang, afterword to *M. Butterfly,* 98–99.

57. Ibid., 100.

58. See, for example, Marjorie Garber, "The Occidental Tourist: *M. Butterfly* and the Scandal of Transvestitism," in *Nationalisms and Sexualities,* ed. Andrew Parker, Mary Russo, Doris Sommer, and Patricia Yaeger, 121–46 (New York: Routledge, 1992), and Dorinne Kondo, "*M. Butterfly*: Orientalism, Gender, and a Critique of Essentialist Identity," *Cultural Critique* 16 (1990): 5–29.

59. Hwang, playwright's notes to *M. Butterfly,* unpag.

60. Arif Dirlik, "Chinese History and the Question of Orientalism," *History and Theory* 35.4 (1996): 116, 117–18.

61. Karl Marx, *Capital* (New York: Vintage Books, 1977), 1:164–65, emphasis added.

62. In a fascinating account of the history of the term "fetish," William Pietz writes that "the fetish, as an idea and problem, and as a novel object not proper to any prior discrete society, originated in the cross-cultural spaces of the coast of West Africa during the sixteenth and seventeenth centuries." Within these spaces, triangulated among Christian feudal, African lineage, and merchant capitalist social systems, there emerged a new "problematic concerning the capacity of the material object to embody—simultaneously and sequentially—religious, commercial, aesthetic, and sexual values . . . the fetish could originate only in conjunction with the emergent articulation of the ideology of the commodity form that defined itself within and against the social values and religious ideologies of . . . radically heterogeneous social systems." He continues that it was this power of a singular social construct able to yoke together heterogeneous elements into an apparently natural unity that in part attracted Marx to the notion of the fetish. Because of its materiality and its repetitive durability in conjoining heterogeneous elements into a singular fixation, the fetish, then, is the locus of social value and subjective formation. See William Pietz, "The Problem of the Fetish, I," *Res* 9 (Spring 1985): 5, 7. In psychoanalytic discourse, the fetish has also been taken up to mean an object that is overinvested with erotic value.

63. Hwang, *M. Butterfly*, 5; further citations to this work will appear in the text.

64. Bruce Cumings, *Parallax Visions: Making Sense of American–East Asian Relations at the End of the Century* (Durham: Duke University Press, 1999), 168–69.

65. John Louis DiGaetani, "'M. Butterfly': An Interview with David Henry Hwang," *TDR* 33.3 (1989): 146.

66. The scramble for the Chinese market reached historic heights in the late nineteenth and early twentieth centuries. Western nations, most notably the United States, England, and France, competed for market penetration and the extraction of raw materials. For a curiously detailed account of how Westerners attempted to attract Chinese customers, see Carl Crow's 1937 book, entitled, appropriately enough, *Four Hundred Million Customers: The Experiences, Some Happy, Some Sad of an American in China, and What They Taught Him* (New York: Harper and Brothers Publishers, 1937).

67. The roots of the hula hoop date back to ancient Egypt, Greece, Rome, and fourteenth-century England. Though the hoops were actually wooden back then, their use was the same. The etymology of the term "hula hoop" dates back to the eighteenth century, when missionaries first visited Hawaii, saw the hula dance, and christened the toy the "hula hoop." Interestingly, hula hooping has made a recent comeback in the United States since the inception of its mass-market version in 1958, which spawned increasingly elaborate national contests to see who could hoop the longest. In the recent trend, however, the hula hoop has transmogrified from child toy to adult fitness tool. Enthusiasts believe there are physical and spiritual benefits to hooping; it is deemed to help tone the abdominals, gluteas maximus, arms, and legs, and to aid digestion and circulation (which releases toxins), while boosting overall energy and mental clarity. See *East West Magazine*, November 18, 2002.

68. Marx, *Capital*, 1:166–67.

69. Robert D. Kaplan, "The Next Cold War: How We Would Fight China," *Atlantic Monthly*, June 2005, 49–50.

70. Ibid., 55.

71. Ibid., 49.

3. Asian America's Japan

1. Alain Resnais, dir., *Hiroshima, Mon Amour* (Argos Films, 1959), 90 minutes.

2. I would like to thank Setsu Shigematsu for pointing out this multiple valence of "You saw nothing in Hiroshima."

3. Steven Okasaki, dir., *Survivors* (Video Project, 1982, updated 1994), 35 minutes; David Mura, *Turning Japanese: Memoirs of a Sansei* (New York: Anchor Books, 1991); Ruth L. Ozeki, *My Year of Meats* (New York: Penguin Books, 1998).

4. Quoted in Michael Schaller, *The American Occupation of Japan: The Origins of the Cold War in Asia* (New York: Oxford University Press, 1985), 100.

5. The term "model minority" came about in the 1960s in newspaper and magazine accounts of perceived Japanese American and Chinese American socioeconomic success. High levels of educational achievement, low rates of mental disorder and criminality, and job mobility were used as factors to measure this success. Subsequently, it was extended to Asian Americans as a whole. Characteristics attributed to the model minority—of hard work, thrift, family cohesion, deference to authority—were explained by pointing to an undifferentiated, essentialized notion of "Asian culture." These Asian values, it was argued, while still alien, were highly compatible with Anglo-American values, especially the Protestant work ethic. How did Asians, who had historically been subject to immigration exclusion, political disenfranchisement, various forms of discrimination, and physical violence as the "yellow peril," become the model minority, seemingly overnight? Turning to the domestic and international historical context at this time sheds light on the apparent shift. In the 1960s, African Americans were actively challenging institutional racism through the civil rights struggle. The figure of the Asian American model minority was constructed as a conservative backlash against these activists, who were deemed to be unruly and underachieving. African Americans were told that if Asian Americans could succeed, why couldn't they? A *U.S. News and World Report* article in 1966 presented a progressive account of the history of Asians in the United States, the road "from hardship and discrimination to become a model of self-respect and achievement in today's America." Asian American "success" was used as evidence to support the claim that American liberalism could indeed function as a multiracial democracy. Therefore, if the system is not flawed, it was argued, the fault must somehow lie with the African Americans themselves. If African Americans "worked" as hard as the Asian Americans, then surely they could become model minorities as well. Indeed, as reported by *U.S. News and World Report*, "At a time when it is being proposed that hundreds of billions be spent to uplift Negroes and other minorities, the nation's 300,000 Chinese-Americans are moving ahead on their own—with no help from anyone else." So the figure of the model minority was less *about* Asian Americans per se and more a lesson to be learned by African Americans and a deflection away from the focus on the problem of institutional racism and racial inequality. It attempted to sublate the contradictions of

the U.S. nation-state. Such a deflection was necessary not only for domestic race relations, but for Cold War international geopolitical relations as well. In the Cold War battle against communist totalitarianism, the United States was very concerned about its international image and sought to counter and mitigate charges of racism. See William Petersen, "Success Story, Japanese-American Style," *New York Times Magazine,* January 6, 1966, 20–43; "Success Story of One Minority Group in U.S.," *U.S. News and World Report,* December 26, 1966, 73ff.; and "Success Story: Outwhiting the Whites," *Newsweek,* June 21, 1971, 24–25.

6. Homi K. Bhabha, "Of Mimicry and Man: The Ambivalence of Colonial Discourse," in *The Location of Culture* (London: Routledge, 1994), 86, 92.

7. I would like to thank Aisha Finch for helping me refine this part of my argument.

8. Quoted in Naoko Shibusawa, *America's Geisha Ally: Reimagining the Japanese Enemy* (Cambridge, Mass.: Harvard University Press, 2006), 1.

9. Schaller, *The American Occupation of Japan,* 4.

10. Shibusawa, *America's Geisha Ally,* 1. For a critical analysis of race in the Pacific War, see also Dower, *War without Mercy.*

11. Quoted in Shibusawa, *America's Geisha Ally,* 2.

12. Mineo, "The Sino–Soviet Confrontation," 207. See also Ronald Takaki, *Hiroshima: Why America Dropped the Atomic Bomb* (Boston: Little, Brown and Company, 1995).

13. McCormick, *America's Half-Century,* 46.

14. Schaller, *The American Occupation of Japan,* 24.

15. John W. Dower, *Embracing Defeat: Japan in the Wake of World War II* (New York: W. W. Norton and Company, 1999), 211.

16. Ibid., 79–80.

17. Yukiko Koshiro, *Trans-Pacific Racisms and the U.S. Occupation of Japan* (New York: Columbia University Press, 1999), 17.

18. Lisa Yoneyama, "Traveling Memories, Contagious Justice: Americanization of Japanese War Crimes at the End of the Post–Cold War," *Journal of Asian American Studies* 6.1 (2003): 58–59.

19. Traise Yamamoto, *Masking Selves, Making Subjects: Japanese American Women, Identity, and the Body* (Berkeley: University of California Press, 1999), 5.

20. Koshiro, *Trans-Pacific Racisms,* 12, 2. Koshiro argues that it was a codependence "within the Western hierarchical order," and that "Japan's Pan-Asianism was well nested within the Western version of a worldwide racial hierarchy. Modern Japan's dualistic racism needed American racism to reinforce the validity of white supremacy, upon which Japan built its own superiority in Asia. Japanese racism also reinforced American racism" (12).

21. Dower, *Embracing Defeat,* 561, 81, 27.

22. Ibid., 205–6. American military and civilian bureaucrats numbered approximately 1,500 in early 1946 and peaked at 3,200 in January 1948.

23. Shibusawa argues that "the ideologies of gender and maturity helped to minimize racial hostility. Feminizing the hated enemy or regarding them as immature youths made it easier to humanize the Japanese and to recast them as an American responsibility" (*America's Geisha Ally,* 5).

24. John W. Dower, "The Bombed: Hiroshimas and Nagasakis in Japanese Memory," in *America's Wars in Asia: A Cultural Approach to History and Memory*, ed. Philip West, Steven I. Levine, and Jackie Hiltz (Armonk, N.Y.: M. E. Sharpe, 1998), 27–48.

25. For histories of the U.S. occupation of Japan, see Schaller, *The American Occupation of Japan*; Dower, *Embracing Defeat*; Takemae Eiji, *Inside GHQ: The Allied Occupation of Japan and Its Legacy*, trans. Robert Ricketts and Sebastian Swann (New York: Continuum, 2002); Robert E. Ward and Sakamoto Yoshikazu, eds., *Democratizing Japan: The Allied Occupation* (Honolulu: University of Hawaii Press, 1987); and Koshiro, *Trans-Pacific Racisms*. For a cultural history of the post–World War II shift in U.S. figurations of Japan as racially savage enemy to Cold War ally, see Shibusawa, *America's Geisha Ally*. For a literary history, see Michael S. Molasky, *The American Occupation of Japan and Okinawa: Literature and Memory* (London: Routledge, 1999).

26. Eventually, about 200,000 people were formally purged, a vast majority coming from military ranks. See Schaller, *The American Occupation of Japan*, 44.

27. Iriye, *Cold War in Asia*, 147.

28. Ibid., 125.

29. Dower, *Embracing Defeat*, 206.

30. Shibusawa, *America's Geisha Ally*, 4.

31. Quoted in Schaller, *The American Occupation of Japan*, 100–101.

32. Although the "reverse course" helped produce a long-standing conservative hegemony, Communists and Socialists continued to be elected to the Diet and held significant roles in voicing serious opposition to U.S. Cold War policy. See Dower, *Embracing Defeat*, 272–73.

33. Schaller, *The American Occupation of Japan*, 132.

34. LaFeber, *America, Russia, and the Cold War 1945–1992*, 66.

35. Lisa Yoneyama, *Hiroshima Traces: Time, Space, and the Dialectics of Memory* (Berkeley: University of California Press, 1999), 21.

36. Chalmers Johnson writes that from 1945 to 1972, Okinawa functioned as a U.S. colony, directly governed by the Pentagon. As such, during this period, Okinawans became stateless, neither American nor Japanese citizens, and were governed by an American lieutenant general. Okinawa was sealed off from the outside world, a secret enclave of U.S. military and intelligence operations. Those who protested were deemed to be communists, and hundreds were taken to Bolivia and dumped in a remote area of the Amazon and left to fend for themselves. In the 1970s, when the Okinawans openly revolted against the use of their island as a bomber base for the Vietnam War (in light of revelations that the United States was storing nerve gas and nuclear weapons there without warning the people), the United States reluctantly agreed to a pro forma "reversion" of Okinawa to Japan but still maintained its base rights there. The Japanese government has gone through great effort to keep the American military confined to Okinawa. About 75 percent of U.S. military bases in Japan are in Okinawa, even though the island constitutes only 1 percent of the total Japanese land area and is the poorest of its prefectures. Since the Japanese annexation of the Ryukyu Kingdom (of which Okinawa is the largest island) in the late nineteenth century, Okinawa has remained in semicolonial conditions. See Johnson, *The Sorrows of Empire*, 199–200.

37. Iriye, *Cold War in Asia*, 183.

38. Quoted in Dower, *Embracing Defeat*, 553.

39. Ibid., 553.

40. According to Schaller, during 1951–52 American military orders (known as off-shore procurements) reached $800 million per year, and by the end of 1954, Japan had received almost $3 billion in orders. Between 1945 and 1955 the $6.2-billion gap was balanced by $2 billion in economic aid and $4 billion in military procurements. (Dower notes that after the Korean War ended, military-related U.S. purchases continued under "New Special Procurements," a "prolonged windfall" that allowed Japan to increase its imports significantly and almost double its scale of production in key industries [*Embracing Defeat*, 542].) From 1965 to 1970, as America's war in Vietnam escalated, these procurements rose by another $3 billion. This averaged out to be about $500 million per year over twenty years. Since the bulk of these orders was for "nonlethal" supplies and not weapons (such as clothing, electronics, transportation vehicles, etc.), production could easily be shifted and applied to consumer and export sectors. See Schaller, *The American Occupation of Japan*, 288, 295, 296.

41. Quoted in Schaller, *The American Occupation of Japan*, 289.

42. Ibid., 296.

43. Johnson, *The Sorrows of Empire*, 202.

44. Chalmers Johnson, *Blowback: The Costs and Consequences of American Empire* (New York: Henry Holt and Company, 2000), 21.

45. Pease, "Hiroshima, the Vietnam Veteran's Memorial, and the Gulf War," 562. Similarly, Rey Chow writes that the image of the mushroom cloud has itself become a "sign of terror, a kind of gigantic demonstration with us, the spectators, as the potential target" ("The Age of the World Target," in West, Levine, and Hiltz, *America's Wars in Asia*, 205).

46. Pease, "Hiroshima, the Vietnam Veteran's Memorial, and the Gulf War," 563.

47. David E. Sanger and Eric Schmitt, "U.S. Has a Plan to Occupy Iraq, Officials Report," *New York Times*, October 11, 2002.

48. Lisa Yoneyama, "Liberation under Siege: U.S. Military Occupation and Japanese Women's Enfranchisement," in "Legal Borderlands: Law and the Construction of American Borders," ed. Mary L. Dudziak and Leti Volpp, special issue, *American Quarterly* 57.3 (2005): 886.

49. The video of Rob Corddry's May 6, 2004 segment, titled "Prison Abuse Scandal," can be accessed and viewed on the *The Daily Show with Jon Stewart* Web site at http://www.thedailyshow.com/watch/thu-may-6-2004/prison-abuse-scandal (accessed November 16, 2009).

50. It is estimated that approximately 3,200 second-generation Japanese Americans were in Hiroshima when the bomb was dropped. Extrapolating from overall casualty rates, it is then probable that 2,000 of these American citizens were killed. Moreover, thousands of Koreans, colonized subjects who had been conscripted to labor for the Japanese, were also killed in Hiroshima (between 5,000 and 8,000) and Nagasaki (between 1,500 and 2,000). See Dower, "The Bombed," 41. For an analysis of the Korean survivors of Hiroshima, see Toyonaga Keisaburo, "Colonialism and Atom Bombs: About Survivors of Hiroshima Living in Korea," in *Perilous Memories: The*

Asia-Pacific Wars, ed. T. Fujitani, Geoffrey M. White, and Lisa Yoneyama (Durham: Duke University Press, 2001), 378–94.

51. A film such as *Survivors* goes against the grain of dominant memories and commemorations of the end of World War II. For example, as Lisa Yoneyama observes, after much debate and controversy, the Smithsonian National Air and Space Museum exhibit of the *Enola Gay* (the bomber that dropped the atomic bomb on Hiroshima), in commemoration of the fiftieth anniversary of the end of World War II, ultimately omitted the following details from the exhibit: the debates surrounding the decision to use the atom bombs; photographs and descriptions of Japanese military and colonial atrocities in Asia and the Pacific Islands; photographs of physical and human damage in Hiroshima and Nagasaki; and a discussion of the atomic age and nuclear weapons proliferation inaugurated by the bombings. See Lisa Yoneyama, "For Transformative Knowledge and Postnationalist Public Spheres: The Smithsonian *Enola Gay* Controversy," in Fujitani, White, and Yoneyama, *Perilous Memories,* 324–25.

52. After the war, Americans channeled their "atomic guilt" without explicitly acknowledging it as such through privately initiated and sponsored programs such as those of *Saturday Review of Literature* editor Norman Cousins: the Hiroshima Maidens Project (1955–56), which provided plastic surgery in New York City for twenty-five Japanese women disfigured by the bomb, and the "moral adoptions" program (1949 to the mid-1960s), which assisted about three hundred children orphaned by the bomb. See Shibusawa, *America's Geisha Ally,* 213–54. See also Caroline Chung Simpson, *An Absent Presence: Japanese Americans in Postwar American Culture, 1945–1960* (Durham: Duke University Press, 2001), 113–48.

53. By December 1945 an estimated 140,000 people had died in Hiroshima and 70,000 in Nagasaki, leaving thousands of children and elderly without caretakers and driving many to suicide. By 1950 another 140,000 had died from the ongoing effects of radiation exposure, and since then, radiation-related cancer deaths have been estimated to be as high as 100,000.

54. I would like to thank Grace Kyungwon Hong for pointing this out to me.

55. I would like to thank Grace Kyungwon Hong for helping me articulate this point about the transfer of patriarchal authority.

56. Lye, *America's Asia,* 142.

57. In 1913 California passed the Alien Land Law prohibiting "aliens ineligible for citizenship" from buying agricultural land or leasing it for more than three years. This law selectively targeted Asian "aliens" and Japanese immigrants in particular. A subsequent 1920 law made it illegal for them to lease land altogether, to purchase land in the name of corporations in which they held more than 50 percent of the stock, or to buy land in the names of their American-born (and thus citizen) children. Arizona, Washington, Louisiana, New Mexico, Idaho, Montana, Oregon, and Kansas passed similar alien land laws. See Chan, *Asian Americans,* 47. For an analysis of how Japanese immigrants in the United States, the Issei, forged transnational identities that negotiated and contested American racism (such as the Alien Land Laws) as well as imperial Japan's nationalist protocols in the period before World War II, see Eiichiro Azuma, *Between Two Empires: Race, History, and Transnationalism in Japanese America* (New York: Oxford University Press, 2005).

58. Lye, *America's Asia,* 161.

59. Ibid., 202.

60. Chuh, *Imagine Otherwise,* 59.

61. Simpson, *An Absent Presence,* 9, 43.

62. Quoted in ibid., 74.

63. Mura, *Turning Japanese,* 8; further citations to this work will appear in the text.

64. In January 1943 the U.S. government announced that Japanese Americans, including those interned, could volunteer for a racially segregated U.S. army unit. Those interned were subjected to a loyalty questionnaire. Given that their civil liberties as U.S. citizens had been abrogated, many found two particular questions to be absurd. These questions were number 27: "Are you willing to serve in the armed forces of the United States on combat duty, wherever ordered?" and number 28: "Will you swear unqualified allegiance to the United States of America and faithfully defend the United States from any and all attack by foreign or domestic forces, and forswear any form of allegiance to the Japanese Emperor or any other foreign government, power, or organization?" Those who answered "no" to both these questions came to be known as "no-no boys."

65. For histories of the World War II internment of Japanese Americans, see Roger Daniels, *Prisoners without Trial: Japanese Americans in World War II* (New York: Hill and Wang, 1993), and *Concentration Camps, U.S.A.: Japanese Americans and World War II* (New York: Holt, Rinehart, and Winston, 1970); and Richard Nishimoto, *Inside an American Concentration Camp: Japanese American Resistance at Poston* (Tucson: University of Arizona Press, 1995). For analyses of Japanese American legal challenges to internment, see Peter Irons, *Justice at War: The Story of the Japanese American Internment Cases* (New York: Oxford University Press, 1983); and Peter Irons, ed., *Justice Delayed: The Record of the Japanese American Internment Cases* (New York: Oxford University Press, 1989). For an analysis of popular representations of Japanese American internment and the formation of Cold War culture, see Simpson, *An Absent Presence.*

66. Cynthia Franklin, "Turning Japanese/Returning to America: Problems of Gender, Class, and Nation in David Mura's Use of Memoir," *LIT (Literature, Interpretation, Theory)* 12 (2001): 242. For an analysis of how Mura's narratives challenge and rework "the heteronormative logic through which Asian-American masculinity has been formulated," see Crystal Parikh, "'The Most Outrageous Masquerade': Queering Asian American Masculinity," *Modern Fiction Studies* 48.4 (2002): 858–98.

67. David L. Eng, *Racial Castration: Managing Masculinity in Asian America* (Durham: Duke University Press, 2001).

68. Whereas many Asian groups in the United States, especially Chinese and Filipino immigrant communities, were not able to form normative families in great numbers due to exclusionary immigration laws, Japanese Americans were able to form families in greater numbers. The gender ratio among Japanese Americans was not as skewed, because agreements between the United States and a geopolitically ascending Japan allowed the migration of Japanese women to the United States. See Chan, *Asian Americans;* and Ronald Takaki, *Strangers from a Different Shore: A History of Asian Americans,* rev. ed. (Boston: Little, Brown and Company, 1998).

69. Simpson, *An Absent Presence,* 17.

70. Christine Hong, "Flashforward Democracy: American Exceptionalism and the Atomic Bomb in *Barefoot Gen,*" *Comparative Literature Studies* 49.1 (2009): 130.

71. Yoneyama, *Hiroshima Traces,* 20.

72. David Mura, *After We Lost Our Way* (New York: E. P. Dutton, 1989), 5. The poem was previously published in *Breaking Silence: An Anthology of Contemporary Asian-American Poets,* ed. Joseph Bruchac (Greenfield Center, N.Y.: Greenfield Review Press, 1983).

73. Avery F. Gordon, *Ghostly Matters: Haunting and the Sociological Imagination* (Minneapolis: University of Minnesota Press, 1997), 18. I would like to thank Erica Edwards for suggesting that I emphasize the ghostly.

74. For an analysis of miscegenation discourse and Asian Americans, see Susan Koshy, *Sexual Naturalization: Asian Americans and Miscegenation* (Stanford: Stanford University Press, 2004).

75. I would like to thank Jayna Brown for pointing this out to me.

76. I would like to thank Arlene Keizer for helping me note this.

77. Marianne Hirsch, *Family Frames: Photography, Narrative, and Postmemory* (Cambridge, Mass.: Harvard University Press, 1997).

78. For an analysis of how the memory of the camps—"bracketed by the twin catastrophes of Pearl Harbor and Hiroshima"—has shaped Japanese American identity and literary expression, see Gordon O. Taylor, "'The country I had thought was my home': David Mura's *Turning Japanese* and Japanese-American Narrative since World War II," *Connotations* 63 (1996): 283–307.

79. Joshua Logan, dir., *Sayonara* (MGM, 1957), 147 minutes, adapted from James Michener's 1953 novel of the same title.

80. In her analysis of *Sayonara,* Gina Marchetti writes that the film "can be looked at as structured by a series of narrative transpositions that serve to obscure a good deal of the film's apparent social criticism. Through these narrative twists, the film manages to voice and then ignore ideological contradictions by transforming them into more distant but related problems" (*Romance and the "Yellow Peril": Race, Sex, and Discursive Strategies in Hollywood Fiction* [Berkeley: University of California Press, 1993], 128).

81. Dower, *Embracing Defeat,* 70.

82. Ibid., 254. May Day, now also known as International Workers' Day, was established by the International Socialist Congress of 1889 as an expression of worker solidarity. Starting in 1920, it had been observed by Japanese workers annually until the government banned it in 1936.

83. Ozeki, *My Year of Meats,* 124–27; further citations to this work will appear in the text.

84. Yoneyama, "Liberation under Siege," 887.

85. Ibid., 889–90.

86. Mire Koikari, *Pedagogy of Democracy: Feminism and the Cold War in the U.S. Occupation of Japan* (Philadelphia: Temple University Press, 2008), 5.

87. See, for example, Elaine Tyler May, *Homeward Bound.*

88. See, for example, Indra Levy's *Sirens of the Western Shore: The Westernesque*

Femme Fatale, Translation, and Vernacular Style in Modern Japanese Literature (New York: Columbia University Press, 2006), which traces the figure of the Japanese woman who invokes a "Westernesque femme fatale" in literature and theater.

89. Yoneyama, "Liberation under Siege," 895. This discursive reversal from warrior woman to anticommunist liberated woman reveals how World War II bled into the Cold War, but also obscures related histories, such as that of the conviction of Iva Toguri d'Aquino, a U.S.-born Japanese American who had gone to Japan at the start of the war and could not return to the United States after the bombing of Pearl Harbor. She was accused of being Tokyo Rose, the mythical radio personality who was reputed to have demoralized American soldiers in the Pacific War with her subversive broadcasts. Convicted within the context of the U.S. occupation's Tokyo War Trials, this "oriental vixen" also represented American fears of gender transgressions. See Simpson, *An Absent Presence*, 76–112.

90. Monica Chiu, "Postnational Globalization and (En)gendered Meat Production in Ruth L. Ozeki's *My Year of Meats*," *LIT (Literature, Interpretation, Theory)* 12 (2001): 102–3.

91. This incident in the novel is based on an actual case.

92. For an analysis of how a vision of "cosmofeminism" emerges in the novel, see Shameem Black, "Fertile Cosmofeminism: Ruth L. Ozeki and Transnational Reproduction," *Meridians: Feminism, Race, Transnationalism* 5.1 (2004): 226–56. For an analysis of how the novel is ultimately unsuccessful in its attempt to unhinge adherences to nation and patriarchy within the context of globalization, see Chiu, "Postnational Globalization and (En)gendered Meat Production." David Palumbo-Liu agrees with both of these contrasting interpretations and suggests that the novel is more complex and self-conscious than it might appear, displaying a tension between its calculated ethical critique and a skepticism toward the ability to narrate that critique in any pristine, uncompromised manner ("Rational and Irrational Choices: Form, Affect, and Ethics," in *Minor Transnationalism*, ed. Francoise Lionnet and Shu-mei Shih, 41–72 [Durham: Duke University Press, 2005]).

93. Quoted in Schaller, *The American Occupation of Japan*, 232.

4. The Forgotten War

1. Suji Kwock Kim, "Fragments of the Forgotten War," in *Notes from the Divided Country* (Baton Rouge: Louisiana State University Press, 2003), 30.

2. Ibid., 31.

3. Ibid., 31, emphasis added.

4. Ramsay Liem, Seung-Hee Jeon, Channing and Papai Liem Education Foundation, and Korean American Memories of the Korean War Oral History Project, *Still Present Pasts: Korean Americans and the "Forgotten War,"* exh. cat. (Chestnut Hill, Mass.: Still Present Pasts, 2005), 8. Ramsay Liem is also a professor of psychology at Boston College and director of the Korean American Memories of the Korean War oral history project. The exhibition opened in Boston in January 2005 and has since traveled to cities including New York, Oakland, Minneapolis, and Los Angeles. For information, see the exhibition Web site, http://www.stillpresentpasts.org (accessed

November 18, 2009), which includes downloadable exhibit study guides for high school students and teachers.

5. Ibid., 2.

6. David Halberstam, *The Coldest Winter: America and the Korean War* (New York: Hyperion, 2007), 2. Unlike Vietnam, Halberstam continues, the Korean War was not a heavily televised war; it was largely a print war "reported in newspapers in black and white, and it remained black and white in the nation's consciousness" (3).

7. Susan Choi, *The Foreign Student* (New York: HarperFlamingo, 1998); Heinz Insu Fenkl, *Memories of My Ghost Brother* (New York: Plume, 1996); and Deann Borshay Liem, dir., *First Person Plural* (National Asian American Telecommunications Association, 2000), 56 minutes.

8. For substantive and detailed histories of the war, see I. F. Stone, *The Hidden History of the Korean War* (New York: Monthly Review Press, 1971); Peter Lowe, *The Origins of the Korean War*, 2nd ed. (London: Longman, 1997); Bruce Cumings, *The Origins of the Korean War*, 2 vols. (Princeton: Princeton University Press, 1981, 1990); Clay Blair, *The Forgotten War: America in Korea* (New York: Anchor Books, 1987); Jon Halliday and Bruce Cumings, *Korea: The Unknown War* (New York: Pantheon Books, 1988); Allan R. Millett, "The Korean War: A 50-Year Critical Historiography," *Journal of Strategic Studies* 24.1 (2001): 188–224; and Halberstam, *The Coldest Winter*.

9. Suji Kwock Kim, "Fragments of the Forgotten War," 30.

10. One day after the bombing of Nagasaki, three Americans—John J. McCloy, Lieutenant Colonel Dean Rusk, and Colonel Charles H. Bonesteel—unilaterally divided Korea at the 38th parallel without consulting any Koreans or allies.

11. Okonogi Masao writes, "The domestic power struggle became 'internationalized' when the waves of the Cold War reached the shores of Korea in the late forties. The 'internationalization' of the Korean conflict, however, because it was ex post facto, does not justify the popular view that domestic factors were largely irrelevant and war was imposed from outside. A balanced understanding of the Korean War can be achieved only by analyzing, on the one hand, the way in which world events impinged upon the Korean peninsula to 'internationalize' the domestic independence struggle and, on the other, the way domestic political forces drew in, or 'internalized,' the international environment in the course of pursuing those goals" ("The Domestic Roots of the Korean War," in Nagai and Iriye, *The Origins of the Cold War in Asia*, 299).

12. LaFeber, *America, Russia, and the Cold War 1945–1992*, 99–100. He writes that the main struggle was not between the Soviet Union and the United States, but between the left-wing Koreans (both communists and noncommunists) and right-wing Koreans.

13. Bruce Cumings, "Decoupled from History: North Korea in the 'Axis of Evil,'" in *Inventing the Axis of Evil: The Truth about North Korea, Iran, and Syria*, ed. Bruce Cumings, Ervand Abrahamian, and Moshe Ma'oz (New York: The New Press, 2004), 3, 13.

14. For example, a letter written by Syngman Rhee in April 1949 indicated that in exchange for America's withdrawal of its troops from South Korea, he sought American weapons supplies. This was a prerequisite for his plan to reunify Korea by attacking the North. See Masao, "The Domestic Roots of the Korean War," 308, 312, 316.

15. Bruce Cumings, *Korea's Place in the Sun: A Modern History* (New York: Norton, 1997), 185.

16. Pease, "Moby Dick and the Cold War," 113.

17. According to Cumings, there is no evidence of an increase in Soviet military shipments to North Korea after June 25. Rather, a decrease was registered. See Cumings, *Korea's Place in the Sun*, 266. Moreover, Thomas J. McCormick argues, "Russian aid was limited in extent and kind, partly because of Russian fears of any direct encounter with the United States, partly because it may have been that North Korea angered the USSR by crossing the 38th parallel prematurely. Rather than moving in August 1950, in tandem with an expected Chinese invasion of Taiwan, North Korea attacked South Korea in June to head off Rhee's attempt to crush southern resistance forces, which were deemed essential to the northern military effort" (*America's Half-Century*, 102–3).

18. The military command in Korea took its orders from Washington, not the UN. General MacArthur later recalled the following: "The entire control of my command and everything I did came from our own Chiefs of Staff. Even the reports which were normally made by me to the United Nations were subject to censorship by our State and Defense Departments. I had no direct connection with the United Nations whatsoever" (quoted in LaFeber, *America, Russia, and the Cold War 1945–1992*, 105). Further, LaFeber writes that ultimately, "sixteen nations contributed to 'United Nations' forces, but the United States provided 50 percent of the ground forces (with South Korea providing most of the remainder), 86 percent of the naval power, and 93 percent of the air power. In October, during the Truman-MacArthur conference at Wake Island, a dozen American officials prepared plans for the reconstruction of all Korea without consulting anyone, not even the United Nations or Syngman Rhee. The United States suffered . . . casualties in Korea not for the sake of 'collective security' or the United Nations, but because the Executive Branch of the government decided that the invasions signaled a direct threat to American interests in both Asia and Europe" (105).

19. Every major town and city was destroyed during the Korean War, at least 10 percent of Korea's population was dead by the end of the war, and the vast majority of those surviving were homeless. Casualty figures are reported to be the following: 3 million Korean civilians (2 million in the North and 1 million in the South); 36,949 U.S. military forces; 175,000 South Korean forces; 500,000 North Korean soldiers; 1 million Chinese volunteers; and 150,000 UN forces, 35,000 of whom were from the United States. In addition, 2 million were missing or wounded. Almost 10 million Koreans were separated from friends and relatives, and fewer than 10,000 of them have been reunited with their families. See Ramsay Liem, "History, Trauma, and Identity: The Legacy of the Korean War for Korean Americans," *Amerasia Journal* 29.3 (2003–4): 114. David Halberstam puts the South Korean casualty figure at 415,000 (*The Coldest Winter*, 4).

20. Halberstam, *The Coldest Winter*, 5.

21. Quoted in Cumings, *Korea's Place in the Sun*, 298. This leveling of North Korean towns involved targeting massive irrigation dams that provided over 75 percent of the North's food production (296).

22. In 2002, according to the Department of Defense, the United States' military

presence in South Korea includes 101 separate military installations staffed by 37,605 American troops, 2,875 U.S. civilians employed by the military, and 7,027 resident American dependents. These American bases were established during the Korean War, and since the armistice in 1953, the large number of troops based there has had "nothing to do" (Johnson, *The Sorrows of Empire*, 92, 202–3).

23. In particular, the war strengthened NATO and rearmed Germany as part of the defense system. See Lloyd C. Gardner, Walter F. LaFeber, and Thomas J. McCormick, eds., *Creation of the American Empire: U.S. Diplomatic History* (Chicago: Rand McNally and Company, 1973), 468.

24. U.S. military expenditures were about 10 percent of GNP in the 1950s, peaking at 12.7 percent in 1954. See Painter, *The Cold War*, 34.

25. Quoted in LaFeber, *America, Russia, and the Cold War 1945–1992*, 116.

26. Samuel F. Wells, quoted in Ernest R. May, *American Cold War Strategy*, 139.

27. Choi, *The Foreign Student*, 34; further citations to this work will appear in the text.

28. Naoki Sakai, *Translation and Subjectivity: On "Japan" and Cultural Nationalism* (Minneapolis: University of Minnesota Press, 1997), 3. Elaborating what he calls the "schema of cofiguration," Sakai writes that in the process of translation, relating two terms to each other via equivalence and resemblance actually generates the possibility of "extracting an infinite number of distinctions between the two." He argues that in the cofiguration of "the West and the Rest," for example, "conceptual difference allows for the evaluative determination of the one term as superior over the other" (16).

29. Theresa Hak Kyung Cha, *Dictee* (1982; Berkeley: Third Woman Press, 1995).

30. Lowe, *Immigrant Acts*, 146.

31. Walter Benjamin, "The Task of the Translator," in *Illuminations: Essays and Reflections* (New York: Shocken Books, 1968), 78.

32. In a resonant testimonial, a Korean American immigrant who was interviewed by Ramsay Liem as a part of the "Korean American Memories of the Korean War" oral history project recalls, "If there is no Korean War, you are not here and I am not here!" ("History, Trauma, and Identity," 118).

33. For a history of Korean military brides in the United States, see Ji-Yeon Yuh, *Beyond the Shadow of Camptown: Korean Military Brides in America* (New York: New York University Press, 2002). For analyses of military prostitution in Korea and Asia, see Katharine H. S. Moon, *Sex among Allies: Military Prostitution in U.S.–Korea Relations* (New York: Columbia University Press, 1997); Saundra Pollack Sturdevant and Brenda Stoltzfus, *Let the Good Times Roll: Prostitution and the U.S. Military in Asia* (New York: The New Press, 1992); and Alexandra Suh, "Military Prostitution in Asia and the United States," in *States of Confinement: Policing, Detention, and Prisons*, ed. Joy James, 144–58 (New York: St. Martin's Press, 2000). For documentary films, see *The Women Outside: Korean Women and the U.S. Military*, dir. J. T. Takagi and Hye Jung Park (Third World Newsreel, 1995), 52 minutes; and *Camp Arirang*, dir. Diana S. Lee and Grace Yoon Kyung Lee (National Asian American Telecommunications Association, 1995), 28 minutes.

34. Ji-Yeon Yuh, "Moved by War: Migration, Diaspora and the Korean War," *Journal of Asian American Studies* 8.3 (2005): 277. She writes that U.S.-based scholars, whether

working in the fields of Asian American, immigration, or assimilation studies, as well as Korean studies scholars, pose questions of Korean migration that privilege the nation-state as the point of reference.

35. Ibid., 281.

36. Yuh also includes labor migrants, political exiles, and international students turned immigrants in this category. Transnational adoptees are a notable exception, but historically, even this group—as a group of orphans who needed to be adopted—came about as a result of the Korean War.

37. Ibid., 278. At its peak in the 1970s and 1980s, more than four thousand military brides came to the United States annually, and now, an estimated two thousand arrive per year.

38. Yuh, *Beyond the Shadow of Camptown*, 4.

39. Grace M. Cho, "Prostituted and Invisible Bodies," in *Gendered Bodies: Feminist Perspectives*, ed. Judith Lorber and Lisa Jean Moore (Los Angeles: Roxbury Publishing Company, 2007), 211. For an excellent analysis of the figure of the *yanggongju* (literally meaning "Western princess" and referring broadly to a Korean woman who has sexual relations with Americans) as the ghostly figure of the repressed collective traumas of Japanese imperialism, the Korean War, and U.S. militarism and neoimperialism in Korea, see also Cho's *Haunting the Korean Diaspora: Shame, Secrecy, and the Forgotten War* (Minneapolis: University of Minnesota Press, 2008).

40. For an important feminist critique of militarization, see Cynthia Enloe, *Bananas, Beaches, and Bases: Making Feminist Sense of International Politics* (1989; Berkeley: University of California Press, 1990). For an incisive critique of militarization and colonialism across the Asia-Pacific, see Setsu Shigematsu and Keith L. Camacho, eds., *Militarized Currents: Toward a Decolonized Future in Asia and the Pacific* (Minneapolis: University of Minnesota Press, 2010).

41. Elaine H. Kim, "Myth, Memory, and Desire: Homeland and History in Contemporary Korean American Writing and Visual Art," in *Holding Their Own: Perspectives on the Multi-Ethnic Literatures of the United States*, ed. Dorothea Fischer-Hornung and Heike Raphael-Hernandez (Tübingen: Stauffenburg Verlag, 2000), 81.

42. Fenkl, *Memories of My Ghost Brother*, 7; further citations to this work will appear in the text.

43. Between 1965 and 1973 the ROK sent more than three hundred thousand combat troops to Vietnam, second only to the United States itself and greatly exceeding the number sent by all other Allied nations combined. It was not until the 1990s that public discourse—in novels, films, the media, and to a small extent the Ministry of National Defense—about the legacy of Korea's participation in the Vietnam War surfaced. Novels available in English translation include Hwang Suk-young's autobiographical *Shadow of Arms*, trans. Chun Kyung-ja (Ithaca: Cornell University, East Asia Program, 1994), which reveals the large number of "entertainment women" who were sent to Vietnam from South Korea to service both Koreans and Americans. This historical occurrence and its attempted erasure are ironic, to say the least, given the experience of Korean "comfort women" who were conscripted by Japan during World War II to service the Japanese military. Also available in English translation is Ahn Junghyo's novel *White Badge* (New York: Soho Press, 1989), which was adapted into

a film in 1992. Although the Korean title of the novel and film translates to "White War," with explicit racial implications, the author himself chose to translate it differently as "White Badge." See Charles K. Armstrong, "America's Korea, Korea's Vietnam," *Critical Asian Studies* 33.4 (2001): 527–39. For an analysis of Korea's "Vietnam question" in terms of how Vietnam can be critically incorporated into Korea's national memory, how such an incorporation can reshape Korea's collective identity and consciousness, and of what new forms of praxis can facilitate reconciliation between Korea and Vietnam, see Hyun Sook Kim, "Korea's 'Vietnam Question': War Atrocities, National Identity, and Reconciliation in Asia," *positions* 9.3 (2001): 621–35.

44. Armstrong, "America's Korea, Korea's Vietnam," 532, 533. War-related income (direct aid, military assistance, procurements, and soldiers' salaries) totaled over $1 billion; South Korea's new heavy-industry sector (steel, transportation equipment, chemical exports, etc.) was given an immeasurable boost; and the war largely financed the building of South Korea's first expressway, the Seoul–Pusan highway, between 1968 and 1970. This economic boom sustained President Park's dictatorship; in fact, Park's first five-year plan for the development of Korea's economy was constructed with Vietnam in mind.

45. Ibid., 535.

46. Jinim Park, *Narratives of the Vietnam War by Korean and American Writers* (New York: Peter Lang, 2007), 77.

47. Robert M. Blackburn, quoted in ibid., 78.

48. Quoted in ibid., 83.

49. Toby Alice Volkman, "Introduction: New Geographies of Kinship," in *Cultures of Transnational Adoption*, ed. Toby Alice Volkman, 1–22 (Durham: Duke University Press, 2005). Between 1985 and 2003 in the United States, there were 40,496 adoptions from China alone. See Helena Grice, "Transracial Adoption Narratives: Prospects and Perspectives," *Meridians: Feminism, Race, Transnationalism* 5.2 (2005): 124.

50. Eleana Kim notes that while there are "no international bodies that track the global transfer of children through adoption . . . demographer Peter Selman's estimates show that the numbers of children have nearly doubled from a mean annual rate of approximately 16,000 children in the 1980s to nearly 32,000 in 1998 . . . and these numbers have no doubt increased in the past several years." The United States has been the primary "receiving" country throughout the history of transnational adoption, and according to U.S. State Department statistics on "orphan visas" or more recently, beneficiaries of the Child Citizenship Act (which confers immediate U.S. citizenship to a child adopted by a U.S. citizen), the number of U.S. adoptions from foreign countries has exceeded 20,000 per year since 2001. See Eleana Kim, "Our Adoptee, Our Alien: Transnational Adoptees as Specters of Foreignness and Family in South Korea," *Anthropological Quarterly* 80.2 (2007): 527.

51. Adoption discourses have typically separated interracial domestic adoptions, labeled *transracial,* from international or intercountry adoptions, labeled *transnational.* This obscures the extent to which most transnational adoptions, particularly from Asia, have historically also been transracial. As such, the editors of *Outsiders Within: Writing on Transracial Adoption,* who are transnational adoptees, have chosen to redefine themselves as transracial to forge solidarities among adoptees of color and to

emphasize the salience of racialization across national borders. Moreover, adoption of Native Americans is rarely labeled transnational, erasing the nation-to-nation relationship between the United States as a settler state and sovereign indigenous nations. See Jane Jeong Trenka, Julia Chinyere Oparah, and Sun Yung Shin, Introduction to *Outsiders Within: Writing on Transracial Adoption,* ed. Jane Jeong Trenka, Julia Chinyere Oparah, and Sun Yung Shin (Cambridge, Mass.: South End Press, 2006), 3, 5. I have thus chosen to use the term transracial in most instances throughout my discussion, rather than transnational, to emphasize, as the editors of *Outsiders Within* do, the significance of race. When I do use transnational, I do so to reference transnational adoption more broadly as a practice that is mostly but not exclusively transracial.

52. After World War II, Americans began adopting European war orphans, but it was the aftermath of the Korean War that inaugurated transnational adoption as a continuous, institutionalized practice in the United States. Since then, the "sending" countries have tended to be the sites of America's Cold War military operations and covert actions, not only in Asia, but also in Latin America. Between the 1950s and 1970s South Korea allowed, as Eleana Kim notes, the "almost unrestricted adoption" of orphaned and abandoned children. This history of adoption from South Korea spans five decades, which makes it "the country with the longest continuous foreign adoption program in the world." Since 1954 over 200,000 children have been adopted from South Korea, including 150,000 sent to America and the remaining to Europe, and more recently, Australia. In the 1980s and early 1990s this constituted over half of all international adoptions in the United States. Until 1991 South Korea sent the largest number of adoptees to the United States. In 2000 it ranked third after China and Russia (with upwards of 5,000 adoptions from these countries), and in 2002 it ranked fourth after China, Russia, and Guatemala. Since the early 1990s, particularly in the wake of negative media attention during the 1988 summer Olympics in Seoul of South Korea being an "orphan-exporting-nation," Korean adoptions have been tightly regulated, numbering about 2,000 per year. More recently, as reported in an October 9, 2008, *New York Times* article, the South Korean government has made concerted efforts to encourage local adoptions by offering such incentives as monthly allowances and greater health benefits. In 2007, for the first time, the number of babies adopted locally by South Koreans (1,388) exceeded the number adopted transnationally (1,264), and the government has established a goal of eliminating foreign adoptions altogether by 2012. Significantly, other countries in Asia with strong military, political, and/or economic ties to the United States (such as Vietnam, Cambodia, and China) have followed South Korea's practice of transnational adoption. See Eleana Kim, "Wedding Citizenship to Culture: Korean Adoptees and the Global Family of Korea," in Volkman, *Cultures of Transnational Adoption,* 58–59. See also her "Our Adoptee, Our Alien"; and Norimitsu Onishi, "Korea Aims to End Stigma of Adoption and Stop 'Exporting' Babies," *New York Times,* October 9, 2008. For an analysis of transnational adoption and Latin America, see Laura Briggs, "Making 'American' Families: Transnational Adoption and U.S. Latin American Policy," in *Haunted by Empire: Geographies of Intimacy in North American History,* ed. Ann Laura Stoler, 344–65 (Durham: Duke University Press, 2006).

53. While the focus of my analysis is thus transnational, transracial adoptions out

of Asia and to the United States as impelled by and in the wake of the Cold War, this is not to suggest that these sending and receiving countries are the only sites implicated in what is now a global phenomenon and practice. Children from Korea and Vietnam, for example, were not only sent to the United States but also to such countries and regions as Australia, New Zealand, and Western Europe. In terms of per capita figures, Sweden adopted the highest number of South Korean children, and the country that adopts the most transnationally is Spain.

54. This is especially the case with more recent adoptions of Chinese girls in the wake of China's one-child policy, in effect since 1980. Almost all transnationally adopted Chinese babies are abandoned girls.

55. I would like to thank Maylei Blackwell for helping me note how liberal feminism is implicated.

56. I borrow the term "social death" from Orlando Patterson's classic analysis, *Slavery and Social Death: A Comparative Study* (Cambridge, Mass.: Harvard University Press, 1982). Patterson argues that slaves are "socially dead" because of their natal alienation, or "loss of ties of birth in both ascending and descending generations," as well as "the important nuance of a loss of native status," of having been born in a particular time and place to a particular people. Natal alienation severs the slave from belonging to, or having rights within, any formally recognized community or sociality (7). According to Patterson's analysis, in addition to such natal alienation, social death is also constituted by processes of general dishonor and violent domination. In using this term, I am not, of course, arguing that transracial adoptees and birth mothers are slaves. Rather, I am building on extensions of Patterson's work that take up "social death" to index the persistence of gendered racial domination, violence, and the production of degrees of social nonpersonhood within the context of formal emancipation, freedom, or sovereignty. That is, I am pointing to the ways in which natal alienation and gendered racial governmentalities outside the space of formal slavery persist in creating a variety of "social deaths" for subjugated groups.

57. For a discussion of how this operates specifically in Korea, see Eleana Kim, "Our Adoptee, Our Alien."

58. For a discussion of such an expanded notion of reproductive justice, see Trenka, Oparah, and Shin, Introduction, 13.

59. For a useful analysis of how *Seeds from a Silent Tree,* an anthology of writing by Korean adoptees, disrupts such fantasies, see Catherine Ceniza Choy and Gregory Paul Choy, "Transformative Terrains: Korean Adoptees and the Social Construction of an American Childhood," in *The American Child: A Cultural Studies Reader,* ed. Caroline F. Levander and Carol J. Singley, 262–79 (New Brunswick: Rutgers University Press, 2003).

60. In 1978 the Indian Child Welfare Act was enacted to restore tribal jurisdiction over the adoption of Native American children. See Pauline Turner Strong, "To Forget Their Tongue, Their Name, and Their Whole Relation: Captivity, Extra-Tribal Adoption, and the Indian Child Welfare Act," in *Relative Values: Reconfiguring Kinship Studies,* ed. Sarah Franklin and Susan McKinnon (Durham: Duke University Press, 2001), 469, 471. For an example of efforts to address the long-term legacies of the physical, sexual, and emotional violence that occurred in the Christian boarding

schools that Native American children were forced to attend as a matter of government policy, see the Boarding School Healing Project (http://www.boardingschool
healingproject.org [accessed November 20, 2009]). According to its Web site, "The
Boarding School Healing Project, a coalition of several organizations around the
country, seeks to document Native boarding school abuses so that Native communities can begin healing from boarding school abuses and demand justice." For an
analysis of the connections among the conquest of Native Americans, sexual violence,
and the control of women's reproductive rights, see Andrea Smith, *Conquest: Sexual
Violence and American Indian Genocide* (Cambridge, Mass.: South End Press, 2005).

   61. Sara K. Dorow, *Transnational Adoption: A Cultural Economy of Race, Gender,
and Kinship* (New York: New York University Press, 2006), 3, 17, 19, 21.

   62. For further examples of such interdisciplinary work, see Volkman, *Cultures of
Transnational Adoption,* and Trenka, Oparah, and Shin, *Outsiders Within.*

   63. Borshay Liem's adoption documents and identity papers are connected to a
social history of the document and how "papering" creates complex identities and
processes for Asian and other immigrants. In the context of Asian American immigration history, for example, so-called "paper sons," who were not biological sons of
Chinese already residing in the United States, attempted to seek entrance based on
"paper" identities they had created. While this might have created a condition of possibility for immigration within the context of strict immigration exclusion, of course
in the more contemporary context, the focus on documents and the discourse of
"undocumented immigrants" constitute an apparatus of racial surveillance and crim-
inalization. I would like to thank Maylei Blackwell for pointing out the connection
between Borshay Liem's (forged) identity papers and a social history of the document.

   64. David L. Eng uses the term "privileged" to describe the transnational adoption of Asian babies as a particular kind of immigration in "Transnational Adoption
and Queer Diasporas," *Social Text* 21.3 (2003): 7.

   65. Ibid., 11.

   66. Laura Briggs, "Mother, Child, Race, Nation: The Visual Iconography of Rescue
and the Politics of Transnational and Transracial Adoption," *Gender and History* 15.2
(2003): 179–200.

   67. Lisa Cartwright, "Images of 'Waiting Children': Spectatorship and Pity in the
Representation of the Global Social Orphan in the 1990s," in Volkman, *Cultures of
Transnational Adoption,* 187.

   68. Klein, *Cold War Orientalism,* 152

   69. Ibid., 157.

   70. Ibid., 153, 158.

   71. Briggs argues that "Madonna-and-child and waif" images constituted a "visual
iconography of rescue" during the Cold War, producing a "secular salvation theology"
marshaled in the service of various Cold War development and interventionist projects, ranging from child-feeding programs to military intervention. These images were
recycled from earlier ones, such as Dorothea Lange's famous photograph "Migrant
Mother," used within the domestic context in the service of New Deal programs. See
Briggs, "Mother, Child, Race, Nation."

   72. Volkman, "Introduction," 7, 13. For further analyses of this commodity logic

implicated in transnational adoption, see Barbara Yngvesson, "Placing the 'Gift Child' in Transnational Adoption," *Law and Society Review* 36.2 (2002): 227–56; and Kim Park Nelson, "Shopping for Children in the International Marketplace," in Trenka, Oparah, and Shin, *Outsiders Within,* 89–104. Nelson notes that in 2000, "the adoption industry generated $1.5 billion in adoption spending, with costs for transnational adoptions ranging from $15,000 to $50,000, up from about $1000 in the early 1970s. . . . [O]ne US adoption agency reported revenues of $4.1 million with a profit of $937,515 in 1998" (94).

73. Eng, "Transnational Adoption and Queer Diasporas," 8.

74. I take this from the title of George Lipsitz's *The Possessive Investment in Whiteness: How White People Profit from Identity Politics* (Philadelphia: Temple University Press, 1998).

75. Dorow, *Transnational Adoption,* 21.

76. Eleana Kim estimates that the female to male ratio of Korean adoptees was 2 to 1 until the mid-1990s, by which point single motherhood replaced poverty as the main reason for child relinquishments. This, combined with a mirroring by Korean adopters of the Western preference for girls, and with the priority given to domestic Korean adopters, has led to more boys than girls being placed overseas since the mid-1990s. The gender ratio is different for Chinese adoptions, in which almost all children are girls. See Eleana Kim, "Our Adoptee, Our Alien," 525.

77. Dorothy Roberts, "Adoption Myths and Racial Realities in the United States," in Trenka, Oparah, and Shin, *Outsiders Within,* 49–56.

78. Trenka, Oparah, and Shin, Introduction, 15.

79. George E. Ogle notes that from "dire poverty" in 1960 Korea became the world's tenth-largest economy by 1987 and asks how such a "wondrous thing" occurred. He responds by arguing that "the success of Korea's march to modernization is best accounted for by five innovating actors . . . : a strong centralized government, a system of centralized economic planning, a generous supply of foreign investments, a model of export development and a small number of huge conglomerates called *chaebol*" (*South Korea: Dissent within the Economic Miracle* [Atlantic Highlands, N.J.: Zed Books, 1990], 29). He continues, "Korea's economic transformation was so remarkable that few bothered to look at the underside of the 'miracle . . . ' Ironically and sadly, [it was] built upon a labor policy that violated the human rights of workers, a labor policy that required pervasive, and often cruel suppression of the nation's working people" (47). Politically, this labor policy of South Korea's export-led industrialization required a strong central government, one that was constructed by President Park Chung Hee upon his seizure of power in 1961. After serving two terms, however, he reneged on his earlier promises to step down, and in Ogle's words, "threw out his own democratic constitution, and set up a military dictatorship which he euphemistically called *Yushin,* meaning 'restoration' or 'making new.' [He] liked to call it a 'revitalizing reform'" (32). Interestingly, in rationalizing this move, Park made recourse to familiar Cold War logics: that the military dictatorship was necessary in order to save South Korea from communism.

80. For a discussion of the role of the state in "*producing* the physically abandoned child," see Yngvesson, "Placing the 'Gift Child' in Transnational Adoption," 236.

81. Tobias Hübinette, "From Orphan Trains to Babylifts: Colonial Trafficking, Empire Building, and Social Engineering," in Trenka, Oparah, and Shin, *Outsiders Within,* 139–49. Hübinette argues that the Atlantic slave trade and transnational, transracial adoption, as types of forced migration, share several parallel features and effects.

82. Eleana Kim, "Our Adoptee, Our Alien," 521.

83. Christine Ward Gailey, "Race, Class and Gender in Intercountry Adoption in the USA," in *Intercountry Adoption: Developments, Trends and Perspectives,* ed. Peter Selman (London: British Agencies for Adoption and Fostering, 2000), 305.

84. Trenka, Oparah, and Shin, Introduction, 13.

85. E. J. Graff, "The Lie We Love," *Foreign Policy,* November/December 2008, http://www.foreignpolicy.com/story/cms.php?story_id=4508=1 (accessed December 9, 2009).

86. Deann's birth mother's name is not revealed in the film. Whether or not this was an intentional omission on Deann's part, it is true that Korean family members do not usually refer to one another by their given names, but rather to the term that designates the kin relation. Siblings, for example, call one another "sister" or "brother" and not by their given names.

87. Eng, "Transnational Adoption and Queer Diasporas," 12.

88. For a discussion of this incorporation, see Eleana Kim, "Our Adoptee, Our Alien" and "Wedding Citizenship to Culture."

5. The War-Surplus of Our New Imperialism

1. Tiana (Thi Thanh Nga), dir., *From Hollywood to Hanoi* (Friendship Bridge Productions, 1993), 80 minutes, distributed by Indochina Film Arts Foundation.

2. In the Academy Award–winning documentary *Hearts and Minds,* General William Westmoreland, Commanding General of Vietnam (1964–68), has this to say: "You know Vietnam reminds me of a child, a developing child. The laws of nature control the development of this child. A child has to sit up before it crawls, it has to crawl before it walks, it has to walk before it runs." Later in the film, he adds: "Well the Oriental doesn't put the same high price on life as the Westerner. Life is plentiful, life is cheap in the Orient, and as the philosophy of the Orient expresses it, life is not important." See Peter Davis, dir., *Hearts and Minds* (BBS, 1974), 115 minutes.

3. Rick Berg and John Carlos Rowe, "The Vietnam War and American Memory," in *The Vietnam War and American Culture,* ed. John Carlos Rowe and Rick Berg (New York: Columbia University Press, 1991), 2–3.

4. For an overview of representations of the Vietnam War in American popular culture and politics since the war's conclusion to recent years, see Gordon Arnold, *The Afterlife of America's War in Vietnam: Changing Visions in Politics and on Screen* (Jefferson, N.C.: McFarland, 2006). For an analysis of popular culture during the war, see Mitchell K. Hall, *Crossroads: American Popular Culture and the Vietnam Generation* (Lanham, Md.: Rowman and Littlefield Publishers, 2005).

5. Gail Dolgin and Vicente Franco, dirs., *Daughter from Danang* (Distributed by PBS Home Video, a copresentation of ITVS and NAATA with *American Experience,* WGBH Boston, 2002), 81 minutes; Aimee Phan, *We Should Never Meet: Stories* (New

York: Picador, 2004); and Trinh T. Minh-ha, dir., *Surname Viet Given Name Nam* (Women Make Movies, 1989), 108 minutes.

6. Between 1950 and 1954, the United States gave France $1.2 billion, paying for over 70 percent of the French military budget, and sent several hundred American military advisors and technicians to Vietnam. By September to October 1954, aid was being sent directly to the South Vietnamese and not through the French, allowing American allies like Japan to sell goods directly to the Vietnamese and shifting the previous "open door" policy in Asia to an extension of the Monroe Doctrine. See LaFeber, *America, Russia, and the Cold War 1945–1992,* 161, 165, 167. Indeed, as early as 1951, arguments were made before Congress advocating the strategic case for intervention in Southeast Asia. For example, Dean Rusk, then head of the Far Eastern Affairs Office, argued, "Even without a communist threat . . . it seems to us that we should have to be deeply interested in the strength and stability of these nations and we would want to bind them to us in ties of friendship in whatever ways we could, and in a more practical sense to serve our mutual advantage by developing a lively exchange of goods and services with them." The "loss" of Southeast Asia, he cautioned, would embolden the communists and close off a valuable source of Western raw materials resources. Quoted in Borden, *The Pacific Alliance,* 195.

7. Hammond, "From Rhetoric to Rollback," 8.

8. Although the Vietnam conflict spanned two decades (beginning with escalating levels of American involvement in 1950 but officially running from 1959 to 1975), it was waged without an official declaration of war from U.S. Congress. In particular, the Golf of Tonkin Resolution (officially called the Southeast Asia Resolution), following the *putative* North Vietnamese attacks on two U.S. destroyers in the Gulf of Tonkin in August 1964, essentially gave President Johnson unlimited powers in Vietnam and circumvented the official declaration of war. Casualty figures are still debated and not fully known, especially the numbers of Vietnamese, Laotians, and Cambodians killed. The United States started secret, systematic bombing raids on Laos in 1964, and later in Cambodia in 1969, to destroy North Vietnamese supply lines along the Ho Chi Minh Trail.

9. Quoted in Mark Bradley, "Slouching toward Bethlehem: Culture, Diplomacy, and the Origins of the Cold War in Vietnam," in Appy, *Cold War Constructions,* 22.

10. Ibid., 23.

11. Ibid., 14–15.

12. Quoted in Borstelmann, *The Cold War and the Color Line,* 215.

13. Bradley, "Slouching toward Bethlehem," 25.

14. Quoted in LaFeber, *America, Russia, and the Cold War 1945–1992,* 252.

15. Borstelmann, *The Cold War and the Color Line,* 215.

16. Bradley, "Slouching toward Bethlehem," 28.

17. Quoted in Borstelmann, *The Cold War and the Color Line,* 216.

18. Quoted in ibid., 230.

19. Ibid., 230.

20. Ibid., 217. Borstelmann notes further that not a single television story during the war provided an in-depth examination of the history, politics, or program of the North Vietnamese. In terms of the racial politics of the American army and its

institutionalized racism against soldiers of color, a telling statistic is that in 1971, while African Americans constituted 11 percent of the American population, they made up about 20 percent of military personnel and only 2.3 percent of officers (229). We are by now familiar with the knowledge that GIs of color were overrepresented in the military, especially on the dangerous front lines, while often passed over for promotions and more desirable occupations. As such, they are also unfortunately overrepresented in terms of casualties.

21. Ibid., 216. Borstelmann also observes the Johnson administration's lack of respect for the South Vietnamese government. For example, when Johnson visited American bases in Vietnam, he did not "bother to consult with his Saigon allies while in their country. By contrast, it is impossible to imagine Franklin Roosevelt avoiding Winston Churchill were he to have visited U.S. bases in England in 1944" (216).

22. Kramer, *The Blood of Government*, 138.

23. Ibid., 139.

24. McCormick, *America's Half-Century*, 151.

25. David Trask, "The Indian Wars and the Vietnam War," in West, Levine, and Hiltz, *America's Wars in Asia*, 255.

26. Milton J. Bates, *The Wars We Took to Vietnam: Cultural Conflict and Storytelling* (Berkeley: University of California Press, 1996), 10.

27. Quoted in Marilyn Young, "Introduction: Why Vietnam Still Matters," in *The War That Never Ends: New Perspectives on the Vietnam War*, ed. David L. Anderson and John Ernst (Lexington: University Press of Kentucky, 2007), 5.

28. Katherine Kinney, *Friendly Fire: American Images of the Vietnam War* (Oxford: Oxford University Press, 2000), 4.

29. Susan Jeffords, *The Remasculinization of America: Gender and the Vietnam War* (Bloomington: Indiana University Press, 1989).

30. See Bates, *The Wars We Took to Vietnam*. For additional literary and cultural analyses, see Keith Beattie, *The Scar That Binds: American Culture and the Vietnam War* (New York: New York University Press, 1998), which focuses on texts representing the impacts of the war rather than the war itself; Philip D. Beidler, *American Literature and the Experience of Vietnam: With a New Afterword* (1982; Athens: University of Georgia Press, 2007), and *Re-Writing America: Vietnam Authors in Their Generation* (Athens: University of Georgia Press, 1991); H. Bruce Franklin, *Vietnam and Other American Fantasies* (Amherst: University of Massachusetts Press, 2000); Arnold R. Isaacs, *Vietnam Shadows: The War, Its Ghosts, and Its Legacy* (Baltimore: Johns Hopkins University Press, 1997); Philip K. Jason, *Acts and Shadows: The Vietnam War in American Literary Culture* (Lanham, Md.: Rowan and Littlefield Publishers, 2000); Jim Neilson, *Warring Fictions: American Literary Culture and the Vietnam War Narrative* (Jackson: University Press of Mississippi, 1998); and Jinim Park, *Narratives of the Vietnam War*.

31. Marita Sturken, *Tangled Memories: The Vietnam War, the AIDS Epidemic, and the Politics of Remembering* (Berkeley: University of California Press, 1997), 2, 7.

32. Ibid., 82. Even in *Heaven and Earth* (1993), director Oliver Stone's filmic adaptation of Vietnamese American Le Ly Hayslip's memoirs *When Heaven and Earth Changed Places* and *Child of War, Woman of Peace*, Hayslip's journey is overshadowed

by that of her husband Steve, an American Vietnam veteran, played by Academy Award–winning actor Tommy Lee Jones (see 117).

33. Ibid., 75.

34. Volkman, "Introduction," 1–22.

35. For a triumphalist history of Operation Babylift as "heroic," "colossal," and "one of the most noteworthy and humanitarian efforts in our lifetime," see Shirley Peck-Barnes, *The War Cradle: The Untold Story of "Operation Babylift"* (Denver: Vintage Pressworks, 2000). For a useful Web site on Operation Babylift, and U.S. adoption history more broadly, see "The Adoption History Project," http://darkwing .uoregon.edu/~adoption/ (accessed November 27, 2009). There is also a documentary on Operation Babylift that includes interviews with the adoptees and their adoptive parents, as well as footage of a group's trip back to Vietnam: Janet Gardner, dir., *Precious Cargo* (Filmmakers Library, 2001), 56 minutes.

36. A series of lawsuits was later filed against Lockheed, the manufacturer of the C-5A plane that crashed, and the U.S. government, resulting in settlements of over $36.7 million paid to 52 survivors living in the United States and 78 living abroad.

37. Karen Dubinsky, "Babies without Borders: Rescue, Kidnap, and the Symbolic Child," *Journal of Women's History* 19.1 (2007): 147.

38. Ibid., 143, 146.

39. Since its 2002 release, the film has garnered eight film festival awards and honors, received an Academy Award nomination for Best Documentary feature, and aired on PBS's program *American Experience*. The film's official Web site is http://daughter fromdanang.com/ (accessed November 27, 2009), and the extensive PBS educational Web site is http://www.pbs.org/wgbh/amex/daughter/ (accessed November 27, 2009).

40. Gregory Paul Choy and Catherine Ceniza Choy, "What Lies Beneath: Reframing *Daughter from Danang*," in Trenka, Oparah, and Shin, *Outsiders Within*, 222–23. Similarly, Soo Na criticizes the film's "imperial camera lens" for silencing Heidi's voice and agency ("Daughter from Danang: The Imperial Camera Lens as Documentary Form," *ChickenBones: Journal for Literary and Artistic African-American Themes* [2002], http://www.nathanielturner.com/daughterfromdenang.htm [note: Danang is misspelled as "denang" in the actual URL; accessed November 27, 2009].

41. Briggs, "Mother, Child, Race, Nation," 182.

42. Dubinsky, "Babies without Borders," 142.

43. Yngvesson, "Placing the 'Gift Child' in Transnational Adoption," 230.

44. Eleana Kim, "Our Adoptee, Our Alien," 521.

45. Fiona I. B. Ngô, "A Chameleon's Fate: Transnational Mixed-Race Vietnamese Identities," *Amerasia Journal* 31.2 (2005): 57.

46. Choy and Choy, "What Lies Beneath," 222.

47. Ibid., 223.

48. Ibid., 225, 223.

49. Kim Park Nelson, "Shopping for Children in the International Marketplace," in Trenka, Oparah, and Shin, *Outsiders Within*, 90.

50. Phan, *We Should Never Meet*, 12, emphasis added; further citations to this work will appear in the text.

51. Christopher Connery, "On the Continuing Necessity of Anti-Americanism," *Inter-Asia Cultural Studies* 2.3 (2001): 399.

52. Yen Le Espiritu, "The 'We-Win-Even-When-We-Lose' Syndrome: U.S. Press Coverage of the Twenty-Fifth Anniversary of the 'Fall of Saigon,'" *American Quarterly* 58.2 (2006): 329, 330.

53. Dubinsky, "Babies without Borders," 144. Dubinsky quotes Vivan Zelizer on the "sacralized" child.

54. The interviews are adapted from Mai Thu Van's *Viêtnam: Un peuple, des voix* (Paris: P. Horay, 1983). Born in New Caledonia, Mai arrived in Paris at the age of twenty-three in the mid-1960s to work and study. In the fall of 1978, she went to Vietnam to conduct research on Vietnamese women. Because it took her some time to earn the trust of her interviewees, most of the interviews in her book took place between 1981 and 1982. See Peter X. Feng, *Identities in Motion: Asian American Film and Video* (Durham: Duke University Press, 2002), 194.

55. Amy Lawrence, "Women's Voices in Third World Cinema," in *Multiple Voices in Feminist Film Criticism,* ed. Diane Carson, Linda Dittmar, and Janice R. Welsch (Minneapolis: University of Minnesota Press, 1994), 417.

56. For ease of reference, I will be citing the page numbers from the script of the film, printed in Trinh T. Minh-ha, *Framer Framed* (New York: Routledge, 1992), 49–91.

57. Quoted in Lynn J. Turner, "Documentary Friction: Vocal and Visual Strategies in *Surname Viet Given Name Nam,*" *parallax* 3 (September 1996): 82. This article originally appeared in Trinh's *When the Moon Waxes Red* (London: Routledge, 1991), 54.

58. Quoted in Turner, "Documentary Friction," 90, from Bill Nichols, *Representing Reality: Issues and Concepts in Documentary* (Bloomington: Indiana University Press, 1991), 254.

59. Trinh T. Minh-ha, "'Who Is Speaking?' Of Nation, Community, and First-Person Interviews (an interview conducted by Isaac Julien and Laura Mulvey)," in *Feminisms in the Cinema,* ed. Laura Pietropaolo and Ada Testaferri (Bloomington: Indiana University Press, 1995), 46–47.

60. Indeed, Turner reads the film as an elaboration of the complicity of what Gayatri Spivak in "Can the Subaltern Speak?" argues are the two senses of representation: the political (*vertreten*), or representation as proxy, and that indicating subject-predication (*darstellen*), or identification and portrait. See Turner, "Documentary Friction," 83–84.

61. Benjamin, "The Task of the Translator," 73, emphasis added.

62. He writes, "The task of the translator consists in finding that intended effect [*Intention*] upon the language into which he is translating which produces in it the echo of the original" (ibid., 76).

63. In addition to Lawrence, "Women's Voices in Third World Cinema," and Turner, "Documentary Friction," see, for example, Katherine Gracki, "True Lies: Staging the Ethnographic Interview in Trinh T. Minh-ha's *Surname Viet Given Name Nam* (1989)," *Pacific Coast Philology* 36 (2001): 48–62; Susan Pui San Lok, "Staging/Translating *Surname Viet Given Name Nam,*" *Third Text* 46 (Spring 1999): 61–72; and Linda Peckham, "*Surname Viet Given Name Nam:* Spreading Rumors and Ex/Changing Histories," in *Screening Asian Americans,* ed. Peter X Feng (New Brunswick: Rutgers University Press,

2002), 235–42, originally published in *Frame/work: A Journal of Images and Culture* 2.3 (1989): 31–35.

64. Gayatri Chakravorty Spivak, "Can the Subaltern Speak?" in *Marxism and the Interpretation of Culture*, ed. Cary Nelson and Lawrence Grossberg, 271–313 (Urbana: University of Illinois Press, 1988).

65. Lawrence, "Women's Voices in Third World Cinema," 417.

66. Louis Althusser, "Ideology and Ideological State Apparatuses: Notes towards an Investigation," in *Lenin, Philosophy, and Other Essays*, 127–86 (New York: Monthly Review Press, 1971).

67. Trinh, "'Who Is Speaking?'" 51.

68. Gordon, *Ghostly Matters*, 8.

69. Ibid., 18.

70. The four virtues are "*Cong Dung Ngon Hanh*. What are these four virtues persistently required of women? First, *Cong:* you'll have to be able, competent and skillful—in cooking, sewing, managing the household budget, caring for the husband, educating the children—all this to save the husband's face. Second. *Dung:* you'll have to maintain a gracious, compliant and cheerful appearance—first of all for the husband. Third, *Ngon:* you'll have to speak properly and softly and never raise your voice—particularly in front of the husband or his relatives. Then fourth, *Hanh:* you'll have to know where your place is; respect those older than you and yield to those younger or weaker than you—moreover, be faithful and sacrifice for the husband" (Trinh, *Framer Framed*, 90). The three submissions are: "Daughter, she obeys her father/Wife, she obeys her husband/Widow, she obeys her son" (83).

71. Nguyên-Vo Thu Huong, "Forking Paths: How Shall We Mourn the Dead?" *Amerasia Journal* 31.2 (2005): 159. For another analysis of the politics and ethics of remembering and mourning the dead in the aftermath of the Vietnam War, see Viet Thanh Nguyen, "Speak of the Dead, Speak of Viet Nam: The Ethics and Aesthetics of Minority Discourse," *CR: The New Centennial Review* 6.2 (2006): 7–37.

72. Nguyên-Vo, "Forking Paths," 171.

Epilogue

1. Yuh, "Moved by War," 281.

2. Fukuyama, *The End of History and the Last Man*.

3. Jonathan Demme, dir., *The Manchurian Candidate* (Paramount Pictures, 2004), 129 minutes.

4. David Palumbo-Liu writes, "The events of September 11th and following have been shocking beyond belief. For me, part of the shock has been the almost instantaneous contradiction in public-speak: the simultaneous evocation of the notion that the world has changed, that the war we will fight will be a 'new' war, and the rearticulation of only slightly modified Cold War rhetoric and 'civilizational' discourse" ("Multiculturalism Now: Civilization, National Identity, and Difference Before and After September 11th," *boundary 2* 29.2 [2002]: 109).

5. Quoted in Field, Introduction, 1–2, emphasis added.

6. Although the State Department distributed the sixty-page booklet of fifteen

essays, free of charge, to American embassies worldwide, such distribution is interestingly illegal in the United States. The Smith-Mundt Act (officially called the U.S. Information and Educational Exchange Act) of 1948, renewed when the United States Information Agency became part of the State Department under a new Bureau of Public Diplomacy and Public Affairs, effective October 1999, bars the domestic distribution of American material produced specifically for foreign audiences. See Michael Z. Wise, "U.S. Writers Do Cultural Battle around the Globe," *New York Times,* December 7, 2002.

7. James Gersgenzang and Tyler Marshall, "Bush Likens War on Terrorism to Cold War," *Los Angeles Times,* October 6, 2005, emphasis added.

8. Mahmood Mamdani, *Good Muslim, Bad Muslim: America, the Cold War, and the Roots of Terror* (New York: Pantheon Books, 2004), 11, 13.

9. Cumings, "Decoupled from History," 3.

10. Smith, *Native Americans and the Christian Right,* xxvii.

11. Ruth Wilson Gilmore offers a rigorous conceptualization of racism as "the state-sanctioned or extralegal production and exploitation of group-differentiated vulnerability to premature death." See her *Golden Gulag: Prisons, Surplus, Crisis, and Opposition in Globalizing California* (Berkeley: University of California Press, 2007), 28.

12. Dylan Rodríguez, *Forced Passages: Imprisoned Radical Intellectuals and the U.S. Prison Regime* (Minneapolis: University of Minnesota Press, 2006), 25.

INDEX

Acheson, Dean, 52, 56, 69–70; China Lobby and, 69; Greek revolution and, 51; Korean War and, 26; Mao/recognition and, 71; NSC 68 and, 53, 54; patronizing logic of, 70; Soviet expansion and, 71

adoption agencies, 177, 182, 183, 187, 209–10, 283n72

adoptions, 34, 167, 170, 279n49; African American, 181; Amerasian, 205; Chinese, 283n76; complexities of, 169, 171, 180, 183; happiness/sadness of, 182; Korean War and, 183, 184, 278n36; subjectivity of, 170, 174; successful, 170; transnational, 161, 168, 169, 171, 174, 176, 177, 180, 186, 190, 191, 203, 205, 206, 208, 215, 218, 223, 278n36, 279n51, 280n52, 280–81n53, 281n54, 282n64, 283n72, 284n81; transracial, 107, 168, 169, 171, 172, 174, 176, 177, 180, 181, 184, 185, 186, 189, 190, 191, 208, 215, 223, 280n51, 280–81n53, 281n56, 284n81

Adorno, Theodor, 250n15

African Americans: adoption of, 181; disenfranchisement of, 50

agency, Asian, 60, 61, 91, 201, 233

Agent Orange, 29, 149, 194

Ahn, Chang "Chuck," 150, 151, 152, 155–59, 165, 167; doubling/splitting of, 153–54; nonalignment and, 159; revisionist history and, 153

Ahn Junghyo, 278–79n43

Alien Land Law (1913), 118, 271n57

al-Qaeda, 109, 240

Alsop, Stewart, 140, 141

Amerasian Homecoming Act (1987), 19

Amerasian Immigration Act (1982), 19

American Asiatic Association, 67

"American Century, The" (Luce), 20, 21

American Dream, 158, 220, 238

Americanness, 119–20, 121, 128, 182

Anglo-Saxon traditions, 22, 46

anticolonialism, 16, 22, 62, 67, 150, 254n41

anticommunism, 38, 64, 104, 204, 248n8; Cold War liberalism and, 257n87; logics of, 29, 92; Orientalism of, 32

antiracism, 14, 22, 254n41

Aristophanes, 50

Armstrong, Charles, 164

Arrighi, Giovanni, 24

Asian Americans, 6, 249n14; coherent incoherence of, 7; as exiles/refugees, 9; as racialized minority, 9

assimilation, 128, 146, 170, 171, 182, 278n34

atomic bomb, 124, 148; ghosts of, 125; peace and, 123; victims of, 138

as object of desire/means of escape, 165; violence of, 165

globalization, 14, 15, 18, 24, 88, 100, 190, 241, 274n92

global third ways, 9–16

good, 32, 83; logics/grammars of, 8

gooks, 1, 21, 51, 63, 139, 159, 164–65, 199, 200; etymology of, 2–3; explanation of, 247n5; Japanese women as, 102

Gordon, Avery, 124, 231

Gore, Al, 263n34

Government and Relief in Occupied Areas (GARIOA), 106

Grapes of Wrath, The (Steinbeck), 118

gross national product (GNP), military spending and, 57, 149

guerilla warfare, 157, 200

Halberstam, David, 275n6

Halliburton, 238

Hamby, Alonzo L., 261n53

Hammond, Andrew, 17, 250n16

Hardt, Michael, 29, 248n8

Harvey, David, 14

Hay, John, 66, 70

Hayslip, Le Ly, 286–87n32

Hayslip, Steve, 287n32

Hearts and Minds (documentary), 284n2

Hill, Lister, 101

Hirohito, Emperor, 100, 105

Hiroshima, 19, 33, 93, 138, 175, 203; aftermath of, 110; bombing of, 95, 97, 98, 99, 101, 102, 109, 112, 116, 122, 123, 162; encounter with, 123, 125, 126, 127; future anterior of, 108–17; gendered racial rehabilitation and, 129, 133; photo of, 97; as transcendental signifier, 110, 123

Hiroshima Maidens Project, 175, 271n52

Hiroshima, Mon Amour (Resnais), 95, 97, 98, 125, 126; scenes from (photos), 96, 97

Hirsch, Marianne, 128

history, 4, 10; end of, 23, 238; immigration, 20, 237; proliferation of, 174

Hitler, Adolf, 101

Hobson, J. A., 30, 257n82

Ho Chi Minh, 40

Ho Chi Minh Trail, 285n8

Hodge, John R., 147, 154, 155, 156

Hofstadter, Richard, 249n15, 250n15

Holt, Harry, 183

Holt International, 176

Hong, Christine, 123

Hong, Grace Kyungwon, 10, 253n39

Horkheimer, Max, 250n15

hot wars, 19, 32, 33, 56, 147

House Un-American Activities Committee, 264n43

Ho Xuan, 231, 232

hula hoops, Cold War and, 82–93

human conservation, 119

human rights, 187

Hunter, Edward, 75–76, 78, 264n40

Hwang, David Henry, 33, 78, 81, 87, 88, 92; Chinese communism and, 91; Madame Butterfly and, 82; Pinkerton and, 85–86; stereotypes and, 84; work of, 65, 83

Hwang Suk-young, 165, 278n43

identification, 10, 100, 120, 125, 251n21

identities, 125, 237, 251n21, 279n43, 282n63; domestic, 15; gendered racial, 122, 126; Japanese, 121; Korean, 179, 182; mistaken, 171; Native American, 10; proliferation of, 174; self-, 2, 10, 48, 137; sexual, 82, 83; social, 169–70, 186; Vietnamese, 193–94

ideology, 11, 23, 150, 242

immigrants, 255n56, 278n36; disenfranchisement of, 50; Japanese, 271n57; Korean, 2

immigration, 238, 278n34; Asian, 80; Chinese, 66; Korean, 159–60; privileged, 176, 282n64; sponsorship for, 215

Immigration Act (1965), 19, 255–56n56

immigration laws, 20, 121, 176, 272n68

imperialism, 4, 60, 65, 81, 109, 133, 186, 191, 195, 216; capitalist, 14; charges of,

Tadashi, Aruga, 72
Taka, Miiko, 131; photo of, 130
Tale of Kieu, The, 234, 235
Taliban, 240
taxonomies, gendered racial, 49, 126, 216
Teahouse of the August Moon (film), 129
Team America: World Police (film), 240
ten pin theory, 26, 27, 140, 141
terrorism, racial, 118
Tesutaro, Kawakami, 131
Tet Offensive, 162, 163
Thatcher, Margaret, 265n51
Third Cinema, 15
Third World: bodies/commodification of, 189; exploitation of, 88–89; movements, 13–14, 21
Third World women, racialized/gendered economy of, 189
Tiana (Thi Thanh Nga), 193–94
Tokyo Rose, 274n89
Tokyo War Trials, 274n89
topographies, gendered/racialized, 49
totalitarianism, 28, 32; battle against, 51; Cold War and, 27; communist, 51; cultural, 14; evils of, 27; political, 14
trade, 23, 24, 81, 82, 86, 133
transcendental signifier, 109, 110, 123
translation, 156; cultural, 214; interpretation and, 228; limits of, 224–35
Tran Tuong Nhu, 209, 211
Trask, David, 201
Treaty of Wanghia (1844), 65, 66
Trenka, Jane Jeong, 186
triangulations, 5, 39, 87, 164, 174
Trilling, Lionel, 249n15, 250n15
Trinh T. Minh-ha, 34, 196, 225, 228, 230, 231, 232, 234; bad commies and, 229; documentary desire and, 227; on patriarchal system, 226; work of, 224
Truman, Harry S., 68, 147, 255n49, 255n53; Asia and, 67; Cold War and, 52, 261n53; on colonialism, 1; Korean War and, 148, 199; MacArthur and, 153, 276n18; Mao/recognition and,

71; nation building and, 59; New Deal and, 24; NSC and, 54; NSC 68 and, 57; reverse course and, 105
Truman Doctrine, 32, 51, 52, 68, 255n53
"Turning Japanese" (Vapors), 120, 121
Turning Japanese: Memoirs of a Sansei (Mura), 33, 98, 100, 117, 120, 129, 131, 140
two-China policy, 107

Ueno, Akiko, 135
ultranationalism, 102, 106
United Nations, 18, 40, 276n18
United Nations Charter, 70
United Nations Declaration of Human Rights, 20
United States Information Agency (USIA), 255n55, 290n6
U.S. Information and Educational Exchange Act (1948), 290n6
United States Information Service (USIS), 156–57, 158
U.S.–Japanese Mutual Security Pact (1951), 107
United States Relations with China (Acheson), 69
U.S.–Soviet relations, 8, 47, 50–51, 72
unsettling hermeneutic, 5, 7, 10, 30, 32

Vandenburg, Arthur, 51
Vapors, 120
Viaud, Louis-Marie-Julien, 79
Viet Cong, 91, 163, 164, 207
Viet Cong women, use-value of, 232–33
Vietnamese, as identity/ideology, 193–94
Vietnamese Americans, 193
Vietnamese Communist Party, 229
Vietnamese women: oppression of, 226; photo of, 209, 234; pressure on, 208–9; rape of, 218; roundup of, 232
Vietnam Veterans Memorial, 202
Vietnam War, 1, 191, 195, 198, 269n36, 270n40; Asians/Asian Americans and, 63; Cold War and, 203; escalation of, 196; Korean involvement in,

Jodi Kim is assistant professor of ethnic studies at the University of California, Riverside.